R0006462829

D1418505

Knowledge and Technology Management in Virtual Organizations:

Issues, Trends, Opportunities and Solutions

Goran D. Putnik
University of Minho, School of Engineering, Portugal

Maria Manuela Cunha
Polytechnic Institute of Cávado and Ave, Higher School of Technology, Portugal

IDEA GROUP PUBLISHING
Hershey • London • Melbourne • Singapore

Acquisition Editor:	Kristin Klinger
Senior Managing Editor:	Jennifer Neidig
Managing Editor:	Sara Reed
Assistant Managing Editor:	Sharon Berger
Development Editor:	Kristin Roth
Copy Editor:	Julie LeBlanc
Typesetter:	Sharon Berger
Cover Design:	Lisa Tosheff
Printed at:	Yurchak Printing Inc.

Published in the United States of America by
   Idea Group Publishing (an imprint of Idea Group Inc.)
   701 E. Chocolate Avenue
   Hershey PA 17033
   Tel: 717-533-8845
   Fax: 717-533-8661
   E-mail: cust@idea-group.com
   Web site: http://www.idea-group.com

and in the United Kingdom by
   Idea Group Publishing (an imprint of Idea Group Inc.)
   3 Henrietta Street
   Covent Garden
   London WC2E 8LU
   Tel: 44 20 7240 0856
   Fax: 44 20 7379 0609
   Web site: http://www.eurospanonline.com

Library of Congress Cataloging-in-Publication Data

Knowledge and technology management in virtual organizations : issues, trends, opportunities and solutions / Goran D. Putnik and Maria Manuela Cunha, editors.
      p. cm.
   Summary: "This book explains the infrastructures and technologies to support technology and information integration standards and protocols. It highlights the social dimension, including human resources management, human resources integration, social issues, social impact, social requirements, and communities of knowledge"--Provided by publisher.
   Includes bibliographical references and index.
   ISBN 1-59904-165-0 (hbk.) -- ISBN 1-59904-166-9 (softcover) -- ISBN 1-59904-167-7 (ebook)
   1. Virtual reality in management. 2. Virtual corporations--Management. 3. Information technology--Management. 4. Knowledge management. I. Putnik, Goran, 1954- II. Cunha, Maria Manuela, 1964-
   HD30.2122.K66 2007
   658.4'038--dc22
                              2006033661

British Cataloguing in Publication Data
A Cataloguing in Publication record for this book is available from the British Library.

Knowledge and Technology Management in Virtual Organizations:
Issues, Trends, Opportunities and Solutions

Table of Contents

Section II:
Models and Architectures

Section III:
Virtual Organization Management

Preface

About the Subject

This book addresses the virtual organization (VO) model, a new organizational paradigm, virtually the most advanced organizational paradigm today.

The implementation of this organizational model is complex and challenging, and although we have VO implemented in compliance with a number of theoretical models that were developed in the last few years, we can observe that the implementations still represent a lot of potential for further improvements, as well as that there are needs for new, more advanced, more effective, more efficient, more competitive, and more sustainable. Considering this, the editors have conceived this book with the objective of collecting recent contributions at the several dimensions that can be identified in organization, knowledge, and technology management in the context of VO:

- **Organizational dimension:** Includes approaches, concepts, organizational models, and knowledge management models
- **Managerial dimension:** Includes the process management, integration management, relationship management, process integration, performance measurement, knowledge management, technology integration management, and information integration
- **Technological dimension:** Includes the infrastructures and technologies to support process management, integration management, relationship management, process integration, knowledge management, technology integration management, and information integration, standards, and protocols
- **Organization, knowledge, and technology management applications in virtual organizations**, through case studies and solutions

The mission of the book is to contribute to the discussion of the main issues, trends, and opportunities related to knowledge and technology management in virtual organizations, from the above-mentioned perspectives or dimensions, and to disseminate proposals, solutions, and conclusions that we believe are relevant to practice.

It is necessary to mention that this book does not cover the whole area of knowledge and technology management in VO. In fact, and besides the effort of the editors, the continuous emerging of solutions made it impossible to totally cover the current state-of-the-art. On the other side, several relevant contributions were not included due to book size restrictions.

However, in its 16 chapters authored by 32 internationally renowned and experienced researchers and professionals in the domain of virtual organizations, the book collects recent models and solutions advanced both by academe and business. It includes different but complementary aspects, such as organizational models, VO models and architectures, VO management, and VO-supporting technologies and infrastructures, all these contributing to make possible the VO model. In this way, *Knowledge and Technology Management in Virtual Organizations: Issues, Trends, Opportunities and Solutions* presents a good representation of emerging contributions that complements the editors' previous book, *Virtual Enterprise Integration: Technological and Organizational Perspectives*, also published by Idea-Group Publishing.

The book is both for an academic audience (teachers, researchers, and students, mainly of post-graduate studies) and professionals (managers, organizational and system developers, and IT specialists) in terms of explaining the requirements and frameworks for the development of solutions.

Organization of the Book

The book contains sixteen chapters, written by a group of internationally-renowned and experienced authors in the VO field, as well as a set of younger authors showing a high potential for research and development. Contributions came from the USA, Latin America, several countries of Eastern and Western Europe, Australia, Taiwan, and Japan. At the same time, the book integrates contributions from academe, research institutions, and industry, representing a good and comprehensive representation of the state-of-the-art adaptive technologies and knowledge management to address the several dimensions of this fast evolutionary area of knowledge.

The sixteen book chapters are organized in four sections:

"Section I: Organizational Requirements" introduces the present business requirements for inter-enterprise integration, namely virtual enterprises or virtual organizations integration and organizational models.

- Why inter-enterprise integration?
- Why virtual enterprise or networked and collaborative organizations integration?
- Which are the integration enablers?

The first three chapters of the book contribute to answering these questions.

Chapter I, "Environments for Virtual Enterprise Integration," introduces the virtual enterprise model as an emerging approach relying on dynamically-reconfigurable partnerships, with extremely high performances, strongly time-oriented while being highly focused on cost and quality, in permanent alignment with the market, and strongly supported by information and communication technology, dictating a paradigm face shift to the traditional organizational models. Networking and reconfiguration dynamics are the main characteristics of this model, which make the claim for enabling and supporting environments, at bearable costs. Some existing technologies and Internet-based environments can partially support this organizational model, but the reconfiguration dynamics can only be assured by environments able to manage, control, and enable networking and dynamics in virtual enterprise creation/reconfiguration. Several environments are introduced in the chapter, and particular focus is given to the market of resources, an environment coping with the requirements of the virtual enterprise model.

Chapter II, "Service Engineering and Extended Artefact Delivery" introduces the main challenges that the manufacturing business should satisfy in order to survive in the move to the new context of an economy of scope under global competition. These challenges are: (1) granting the on-duty performance at the point-of-service; (2) addressing value-added intangibles; and (3) lowering life-cycle eco-impact. These changes in industry reflect on the human society; they are driven both through economical and political measures, as well as being increasingly affected by ecological constraints. Servicing and recovering become challenging demands. Besides technical aspects, spur is in enabling economic profits on the supply chain (by new businesses in maintenance, remanufacturing, etc.), with account of legal acts (suppliers responsibility, etc.), ruled by *voluntary agreements* or by *compulsory targets* frames. The chapter emphasizes the following new paradigms: extended virtual enterprise and extended product, service engineering, life-cycle engineering, product life-cycle management, proactive maintenance, recovery, reuse, recycling, ubiquitous computing, and communication.

Chapter III, "Offshoring: Evolution or Revolution?" describes the emergence of *offshoring*, defining relevant concepts and documenting its rapid growth, and discusses the factors differentiating *offshoring* from outsourcing, especially access to markedly lower costs, extra risks, and cultural differences. The chapter proposes a methodology for deciding what processes to offshore, and establishing, maintaining, and renewing offshoring projects. Offshoring is no longer the preserve of organizations; individuals can obtain an increasing variety of services from overseas. Offshoring is contentious because it threatens to replace high-paid jobs in First World countries with less well-paid Third World jobs. Most outsourcing depends on organizations' ability to transfer data instantly, accurately, and at nearly zero marginal cost. This chapter suggests that the ramifications for individuals, organizations, and societies of this technical advance are underestimated.

"Section II: Models and Architectures" is composed by three chapters that contribute through addressing the specification and development of models and architectures to support networking and interorganizational collaboration and integration. These chapters discuss the questions:

- How can one efficiently and effectively promote networking and interorganizational integration?

- How can one promote business processes and information integration in and interorganizational context?
- How can networking and interorganizational integration bring competitive advantages?

Chapter IV, "How should Enterprises Integrate? From the Need to the Solution ... " discusses the new challenge of industrial companies of building relationships with other value chains. While industrial companies have learned to establish added-value relationships and flows with their supply chain satellite companies, now they suffer from the lack of existing know-how and expertise in meta-value chain operation and management (including methodologies, reference models, case studies, best practices, and business and ICT solution maps). Collaboration only becomes a competitive advantage for a meta-value chain when it leads to meta-value chain agility. Customizing and continuously adapting an extended value preposition is mainly achieved by reshaping the composition and geometry of the whole extended enterprise, relying on dynamic agile business models. This meta-value chain agility needs in turn to be based on extended organizational learning, requiring continuous assessment processes and models based on key performance indicators.

Chapter V, "A Generation of Moderators from Single Product to Global E-Supply" presents the concepts and history of *moderator* research, covering the long journey from the first engineering moderator to recent proposals for an *e-supply chains moderator*. The main function of a moderator is to support a design group or team by raising individual members' awareness of the needs and experiences of other team members. Moderators are specialist intelligent software systems which support each individual to perform his particular role from a position of strength, using his preferred methods of working while still understanding the needs of other individuals and the total team. This research addresses demanding and complex business requirements by exploiting the increasingly powerful technologies and infrastructures available for business integration.

Chapter VI, "Integrating Business Processes and Information Systems in an Interorganizational Context," describes the need of organizations engaging in close cooperation to reorganize the business processes that serve the interface between them. This reorganization is often done with the help of business process models and, as a result, the underlying information systems have to be adapted, too. The changes to the latter can be supported by information system models which are typically "written" in a different language from that of the business processes. The authors suggest an approach to facilitate the development of information system models based on the models of the respective business processes, achieved by mapping a suitable business process language to the Unified Modeling Language. This approach is applied in the context of an interorganizational business process.

"Section III: Virtual Organization Management" addresses the organizational and managerial tools to enable networking and interorganizational collaboration implementation (or integration processes). The five chapters of this section present and discuss several organizational and managerial solutions and contribute to the answer to the questions:

- How can one manage process, knowledge, and information integration in networked and collaborative models?

- How can one measure performance in collaborative and networked organizational models?

- How can one manage to fully exploit opportunities and advantages of these organizational models?

Chapter VII, "The Organizations of Performance Measurement in an Extended Enterprise," discusses the administrative requirements for business integration between partnering companies in the extended enterprise who operate a performance measurement system. It argues that, while on the one hand, interorganizational performance measurement is expected to become increasingly significant in the research literature, it is currently difficult to legislate and coordinate the various performance measurement activities that must be taken into account so as to overcome the disparity in geographical location and culture of extended enterprise nodes. Furthermore, while extended enterprise performance measurement concepts are increasingly being promulgated, the complex nature of these models has made business integration of the firms involved a difficult task: There are problems with regulating the policies and behavior of those who participate in the system, as well as assessing their understanding of the process itself. The chapter tackles these problems by the development of a series of questionnaires and assessment checklists, and by their application in an empirical study in an extended enterprise of the automotive industry.

Chapter VIII, "Process-Driven Business Integration Management for Collaboration Networks" develops a framework for cross-enterprise business integration management addressing the organizational and technical dimension. Firstly, the authors identify basic characteristics of cross-organizational business processes whose complexity results in the need for an efficient and effective business integration management. Therefore, a holistic framework is focused, consisting of a view concept for knowledge management in collaboration networks, a three-tier architecture, and a process-oriented life-cycle model. The framework for business integration management offers the required methods to set up enterprise processes and ICT-support in collaboration networks. Finally, the chapter proposes a management guideline for collaboration participants defining what, why, when, and how they might manage their business integration intra- and cross-organizationally.

Chapter IX, "The Role of Ambiguity in the Transfer of Knowledge within Organizational Networks," discusses that the transfer of knowledge between organizations joining multi-organizational networks to mitigate environmental uncertainties and to access knowledge, cannot be assumed simply as a function of network membership. Researchers identified several factors that have been found to affect the transfer of knowledge within, between, and among organizations. This chapter investigates specifically how organizational ambiguity impacts the transfer of knowledge within multi-organizational networks. The authors explore the effects of causal ambiguity, defined as the ambiguity related to inputs and factors, in a multi-organizational context and discuss the existence of a previously undefined ambiguity, the ambiguity related to outcomes or "outcome ambiguity." The chapter provides a discussion on why outcome ambiguity is particularly relevant when multiple organizations are engaged in a network, where the objective is access to knowledge.

Chapter X, "Systemic Innovation Capability: The Case Study of Embraer, the Brazilian Aircraft Manufacturer," proposes the concept of systemic innovation capability, which is the ability to effectively combine knowledge from a variety of internal and external sources into innovative products, services, efficient business processes, and valuable new combinations of knowledge, holistically taking into consideration business, marketing, operations, and technological aspects. Additionally, the author validates the concept by presenting the case of Embraer, a Brazilian commercial aircraft manufacturer successfully competing in the global marketplace. Based on an extensive literature review with support from Embraer's case, the author proposes the knowledge partnership model and the concept of "knowledge relevance," which is roughly a mutually-attractive force between partners' knowledge pools. The chapter concludes with practical considerations about concepts and models.

Chapter XI, "I-Accounting: An Adaptive Approach (Method + Practices) to Account for Intangibles," introduces the core aspects of an approach facilitating the valuation of intangible assets created by virtual organizations. The approach presented relies on established simple unified procedures which can drastically reduce problems caused by handling each situation individually, especially if there is no previous experience of similar cases. At the same time, the volume, value, and visibility of transactions between the various stakeholders and involved parties is increased. The authors conclude with an example case analysis related to the reality faced in collaborative research projects, which are carried out by diverse partners operating as a virtual organization whose different intellectual assets and the value thereof need to be recognized in order to prepare the ground for successful project completion.

"Section IV: Technologies and Infrastructures" consist of five chapters describing and discussing the development of solutions for processes, knowledge, and information integration in a VE/VO context. It helps with answering the questions:

- Which are the main technologies and infrastructures enabling the VO model?
- Which are the main technologies and infrastructures to support knowledge creation and management in an interorganizational context?
- Which are the main technologies and infrastructures to support process and information integration in VO?
- Which are the main technologies and infrastructures to support technology management in VO?

Chapter XII, "Enabling the Virtual Organization with Agent Technology," introduces the emerging agent-based systems as offering new means of effectively addressing complex decision processes and enabling solutions to business requirements associated with virtual organizations. Intelligent agents can provide more flexible intelligence and expertise and help the smooth integration of a variety of system types (i.e., Internet applications, customer relationship management, supplier network management, enterprise resources management, expert systems). This chapter presents an overview of expert systems as the most widely-used approach for domain knowledge management today and agent technology, and shows the latter as a superior systems development vehicle providing flexible intelligence/expertise and the integration of a variety of system types. To illustrate, a system is developed first by an expert system approach and then by an agent-based approach, in order to identify the strengths and weaknesses of the agent-based approach. Last, the chapter addresses the practical implications of a company adoption of agent-based technology for systems development.

Chapter XIII, "Enterprise Organisational Structure Integration and Service-Oriented Architectures," examines the service-oriented architectures (SOA) in conjunction with the enterprise organizational structure integration problem, applied to innovative organizational models such as virtual enterprises. The chapter presents the evolution of software architectures, from traditional to SOA, along with the characteristics, advantages and disadvantages, and problems and difficulties in applying the SOA, while also focusing on the compatibility between SOA and modern organizational structures. It also examines the new standard in the service orchestration level BPEL and its impact to the integration problem, and also examines new messaging protocols and frameworks such as the enterprise service bus or messaging service bus. The main focus of the chapter is on the SOA technology trends of modern organizational structures, regarding their formation and integration. The comparison between SOA and traditional architectures provides a clear path to their adoption in various cases.

Chapter XIV, "Knowledge Creation and Adaptive Collaboration Based on XML Web Services," introduces the adaptive collaboration (AC) and its potentials in the new paradigm of the 21st century networked society. It is an innovative information technology system for knowledge creation based on the XML Web services, which is essential to promptly meet the increasingly diverse needs and kaleidoscopic changes in economy. The AC is critical in the ubiquitous society, where constant improvement of business processes and cooperation and collaboration with both existing and new systems are required. Today's knowledge is considered ecological and organic in a way that it is flexible enough to swiftly sense numeral shifts in the environment. The new method that integrates a number of different systems and applications into one system to enable the AC has been generating much attention as it may meet the diverse and growing demands in the future of the ubiquitous society.

Chapter XV, "Software Agent Technology for Supporting Ad Hoc Virtual Enterprises," introduces a new idea of using software agents for supporting ad-hoc virtual enterprises and similar forms of temporal business-to-business collaboration. The authors argue that current information and telecommunication technologies, based on information interchange and local data processing, are not flexible enough to deal with modern business requirements, especially dynamic and temporal business relations, heterogeneity of hardware, software and communication means, and data complexity. The proposed approach, consisting of distributed and remotely-executed programs—software agents—working in the name and under the authority of their owners, differs in the distribution of both data and programs for data treatment at-the-place and just-in-time. The proposed techniques for agent preparation, distribution, and execution should make the whole system safe and secure, providing an efficient environment for wide spectrum of temporal and ad-hoc business collaboration.

Chapter XVI, "Business Networking: The Technological Infrastructure Support," discusses that enterprises are impelled to adapt their way of undertaking business, from traditional practices to e-business, and to participate in new forms of collaboration, such as networked organizations. In this context, standards, frameworks, technologies, and infrastructures supporting collaborative business become key factors in achieving environments with a desired high level of collaboration and inter- and intra-organization business processes alignment. The chapter underlines the main issues, trends, and opportunities related to business integration from a technological perspective, analyzing and discussing the most relevant (existing and still under development) business integration reference models, frameworks, standards, technologies, and supporting infrastructures, and to briefly present relevant research projects in the area of business networking developed in Europe and USA. A special emphasis is made on frameworks such as ebXML and RosettaNet, and the importance of papiNet, BPLE4WS, and freebXML is underlined. Challenges regarding self-forming networked organizations are also advanced.

Expectations

The book provides researchers, scholars, and professionals with some of the most advanced research developments, solutions, and implementations. It will provide a better understanding of knowledge and technology management in virtual organizations, from an organizational, managerial, and technological perspective. We expect that this book will be read by academics (i.e., teachers, researchers and students), technology solutions developers, and enterprise managers (including top level managers). We believe that this book will help and support teachers of several graduate and postgraduate courses, from management to information technology.

The Editors,

Goran D. Putnik
Maria Manuela Cunha

Guimarães, April, 2006

Acknowledgments

Editing a book is a hard but compensating and enriching task, as it involves an array of different activities like contacts with authors and reviewers, exchange of ideas and experiences, process management, organization and integration of contents, and many others, with the permanent objective of creating a book that meets the public expectations. And this task cannot be accomplished without a great deal of help and support from many sources. The authors would like to acknowledge the help, support, and belief of all who made possible this creation.

First of all, this book would not have been possible without the ongoing professional support of the team of professionals at Idea Group Inc. We are most grateful to Mehdi Khosrow-Pour, senior academic editor, and to Jan Travers, managing director, for the opportunity. A special word of gratitude is due to Kristin Roth, development editor, for her guidance and friendly words of advise, encouragement, and prompt help.

Special thanks go also to all the staff at Idea Group Inc., whose contributions throughout the process of making this book available all over the world was invaluable.

We are grateful to all authors, who simultaneously served as referees for chapters written by other authors, for their insights, valuable contributions, prompt collaboration, and constructive comments. The communication and exchange of views within this truly global group of recognized individualities from the scientific domain and from industry was an enriching and exciting experience for us, the editors. We wish to thank all the authors for their insights and excellent contributions to this book, which made of this book the book we wanted.

The authors would like to acknowledge the support of the Network of Excellence I*PROMS —*Innovative Production Machines and Systems*, http://www.iproms.org/, an EU FP6 project, N° NMP2-CT-2004-500273, whose partner is University of Minho.

A special thanks to our institutions, the University of Minho and the Polytechnic Institute of Cávado and Ave, in Portugal, for providing the material resources and all the necessary logistics.

Thank you.

The Editors

Section I

Organizational Requirements

Chapter I

Environments for Virtual Enterprise Integration

Maria Manuela Cunha,
Polytechnic Institute of Cávado and Ave, Higher School of Technology, Portugal

Goran D. Putnik, University of Minho, School of Engineering, Portugal

Paulo Silva Ávila, Polytechnic Institute of Porto, Institute of Engineering, Portugal

Abstract

The virtual enterprise model is an emerging approach in answer to the new requirements of the business environment, relying on dynamically-reconfigurable partnerships, with extremely high performances, strongly time-oriented while being highly focused on cost and quality, in permanent alignment with the market, and strongly supported by information and communication technology, dictating a paradigm face shift to the traditional organizational models. Networking and reconfiguration dynamics are the main characteristics of this model, requiring enabling and supporting environments, at bearable costs. Some existing technologies and Internet-based environments can partially support this organizational model, but the reconfiguration dynamics can only be assured by environments able to manage, control, and enable networking and dynamics in virtual enterprise creation/reconfiguration. Several environments are introduced in the chapter, and particular focus is given to the market of resources, an environment coping with the requirements of the virtual enterprise model.

Introduction

A main feature of the "New Economy" consists of an increased emphasis on inter-enterprise collaboration within networked supply chains (Euroma, 2002). Enterprises are no longer confined to their four walls, and the networked value chain concept is extending to several organizational approaches, with extremely high performances, strongly time-oriented while being highly focused on cost and quality, and permanently aligned with business opportunities, in answer to the new requirements of the business environment. Some of these approaches rely on dynamically-reconfigurable business networks, in permanent alignment with the market, and strongly supported by information and communication technology, dictating a paradigm face shift to the traditional organizational models. The leading organizational model introducing these characteristics is the virtual enterprise (VE) organizational model, characterized as a dynamic organizational model.

Virtual enterprise integration (VEI) is one of the most (if not the most) important requirements for making the virtual enterprises a real, competitive, and widely-implemented organizational and management concept.

Several VE definitions and similar models exist, and several taxonomies could be tried. Terminology varies frequently, and many expressions are used: collaborative networks, collaborative supply chains, networked enterprise, star alliances, extended enterprises, agile virtual enterprises, and so forth. These are all forms of virtual enterprises, in a broad sense. What makes the distinction is the duration and the links established or intended to establish, the legal formalities, scope, sharing of responsibilities and results, coordination, reconfiguration dynamics, and so forth. Concerning duration, such networks can be established on a temporary or a long-term basis. Temporary organizations seem to better fit the dynamics of the market and the typically short duration of business opportunities, while long-term organizations better cope with the trust-building process and the investment on common infrastructures and practices. However, we will not be concerned with the particularities of these labels, their overlapping, and differences in structure, organization, or operation.

Dynamic organizational models represent solutions for highly-customized products, small series, in highly competitive and changing environments where permanent business alignment is crucial. Partnership stability is low (sometimes very low), dependency between partners is very weak, and reconfiguration dynamics should be as high as possible, given the permanent monitoring of the structure to introduce the most competitive solution at every moment of the product life cycle (Cunha & Putnik, 2005b). Some forms of extended enterprises in stable mass production-oriented businesses, in long- to medium-sized series for traditional to semi-standardized products, are examples of more stable, sometimes long-term, organizations (Cunha & Putnik, 2005b).

Most definitions of virtual enterprise (VE) incorporate the idea of extended and collaborative outsourcing to suppliers and subcontractors, in order to achieve a competitive response to market demands (Webster, Sugden, & Tayles, 2004). As suggested by several authors (Browne & Zhang, 1999; Byrne, 1993; Camarinha-Matos & Afsarmanesh, 1999; Cunha, Putnik, & Ávila, 2000; Davidow & Malone, 1992; Preiss, Goldman, & Nagel, 1996), a VE consists of a network of independent enterprises (resources providers) with reconfiguration capability in useful time, permanently aligned with the market requirements, created to take profit from a specific market opportunity, and where each participant contributes with its best practices and core competencies to the success and competitiveness of the structure as a whole. Even during the operation phase of the VE, the configuration can change, to assure business alignment with the market demands, introduced by the identification of reconfiguration opportunities and constant readjustment or reconfiguration of the VE network, to meet unexpected situations or to keep permanent competitiveness and maximum performance (Cunha & Putnik, 2002, 2005a, 2005b).

A particular model characterized by a high reconfiguration dynamics is the agile/virtual enterprise (A/V E) model (Cunha & Putnik, 2005b, 2006a, 2006b; Putnik, 2001; Putnik, Cunha, Sousa, & Ávila, 2005).

The implementation of the VE model should assure the required reconfiguration dynamics, which as we will see in the chapter is dependent on: (1) the reduction of reconfiguration costs and effort, that is, requires a balancing between reconfiguration dynamics and reconfiguration time and costs, and (2) the capability to preserve the firms' private knowledge of products or processes.

Considering that the VE concept aims to represent a new organizational paradigm for enterprises in general, and, in that way, permeating virtually the whole economy and even society (through the concept of virtual organizations), we could talk about the social costs of ineffective and inefficient integration of VE. However, many authors recognize that the present solutions for VEI are either inexistent or insufficient. Therefore, there is a need for further effort by the community towards satisfactory and competitive solutions. This chapter introduces a part of this effort. It alerts the reader to the development of a new generation of electronic marketplaces, designated as market of resources, which supposedly should cope with the high reconfigurability of the VE model, at a low transaction cost while preserving the firms' private knowledge; it also introduces other undergoing developments that give hope to be on the way to the VE model.

In the chapter, we discuss the VE reconfigurability requirement and the requirements of reconfiguration dynamics, introduce some of the most recent developments and environments to cope with these requirements, such as the electronic marketplaces, including the recent generation of collaborative electronic marketplaces, breeding environments, virtual clusters, and so forth, and present the market of resources as a tool for managing, controlling, and enabling networking and dynamics in VE integration.

This chapter makes two contributions: (1) To industry managers, it highlights the importance of dynamic organizational models as the ultimate paradigm; and (2) to IS technologists, it alerts them to the development of a new generation of environments, which are able to cope with the high reconfigurability of the VE model, at a low transaction cost while preserving the firms' private knowledge.

Requirements for Virtual Enterprise Integration

A few important trends have been identified in the strongly competitive business environment, which according to several experts will lead to dramatic changes in present and future productivity and approaches. Altogether, the combination of the shorter life span of new products, increasing product diversity over time, rapid technological developments, increased technological complexity, market globalization, frequent changes in demand, uncertainty, and strong competition are the main trends of the actual worldwide economic context.

"Fast adaptability" or "fast reconfigurability" of the enterprise, globalization and integration, adoption of technological developments, and the adoption of new organizational models can be seen as main enablers of business alignment, the main requirement for competitiveness. In its BM_virtual enterprise architecture reference model, Putnik (2000) presents "fast adaptability" or "fast reconfigurability" as a characteristic for the competitive enterprise, considering that the recent concepts of "agile enterprise" and "virtual enterprise" are the organizational paradigms incorporating this characteristic.

In the dynamic economy which we live today, it is usual for people entering the world of labor to expect to have several career changes during their working lives. It is a dynamic labor market. Organizations can no longer provide a long-term secure relationship as in the past; we live in the portfolio worker era, as Handy (1996) called it.

Networking and reconfigurability dynamics are the main requirements for virtual enterprise integration. However, the main factors against networking and reconfigurability dynamics are the reconfiguration costs and the leakage of private information.

Networking and Reconfiguration Dynamics: The VE Enablers

For the last years, global competition has strengthened the significance of a company's ability to introduce new products, while responding to increasingly dynamic markets with customers' rapidly changing needs, and thus making a claim for shortening the time required to design, develop, and manufacture, as well as for cost reduction and quality improvement. In the past a product could exist without great changes (adaptations, redesigns). Faced with the challenges of today, besides the shorter duration of a product, it usually suffers several redesigns in order to be competitive, that is, aligned with the market demands.

These trends require enterprises to have the capability to incorporate into their products or processes the best resources available in the market, and to dynamically adjust its interorganizational structure to keep its maximum alignment with the business opportunity.

Let us use Figure 1 to illustrate the importance of networking. Multi-product companies, that is, those whose organizational model consists of the production of various products, present different performance levels for the different products, as represented in Figure 1a, as a consequence of the different performances of its resources in the execution of the different operations of a given product, as in (c). In general, the operations performed with larger efficiency correspond to the core competencies of the company. Contrarily, under the concept of a network organization, it is possible to conceive a new physical structure of the production system for each new product (in Figure 1b, one network created for each product), where all the processes to produce a product are decomposed in operations performed by partners of the network. For each operation is selected the partner presenting the highest possible performance, so that the overall performance of the network is optimized (ideally 100%), as in Figure 1d.

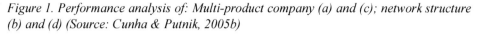

Figure 1. Performance analysis of: Multi-product company (a) and (c); network structure (b) and (d) (Source: Cunha & Putnik, 2005b)

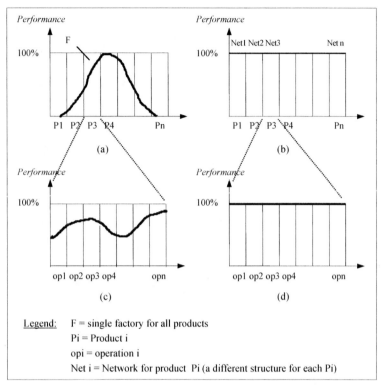

But the changing business environment requires also the permanent adaptation of the partner organizations (VE), that is, alignment with business opportunities. By alignment, in this context, we mean the actions to be undertaken to gain synergy between business, that is, between a market opportunity and the delivery of the required product, with the required specifications, at the required time, with the lowest cost and with the best possible return (Cunha & Putnik, 2005a).

Reconfigurability, that is, the ability to quickly react to the unpredictable changes in the environment (market) is a requirement of the VE to keep the partnership aligned with business requirements, and is a consequence of product life cycle dynamics, that is, business and market dynamics. This requirement implies the ability of:

1. Flexible and almost instantaneous access to the optimal *resources* to integrate in the enterprise
2. Design, negotiation, business management, and manufacturing management functions independently from the physical barrier of space
3. Minimization of the reconfiguration or integration time

Reconfiguration, meaning the substitution of resources providers, generating a new instance of the network, can happen mainly from four reasons:

1. Reconfiguration during the network company life cycle is a consequence of the product redesign in the product life cycle, to keep the network aligned with the market requirements, that is, to deliver the right product.

2. Reconfiguration as a consequence of the nature of the particular product life cycle phase (the evolutionary phases of the product).

3. Reconfiguration can happen also as a consequence of the evaluation of the resources performance during one instantiation of the network, or as a consequence of voluntary contract rescission by a participating resources provider, willing to disentail from the network.

4. Reconfiguration can also be a consequence of fluctuation in the demand side, or even a consequence of the so-called "bullwhip effect" phenomenon in the supply chain, where a little fluctuation in end customer demand can be dramatically amplified at the upstream company, requiring a fast adaptation for a short period of time. Supply chain dynamics is a strong cause of possible and unexpected reconfiguration needs in the A/V E, originating a new instantiation of the A/V E, substituting or reinforcing the provision of any resources, which is independent from the integrated resources performance, or from the product or business lifecycle.

A VE is defined as a reconfigurable network to assure permanent business alignment, in transition between states or instantiations (configurations) along time, as represented in Figure 2. VE dynamics considers a succession of a network's states (physical configurations of the VE) along the time, that is, the network reconfiguration dynamics. Dynamics means precisely the intensity of change to which the VE is subject.

Figure 2. Networking dynamics considers a succession of a network's states along the time (Source: Cunha & Putnik, 2005b)

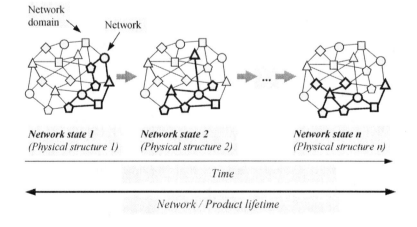

Figure 3. Organizational dynamics: A network configuration parameter (F) as a function of time (t)

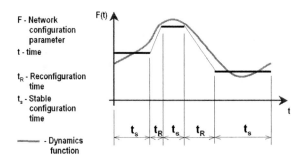

In Cunha and Putnik (2006c), the authors propose two parameters of *reconfigurability dynamics*: the number of requested reconfigurations per unit of time (*reconfiguration request frequency*) and the time to reconfigure (*reconfiguration time*). *Reconfigurability dynamics* is directly proportional to the number of requests and inversely proportional to the time to make operational the reconfiguration (selection, negotiation, and integration of resources in the VE).

Ideally, reconfiguration time (t_R in Figure 3) should tend to zero, and stable configuration durations (t_S) should be dictated by business alignment needs, to keep VE performance at its maximum level.

Transaction Costs and Leakage of Private Information: The VE Disablers

The main factor against reconfigurability dynamics, that is, the main factor disabling reconfiguration frequency is reconfiguration cost and time, reducing dynamics by increasing the duration of stable and sometimes less performing configurations.

The costs of outsourcing are composed of both the explicit cost of carrying out the transaction as well as hidden costs due to coordination difficulties and contractual risks. The major costs associated with outsourcing include: (1) the transaction costs and (2) the leakage of private information. In dynamic organizations, *transaction costs* are the firm reconfiguration costs, associated to partners search, selection, negotiation, and integration as well as permanent monitoring and the evaluation of the partnership performance (Cunha & Putnik, 2003b).

A firm's private information is information that no one else knows, and which gives a firm an advantage in the market. In many situations this private information is a core competitive advantage which distinguishes a firm from its competitors. Networking or partitioning tasks between resources providers increases the risk of losing control of such type of information, which only through complete contractual agreements could be safeguarded, and furthermore, through an environment assuring trust and accomplishment of the duty of seal. The implementation of the networked structures requires tools to enable the preservation of the firm's knowledge. When considering dynamically-reconfigurable networks, the risk of leakage of private information increases.

The implementation of the dynamic organizations requires the existence of tools and environments that, by reducing reconfiguration costs and reconfiguration time, overcome these two disabling factors, allowing dynamics as high as required to assure business alignment.

Environments for Virtual Enterprise Integration

Value chains have been supported by a wide variety of technologies to communicate, but the pace of competition requires more intelligent and effective information and communication systems and technologies. Literature suggests that "traditional" Internet-based tools (such as WWW search engines, directories, e-mail, electronic marketplaces, etc.), can support some activities of VE integration, helping from procurement processes until the search of partners for a partnership, including electronic automated negotiation, electronic contracting, and market brokerage (Cunha & Putnik, 2003a; Dai & Kauffman, 2001; Dogac, 1998; Hands, Bessonov, Blinov, Patel, & Smith, 2000; O'Sullivan, 1998; Wang, 2001).

Khalil and Wang (2002) have proposed ways for information technology to enable the VE model, by providing:

1. Web-based information systems, supporting B2B and B2C applications
2. Sophisticated customer databases, supporting data mining, enhancing business intelligence, and decision support
3. Support for organizational learning
4. Groupware-supported coordination and decision-making

Several authors (Carlsson, 2002; Martin, 1999) refer that the new VE paradigm requires intelligent support for transactions, new effective methods for finding partners, intelligent support to virtual teams, knowledge management support systems, reliable decision support in VE/network design/configuring, effective tools for information filtering and knowledge acquisition, and support in the identification of the best alternatives to keep the network aligned with the market, that is, competitive.

Several supporting infrastructures and applications must exist before we can take advantage of the VE organizational model, such as: electronic markets of resources providers, legal platforms, brokerage services, efficient and reliable global and intelligent information systems, electronic contractualization and electronic negotiation systems, and decision support systems and tools.

This section introduces some examples of the recent generation of electronic marketplaces, the collaborative e-marketplaces, and introduces the recent concept of breeding environments, virtual clusters, electronic institutions, and the market of resources. We will dedicate a different section to the market of resources, a solution proposed by the authors, to fully support VE implementation, operation, and management, which is deeply documented in Cunha and Putnik (2006a).

Electronic Marketplaces

To contribute to the reduction of search time in procurement and engineering, and to reduce transaction costs, manufacturers in several industries created electronic marketplaces (e-marketplaces), to pool their purchasing power and to develop technology platforms to exploit networked technologies. Electronic markets like *Covisint* (http://www.covisint.com) in the auto industry or *Elemica* in the chemicals industry (http://www.elemica.com) or ManufacturingQuote (http://www.mgfquote.com) in the engineering domain in general, provide environments to help collaboration, networking, and at a certain extent, VE dynamics.

Elemica was founded in August 2000, by 22 of the world's largest chemical firms. It was the premier global neutral information network built to facilitate the order processing and supply chain management, offering an integrated suite of product solutions that enable buyers and sellers of chemicals to streamline their business processes and to collaborate to achieve savings (Elemica, 2005).

Its core business is an interoperable data exchange service capable of routing messages (such as purchase orders and shipping notices) between participants. In 2003, Elemica was able to connect the chemical industry by offering integration of participants' ERP systems into a hub-and-spoke network (Metcalfe, 2004). Elemica is an example of a collaboration e-market-place, that is, it emphasizes interaction services (Christiaanse & Markus, 2003). Collaboration e-marketplaces are expected to benefit participants by reducing the costs and increasing the quality of multiparty information exchange (Christiaanse & Markus, 2003).

Covisint (http://www.covisint.com), officially announced in December 2000, as an independent company, created by Ford, Chrysler, General Motors, Renault, Nissan, and a number of development partners, was projected to be a one-stop-shop for the automotive supply chain, supporting buying, selling, and collaboration on a global platform: Buyers can access all their suppliers in one site, and in the same way, suppliers can have all their clients in one site, all sharing common procedures and processes.

Covisint consists of a virtual supplier network specifically created for the automotive industry. Its extension to other industries by strategic partnerships was planned since their creation; at present Covisint is applying its *Industry Operating System* to the healthcare sector.

Covisint (Covisint, 2001) project scope includes three major areas:

- **Procurement:** It hosts a global marketplace where industry participants can purchase and sell a wide range of items and services via the Internet.
- **Product development:** It provides customers with the ability to develop products via real-time collaboration and to strengthen global integration among partners, creating a secure environment.

- **Supply chain:** It allows individual organizations to see the current and future status of their supply chain inventory levels, material flows, and capacity constraints via the Internet.

The service encompasses the complete interaction between suppliers or between suppliers and their customers, and includes procurement transactions, pre-production collaborative engineering, and exchange of information during production or for supply chain management.

The neutral e-marketplace Manufacturing Quote (http://www.mfgquote.com) was founded in 1999, and facilitated its first online sourcing transactions in February, 2000. It is an online *sourcing management system* with automated supplier discovery and a global network of independent participating suppliers.

MfgQuote uses its proprietary technology to intelligently connect buyers with suppliers of manufacturing services while facilitating the collaboration, quoting, due diligence, and analysis processes. This technology supports the request for quotations or proposals process, supplier discovery, engineering data exchange, revision control, collaboration, due diligence, analytics, and supplier management.

Buyers using MfgQuote are typically original equipment manufacturers (OEMs) requiring the services of contract manufacturers and job-shops. As a general rule, if an item needs to be manufactured in accordance with a drawing, computer-aided design (CAD) model, or technical specification, it is appropriate to be sourced via MfgQuote.

Another crucial example of an electronic marketplace is given by the European Union through EURES, European Employment Services (http://europa.eu.int/eures/home), and its project called "The European Job Mobility Portal, especially as 2006 is the European Year of Workers' Mobility. The service is pretended as "the easy way to find information on jobs and learning opportunities throughout Europe," where both jobseekers and employers can meet and personalize the service according to their individual needs. EURES offers a human network of advisers to provide the information required by jobseekers and employers through personal contacts. In March 2006, there were about 700 EURES advisers across Europe.

This field of intervention is also fundamental when we are addressing VE dynamics.

The SEEMSeed project, funded by the European Commission (Information Society Directorate-general) in the frame of the "policy-orientated research" priority, pretends to contribute for a single european electronic market (SEEM) "accessible and affordable to all businesses, organisations and individuals of any nature, size and geographic location, with no technological, cultural or linguistic restraints" (SEEMseed_Consortium, 2005). The SEEM will allow the dynamic creation and operation of collaborative structures, to trade goods, services, or work, in a peer-to-peer manner in the knowledge economy.

The SEEM concept is driven by the changing work paradigms in business. The IST vision is based on ambient intelligence, which will be available in the near future. But making use of it requires not only technological development but also development of business models and behavioral models adapted to the new situation.

In fact, several technologies and valuable applications have been developed that can support activities of the VE model, such as the e-marketplaces; however, they do not cope with the requirements of the VE model, that is, they do not implement the indispensable functionalities to assure the fast reconfigurability requirement.

Virtual Clusters

A virtual industry cluster (VIC) consists of an aggregation of companies from diverse industries, with well-defined and focused competences, with the purpose of gaining access to new markets and business opportunities by leveraging their resources (Molina & Flores, 1999). The intention of the formation of VIC is to enable search and selection of partners for the formation of virtual enterprises. Virtual enterprise brokers are intermediaries that possess the ability to look for core competences in a virtual industry cluster and to integrate the competences of partners into successful virtual enterprises (Molina & Flores, 1999).

Electronic Institutions

An electronic institution is a framework that, based on communication network, enables automatic transactions between parties, according to sets of explicit institutional norms and rules, ensuring the trust and confidence needed in any electronic transaction (Rocha, Cardoso, & Oliveira, 2005). The electronic institution is a meta-institution, which is a shell for generating specific electronic institutions for particular application domains. The meta-institution includes general modules related to social and institutional behavior norms and rules, ontology services, as well as links to other institutions (financial, legal, etc.). The main goal of a meta-institution is to generate specific electronic institutions through the instantiation of some of these modules that are domain dependent according to the current application domain (Cardoso & Oliveira, 2005; Rocha et al., 2005).

Breeding Environments

The virtual organization breeding environment represents a long-term cluster/association/pool of organizations that are supported and facilitated for the establishment of virtual organizations and other forms of dynamic collaborative networked organizations (Camarinha-Matos & Afsarmanesh, 2004). If traditionally, such clusters were established in a given geographic region, having a common business culture and typically focused on a specific sector of the economical activity of that region, today, the challenge is the replacement of these clusters by a new "support-environment" called by the authors as a breeding environment. This environment is supposedly based in effective information and communication infrastructures to provide common grounds for collaboration, facilitation of the establishment of virtual organizations, and assisting with the operation of virtual organizations (Camarinha-Matos & Afsarmanesh, 2004)

Market of Resources for
Virtual Enterprise Integration

In this section, the market of resources is introduced, firstly with a description of the main activities involved in VE integration, secondly with a brief specification of its overall structure, functioning, and services offered, and finally a prototype of the market of resources is partially presented.

Virtual Enterprise Integration Using the Market of Resources

This section explains the main activities involved in VE creation or VE reconfiguration using the Market of Resources. The activities to perform in order to create or reconfigure a VE are the following:

- **VE request:** Request involves the negotiation with the market of resources, broker allocation, and VE design. The VE design complexity is a function of product complexity and requires time to answer (by the market). There is an amount of resources needed to completely define the VE (creation or reconfiguration) project. These resources are broker time, knowledge, and effort (human and computational). This VE project consists of a number of instructions and specifications that will drive the search, negotiation, and integration, and is associated with a degree of complexity. VE design is an activity to be undertaken by the client, and after validated by the market of resources (broker), or alternatively, undertaken interactively by the client (the owner of the VE) and the broker, depending of the request complexity, or of the client ability/knowledge to define the VE project.

- **Resources search and selection:** Search, negotiation, and selection consist of several steps: the identification of potential resources, separation of eligible resources, negotiation within these to the identification of candidate resources, and finally the selection among these to find the best combination for integration. The identification of the potential resources and, within this set, the separation of the eligible ones is made automatically by the market from its knowledge base, and without intervention of the client (VE owner). In the market, the negotiation can be done using different approaches (automated, reverse auction, and direct negotiation). The final selection is a computer-aided activity, controlled by the broker, with an eventual intervention of the VE owner, if necessary.

- **VE integration:** In this activity we will consider only the contractualization aspect. The market of resources assures an automated contractualization.

These activities are systematized in Table 1.

Table 1. Description of VE creation/reconfiguration activities

Activity	Activity Description
VE Request	
Request Negotiation	• Registration of the VE owner, specification of the request, broker allocation, and contractualization with the market
VE Design	• Computer-aided VE design, with specification of the resources requirements and of negotiation parameters
	• The selected broker will validate the VE design, or will support the design, in complex products or when complex negotiation methods are required.
Resources Search and Selection	
Eligible Resources Identification	• Identification of the subset of the market of resources knowledge base where it is intended to perform the search (focused domain)
	• Focused domain filtering, automatically, from the requirements of the VE design to identify eligible resources (eligibility is automatically driven from the catalogs/resources database)
Negotiation	• Computer-aided (more or less automated) negotiation with the eligible resources providers, to identify the candidate resources for integration; we distinguish between automatic search, inverse auction, and direct negotiation.
Selection	• Computer-aided and broker-mediated decision-making for final selection of resources to integrate; sorting of the negotiation results; and identification of the best combination of resources providers, followed by confirmation with the selected ones; depending on the complexity, it involves more or less broker dedication.
VE Integration	
Contractualization	• Automatically, when a selected resources provider confirms its participation
	• Selection of the adequate contract from a standardized collection (for request formalization, integration, etc.)
	• The market also offers integration procedures, not considered here.

The Market of Resources Structure

The Market of Resources is an institutionalized organizational framework and service assuring the accomplishment of the competitiveness requirements for VE dynamic integration and business alignment (Cunha & Putnik, 2005c; Cunha, Putnik, & Gunasekaran, 2002; Cunha, Putnik, Gunasekaran, & Ávila, 2005). The operational aspect of the market of resources consists of an Internet-based intermediation service, mediating offer and demand of resources to dynamically integrate in an VE, assuring low transaction costs (as demonstrated in Cunha & Putnik, 2003b, 2003c) and the partners' knowledge preservation.

The service provided by the market of resources is supported by Cunha and Putnik (2005c); Cunha, Putnik, and Gunasekaran (2003); and Cunha et al. (2005):

- A knowledge base of resources providers and results of their participation in previous VE (historic information)
- A normalized representation of information
- Computer-aided tools and algorithms
- A brokerage service
- Regulation, that is, management of negotiation and integration processes, as well as contract enforcement mechanisms

The market of resources is able to offer (Cunha & Putnik, 2005c; Cunha et al., 2003):

- Knowledge for VE selection of resources, negotiation, and its integration
- Specific functions of VE operation management
- Contracts and formalizing procedures to assure the accomplishment of commitments, responsibility, trust, and deontological aspects, envisaging that the integrated VE accomplishes its objectives of answering to a market opportunity

The overall functioning of the market of resources is represented by an IDEF0 diagram[1] in Figure 4. It consists of the creation and management of the market of resources itself (Process A.1.), as the environment to support the design and integration of the VE (Process A.2.) that, under the coordination of the environment, operates to produce a product to answer to a market opportunity (Process A.3.). The market offers technical and procedural support for the activities of identifying potential partners, qualifying partners, and integrating the VE, as well as coordination and performance evaluation mechanisms.

Process A.2. (VE Design and Integration) is detailed in Figure 5.

This operation is the one that is most effort-consuming for the user in its interface with the Market. The request for VE creation (or reconfiguration or dissolution), is composed by request negotiation, VE design, and request formalization.

A Prototype for the Market of Resources

From the several functionalities offered, we have chosen the "client request for A/V E creation" to illustrate this service.

In the prototype of Figure 6, we partially represent the negotiation of VE creation request, where in the first step the overall aspects of the required project are defined, client search constraints, overall negotiation parameters and a first attempt to fit the project in one or more

Figure 4. IDEF0 representation of the global process for the creation of a market of resources and for VE design, integration, and operation (Source: Cunha et al., 2003; Cunha et al., 2005)

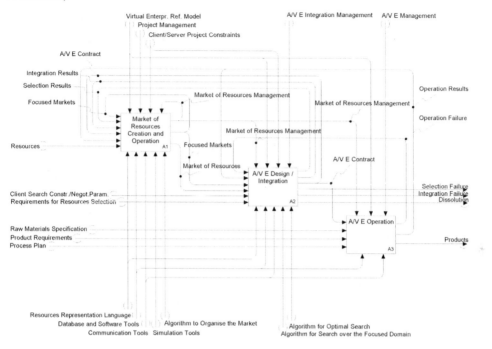

Figure 5. IDEF0 representation of Process A.2: VE design and integration

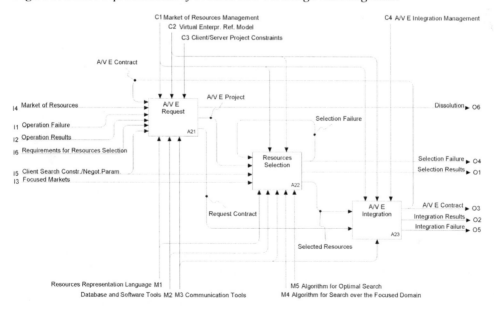

Figure 6. Request negotiation for VE creation: Step 1

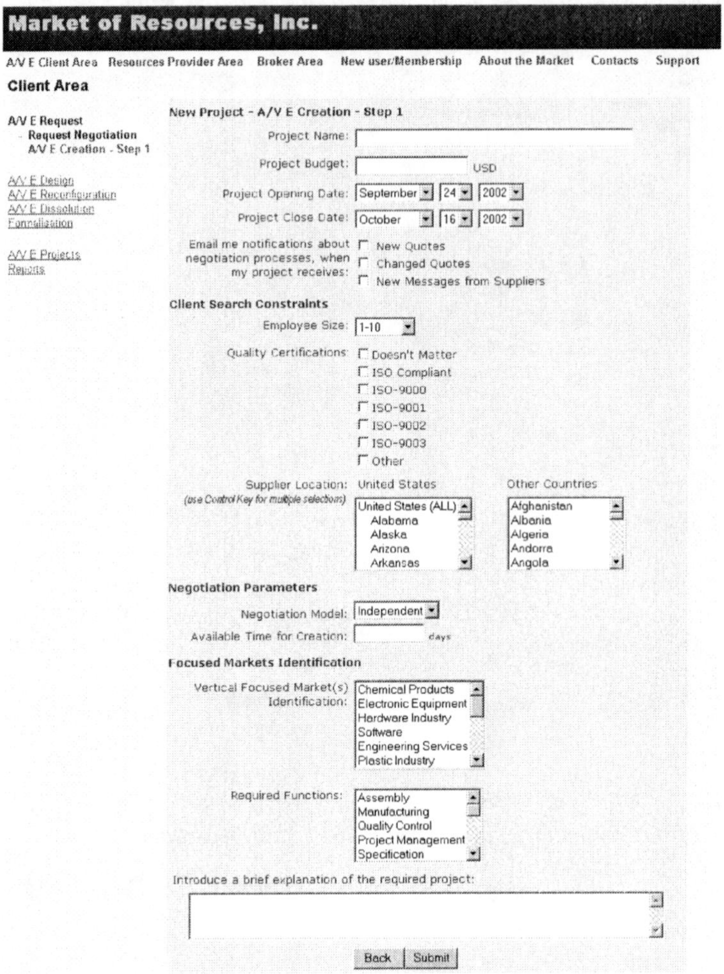

focused markets (to facilitate the identification of a broker) and in the second step (Figure 7) the broker is allocated. At this phase, the client could require an estimation of the cost of the service he is requiring, but the exact cost can only be calculated after the conclusion of the VE design.

The request for VE creation continues with the VE design, where, for each of the required resources, in two steps, the client specifies the requirements for resources selection and negotiation parameters (Figure 8), followed by a corresponding validation face to the grammar associated to the resources representation language (Figure 9). It is intended that the broker can *chat* with the client to provide guidance in the design process. After the request

Figure 7. Request negotiation for VE creation: Step 2

Figure 8. VE design: Step 1

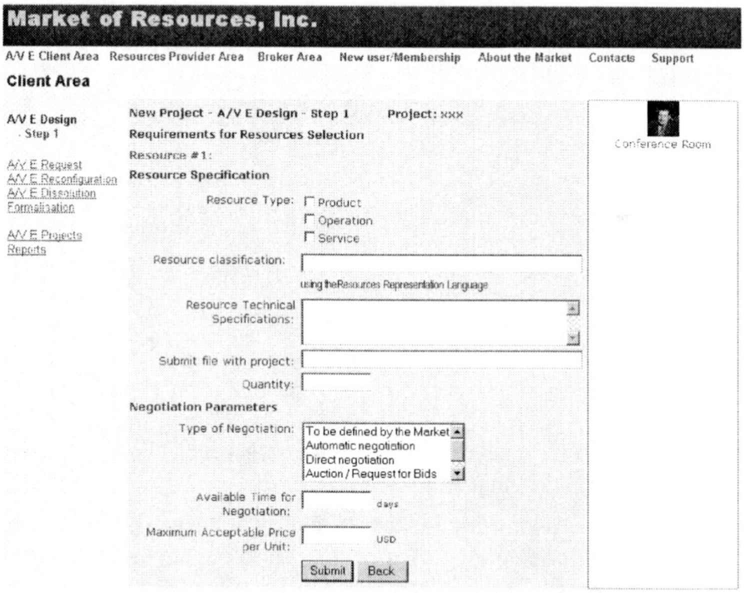

for validation, the client receives a list of errors detected on the overall project evaluation, until the VE project is fully designed and valid.

Finally, after the validation of the project, the request for the service of creating a VE according to the project can be formalized (Figure 10).

Figure 9. VE design: Step 2

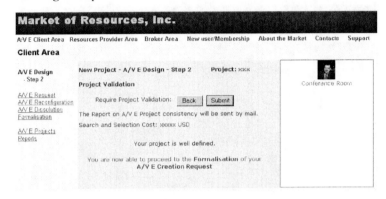

Figure 10. VE request formalization

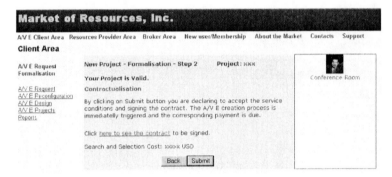

Conclusion

The full potential of the VE model can only be achieved through supporting environments, such as those presented in the chapter.

A study undertaken by the authors to validate the ability of the market of resources to support the high dynamics intrinsic to the VE model, based on an analytical cost and effort model and on the prototype of the market of resources, revealed its high performance when compared with the traditional Internet-based solutions such as World Wide Web search engines and directories, and traditional electronic marketplaces. Results and discussion of this validation can be found in Cunha and Putnik (2003b, 2003c).

Consider K to be the number of required resources to integrate in a VE project (creation or reconfiguration). Based on analytical simulation results based on the already-mentioned cost and effort models, the authors identified the domain of opportunities for the market of resources, in function of the number of required resources (K) and of the search domain

Figure 11. Break-even points based on search and selection cost and time

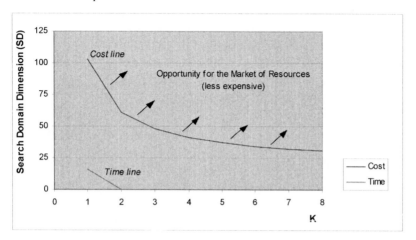

dimension (Figure 11). The Figure identifies the region where the market of resources presents increased efficiency when compared with the traditional Internet-based technologies, in function of the number of required resources and the search domain dimension, considering time and cost parameters.

The market of resources revealed the ability to support higher reconfiguration requirements than the traditional tools (due to the more reduced reconfiguration time and the cost it allows) and its suitability increases with product complexity (introduced by the number of required resources). Traditional tools only support simple products (one at each time) and do no support dynamics. By reducing reconfiguration time and cost, the market of resources is an enabler of reconfiguration dynamics, and an enabler of dynamic organizational models such as the virtual enterprise one.

Obviously, dynamic organizational models are not general and "all-purpose" solutions. This model represents an adequate solution for highly-customized products, with small series, in highly-competitive and changing environments where permanent business alignment is crucial, that is, situations where partnership stability is low (sometimes very low), dependency between partners is very weak, and reconfiguration dynamics should be as high as possible, given the permanent monitoring of the structure to introduce the most competitive solution at every moment of the product life cycle.

References

Browne, J., & Zhang, J. (1999). Extended and virtual enterprises: Similarities and differences. *International Journal of Agile Management Systems, 1*(1), 30-36.

Byrne, J. A. (1993). The virtual corporation: The company of the future will be the ultimate in adaptability. *Business Week*, 98-103.

Camarinha-Matos, L. M., & Afsarmanesh, H. (1999). The virtual enterprise concept. In L. M. Camarinha-Matos & H. Afsarmanesh (Eds.), *Infrastructures for virtual enterprises* (pp. 3-14). Porto, Portugal: Kluwer Academic Publishers.

Camarinha-Matos, L. M., & Afsarmanesh, H. (2004). The emerging discipline of collaborative networks. In L. M. Camarinha-Matos (Ed.), *Virtual enterprises and collaborative networks*: Kluwer Academic Publishers.

Cardoso, H., & Oliveira, E. (2005). Virtual enterprise normative framework within electronic institutions. In M. -P. Gleizes, A. Omicini, & F. Zambonelli (Eds.), *Engineering Societies in the Agents World V: 5th International Workshop* (LNCS 3451, pp. 14-32). Heidelberg, Germany: Springer Berlin.

Carlsson, C. (2002). Decisions support in virtual organizations: The case for multi-agent support. *Group Decision and Negotiation, 11*, 185-221.

Christiaanse, E., & Markus, M. L. (2003). Participation in collaboration electronic marketplaces. In *Proceedings of the 36th Hawaii International Conference of Systems Sciences (HICSS)*.

Covisint. (2001). Retrieved August 2001, from http://www.covisint.com

Cunha, M. M., & Putnik, G. D. (2002). Discussion on requirements for agile/virtual enterprises reconfigurability dynamics: The example of the automotive industry. In L. M. Camarinha-Matos (Ed.), *Collaborative business ecosystems and virtual enterprises* (pp. 527-534). Boston: Kluwer Academic Publishers.

Cunha, M. M., & Putnik, G. D. (2003a). Agile/virtual enterprise enablers: A comparative analysis. In D. N. Sormaz & G. A. Süer (Eds.), *Proceedings of Group Technology/Cellular Manufacturing—World Symposium 2003* (pp. 243-247). Columbus, OH: Ohio University.

Cunha, M. M., & Putnik, G. D. (2003b, June 10-13). Market of resources versus e-based traditional virtual enterprise integration—Part I: A cost model definition. In G. D. Putnik & A. Gunasekaran (Eds.), *Proceedings of the First International Conference on Performance Measures, Benchmarking, and Best Practices in New Economy* (pp. 664-669). Guimarães, Portugal: University of Minho.

Cunha, M. M., & Putnik, G. D. (2003c, June 10-13). Market of resources versus e-based traditional virtual enterprise integration—Part II: A comparative cost analysis. In G. D. Putnik & A. Gunasekaran (Eds.), *Proceedings of the First International Conference on Performance Measures, Benchmarking, and Best Practices in New Economy* (pp. 667-675). Guimarães, Portugal: University of Minho.

Cunha, M. M., & Putnik, G. D. (2005a). Business alignment in agile/virtual enterprise integration. In M. Khosrow-Pour (Ed.), *Advanced topics in information resources management* (Vol. 4, pp. 26-54). Hershey, PA: Idea-Group Publishing.

Cunha, M. M., & Putnik, G. D. (2005b). Business alignment requirements and dynamic organizations. In G. D. Putnik & M. M. Cunha (Eds.), *Virtual enterprise integration: Technological and organizational perspectives* (pp. 78-101). London: Idea Group Publishing.

Cunha, M. M., & Putnik, G. D. (2005c). Market of resources for agile/virtual enterprise integration. In M. Khosrow-Pour (Ed.), *Encyclopedia of information science and technology* (pp. 1891-1898). Hershey, PA: Idea-Group Publishing.

Cunha, M. M., & Putnik, G. D. (2006a). *Agile/virtual enterprise: Implementation and implementation management.* Idea Group Publishing.

Cunha, M. M., & Putnik, G. D. (2006b). Identification of the domain of opportunities for a market of resources for virtual enterprise integration. *International Journal of Production Research, 44*(12), 2277-2298.

Cunha, M. M., & Putnik, G. D. (2006c). On the dynamics of agile/virtual enterprise reconfiguration. *International Journal of Networking and Virtual Organisations, 3*(1), 102-123.

Cunha, M. M., Putnik, G. D., & Ávila, P. (2000). Towards focused markets of resources for agile/ virtual enterprise integration. In L. M. Camarinha-Matos, H. Afsarmanesh, & H. Erbe (Eds.), *Advances in networked enterprises: Virtual organisations, balanced automation, and systems integration* (pp. 15-24). Berlin: Kluwer Academic Publishers.

Cunha, M. M., Putnik, G. D., & Gunasekaran, A. (2002). Market of resources as an environment for agile/virtual enterprise dynamic integration and for business alignment. In A. Gunasekaran (Ed.), *Knowledge and information technology management in the 21st century organisations: Human and social perspectives* (pp. 169-190). London: Idea Group Publishing.

Cunha, M. M., Putnik, G. D., & Gunasekaran, A. (2003). Market of resources as an environment for agile/virtual enterprise dynamic integration and for business alignment. In A. Gunasekaran & O. Khalil (Eds.), *Knowledge and information technology management in the 21st century organisations: Human and social perspectives* (pp. 169-190). London: Idea Group Publishing.

Cunha, M. M., Putnik, G. D., Gunasekaran, A., & Ávila, P. (2005). Market of resources as a virtual enterprise integration enabler. In G. D. Putnik & M. M. Cunha (Eds.), *Virtual enterprise integration: Technological and organizational perspectives* (pp. 145-165). London: Idea Group Publishing.

Dai, Q., & Kauffman, R. (2001). *Business models for Internet-based e-procurement systems and B2B electronic markets: An exploratory assessment.* Paper presented at the 34th Hawaii International Conference on Systems Science, Maui, HI.

Davidow, W. H., & Malone, M. S. (1992). *The virtual corporation: Structuring and revitalizing the corporation for the 21st century.* New York: HarperCollins Publishers.

Dogac, A. (1998, March). *A survey of the current state-of-the-art in electronic commerce and research issues in enabling technologies.* Paper presented at the Euro-Med Net '98 Conference, Electronic Commerce Track.

Elemica (2005). *Elemica Overview.* Retrieved April, 2005, from http://www.elemica.com

Euroma (2002, June). Operations management and the new economy. *Call for Papers and Announcement of the 9th International Conference of the European Operations Management Association.* Copenhagen.

Hands, J., Bessonov, M., Blinov, M., Patel, A., & Smith, R. (2000). An inclusive and extensible architecture for electronic brokerage. *Decision Support Systems, 29*, 305-321.

Handy, C. (1996). *Beyond uncertainty. The changing words of organisations*. Boston: Harvard Business School Press.

Khalil, O., & Wang, S. (2002). Information technology enabled meta-management for virtual organizations. *International Journal of Production Economics, 75*(1), 127-134.

Martin, C. (1999). *Net future*. New York: McGraw-Hill.

Metcalfe, D. (2004). Surging elemica signals the rise of the networks. *Forrester Research*. Retrieved from http://www.forester.com

Molina, A., & Flores, F. (1999). A virtual enterprise in Mexico: From concepts to practice. *Journal of Intelligent and Robotic Systems, 26*, 289-302.

O'Sullivan, D. (1998). Communications technologies for the extended enterprise. *International Journal of Production Planning and Control, 9*(8), 742-753.

Preiss, K., Goldman, S., & Nagel, R. (1996). *Cooperate to compete: Building agile business relationships*. New York: van Nostrand Reinhold.

Putnik, G. D. (2000). BM_virtual enterprise architecture reference model. In A. Gunasekaran (Ed.), *Agile manufacturing: 21st century manufacturing strategy* (pp. 73-93). UK: Elsevier Science Publ.

Putnik, G. D. (2001). BM_virtual enterprise architecture reference model. In A. Gunasekaran (Ed.), *Agile manufacturing: 21st century manufacturing strategy* (pp. 73-93). UK: Elsevier Science Publ.

Putnik, G. D., Cunha, M. M., Sousa, R., & Ávila, P. (2005). BM virtual enterprise: A model for dynamics and virtuality. In G. D. Putnik & M. M. Cunha (Eds.), *Virtual enterprise integration: Technological and organizational perspectives* (pp. 124-144). London: Idea Group Publishing.

Rocha, A. P., Cardoso, H., & Oliveira, E. (2005). Contributions to an electronic institution supporting virtual enterprises' life cycle. In G. D. Putnik & M. M. Cunha (Eds.), *Virtual enterprise integration: Technological and organizational perspectives* (pp. 229-246). London: Idea Group Publishing.

SEEMseed_Consortium. (2005). *European Commission—Information Society Directorate-General*. Report of the SEEMseed Workshop held at the European Commission in Brussels on May 30, 2005. Retrieved from http://www.seemseed.org/default.aspx

Wang, C. X. (2001). Supply chain coordination in B2B electronic markets. In *Proceedings of the 32nd Annual Meeting of the Decision Sciences Institute*, San Francisco.

Webster, M., Sugden, D. M., & Tayles, M. E. (2004). The measurement of manufacturing virtuality. *International Journal of Operations & Production Management, 24*(7), 721-742.

Endnote

[1]   IDEF stands for ICAM DEFinition methodology (ICAM—Integrated Computer-Aided Manufacturing). IDEF diagrams illustrate the structural relations between two processes and the entities present in the system. The processes (represented as boxes) transform the *inputs* into *outputs* (respectively the left and the right arrows of a process), using the *mechanisms* for the transformation (the bottom arrows of a process) and constrained by *control information or conditions* under which the transformation occurs (the top arrows).

Chapter II

Service Engineering and Extended Artefact Delivery

G. M. Acaccia, PMAR Lab, DIMEC, University of Genova, Italy

S. Kopácsi, CIMLAB, Computer and Automation Institute, Hungary

G. L. Kovacs, CIMLAB, Computer and Automation Institute, Hungary

R. C. Michelini, PMAR Lab, DIMEC, University of Genova, Italy

R. P. Razzoli, PMAR Lab, DIMEC, University of Genova, Italy

Abstract

Recently, the manufacturing business is moving from an economy of scale to an economy of scope, under global competition for customers' satisfaction. Under those conditions, for companies around the world, surviving in business means to satisfy at least three challenges: granting the on-duty performance, at the point-of-service; addressing value-added intangibles; and lowering life-cycle eco impact. These changes in industry reflect on the human society; they are driven both through economical and political measures, as well as being increasingly affected by ecological constraints. Servicing and recovering become challenging demands. Besides technical aspects, the emphasis is in enabling economic profits on the supply chain (by new businesses in maintenance, remanufacturing, etc.), with account of legal acts (suppliers responsibility, landfill regulation, etc.), ruled by voluntary agreements or by compulsory targets frames. Our emphasis is on the following new paradigms: extended virtual enterprise and extended product, service engineering, life-cycle engineering, product life-cycle management, proactive maintenance, recovery, reuse, recycling, ubiquitous computing and communication, and so forth.

Introduction

The affluent society, brought forth by the industrial revolution through the economy of scale, cannot last for long, being based on the ceaseless replacement of tangible goods, manufactured by depleting the earth's resources, transformed into pollution and wastes. The eco-consistency requires new business paradigms. At this time, the measures for sustainable growth are not fully acknowledged; to address pollution and dumping minimisation is only an attempt to establish more conservative supply-chains, looking back to the thrifty society. Indeed, the earth is an almost isolated system, with limited input taken from sunlight and a limited output released into space (this is an *energy*, not an *entropy*, balance). In time, the eco-decay will limit the *industrial* growth unless upgrading ecological issues are found, nondependent on entropy (e.g., by information value-added chains, such as information communication technology [ICT] aids; or by bio-mimesis, such as restoration processes emulating the living beings).

Manufacturing and the corresponding business are moving from an economy of scale to an economy of scope, under global competition for customers' satisfaction (Michelini & Kovacs, 2004; Michelini & Razzoli, 2005). To stay in the global competition, the following main challenges should be met:

- Meet customer requirements, granting the on-duty performance, at the point-of-service.
- Diversify the offers by information which is value-added (e.g., supplying lifelong servicing).
- Manufacture products with lower life-cycle (on-duty and at dismissal) impact.

These changes in industry reflect on the human society; they are driven both through economical and political measures, as well as being increasingly affected by ecological constraints. Service, recovery, maintenance, remanufacturing, and so forth, are getting more and more important even in the profit-making procedures. These all are widely stimulated by law-enforced recovery quotas and taxation policies in commodities procurement, or by waste disposal restrictions and corresponding charges. Thereafter, the vision of technology-driven solutions will move with factual checks of their financial appropriateness. The emerging industrial fields will track reciprocal ways:

- Modify the forward value chain, expanding the intangibles delivery for more efficiently satisfying the clients' needs, while watching the eco-impacts; profitability is achieved by selling products and services.
- Resort systematically to the backward value chain, for effective utilisation of the pawned natural capital; profitability is deferred to reverse logistics activities, rewarded by taxing actual net burdens.

These added challenges have been the object of special concern, with pertinent investigations included, for example, by the IV and V EU Framework Programmes, aiming at supply chains providing *products and services*, or *extended artefacts* (EXPIDE, 2003; Jansson & Thoben, 2002), namely, any deliveries joining manufactured commodities and enabling utilities (*artefact*: an object made by man, especially with a view of subsequent use). The idea is that an *extended artefact* blends commodity and utility, through information-intensive supply, to grant specified functions, by means of lifelong indenture binding sellers to buyers. The ICT aids represent the technical divide between previous and emerging challenges; an extended artefact requires the manufacturers' responsibility at the points of *sale*, of *service*, and of *dismissal*. In this type of trade organisations, the value is added by the supplier on the lifelong steps of the provision, aiming at new business paradigms types. The approach has been acknowledged, and product life-cycle management (PLM) (Ameri & Dutta, 2005; Garetti, 2004) tools are noteworthy achievements. By PLM, knowledge and technology keep the manufacturing internality, and exploit virtuality to deal with life-cycle *product responsibility*.

Growth sustainability requires focussing on externalities, and expanding the *producers' responsibilities*; the *extended enterprise* organisation offers opportunities. For the thrifty society, servicing and recycling play a relevant role: The traded artefacts are replaced by products and services, supported by networked partners (Michelini & Kovacs, 2004), and variably connected in terms of duties and competencies. These setups make possible supply chains complying with eco-conservative demands, due to transparent recognition and control on resources decay and environmental burden. The EU environmental protection policy, accordingly, directly addresses the pertinent manufacturer/supplier interventions, mainly by two approaches:

1.   Establish stringent conformance-to-use requirement for minimal eco-impact, thus implicitly to foster voluntary agreements towards a product and service market.

2.   Enact compulsory recovery targets at artefact dismissal, with economic instruments focussed on free-take-back policies and explicit suppliers' involvement.

The content of the chapter aims at both externalities, namely, the challenges of the service engineering for the extended artefact deliveries, supported by extended enterprises. The role of the ICT bears utmost relevance, being an instrumental enabler for the market conversion into products and services, managed by networked organisations. These aspects are duly recalled with, in the last section, special focus on opportunities offered by *ambient intelligence* to provide effectiveness to the many incumbents of *service engineering*.

Business Paradigm Shifts for Eco-Consistency

The added challenges in the global manufacturing world, faced as severe charges by back-looking firms, open the opportunities of the so called knowledge entrepreneurship, which exploits new rules on the market, aiming at extended artefacts, supported by extended enterprises, namely:

- **Rule 1:** The manufacturers' responsibility assumes mandatory delivery of product and service technicalities for *on-duty conformance-to-use*, and law-compulsory *end-of-life* withdrawal of subsets of mass-produced durables, on the *free-take-back* scheme.

- **Rule 2:** It is not enough to deliver the required product, but the most important thing is to supply after-sales services, which satisfy or, in some cases, predict, as well, the customer requirements, complying to the enacted environment protection rules.

- **Rule 3:** The enterprise profitability shall focus on intangibles and services, supplied as an integral part of delivery, with concern on their time-to-market and technological sustainability, through offers enhanced by information-intensive additions.

- **Rule 4:** Not only goods should satisfy demands of cost-competitive and eco-consistent quality, but accompanying services as well shall satisfy these demands, further providing visibility and recording of the impact on the human/nature surroundings.

The farther our community will turn from the affluent to the thrifty society, the more relevance will be given to the products-related services in companies' competition. In other words, if in the affluent society, the competition between companies made emphasis on the "*manufacturing* phase," today the focus should turn to the binding eco-thresholds. In the future thrifty society, effectiveness will make emphasis on the "*life-cycle* service" part of the delivery. This does not mean that tangible components could be totally replaced, but that the knowledge entrepreneurship will simultaneously deal with commodities and utilities to satisfy clients' needs. The role of the second part of the product and service supply is getting more relevant, and companies can buildup their businesses in the area of providing accompanying services for products manufactured by another company. The context, thereafter, has recently led to the appearance of a novel field, namely, *service engineering* (SE), developed to expand the mainly intangible provisions for enhanced use of conventional goods. These rules are basic drivers of the knowledge-intensive restructuring of the manufacturing economy, promoted by ICT aids and leading to the systemic re-thinking of the entrepreneurship characterised by *method innovation*, where the main role is played by Web-interconnected organisations.

Service Engineering and Manufacturer Responsibility

Service engineering is a new research discipline (Liestmann, Gudergan, & Gill, 2004), which deals with: improving the functions of the enabling processes; developing and implementing the supporting frames; and providing and executing the services, as corporate duty. Moreover, it has to tackle service-oriented human resource management. In some aspects, service engineering is very similar to the PLM concept. The service engineering assumes that services can be designed and developed in a similar manner as physical products. Based on Liestmann et al. (2004), the process of service design and development has three major phases: service planning, service conception, and service implementation. The graphical picture for SE is given on the right-hand side of Figure 1. Now, methodologies related with service-providing organisations are covered in PLM, but are focused on integration of services with manufacturing processes. On the contrary, product and service supply develops with emphasis either on the *product* part or on the *service* part (see Figure 1.). If the importance is on the *product* part, the PLM model is applicable for several business cases; but for post-manufacturing businesses, the service engineering (SE) is more appropriate. The SE description makes the stress on the *service* part of product and service supply, and opens opportunities to upgrade the traditional industrial world by means of the rules of the knowledge-driven entrepreneurship.

From a factual point of view, the SE will progressively expand, in conjunction with the widening of the manufacturers/suppliers responsibility enacted through the EU directives. Up to quite recent years, the point-of-sale represented a divide, after which buyers could little argue if purchased items would not correspond to the desired properties, due to ineffective provision of expected functions. The want of properties increasingly comes from conformance-to-use assessments, established by environment protection acts, with restriction or prohibition to take benefit of deliveries; then, manufacturers profit by supplying goods, only *virtually* exploited, and will lose clients for scarcely usable goods. This will result in changing clients' satisfaction, from the point-of-sale, to point-of-service. As a consequence, the enterprises, to face world-wide competition, are compelled to modify their strategies, looking for life-cycle supply chains, and supporting commodities and utility mixes, according to alternative prospects:

- A single supplier keeps in charge all incumbents along the *product and service* delivery (dismissal included).
- A team of dealers grants *special provisions*, due to oriented qualification and infrastructure-based setups.

In both cases, as for sustainability, the seller-to-buyer indenture specifies a life-cycle bond, as the two parties together (*consumers*) oppose to all other people (*eco-resource inherent holders*), locally represented through governmental regulations, and globally protected by international treaties.

The life-cycle relationship obliges the supplier to the buyers, for conformance-to-use at the point-of-service. The traded goods are characterised by: The market-driven *quality* aims at customers' satisfaction by a mix of lifelong operation properties; and the sustainable *quality* becomes monitored attributes, under transparently-acknowledged schemes. These options are considered by the EU environmental policy, and distinguish alternative measures:

- Foster eco-conservative behaviours, by promoting the drawing-up of *voluntary agreements*.
- Force eco-sustainability achievements, by enacting recovery *compulsory targets*.

Thus, the legal frame modifies: *from* mainly bilateral supplier-to-customer responsiveness; *through* jointly-liable consumers' commitment (to reach eco-consistency); and *to* explicit manufacturers' responsibility (to comply with regulations). Depending on the commodities and supply chain steps, the legal frames evolution follows tracks, more or less smooth, in view of the expected impact, the strength of the opposing lobbies, and the effectiveness of the enabling facilities. Anyway, the millennium shows the expansion of:

Figure 1. PLM and SE business paradigms

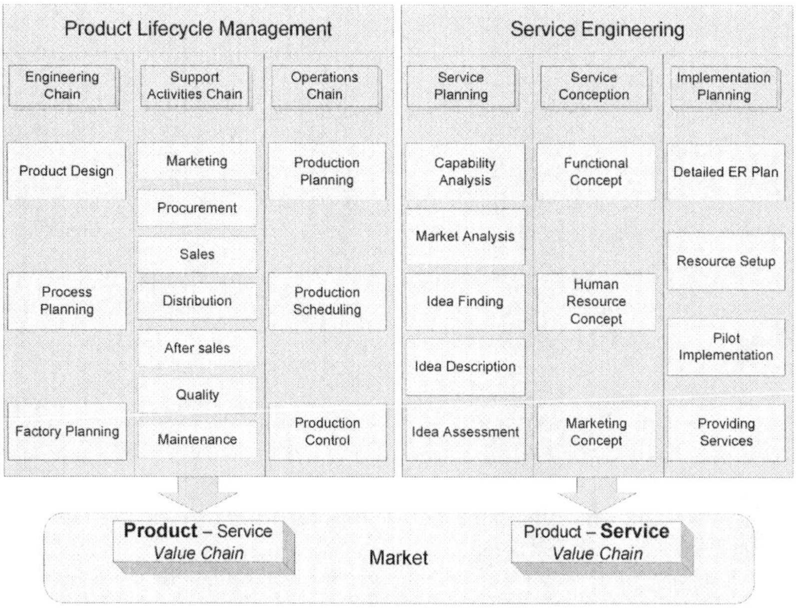

Product Lifecycle Management			Service Engineering		
Engineering Chain	Support Activities Chain	Operations Chain	Service Planning	Service Conception	Implementation Planning
Product Design	Marketing	Production Planning	Capability Analysis	Functional Concept	Detailed ER Plan
	Procurement		Market Analysis		
	Sales				Resource Setup
Process Planning	Distribution	Production Scheduling	Idea Finding	Human Resource Concept	
	After sales		Idea Description		Pilot Implementation
	Quality				
Factory Planning	Maintenance	Production Control	Idea Assessment	Marketing Concept	Providing Services

Product – Service *Value Chain*   **Market**   Product – **Service** *Value Chain*

- **Voluntary agreements:** under consumers' joint liability for product life-cycle operations
- **Compulsory targets:** under producers' responsibility for end-of-life dismissal incumbents

Basically, it is acknowledged that on-duty and dismissal properties of extended artefacts come up to affect third parties sphere and safeguard. The provision of eco-conformance certificates becomes relevant business, in the value chain, with the joint liability of suppliers and users for the protection of the eco-system, according to the enacted rules.

Delivery of Extended Artefacts by Extended Enterprises

This EU demand suggests a number of manufacture/service industries to apply new strategies to join product design and manufacture, with life-cycle and dismissal management. For the last decade, the information technology sector made big advances. It made it possible to address value chains, delivering products and services, supported by cooperating organisations. This type of change opened horizons to enable new businesses, such as SE, embedding high-intensity information, with enhanced transparency of the material resources decay and with increased intangible added value. These paradigms make it possible for networked companies to be more competitive, improving after-sale service, products duty upgrading, and recovery. In some cases, to excel in servicing, maintenance and recycling areas are the critical means for a company to be a winner on the market. Indeed, the full acknowledgement of the technical conformance of a product at the *point-of-use* is a non-eliminable request, to comply with eco-consistency incumbents, and the reliable assessment and recording of life cycle falls-off become standard duty, to certify items sustainability achievements. Actually, economical return is standard reference to support remuneration to the whole flow:

- **Forward value chain:** materials procurement, product design manufacture and testing, items distribution, selling, and conformance upkeeping and maintenance
- **Backward value chain:** exhausted goods collection and forwarding to dismissal; selective dismantling with recovering/shredding; second-hand materials sorting and enhancement; and residuals dumping

Now, the single steps have consignors and assignors, but, most of the backward chain outcomes do not have explicit purchasers, lacking links to actual needs. Thus, separating backward, from forward chain will authorise deviating issues, to keep benefits within a subset of actors, while damaging third (and future) parties. The cost/profit ratio is, then, to be assessed balancing the advantage of stakeholders (manufacturers and users) *against* protection of all the people not involved by the specific value chain. In that sense, regulation for eco-impact is a peremptory task that governments need to undertake, enacting sets of rules for charging the consumers' side for environmental fall-offs linked to the whole supply chain, dismissal and recycling incumbents included. These are leading the EU Council to expand the suppliers' responsibility to the *point of withdrawal* of basic mass products (white and brown household appliances, automotive vehicles, etc.), as shared commitment, established at *the point of sale*, when suppliers earn for their work, and clients purchase to satisfy their whims. A similar rule does not appear for conformance-to-use requests, and these are left to the drawing-up of *voluntary agreements*; but, in this case, explicit buyers exist, with largely expressed needs.

All in all, however, the underlying organisations and technologies present noteworthy similarities, with unifying reference in *service engineering*, characterising issue in *extended* artefacts, and enabling support in extended enterprises. Basically, today one should mainly distinguish the economical instruments: *voluntary agreements*, for on-duty conformance management; and *compulsory regulations*, for recovery targets. The latter, *enforceable* market, in this way, could anticipate the former, unless pioneering enterprises establish. The ICT aids play a fundamental role in developing the whole. Moving to lifelong concern, knowledge-driven frames are a necessary prerequisite, to make possible assessing items impact and resources decay. These frames build up on three facts:

1. Marketing extended artefacts, with collaborative networks to support clients' requests
2. Involvement of extended enterprises, assuring *point-of-service* conformance guarantees
3. Overseeing *third-party* certifying bodies, to record the tangibles yield per unit service

The collaborative networks, thereafter, face hierarchical topologies:

- **Inner cluster:** to link the extended enterprise partners, for extended artefact delivery
- **Specialised links:** to support the *point-of-service* communication with individual buyers
- **Selective data channels:** to give access to the certifying bodies under security protocols

The varying-topology information setup is shared context, sliced into layers, with the:

- **Lowest:** (artefact ideation and construction), within the extended enterprise inner cluster
- **Intermediate:** (artefact life cycle), for the data management at the clients' satisfaction
- **Highest:** (artefact sustainability and tangibles charges), ruled by the certifying bodies

The picture is coherent with a *controlled* collaborative net, connecting extended enterprise to individual clients, so that the supply chain of the delivered extended artefact is available to an accredited certifying body, for conformance assessment purposes. The *e*-maintenance systems and reverse logistics are qualifying features of the new business options. The former is one example of the ICT solutions for the tasks considered in SE. These systems vary from product supported or from engineering/business field of application. Like PLM solutions, their may consist of different modules and tools. Some modules can evaluate the products, machines, or other equipment without human intervention, or adjust the monitored objects to avoid breakdowns or undesirable situations. In the following, details on the technologies and enabling methods are discussed, to understand and implement a very characteristic option: proactive maintenance, based on the ubiquitous computing and communication of ambient intelligence. Moreover, the *backward* value chain could help in explaining how the economical instruments change the business ratability. The *reverse logistics* is the process of designing, planning, and controlling the return and reuse of worn-out products, in order to conserve resources and protect the environment. Profitability through the *backward* value chain requires boosting facts (Acaccia, Michelini, & Qualich, 2005; Dekker, Fleischmann, Inderfurth, & van Wassenhove, 2004; Dyckhoff, Lackes, & Reese, 2004; Michelini & Razzoli, 2003), such as the following:

- **Closed loop supply chains:** grounded on standards for parts/materials recovering
- **Tendency to remanufacture:** based on design for reuse, instead of disposal destination
- **Collection and disassembly organisations:** with effective facilities for worn-out goods

- **Sorting, retrieval, and reintegration processes:** to extract assessed quality resources
- **Account of material and energy whole provisions:** to repay the net caused decay
- **Recognition of every emerging impact:** to pay for the remediation and restoring incumbents
- **Exhaustive information frames:** for product data life cycle certified monitoring and vaulting
- **Objective tax collection:** for all tangibles withdrawals, to establish fair-trade competition

These are a mix of legal and technical prescriptions. The economical return of reverse logistics activities is the current challenge for the coming years, at least, in trading of already regulated durables and consumables. To those goals, it is especially relevant to develop decision aids for backward supply chains, and to compare collecting, dispatching, re-manufacturing, and disposal processes, determining drawbacks/benefits each time they are reached.

Service Engineering and Quality-Certifying Bodies

The critical nature of eco-consistency is differently perceived, today, with stress on weighing current versus future targets, and local versus global needs, according to rather opaque procedures. This results in a wavering gait, with large pressure on given domains or details, and odd thoughtlessness in other cases. The selection of the durables/consumables domains, for example, to regulate by compulsory recover/reuse/recycle targets is, possibly, explained by the impact they are provoking, *negatively*, as for the wreck quantities, and *positively*, as for the psychological issues; indeed, everyone happens, several times in his life, to be involved in waste-electric-and-electronic-equipment and end-of-life vehicles.

The relevance of the ICT tracks emerges with emphasis, *directly*, because of the explicit attention towards high-tech industry and technological excellence promotion, and *indirectly*, because of the instrumental role played in assuring supply chains with maximum value-added in intangibles, and in providing effective technologies for service engineering along goods life cycle, dismissal included. This chapter is especially concerned with the second track, namely, instrumental exploitation of ICT tools. The role is multifarious, with characterising property, the *information intensity*. For the present purposes, the stress is in visibility of the generated eco-impact, with certified assessment of actually-induced effects of *on-duty artefacts* (for allowed exploitation, with positive conformance-to-use checks) and of *end-of-life goods* (for recover/reuse/recycle and dump operations according to law). The business vastness and complexity extent are immediately evident, since progressively all material flows need be monitored and recorded, explicitly associating suppliers and clients. Results ought to be reported to national agencies/authorities (and notified to EU officers, which verify their compliance), in keeping with proper data handling and vaulting caution, granting citizens privacy and security. For the ecological requirements, service engineering shall, accordingly, fulfil two goals:

1. Cover the *servicing* side of the extended artefact supply, such as: the (tangible and intangible) delivery to a client, granting enjoyment of specified *functions*, by life-cycle indentures, ruled by extended enterprises, with return on investment, by recourse to *scope* economy.

2. Accomplish the *monitoring* and *control* of the environmental impact, reporting the results to overseeing certified bodies, namely, *third parties* (independent of dealers and purchasers) with access to thewhole supply chain, charged to assess and record the products life-cycle data.

The two goals are actually deeply connected, since users are, in both cases, the beneficiaries, to keep goods operation reliability and eco-conformance (Blumberg, 2004; Chan & Lee, 2005; Corafas, 2001; Dekker et al., 2004; Michelini & Kovacs, 1999).

To deal with eco-servicing, the information framework lumps together purveyors and users, both subject to the monitoring of independent (and duly accredited) supervisors. The three parties ruling seems to be good compromise to enhance competition, grant privacy, and balance responsibility, under *fair-trade* rules. Then, transparency of the environment impact is achieved by continuous monitoring and recording actual running conditions of the *forward* and the *backward* cycle. The governmental agencies collect charges for consumed tangibles, assessed by the authorised certifying bodies. The three parties scheme includes (Krutwagen & van Kampen, 1999; Vernadat, 1996):

•   **Purveyors:** covering the entire *supply-chain*: materials provision, items manufacture, life-cycle upkeeping, backward recovery; the eco-responsibility is dealt with by clustering several firms within a factual alliance of cooperating multi-sectional interests businesses

•   **Users:** purchasing extended artefacts (*products and services*), to profit of the delivered *functions* with reliability figure close to one; the payments shall include conformance certification at the point of service, after tax collection against tangibles depletion

•   **Supervisors:** assuring *third party* incumbents for (today and tomorrow) environment and society protection; the certifying bodies report to governmental authorities and use objective standards, having access to the extended artefacts life-cycle databases

On such grounds, third party certification builds up as competition-driven service:

•   The joint-consumers' side lets out (on contract) the overseeing incumbents and the related conformance assessments, but can, any time, change the certifying body.

•   The authorities are entitled to rule the legal frames, but without any direct involvement in data keeping and recording, accomplished under proper secrecy by parcelled-out services.

Point-of-Service Eco-Safety Commitment

The knowledge-driven entrepreneurship approach leads to replace the *product-process* design of old simultaneous engineering focused on internalities, by the joint *product-process-enterprise* design conditioned by externalities. This will be basic practice, once life-cycle incumbents, dismissal included, are standard suppliers' responsibility, requiring extended enterprise settings, with integrated design evolving to include the business and operation management domains. The challenges are here more problematic, since the physic-based frames of engineering and manufacture are replaced by economic transactions, human and intellectual activities, and social and legal constraints. Objects and events are specified by texts, frames, graphic, or spreadsheets trends; model validation and simulation testing quickly lead to data reduction in terms of cost propagation and due dates. This provides abstract means to acknowledge business and operation functions, and to help by providing visibility for reliable prediction, on-process control, and steering actions. Moreover, the incorporation of extended enterprise infrastructures is domain-open to new developments, where the ICT aids play strategic roles. However, the chapter is concerned by engineering facts, and the present section addresses a characteristic option: "condition monitoring for proactive maintenance," which offers a noteworthy example for point-of-service eco-safety commitment today, established on voluntary agreements between providers and users. The technology introduces a qualifying competition opportunity between high-tech providers, and the aspects of the underlying ambient intelligence are not dissimilar from the requirements in eco-impact monitoring and vaulting of the enforceable regulations; in such prospects, the voluntary terms simply bring forward tomorrow's obligations.

Besides, the integrated design practice makes deliverables effective, with assessment of the return on investment, and estimation of every after-effect, including tangibles yield (or resource effectiveness), when the eco-consistency paradigms are considered. The tight relationship between design specification and on-duty conformance assessment is covered by proper PLM files. With PLM, the computer aids accomplish the paradigm shift to focus on life-cycle properties, since the ideation steps require, thereafter, powerful information tools, for algorithmic and storing capabilities and for heuristic and storing opportunities. The early merging of *CAD* and *CIME* tools appeared worthy support of intelligent factory, starting the progressive move to interactive design practices, by continuous feedback from artefacts properties. Today, the addition of green-engineering patterns is consistent with the extended artefact concept, with the further requirement of establishing the information surroundings for life-cycle conformance assessments, not limited to the supplier to purchaser indentation, but binding the consumers' side to grant the achieved eco-consistency, with certified record of the whole irreversibility impact. A few PLM properties are recalled, to explain the frame, where condition monitoring and diagnostic data are processed, in view of eco-servicing.

Construction Files and Life-Cycle Management

Following Garetti (2004), PLM defines as: an integrated business model that, using ICT aids, supports the integrated co-operative management of product-related data, along the full product life cycle, dismissal included. PLM originates from PDM, product data management, with two-fold upgrading: to improve the business native effectiveness; and to widen the reach of the involved authorised actors. Key aspects are (Stark, 2005):

- **Product and service unified data-frame:** The delivery of extended artefacts is the primary business achievement, and life-cycle knowledge is a basic requirement, since the earlier design steps.

- **Integrated data-flow management:** Hierarchical, interconnected, parametric product and business models ensure that decisions are made, achieving entrepreneurship-wide impact.

- **Distributed, flexible operability:** Robust communication and shared database and processing resources help in establishing teaming relationships, to face every emerging request.

- **Plug-and-play interoperability:** All technical and business modules need to be seamlessly compatible and self-adapting, to become operational immediately, without integration cost.

- **Total connectedness:** All stakeholders exploit communication infrastructures that deliver the right data at the right time, whenever they are required.

- **Fully-enabled extended artefact transparency:** PLM tools, by science-based and experience-driven knowledge, grants visibility to the decision schemes and achieved performance.

For the enterprise profitability, dependence on the strategic positioning in the market is current admission, and the supply chain concept shall also modify into *value* chain, to join parts and materials delivery, with the related intangibles flow (*value* Web), supporting a main contractor with vital complements. Today, the recourse to off-process design tasks and linked databases is compelled by the enacted product life-cycle regulation constraints, and is made possible by existing ICT aids, once the PLM expands to cover three ranges:

- **Standard product data:** physical specs; operation performance, quality, affordability, and cost; producibility; life-cycle constraints; use and maintenance; and dismissal instructions

- **Standard manufacturing data:** materials procurement and processing, assembly, and disassembly; packaging and delivering; and re-manufacturing

- **Standard enterprise data:** which includes business functions: trade strategies, finance and resource, and so forth; and, operation functions: factory and facilities specs, scheduling and planning, and the likes

A relevant issue in PLM deployment is to link the views, developed for different purposes or by different teams, in order to achieve *model federation*, making it easy to create high-level representations, allowing reuse of existing data and frames, and propagating the knowledge environments by seamless continuity. Designers will be able to assess candidate prototypal deliveries, from virtual factories, for virtual point-of-use setups, up to virtual point-of-dismissal situations, to evaluate and to improve producibility, function performance, operation reliability, maintainability, eco-impacts, dismissal falls-off, and so forth, in actual running conditions. They will be able to perform these checks beforehand, with proper completeness, to quickly reach effective hints, with the ability to zoom-in at the critical details and to compare alternatives. The life-cycle super model, then, distinguishes because of (Michelini & Kovacs, 1999; Michelini & Razzoli, 2005):

- Varying-geometry boundaries, to expand the views to extended artefacts
- Embedded simulation-emulation tools, to allow virtual behavioural checks
- Cooperative infrastructure, to support multiple-domain problem-solving issues
- Automatic propagation of changes, with updating of the super-model data-frame
- Evaluation of alternatives, trends, risks, and so forth, based on reliable relational schemes
- Rapid producibility, affordability, and so forth analyses, through intelligent decision support
- Fast and accurate exploration of life-cycle occurrences, for concept-to-production figures
- Archival of globally-accessible knowledge-bases, available in the current activity
- Ubiquitous service through the extended enterprise, enabling inter-operable tools
- Any similar options of advanced PLM, that today and future ICT tools provide

The unifying super-model for the coherent arrangement of the condition knowledge, needed to deal with extended artefacts, is considered by several research and development initiatives all over the world, with different levels of complexity. The IMTR Inc., (IMTR, 2000), for example, is a noteworthy example, with effective work aimed at joining the modelling and simulation functions, separately used for the description of *products*, *processes,* and *enterprises,* into an unified frame; the project shows the effective achievements at the range of *product-process* integration (by simultaneous engineering) and prospects a list of manufacturing functions deserving specific attention to reach appropriate *enterprise* integration.

The joint *product-process* design is an accepted practice, and has contributed to apply economy of scope by simultaneous engineering techniques. The eco-consistent PLM tools distinguish by a few additions, such as re-manufacturing options, such as processes that support return and reprocessing of products upon completion of original intended use, to take profit from reverse logistics. Actually, design-for-manufacturing (DfM), design-for-assembly (DfA), and so forth, scopes expand over design-for-disassembly (DfD), and design-for-recycling (DfR) ones, since the earlier product ideation steps. The business paradigms include remanufacture, recycle and reuse of products, parts, and materials, to minimise tangibles consumption and to maximise the use of resources. The eco-PLM tools enable designers to analyse reverse logistics as a means to enhance the value chain, for effectiveness, profitability, and environment sensitivity. This is, however, only an intermediate step toward new rules, when suppliers' responsibility encompasses the *product and service* delivery, on the life-cycle span, dismissal included. For *sustainability*, governmental acts will require visibility on the supply chain, to refrain from polluting and to lower consumption. Then competitiveness will turn from the capability of offering new products (fit-for-purpose to *individual* needs) to the ability of providing services, granting functions to full satisfaction, and better tangibles effectiveness (fit-for-purpose to *general* benefits). These emerging businesses will profit from the cooperative organisation by alternative approaches:

- The manufacturers could be spurred to keep in charge all *services*: artefacts supply, life-cycle conformance, and dismissal incumbents.
- New independent enterprises could profit by safety rules and environment acts expansion, to become *service* dealers, with technology-oriented qualification and infrastructure-based organisations.

Both approaches, nevertheless, require to focus on the PLM, moving enterprise profitability to be critically dependent on the design choices. The new market leaders will move within this technical-scientific framework, replacing the economy of *scale*, by the economy of *scope*, with, in any case, two opportunities:

1. **Functions delivery:** with profitability in the business of supplying *products and services*.
2. **Recovering efficiency:** with profitability in *reverse* logistics (from waste, to "raw" materials)

Condition Monitoring and Proactive Maintenance

The evolution in maintenance organisation is usefully characterised by distinguishing (Michelini, Crenna, & Rossi, 2001):

- **Off-process setups:** by restoration rules, when, at *breakdown*, resources are turned-off from duty-state; or by *preemptive* rules, at fixed times or given life consumption, provided by estimated reliability data
- **On-process setups:** by *predictive* rules, as resources are monitored to detect the onset of failures symptoms; or by *proactive* rules, to keep "normal conditions" by controlling on-going functional prerequisites

Breakdown maintenance keeps focus on time-efficient and lower-cost repairing/replacing equipment when a failure occurs. This strategy does not deal with zero failure situations and needs to face the connected falls-off: unpredictable occurrence time and undetermined activity stops (process downtime). To implement the strategy, a basic scenario is the following: A maintenance manager receives malfunction reports or demands for maintenance; this manager allocates engineers, defines time for maintenance activity, and sends the engineer to the field. The decision is affected by several factors like: job priority and constraints between them, ability and availability of engineers, and costs and time uncertainty.

Alternatively, sufficient process knowledge gives the possibility to avoid downtimes, by preemptive rules, based on *a priori* estimation of failure rate figures and pre-setting of operation periods within MTBF bounds; stops are established with proper safety margins, and *preventive* maintenance applies, while resources redundancy grants operation continuity. More elaborate strategies can be devised which detect symptoms of anomalous running and enable proactive maintenance operations, before actual failures develop. For monitoring tasks, they require sensors and links to knowledge databases aimed at on-process diagnoses, respectively, related to:

- **Ill-running situation/trend monitoring:** to prevent breakdown by detection of early symptoms
- **Continuous monitoring and deviation control:** to upkeep conformance-to-specification status

Intelligent modules make feasible monitoring maintenance, with detection of diagnostic signatures, related to operation thresholds, and not simply with detection of symptoms related to established misfits. Upkeeping actions, then, aim at *proactive* mode, as situation/trend monitoring provides knowledge to preserve fit-with-norm conditions. The onset of anomalies is avoided with reliable leads, since trimming or restoring actions are performed as case arises, possibly during idle or hidden times, by resolving at the root of the failure causes. Today, the availability of ICT aids moves *preventive* maintenance to subsidiary/confirmation functions, in view of exploiting the inherent systematic/scheduled arrangements for off-process operations. There are several ways to detect *predictive* rules. A useful architecture (Bengtsson, 2004) slices diagnoses emergence into layers: sensor data, signal processing, signature detection, condition/trend recognition, health assessment, prognostic, decision support, and restitution layers. The conditional maintenance helps to intervene before failure occurs: to reduce the number of failures; to do maintenance only when needed; to reduce maintenance and production lost costs; and to increase the life of equipment/product.

The ICT tools offers smart hardware and software equipment. A big hindrance is efficient exploitation of data, by transforming *diagnoses* into reactive or proactive *retrofit*. The promotion of a conservative running condition requires full understanding of the past, present, and future behaviour of the facilities and execution of redress, compensation, or repair actions, as soon as execution need is recognised, before the degradation symptoms appear. These two steps, to understand for diagnosis and to upkeep for restoring, are *logically* joined, or their separation means such odd issues as (Michelini et al., 2001): maintenance without monitoring is drugs taking with no care on health data; monitoring without maintenance is recording illness and looking for miracles. Predictive retrofit occurs when future evolution data are used to establish restoring actions, for regular or continuous upkeeping. However, the ICT experts easily deal with knowledge processing and buildup; actual redress is then left to *miracles*, unless the suitable outfits are included at the design stage. Condition monitoring, at higher sophistication, is built with support of knowledge-intensive environments; it exploits system hypotheses for feed-forward plans, and uses on-process data for closing proactive measures to preserve safe running situations, or for enabling reactive repair at (planned or unexpected) discontinuities for re-setting purposes. Of course, this strategy cannot eliminate product breakdowns with 100% reliability, but most of them are predicted and the restoring steps can be taken in advance, before failure development. An example of such a system is the MAXIMO product from Projetech Company (Projetech, 2005).

Today's e-maintenance tools, mainly, have resorted to referring to central knowledge-bases, or, to apply agent-based architecture. To enable predictive monitoring, the main duties are (Arnaiz, Arana, Maurtua, & Susperregi, 2004): to detect and identify abnormal situations, defined in terms of features or drifts; to acknowledge the fault situation, level of degradation, type of failure, and so forth; and to troubleshoot, assessing the restoring policy. To develop effective diagnostic knowledge is time/cost consuming and demands a lot of effort; it is especially sensitive, when the e-maintenance aims at generalisation in several businesses, even if the scenarios belong to one company and the tool is planned to be used in similar technical frames. However, unlike the equipment oriented on predefined processes, the knowledge-based system has flexibility to learn and to extend itself; this makes it more and more effective during its exploitation.

The agent based e-maintenance systems are the alternative to the centralised KBS approach. In this case, the intelligence is distributed between agents, specialised to monitor the different parameters. The benefit is that the agents can be technologically oriented on the monitored product, communicate to each other, and provide not spot data, but relational assessments, to the processing blocks. An example of an agent-based solution is found in Lee, Qiu, Ni, and Djurdjanovic (2004), for the predictive maintenance of machine tools. The concept applies for other product and service delivery, as well. The core-enabling element of an intelligent maintenance system is the smart computation agent, which predicts degradation or performance loss, not the mere diagnostics of failure or faults. In case of Lee et al. (2004), these agents are called "watchdog agents" and are mechatronical devices with embedded computer software agent providing the intelligence. Agents may transform data to knowledge, and synchronise decisions with remote systems, embedding the prognostics algorithms for performance degradation assessment. A product's performance degradation trend is often associated with a multi-symptom-domain information cluster. The main drawback of the system described in Lee et al. (2004) and many other agent-based solutions available on the market is that their high level system automation possibilities and human-oriented interfaces are not incorporated enough. The situation drastically changes by implementing *ambient intelligence* (AmI) concepts. As a simplified view, the maintenance can be taken into account as a cross section of PLM and SE (see Figure 2).

Environment Protection and Impact Assessing

The environment protection should not break off the growth of the industrialised countries, with wealth buildup through the *value chain* of manufactured goods. This is an obvious assumption; otherwise, the social acceptation of eco-conservative regulations would face strong political opposition. Then, topics need to address interlinked branches, with high relevance of politico-legal and of socio-economical aspects, which affect current engineering outcomes, as the involved problems move beyond merely technical feasibility. Still, the main features deserve investigation, since to a wide extent, their results are technology-driven, raising a divide in the industrial economy promoted by ICT. This leads to hypothesise a framework, where eco-consistency is faced by balanced knowledge organisations, able to manage the resources preservation to:

Figure 2. Maintenance is a cross-paradigm area

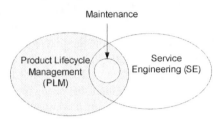

- Acknowledge the *eco-conservative* rules, and to recognise the underlying requirements for growth enhancing
- Suggest viable features for *service engineering* and recovery *inverse logistics*, with data visibility and collaborative networked lay-outs
- Outline the *knowledge organisation* of business involving complementary stakeholders, and enabling decision-making supports

The critical nature of the eco-conservative frameworks depends on two facts: waste, scraps, and pollution are chiefly left to municipal dumps, with community costs which are too often spread by loosely-assigned taxation schemes; and raw materials are paid according to market prices, assuming supply-and-demand balance, without remuneration of third parties and future generations. The EU already explicitly requires to collect taxes of scope for pollution remediation and landfill access, and progressively aims to establish refunds on natural resources withdrawals and the sending out of pollutants (see, the Kyoto protocols). This is equivalent to establish a *cost* of the actually-exploited *natural* capital, exactly as we are accustomed to do, with the *financial* capital and the labour, or *human* capital.

To not break off the growth, the eco-impact assessing, thereafter, could try to balance tangibles costs for the natural resources decay, by equivalent value-added earnings provided by technologies and knowledge-driven sources. A worthy description links the manufacture activity, Q, to four capital contributions (Michelini & Razzoli, 2005):

$$Q = \alpha_o KILT - \alpha_K K - \alpha_I I - \alpha_L L - \alpha_T T,$$

where K is knowledge, know-how, technology, and so forth; I is investments, loans, stocks, and so forth; L is labour, workforce, vocational training, and so forth; and T is tangibles, materials and energy supply, and so forth.

The *affluent society* paradigms have mainly left out eco-consistency: *Investment* and *labour* productivity are the basic concern with, perhaps, the prize on *knowledge* effectiveness, highlighted by the recent ICT achievements. The *tangibles* productivity will become relevant once the whole cost for natural resources depletion is fully charged to the people that actually obtain benefits from it, namely: artefacts suppliers (manufacturing and trading profits) and artefacts buyers (ownership and utilisation enjoyment). *Neutral yield*, with preservation of the *natural capital*, was respected in early times, since technology did not allow too intensive exploitation of non-renewable resources. Now, *thrifty society* could establish *neutrality* again, balancing the *extra cost* of the *T*-factor to pay for tangibles decay, by means of the *value added* by the *K*-factor, based on intangibles supply. The approach, with centrality on the *natural capital*, is enabled by the *technical capital*, on the condition to develop ICT contrivances, with the instrumental duty to help and to manage the growth sustainability.

This *thrifty society* framework quite obviously resorts to new *knowledge aids*, to directly and indirectly benefit from information technologies in the *value chain*, with a life-cycle concern that includes dismissal. The connection with the eco-impact neutrality deserves full visibility and quantitative assessment, thus:

- A metric needs to be selected, for standard measurements of tangibles consumption and environment burden.
- Collaborative, networked organisations shall establish for the resources decay monitoring and control.

The first requirement is suitably met by the *TYPUS*-metrics, *tangibles yield per unit service*, (Michelini & Razzoli, 2005), through which the non-renewable resource depletion is assessed over every product supply chain, from design and materials provisioning, along manufacture and artefacts utilisation, to disposal and tangibles recovery. The *TYPUS*-metrics assumes: to establish a scale, evaluating the *service* supplied by the artefact; and to record the material and energy provisions during *manufacturing, operation,* and *recycling* phases in order to establish the net resources depletion suffered by the *natural capital*, for the specific delivery. This *TYPUS*-metrics directly assesses the *natural capital* productivity for satisfying the needs of individuals; then, a progressive taxation could properly reward conservative choices and behaviours. Other metrics, of course, could be used, each time covering the whole artefact supply chain, to give full account of recycling. The whole is strictly linked to the new opportunities offered by ICT, and preserving from decay the *natural capital* comes to be critically conditioned by the ability of managing pervasive communication infrastructures, once the transparency of the pertinent, on-duty and dismissal, data is granted.

Virtual Organisations and Lifelong Servicing

The eco-sustainability, with the multiple-agents interfacing, dynamic networks reconfiguration, and co-operative or conflicting operation features, naturally leads to experimental new entrepreneurship options. Concepts in virtual enterprises know widely-established interests, and offer effective support to expand the dimension of industrial organisations and to reach economic achievements through method innovation. As a basic rule, virtual corresponds to *potentially real*, meaning that sets of resources could be differently organised, however, always assuring the consistency with the inner and/or outer constraints, with on-going progress. If a given manufacturing flow is addressed, *virtuality* is somehow related to *agility* or to *flexibility*, and becomes a paramount attribute when externalities become critical conditions. It should be pointed out that virtuality does not oppose to *reality* (unless, perhaps, in "virtual reality"), as it simply deals with constraints consistency assuming that the state-equations and/or the driving-actions could further specialise the actual behaviour. In such a process, the latent idea of optimality remains, when one refers to the "virtual-work principle" applied to conservative systems and/or connected variational approaches. Summing up, we would associate virtuality with two properties: dimension expansion, still keeping constraints consistency; and the ability of best choices steering.

These concepts justify the wide recourse to virtual organisations as the natural means supporting extended artefacts, and supplying the related functions of service engineering. Up to now, these issues represent options of advanced enterprises, basically, offered within *voluntary agreement* schemes. Of course, fair trade rules require assessing the actually-delivered functions, according to legal metrology standards, by independent bodies; the wider, networked organisations, thereafter, happen to correspond to heterogeneous stockholders, whose binding reason is the supply chain and related services that grant the given functions and performance. The third party rule becomes central, when dealing with the eco-protection; to such purpose, acknowledging the natural capital productivity (or, reciprocally, material resources consumption per unit delivered function) is non-eliminable duty (by **TYPUS**-metrics, or equivalent means), leading to a preliminary connection among the forward and backward branches of the supply chain, since the net recovery enters in the balance.

Now (and this will explicitly discussed in the next section of the chapter), to speed up the eco-sustainable behaviours, the EU lays down Directives, which aim: (*first priority*) at the prevention of waste; (*in addition*) at the reuse, recycling, and other forms of recovery of end-of-life products or components; and (*as well*) at improving the eco-performance of all economic operators, especially, the ones involved in end-of-life goods treatments. The enacted regulations are grounded on *mandatory targets*, with tight organisational precepts and full operation transparency (otherwise the process believableness disappears). For instance, in the case of end-of-life vehicles, the Member States are required to establish effective *certification-of-destruction* (CoD) procedures, linked to the local automotive registration system, and ruled by *authorised treatment facilities* (ATF) where the backward chain formally begins. The achievement of the *mandatory targets*, however, from the technical point of view, is affected by downstream efficiency (reuse tracks, after-shredding and sorting processes, and so forth), and, from an economic/legal point of view, depends on the upstream carmakers' responsibility. The whole requires adequate infrastructures, such as: for dismantlers' quality; for shedding capacity; for shredder residues treatments; and for process-data reliability. This means local/governmental involvement to promote the appropriate facilities and supporting means, and to establish the pertinent monitoring/controlling outfits. Most of the EU Member States are facing these issues with bureaucratic concern, rather than factual effectiveness, possibly because they are unaware of the potentialities of virtual organisations, in dealing the effective management of dynamic supply chains, joining efficiency and visibility.

The PMAR*RLelv* environment (see Figure 3) is an example of a reference layout, positively established to introduce to acknowledge the buildup and the management of dynamic supply chains, providing visibility to ongoing processes and intermediate achievements. Basically, it exploits interfacing layers, hierarchically above and under the operating modules or agents; the information management is accomplished by brokers, hiding the client and/or the server, and addresses the (each time properly enabled) knowledge mask, which performs the transaction. This way, each agent or partner does not see the actual structure of each operation module; it only addresses its image, consistent with the chosen inner and/or outer constraints. The software is presently developed to deal with the end-of-life

Figure 3. PMARRLelv-environment system concept

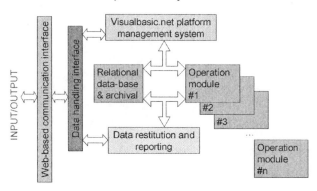

vehicles case, both as investigation tools required by the local/governmental authorities to face *mandatory targets* already enacted by the European Commission, and to consider the *voluntary agreements* that the involved stakeholders could establish for better performance. The implementation explores virtuality also, according to a more powerful track; the constraints consistency provides the full set of *potentially real* setups, most suitably arranged into federated architectures. Then, the recourse to general knowledge-driven layouts gives reference criteria for resource optimisation.

All in all, the Web-based software that we are more generally addressing in the chapter, which deals with three-parties interfacing, might be quoted and described as a winning example of virtual enterprise. Indeed, lifelong servicing, with joint resources recovery at dismissal, cannot strictly be conceived, unless this option exists. Virtual enterprises, virtual organisations, extended enterprises, or dynamic cooperative networked concerns are more or less synonyms from the point of view of our study. These notions mean some or several dynamic partners that form themselves to a goal-oriented alliance according to needs and opportunities of the market, and remain operational as long as these opportunities persist (Camarinha-Matos et al., 2002). All members of such a cooperative effort keep certain independence; they exploit their individual features, and work together in harmony to efficiently achieve their common goals, with highest economic benefits. From the network view, it can be taken into account as an agent-based community, too. Such setups might have several benefits comparing them with "traditional" big, networked, distributed but centrally-controlled enterprises, such as, for example:

- **Agility:** to faster recognize and react to any expected or unexpected changes in their environment, the ability to reorganise themselves if needed and, generally, a shorter time-to-market
- **Complementarity:** the creation of synergies, to better participate in competitive markets
- **Achieving dimension:** to reach "critical mass" together with other "not big enough partners," as SMEs

- **Resource optimisation:** the possibility of optimal sharing of infrastructures, knowledge, and even risks
- **Increased flexibility and reconfigurability:** due to the principles of the set-up of such organisations; this flexibility may mean even the changing of some participating partners to others

The other hand, the "joint" management and operation of such voluntarily-organised co-operations mean several new legal aspects, which should be well defined in appropriate contracts. For example, confidential information management, access rights, and so forth, may be some such problems.

The EU Environmental Compulsory Policy

Eco-conservativeness becomes an imperative demand, once *quality of life* continuation is dealt with. This results in a series of accomplishments, with mainly two scopes, to:

- **Expand intangible contributions in the value chain:** widely exploiting ICT means for wealth creation by value-added enhancements
- **Lower tangibles consumption:** drastically compressing dumping and pollution impacts, through proper recovery/reuse/recycling targets

We address ambient intelligence as an opportunity to enrich the extended artefacts delivery, supported by extended enterprises, with concern for the manufacturers' responsibility, to cover products life-cycle operation, notably, for environment impact and conformance-to-use monitoring. We ought to consider ambient intelligence as the enabling means to fulfil the basic monitoring and vaulting duties, already required by the EU environmental policy with the compulsory recovery/reuse/recycling targets, fixed for mass-product durables, for example, end-of-life vehicles (ELV), or waste electrical and electronic equipment (WEEE). The avoidance or, at least, the drastic reduction of polluting dumping appear to be the driving input of such policy with, however, relevant direct effects on resource recovering, and on restructuring the supply chain by information-intensive deliveries.

On these grounds, the ambient intelligence tools acquire a quite special flavour, since they are invoked to face very demanding incumbents, with ready recourse to frameworks factually providing knowledge-driven entrepreneurship on the reverse logistics loop. This section of the chapter will organise to explore the:

- **Manufacturers' responsibility principle:** as it surfaces from the EU directives, with due regards of the dismissal/dismantling/recovery requirements
- **Information frame:** joined with the enacted recovery/reuse/recycling compulsory targets, as the basic instrument for process effectiveness assessment

- **Operation surroundings:** leading to enhanced usability and reverse logistics achievements, for suitable environment protection and eco-sustainability

Manufacturer/Supplier Responsibility Principle

The wealth growth, based on ceaseless replacing of tangible goods, obtained by transforming natural resources into pollution and waste, grants benefits to specially-involved *consumers*, with penalties to the overall societies and future generations. The *consumers*' side covers the whole supply chain, manufacturer and user; the former establishes the product properties, choosing materials, components, and technologies, specifying operation and surroundings impact, and providing the construction files for maintenance and dismissal; the latter needs to comply with the technical and legal regulations, to be allowed to continue enjoying the purchased item functions. The industrial revolution has widened the manufacture market, by increased process effectiveness, but has also speeded up resource consumption and environment downgrading, so that the growth sustainability faces critical thresholds. We are apparently approaching a bottleneck, and urgent voluntary provisions and legal restrictions shall apply, to alleviate or slow down the world decay. To such purpose, the EU addresses the *manufacturer/supplier responsibility*, considering three phases:

- **Within the production process:** Suitable antipollution regulations are issued at the level of processes and facilities, and promotion of conservative design is fostered by, for example, the *eco-design requirements for energy-using products* (EUP) directive, through a series of advices and warnings (Directive 2005/32/EC, 2005).

- **Along the supply on-duty cycle:** Eco-consistency figures, included in the *construction file*, need to be strictly followed, to reach conformance-to-use assessments, and the service engineering, grounded on ambient-intelligence, comes out as the winning opportunity.

- **From the product dismissal:** Today, most durables, and in the near future, the whole consumables need to fall within suppliers' responsibility, under the *free-take-back* scheme, aiming at reverse logistics treatments for resource recovering and dump avoiding.

The regulation acts look after establishing *eco-costs*, to be included in all tangible goods, when brought into market. These costs shall cover cleaning up, reclamation, and consumption ratios, and will represent a sort of threshold tax, collected from producers/importers and dealers, to refund the supply chain burden.

The concept behind the sketched approach is to turn the earlier users' responsibility, into the more consistent manufacturers' responsibility, so that prospectively the traded goods will become more eco-conservative. The frame originally moved from waste management, with goals such as:

- Avoiding the content of hazardous substances, through measures at the production phase

- Lowering the land-filled quantities, by suitably pre-arranged reuse/recycling processes
- Enacting very stringent environment standards for the disposal and dumping acceptance
- Establishing a certified overseeing frame, for the supply chain monitoring and tax exaction

On these premises, the manufacturer responsibility is a clever measure to foster knowledge-entrepreneurship, expanding the integrated *DfX* practices, over regulation and maintenance (by service engineering, etc.) and over dismantling and recovering (by reverse logistics, etc.) by suitably-enacted economic instruments, such as deposit-refund, recycle-fee, free-take-back, or other schemes, binding the supply chain, from provisioning to dismissal, to accomplish cyclic materials flows. These schemes are made mandatory for some areas, and proposals to extend similar legislation to other cases are being discussed. The producer/importer of the given goods becomes responsible for taking care of all delivered items, once the purchaser no longer has any use of them, and for accomplishing the enacted recovery/dumping incumbents. The economic instruments conveniently spring off the merely passive waste management regulations of the safe landfills running, to tackle enterprises about innovative technologies, along new stimulating paths, such as: eco-conservative products, environmentally sound recycling, and transparent information aids. The approach requires throughout changes of industry habits, with huge falls-off in research and development structures and in market regulation, such as:

- Direct investments by producers, to switch product competition into recoverability figures
- Restructuring the reverse logistics business, into high-tech reuse/recycling companies
- Creation of producers/dismantlers/recyclers clusters, with collaborative organisations
- Growth of certifying bodies, to manage economic instruments, under EU mandatory rules

The factual *technical* and *legislation* drivers originate new effectiveness patterns with possibly the enhanced preeminence of leading manufacturers, and new distributions of factories and facilities in the EU, emerging from how the compulsory regulations are transferred into national laws and the local organisations react with lean reverse logistics organisations.

The Recovery/Reuse/Recycle Compulsory Targets

The economic instruments underlying the EU environment policy attract an increasing research attention. Industrial innovation is the main answer, and how specific measures affect the changes distinguish between "induced offsprings" and "evolutionary upgrading." A great number of projects address the technological and organisational issues of individual areas (automotive, electrical/electronic equipment, etc.) only when the regulations are enacted, and the industrial strategies are specified by the *black-box* approach, recognising input-output flows and experiencing *on-the-path* adjustments. This is the way to exploit flexibility and leanness by pace-wise betterments, leaving aside the method innovation, which only lead to winning competitiveness, as a divide established in the business paradigms. To move a step inside the *black-box*, the EU and national research projects ought to follow an integrated path, joining *technical* and *legislation* drivers, into balanced promotion, with proper wide-range actions. The enabling role of the ICT here again ought to be emphasised, assuring method innovation, along a class of policies characterised by the:

- Recourse to the producers' responsibility, joined to economic instruments drivers
- Involvement of partners, with different technological profiles and capabilities, uneven market position and power, and dissimilar economic interest towards the issues stimulated by the promotion
- Focus on the business paradigm shifts of method innovation, where concepts such as extended artefact and extended enterprise play a critical role

These three characteristics apply when the recovery/reuse/recycle targets are cast into fixed figures, and compulsory regulations are enacted, with sanctions and fines to infringers.

Actually, the waste items (domestic appliances, cars, etc.) quickly reach *negative* value, in face of sound recovery/reuse/recycle targets, as the dismantling and dumping costs are higher than the selling price of reused parts and recycled materials. Any evolutionary upgrading, simply issued by voluntary agreements between private actors, is unable to economically achieve these targets; thus inter-dependent value-chains must be pursued. The induced offsprings shall address the:

- **Creation of *networks* of transporters, handlers, collectors, dismantlers, shredders, sorters, and so forth**, with the related links, upwards, to manufacturers and dealers, and downwards, to secondary users, recyclers, and materials transformers
- **Establishment of *networks* of certified bodies**, duly registered by the national authorities and notified to the European Commission, to assure the overseeing duties, to record the achievements, to draw the eco-fees, and, when the case arises, to inflict the punishments
- **Development of proper *product and service* deliveries**, with high recovery figures (avoiding dangerous substances/parts, good dismantling properties, modularly reused sub-items, etc.), duly supported by the interconnected extended enterprise concern

Separately, the induced offsprings do not have the potential to grant economical return and to attain eco-sound targets. Important upgrading might exploit special tricks (e.g., *cascade recycling*, the using of secondary materials to increase the tangibles yield per unit service, etc.), but only the integrated setup of the listed opportunities leads to method innovation.

Regulatory Schemes and Economic Instruments

Up to today, most of the national industrial and business operators reacted somewhat with irritation at the EU environmental legislation, considering the eco-protection incumbents as a serious burden, with increasing costs and bureaucratic accomplishments. Now, at least in the market domains, where the recovery/reuse/recycle targets are fixed by mandatory figures, the only clever approach is looking at efficient organisations, minimising the drawbacks, and removing the pitfalls of internal struggles. A noteworthy competitiveness benchmark is given by how the local economic instruments will organise, depending on the policy-making and instrument choice of the other EU partners. Common technical goals are: processing the totality of dismissed goods for highest recovery; avoiding release of pollutants in the environment; and minimising shredding residues moved to landfills. The first goal is *reasonably* achieved by eliminating the cost of dismissal; the second, by suitably monitoring the reverse logistics incumbents; and the third, by pushing downstream to new processes and upstream to new design. The addressed cluster of industrial actors should be fostered towards innovation, on the condition to establish legal and societal setups grounded on:

- **Appropriate economic instruments:** to absorb the negative value of tangibles recovering
- **Effective information value-added aids:** to partially balance the value chain deficiency

To figure out general rules answering the two conditions, we make a bird's-eye analysis of the current standard knowledge of policy makers and research leaders. For policy makers, the standard knowledge includes the following options:

- **Tax on virgin materials or subsidies on recycled stuffs:** paid at provisioning or received at recovery (possible distortions on primary/secondary materials market, unless global legal metrology prices are stated)
- **Landfill charges:** paid for waste dumping (possible negative effect: illegal dump)
- **Recycling fee/credit:** paid by artefacts buyers and transferred to subsidise recycling (possible profit for reverse logistics operators)
- **Deposit-refund:** paid by first buyers and returned to the last owners at dismissal (possible negative effect: illegal trade of end-of-life items)
- **Free-take-back:** included in the price of new artefacts and used by producers to subsidise recycling (possible profit for monopolistic manufacturers)

The full impact (short/long terms, direct/indirect outcomes, etc.) of the listed instruments requires a careful analysis, strictly linked to the information value-added path. A mix of the five options exists today, with loose weights assigned by the EU partners legislations, so that when these externalities are summed up, the charges highly vary from one country to another, biasing the common market. For explanatory purposes, we will refer to noteworthy cases already established in Europe and to the basic scheme chosen by the directives.

Well-known cases are *recycling fee* (The Netherlands) or *deposit-refund* (Sweden), for end-of-life vehicles. They assume a foundation/agency, financed by the first purchasers with a *fee* (linked to visible costs) or *deposit* (established by the government), which takes charge of recovering, directly paying dismantlers/shredders (The Netherlands), or supplying a fixed amount to last owners (Sweden) that could be the dismantlers. Both approaches are questioned, as the producers responsibility is bypassed through third-party intervention, interfaced downstream, thus possibly implying state-aid to dismantlers/recyclers. The basic EU scheme aims at *free-take-back* by the sellers; allocating full costs to producers, final owners are relieved from any charges at dismissal. The financial resources are directly transferred from manufacturers to dismantlers/recyclers, with no third party biasing. The incentives, to improve recovery/reuse/ recycle figures, concern producers, leaving bureaucratic out cost or scope tax. This scheme is mainly used in Germany, where, for example, several carmakers compete, making monopolistic drifts unlikely, and externalities could only move to other countries, with no or weaker car-makers. This might be at fault, if transposed into *free price*, *full reimbursement* scheme, such as: the last owner is totally discharged at dismissal, and dismantlers can freely establish recovery costs (acquitted by an agency, directly founded by producers). The interposition of a third party creates higher charges, turned to local buyers, but allows inter-industry incentive transmission for fostering process and method innovations on the whole supply chain (forward and backward loop). Thus, the EU *free-take-back* scheme is consistent with overseeing bodies (foundations or agencies); it simply assumes that: the producers shall internalise all or most of the reverse logistics costs; the established agreements, published in an official document, are enforceable, equally binding all parties; the competent agency ought to monitor the progress and provide transparent records; in case of non-compliance, the local State must strictly apply regulatory and administrative measures. The German carmakers prefer autonomous negotiation of the recycling fees for newly-registered cars, at least. A similar position is taken by the French carmakers, even if established on separate networks. The burden of the scheme can follow stable progression, with possible unequal cost distribution, reflecting the market power of each company more than objective recoverability properties of the individual artefact.

Example Cases: The European Regulation

The recourse to economic instruments, with mandatory recovery/reuse/recycle targets, is becoming standard procedure. In June, 2001, the Economics Ministers of the UE Member States agreed on environmental policy goals, establishing set of priorities, as it follows, to:

- **Lower the recourse to potentially noxious materials (a series of plastics, etc.), and forbid the use of others (mercury, etc.):** See the Directive RoHS, *Restriction on Hazardous Substances* (Directive, 2002 L 0095).

- **Oblige the manufacturers/dealers of electrical and electronic devices to collect the dismissed items and to mark every new product:** See the Directive WEEE, *Waste Electrical and Electronic Equipment* (Directive, 2002 L 0096).

- **Impose on automotive manufacturers/dealers compulsory recover/reuse/recycle targets, with controlled registration of the achievements:** See the Directive ELV, *End of Life Vehicles* (Directive, 2000 L 0053).

- **Promote eco-conservative design, specifying the list of recommendations and warnings:** See the Directive EEE, *Eco-design of End-use Equipment* (Directive 2003).

- **Enact a series of restrictions on landfill management:** on waste handling and processing, and so forth, and to require healing and reclamation operations, with safety thresholds

These are preliminary examples, as environmental acts should progressively cover the totality of durables and consumables on the market. Today goods distinguish into classes, such as: civil artefacts, meaning buildings, houses, roads, bridges, dams, and so forth; instrument buildings, meaning factories, shops, military plants, and so forth; special structures, meaning naval, aeronautic, constructions, and so forth; durables, meaning pieces of furniture, cars, household appliances, and so forth; instrumental deliveries, meaning packaging, spare parts, and so forth; consumables, meaning house-furnishings, linen, clothes, garments, and so forth; commodities, meaning foodstuffs, loose/packed provisions, and so forth; auxiliary deliveries, meaning virgin materials, chemicals, semi-finished items, and so forth; other goods, meaning work-tools, plastic, glass, paper, objects, and so forth . In every case, backward paths exist, from building demolition or rags digestion, to dump or recovery. The preliminary regulations specially address only subsets of artefacts.

Recovery, indeed, is fostered as an antidote of the affluent society, with the inherent task of educating the consumers towards more conservative behaviours. At first, broadband actions are chosen, such as the ones which deal with the ELV or WEEE concerning mass-produced goods, typically feeding the replacement market with high environment impact. Conservativeness is achieved through the manufacturers' responsibility, by setting out regulations with enforceable targets and visible fees, still easy to run and to control. The end-of-life vehicles regulation provides explanatory hints to this new trend. The 2000/53/EC Directive, enacted September 18, 2000, and requiring acknowledgement by the Member States before April, 2002, defines the rules to be followed by national authorities for vehicles dismissal, and by automotive manufacturers for selling cars respectful of the legal requests. The Commission further modified and integrated the rules by special specifications, for example, the 2003/138/EC, to establish standard codes for parts and materials. It needs to be mentioned that the EU is concerned by *final issues*, not about *how* these achievements are obtained according to the different Member States laws. Actually, this creates drawbacks to car-makers, which ought to comply with possibly uneven rules; a Guidance Document is added, to collect harmonisation hints. The literature is fast growing (Michelini & Razzoli, 2003; Stahel, 1989) and, by now, with open doubts. The reading of the documents leads to a few comments, such as the following:

- **Regulation addresses environment protection:** by explicit producers' responsibility charges

- **Design:** for disassembly, for recovering, for recycling, and so forth, become standard request

- **Extensive recourse to re-manufacturing:** to re-use of parts, materials, and so forth, is stimulated
- **Proper aids:** (modularity, identifying codes, etc.) are suggested for easier dismantling, and so forth
- **Life-cycle monitoring and reporting:** disclose on-duty conformance-to-specification checks
- Not-justified high-impact non-consistent behaviours are heavily taxed or totally forbidden.

The sample notices show that new business paradigms are fostered based on different design patterns, with concern on point-of-service performance and commitment for withdrawal. The focus on growth sustainability is the basic driver and, obviously, it leads to the reverse logistics entrepreneurship, with competitiveness played by the incumbents of the backward cycle.

The automotive field is a paradigmatically-noteworthy case, with a widely-spread market of *registered* goods, thus: falls-off affect a large amount of people; and items end-of-life have individual acknowledgement and recording. The EU approach, by already-enacted directives and advices, gives detailed prescribing issues for the end-of-life vehicles operations, such as:

- Member states shall establish collecting systems for exhausted vehicles and parts, at authorised sites, where preliminary treatments will grant safety and security fitting-out, by removing noxious and harmful parts.
- Withdrawal needs to be assured without charge on the final owners (prescription to be fully enabled from January 1, 2007), but included in the product and service delivery, as an inherent attribute.
- Dealers and manufacturers shall bear complete responsibility for the delivery life cycle, dismissal included, answering for the environment impact and resource consumption according to established schemes.
- Users' co-responsibility could be invoked, for special non-conservative behaviours, when critical pieces are damaged, removed, or modified, altering the original setting of the supply.
- The dismantling and destruction incumbents ought to be certified, with full assessment of recovery parts, recycled materials, thermo-recovery and residuals dumping, to be notified to the European Council.

The compulsory targets are quite severe, such as:

- **From January 1, 2006:** 85% by weight of the vehicle ought to be recovered or recycled, 10% can be dumped to landfills (after suitable neutralisation), and 5% can be used as auxiliary fuel.

- **From January 1, 2015:** Figures are modified, allowing 10% for fuel use, but only 5% to landfills.

The WEEE case, already in force since mid-2005, is partially different since it deals with non-registered goods. Without entering into details, producers/dealers again are required for items withdrawal, collection, and dismantling; different recovery and recycling targets apply, depending on appliances size and on lighting rigs; and a visible fee can be collected when a new device is sold. The EU prescriptions, with some modifications, have been transferred to the national acts, and one country is still considering transient alternatives for legal (data registration and vaulting, etc.) and technical (withdrawal, dismantling, recycling, dumping, etc.) incumbents. The role of manufacturers is fundamental to support reverse logistics by product-data management aids for enhanced dismantling and selective recycling, and turns to be critical, in the short term, to enable design-for-recycling paradigms (modularity and material segregation, disassembly pre-setting, etc.) and to take profit of sustainable manufacture (high recourse to recovered or recycled provisions, etc.) and maintenance (proactive upkeeping, reintegration, etc.) options.

The Enhanced Usability and Reverse Logistics

Servicing and recycling address requirements along the supply chain for lower impact in pollution and consumption. The hints, up to now outlined, bring in a few facts, such as:

- In the *affluent* society, conservativeness of behaviour does not support economical trade, due to very low cost of repaying for raw natural resource exploitation, as compared with human and financial costs.
- In our finite Earth surroundings, growth sustainability shall simultaneously deal with *four* capital contributions: natural, human, financial, and technical, with balanced value chains.
- In the *thrifty* society, the abrupt unavailability of rich provisions would drastically endanger the people's quality of life, unless innovative business paradigms could counterbalance the material scarcities.

Several analyses have been undertaken with contrasting issues. Today, the enacted legal frames are far from offering coherent regulations; there is, perhaps, too much emphasis on details, prising slightly significant facets (such as aspects in waste safeguard) or covering only limited sub-classes of artefacts, without a comprehensive attack to the recover/reuse/recycle requirements, in view of sustainability. The critical nature of eco-consistency, then, appears as a consequence of mainly fragmented measures and odd precautions, which result from the EU policy, as the sum of slightly-persuaded Member States acts. This lack of consistency risks to undermine the credibility of the series of rules, when the eco-advantages weighed against the incumbents do not clearly appear, and the procedures opacity does not provide evidence that the onerousness is equally distributed among all citizens and across EU partners. It should also be recalled that the deployment of the affluent society paradigms is conquest non uniform and with uneven achievement times; then, a set of legal provisions, socially and politically correct in some States, could turn ineffective or even self-defeating in other contexts. The whole shows the need to find out shared and enthralling convictions which are capable to:

- Stimulate, in every country, better eco-consistency of the consumers' behaviour
- Discourage or to forbid the use and the selling of highly-penalising tangibles

Indeed, the fair-trade protection in the whole European market cannot do so without common obligations on product usability and end-of-life processing, even when the local habits seem to be an impediment for unified goals. To understand how to modify the value chain, let us refer to current statements:

- At the point-of-sale, the trading price does not include the eco-consistency charges for usage, maintenance, refurbishing, and replacement; a different indenture would oddly result.
- The time to failure of a complex artefact is shorter than that of any of its components, as the reliability characterises the life-span of the whole, and repairing and revamping are not scheduled.
- The consumables replacement is the winning option to expand gross domestic product (clothes refit is becoming an extravagance and their repair is marginal duty), and the likes.

Then, if the supplier has the contract obligation of assuring *free-take-back* of dismissed items and of supporting their *fit-for-purpose* life span, the pricing will include further competition features between offers; this will give rise to the knowledge-entrepreneurship, empowering consumers by involving them in eco-consistent choices. On the other side, looking at individual products, the effectiveness will be rated in terms of *tangibles* productivity or natural *resource* effectiveness (further to *human* productivity or *labour* efficiency), with a lifelong value chain, from material and energy procurement and construction, to operation and maintenance and to dismissal and recycling. The given outlines emphasise that the *artefacts* (at least, instrumental goods, e.g., cars, home appliances) might be replaced by the *functions* they provide (mobility, domestic chores, etc.), provided that the *service* supply establishes at clients' satisfaction and suppliers' profit. Then tangibles are treated as capital assets (rather than consumables) or investments (see the **KILT** model), whose return has to be maximised (by value-added operations, life extension, losses avoidance, wear-out removal). This scenario has multiple issues, even if basic approaches remain to:

- **Enhance usability:** by lower material and energy depletion intensity (at construction, use, and dismissal), and by increased service intensity
- **Improve reverse logistics:** by avoiding toxic dispersion and lowering pollution, and by enhancing recourse to renewable resources and by reusing exhausted tangibles

The EU regulations wish of coherence is possibly removed if appraisal of all *four* capital contributions to the manufacture activity is performed (through the **KILT** model) and if full account of the costs for natural resources decay is accomplished (by the **TYPUS** metrics). To keep the existing quality of life, with no wealth decrease, the idea is to replace the charges for tangibles consumption (**T**-factor), by value-added ICT aids (**K**-factor), such as, by information-intensive supply chains. The new businesses of tangibles recovering suggest a few remarks:

- The need of a logistic network, with collecting and transportation equipment, storage points, handling and processing fixtures, and joint information flow for acquisition and recording

- The establishment of adequate dismantling shops for safe parts recovering, and of suitably located shredding facilities, to grind the left hulks to tiny pieces

- The recourse to specialised sorting plants, to separate the different metals (ferrous alloys, stainless steels, brass, aluminium alloys, etc.) from glass, plastics

- The development of recycled materials tracks, with enhancement of design and manufacture with secondary materials provisioning practices

All four processes lead to innovative setups; the second and third ones deserve high interest, with new robot aids to be conceived and exploited for irksome and dangerous tasks, today, mainly accomplished by front-end personnel. Besides, the material flow, as a whole, deals with a poor but heavy stream; the cost of handling and dispatching could be a serious drawback, with high energy consumption; effectiveness will require distributed processing units, characterised by innovative technologies.

Ambient Intelligence and Sustainability

The role on the growth sustainability of service engineering is related, in the chapter, with the facts that the manufacturers/suppliers (already) have the bylaw obligation to assure *free-take-back* of dismissed goods, and could expand their business by the contract engagement of supporting *fit-for-purpose* operation on their life span. The incumbents, moreover, are linked with eco-consistency checks, requiring the third-party certification of the environment impact, resource consumption, and pollutants remediation, with falls-off transparency and results recording, to provide (in coming years) acknowledged assessment of the actually-exploited natural capital. These facts are dramatic opportunities for the new businesses of knowledge entrepreneurships, which should develop in the shortest time, once people become aware of the enacted regulations (e.g., for ELV, WEEE) and of existing prospects (e.g., *product and service* delivery). Immediacy or delay in enterprises' birth possibly depend on local politico-legal or socio-economical bents as, on the scientific and technological sides, the ICT already provides successful enabling supports. The previous two sections summarise the basic prerequisites of *service engineering* for both opportunities, bylaw obligations or contract engagements; this section addresses the powerful ICT tool of ambient intelligence, for on-duty monitoring and life-cycle data vaulting. Next to the analyses on the recovery/reuse/recycle target incumbents and on the conformance-to-use operations, this tool does not appear anymore a technology-driven option, rather, a factual achievement, to make effective the reaching of the law, or contract debentures.

On-Duty Monitoring and Life-Cycle Data Vaulting

Product and service delivery has an obvious technical instrumental enabler and enhancement aid in the ambient intelligence (AmI). An increasingly high number of the provisions nowadays include more and more elements of ambience intelligence; there is a clear trend towards deliveries, which will include, or will be fully based on forms of AmI. The SMEs in different sectors have to observe carefully and follow this trend to assure their own long-term survival on the market. Many SMEs, therefore, put an improvement of products with AmI elements at the top of their strategic plans. The concept of AmI relies on the provisioning of:

- **Ubiquitous computing:** that is, useful, pleasant, and unobtrusive presence of processing devices everywhere
- **Ubiquitous communication:** that is, availability to interfacing and data-transmission facilities everywhere
- **Intelligent user-adaptive access:** that is, perception of AmI as intelligent by people, who naturally interact with the system that automatically adapts to their preferences

The AmI anticipates that ICT will increasingly become part of the invisible background to peoples' activities and that social interaction and functionality will move to the foreground, resulting in experiences that enhance everyday life. From this anticipation, it is clear that AmI could and should be found everywhere in the human environment. The realisation of AmI concepts leads to establish a collaborative working environment, where virtualised entities communicate to each other. These entities can be (Riva, Vatalaro, Davide, & Alcañiz, 2005) humans, artificial agents, Web/grid services, virtualised-entities representing the real things (not only human beings), descriptions of human knowledge (knowledge-based systems), and the likes. Following Riva (2005), these entities will be able to interact with one another in an AmI environment, to leverage the full potentiality of network-centric environments for creativity improvement, boosting innovation, and productivity gains.

As a general rule, such networks will provide the possibility for individuals to experience interaction with human and artificial agents in their own working environments. Moreover, AmI, by the means of ubiquitous computing and communication technologies, will have a great impact on future overseeing businesses, where PLM and SE represent forward settings of these new organisations. Ambient intelligence is a rapidly increasing field of the ICT with great future impact. The Merriam-Webster's Dictionary (Mish & Morse, 1999) defines "ambient" as: "*existing or present on all sides.*" The Advisory Group to the EU Information Society Technology Programme (ISTAG, 2005) defines "ambient intelligence" as: "*the convergence of ubiquitous computing, ubiquitous communication, and interfaces adapting to the user*" (Gupta, 2003). Ubiquitous should also be defined, since the core domain of AmI envelops this concept. Ubiquity involves the idea that something exists or is everywhere at the same time on a constant level, for example, hundreds of sensors placed throughout a household, or in a factory where some number of agents combined into the network which can monitor the operation of household equipment, the machine tools, or the whole life span supply chain of extended artefacts. This idea is important when trying to understand the future implications that AmI will have on the environments in which we live and function. Indeed, AmI incorporates properties of distributed interactivity (e.g., multiple interactive devices, remote interaction capabilities), ubiquitous computing (the "invisible" computer concept), and nomadic or mobile computing. Thereafter, AmI has the potential to provide the user with a virtual space, enabling unceasing and natural communication with the overseeing frame or with other users, providing input and perceiving feedback by utilising proportionally all the available senses and communication channels, while optimising human and system resources (Stephanidis, 2001). A bird's-eye survey of AmI technicalities follows, separately addressing ubiquitous computing, ubiquitous communication, and users' adaptive interfaces.

Ubiquitous Computing and Communication

Weiser (1991) coined the term "ubiquitous computing," for omnipresent computers that serve people in their everyday lives at home and at work, invisibly and unobtrusively operating in the background and freeing to a large extent from tedious routine tasks. The general definition of ubiquitous computing technology is any equipment that permits human interaction away from a single workstation; this includes pen-based technology, hand-held or portable devices, large-scale interactive screens, wireless networking infrastructure, and voice or vision techno (Abowd, 2004). In its ultimate form, ubiquitous computing means any units which, while moving with you, can build incrementally-dynamic models of its various environments and configure its services accordingly. The devices will be able to either "remember" past environments they operated in, or proactively build up services in new environments (Lyytinen & Yoo, 2002). Ubiquitous computing is roughly the opposite of virtual reality. Where virtual reality puts people inside a computer-generated world, ubiquitous computing forces the computer to live out here in the world with people.

The agent technology is one of the enabling technologies for the realization of AmI concept in life. Following Van Loenen (2003), the agent technology provides distributed architectures and communication strategies for the applications, making easier the information exchange and allowing new modules like sensors or diagnosis algorithms to integrate with less effort from the customer and the machine tool builders' point of view.

User adaptive interfaces, the third integral part of AmI, are also referred to as "intelligent social user interfaces" (ISUIs) (Van Loenen, 2003). These interfaces go beyond the traditional keyboard and mouse, to improve human interaction with technology, by making it more intuitive, efficient, and safe. They allow the computer to know and sense far more about a person, the situation of the person in the interface, the environment and related objects, and so forth, than traditional interfaces can. The ISUIs encompass interfaces that create a perceptive environment, rather than one that relies solely on active and comprehensive user input; they group into five categories: visual-recognition (e.g., face, 3D gesture, and location) and -output; sound-recognition (e.g., speech, melody) and -output; scent-recognition and -output; tactile-recognition and -output; and other sensor technologies. Traditional user interfaces (like PC-controlled touch screens in company environments, and user interfaces in portable units such as PDAs or cellular phones) can also become ISUIs. The key to an ISUI is the ease of use, such as the ability to personalise and automatically adapt to particular user behaviour patterns (profiling) and actual situations (context awareness), by means of intelligent algorithms. In many cases, different ISUIs, such as voice recognition and touch screen, are combined to form multi-modal interfaces (Ailisto, Kotila, & Strömmer, 2003).

These few comments just give preliminary hints of the AmI potential, when explored to support dynamic supply chains, managing extended artefacts with the pervasive (voluntary or mandatory) commitment of the manufacturers, users, and controllers. To that purpose, the chapter briefly moves to summarise existing links of AmI with, respectively, the PLM extensions, and the SE opportunities.

Ambient Intelligence and Extended Artefacts

The main advantage of the PLM solution for a company is that it integrates many enterprise ICT aids in one system and as a result of different processes, can be synchronised. The goal of concurrent engineering can be achieved. Implementing of AmI concepts to support the PLM business paradigm will change the approach. The processes from different chains will be integrated in one virtual environment; the units of this environment will be entities which can be humans, ICT systems (as ERP), intelligent software, or mechatronical agents. These entities will communicate in a peer-to-peer way and build up product-oriented dynamic networks. The networks are dynamic, because on different steps of the product life cycle different entities participate in the product-oriented network. The example of such a network is represented in Figure 4. The Figure shows an example of a network on the step of generating an idea about a product. Two types of graphical representation for entities are used; one is a two-dimensional human sign for human entities and another, cycle-with-line-under-it, for the software agent; the communications between entities are shown as lines with arrows. It is clear that, depending on the product or step in the product life cycle, different entities will join or leave the network. The implementation of ambient intelligent concepts and the integration of it into PLM business paradigm will lead to appearance of a new paradigm and a new environment: the *ambient intelligent product life-cycle manager* (AmI PLM); the main benefits of such an environment will be the following:

- Concentrating information on product and the creation of product-oriented environment for all life-cycle steps
- Enabling information sharing, easier access, and management of product-related data
- Product information updates performed in real-time and in intelligent ways
- Product life-cycle management made easier, and automatically updated
- Enabling products to carry and process information, which influences their destiny

Figure 4. AmI-empowered product-oriented network

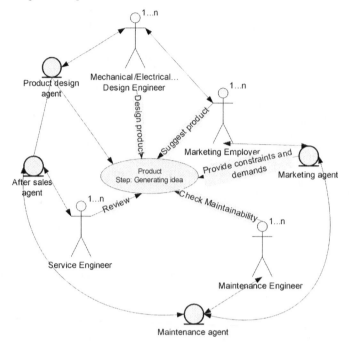

The impact of AmI on service providing and service engineering will be similar to the impact on PLM. The realisation of the AmI vision is required to develop large, complex, heterogeneous, distributed frames. These must be built on multiple-functions platforms capable of providing seamless networking to support the delivery of layers of value-added services or functions to the individual, to industry, and to administrations. The resulting systems, comprising several interacting embedded software components, shall be intelligent, self-configuring, self-healing, self-protective, and self-managed. This leads to a new type of service engineering: *ambient intelligence service engineering* (AmI SE). As pointed out, SE is a new business opportunity, mainly driven by *voluntary agreements* along the product life span, and by *mandatory rules* at dismissal and recovery; these activities, according to the prospected bylaws, request impact monitoring and data vaulting, with third-party certification, and the AmI SE will be the standard ICT solution. Important benefits, already, exist. Maintenance tasks tend to be difficult (Arnaiz et al., 2004), requiring experts; maintenance duties characterise by information overload (manuals, forms, real-time data, etc.), collaboration with suppliers and operators, and integration of data-sources (draws, components, models, historical data, reparation activities, etc.).

Explanatory Example/Demonstration Project

Networked organisations enter today into everyday life, possibly with the mental restriction that the individuals (people or company) have the inherent right to accept/forbid the connections. Actually, as is well known, this is only partially true, and, for example, most of the EU countries' laws permit the generalised recording of the phone links (automatically, for extensions; under special rules, for speech). Likewise, most of us use the car-navigator to find the right destination, or the mobile-phone to be continuously in touch with co-workers or friends, forgetting that this means to be fully tracked (with the uncertainty of a few meters); these data results are effective as an anti-terrorism measure, on the condition, of course, that these instruments are actually exploited with no swindling. This way, most of the ideas behind AmI technologies have already entered into current practice, at least when we recognise that they give useful benefits. In our discussion, however, we have been focusing wider scope objectives, strictly related with trends in the manufacture economy, to achieve the growth sustainability. It might be useful, therefore, to consider explanatory cases, showing how AmI ideas already apply into industrial contexts.

One of our test beds was the European Research Project, called FOKSai (2003). The acronym stands for "SME Focussed KM System to support extended product in Ambient Intelligence domain." The main goal of the project is to develop a knowledge management (KM) system as an extension to Ambient Intelligent products for SMEs in four industrial areas (see Figure 5 and Figure 6). This main goal, common for the four consortium SMEs, is achieved through a sophisticated support to the extended AmI-products of the companies. These SMEs plan to introduce, in the near future (next 1-2 years) new and/or improvements of their current products with even more AmI features, seeing this as their winning competitive edge. A considerable enhancement of business performance of the four SMEs will be reached by introduction of the FOKSai system, mainly by reduction of time and costs for customer support (such as product maintenance, solving customer problems, etc.). For AmI product users, the new support system results in a significant lowering of downtimes of the products and cutting of the maintenance costs. Technically seen, the project will develop:

Figure 5. FOKSai system concept

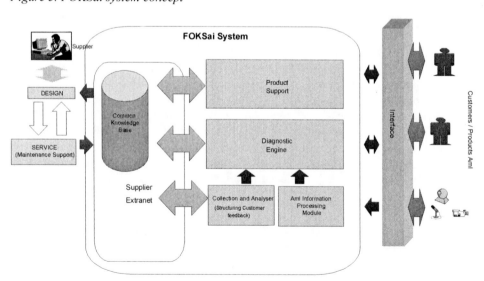

- **A methodology for extension of AmI products:** which will strongly observe business and organisational issues relevant for SMEs
- **A knowledge-based system to support extended AmI products:** which will be affordable for the SMEs manufacturers

The FOKSai solution is planned to be general enough, to be applicable for different products and scalable to support future AmI deliveries, in order to achieve a product (methodology and KM system), which can be offered to a wide spectrum of SMEs intending to introduce AmI options in their portfolios. The topics of supply chain support to be developed and demonstrated as pilot installations within the environments of four SMEs in the project consortium include:

- Remote supervising, problem identification, solving, and maintenance of heterogeneous customer systems, and subsequently reduction of efforts/costs for searching for the reasons of problems in products containing AmI components
- E-supporting manufacturer's staff at remote customer site locations to solve customer/product problems
- Proper integration and sophisticated knowledge-based interpretation of the intelligent ambience information and "reactions"
- Gathering and structuring of the AmI product and process knowledge, from the problem solutions, for the reuse in innovations introduction
- Direct feedback from user to AmI-product/service design and development

Based on the system concept, the business cases have been identified and the user requirements have been specified, by detailing of modules and relations among partners and to the legacy systems. These industrial applications are from four different SMEs, with different profiles from four European countries (Germany, Great Britain, Spain, and Hungary). The dissimilarity ensures that the results of the project can be widely used later. A short description of the business cases helps in showing the expected issues.

The objective of the first business case (RD, Germany) is to establish a new form of customer support by implementing a new methodology and ICT system to support the already-introduced extension in the form of a remote maintenance system, which is the step further in the customer support. The innovation includes not only system status and ambient-related data, but also performance indices, obviously, necessary to achieve full delivery availability and advanced maintainability. The knowledge-based remote access maintenance system provides very fast reaction to customer problems. Especially for real-time critical business or process disturbances, requiring immediate corrective actions, the efficient action, via such a remote access module, is of major importance to reach customer satisfaction and to increase his trust.

In the second business case (LX, Hungary), the need of very high data security, assuring users' trust, is obvious in such a system. Due to the number of measurements and information from the intelligent ambient network, which are analysed continuously as well as their mutual dependencies, it is clear that a rather complex KM system is necessary for proper remote product maintenance. The application of the knowledge-based and Web-based FOKSai system needs to provide the quick reactions to any disturbance, taking into account the relevance of the information processed. Extensions to the products, connected to the monitoring and control frame, have to be scalable, to offer high varieties of services. A proactive customer support has to be addressed, offering to the operator online help and consultancy function. The proactive setting also enables feedback collection from customers, to continuously improve services.

The third business case (DT, Spain) focuses on several activities, which can be summarised as control engineering, technical process automation, remote-management studies, and technical projects. The activity expands around the remote management for technical installations, which allows monitoring, management, and actuation (when required). Furthermore, it can also be applied to different processes, such as chemistry, metallurgy, textile industry, potable and residual waters, control of refrigerator chambers, electrical mini-centrals, and so on.

The SME in the fourth business case (CT, UK) produces process automation and cutting machinery and supplies other companies with turn-key solutions. Installation and setup, backed by problem-solving support provided online (mainly per telephone) either to their own field engineers or to customer maintenance staff, are among the qualifying activities of CT. Thus, CT is often requested to send engineers to solve problems at the customer's site. This 24-hours support involves rather high costs. The firm needs to support their deliveries in more efficient and cost-effective way, that is, it needs to provide problem-solving help to customers (and field engineers), with process full knowledge, but without front-end operators. The complex CT delivery requires a number of built-in measurements and control of machines performance. Recourse to knowledge-based analysis of ambient data enables adjustments to be made when they are required.

Technicalities of the Information Frame

The four business cases cover quite common situations, still, showing even the SMEs are compelled to address *externalities*, as compared to the traditional productivity upgrading which focus on *internalities*. A few technical details of the prototypal development help in explaining how to exploit existing tools. As previously described, the FOKSai system divides into several modules (see Figure 6). The prototype system comprises these modules with a restricted number of realised functionalities, as seen from the modules description, which shortly addresses: the common knowledge-base (CKB); the setup module (SM); the AmI information processing module (AmI IPM); the diagnostic engine (DE); the product support module (PSM); and the knowledge analysis module (KAM).

The common knowledge base (CKB) has the objective of storing all the information that describes products and processes, as well as all the necessary data related to these components. This repository was implemented at the end users as a relational database, using Oracle or MySQL, depending on their individual requests. Further completion of the data in CKB will be done during the full system prototype development, but no refinements and changes are planned in the CKB structure.

The setup module (SM) is an efficient graphical user interface that enables the users to understand the database model and make the best use of it. This module, at early prototype level, is realized as a stand-alone Java application installed at the companies. It supports the definition, modification, and deletion of all data which constitutes the common knowledge base archival. In addition, this Java application will include, at the full prototype stage, the corresponding functionality to administrate the users of the FOKSai system, including users and user groups' definition, and specification of rights for each user, regarding what could be accessed, modified, and/or deleted in the system.

In the early prototype, the main function of the AmI information processing module (AmI IPM) is to map the input XML data (coming from the AmI products) to the common knowledge base (CKB). AmI IPM does not presently have a graphical user interface (GUI), just a command line input, where the input file name is given, and a text-based output, to where it writes certain messages to let the user or tester know what is going on during the operation of the module. This module has been developed using the 1.4 version of J2EE SDK. For the easier development, the Eclipse Project software suite was used as a GUI to help the work. For the parsing of XML files, the SAX XML parser was integrated into this module. The early prototype of the AmI IPM, as a standalone Java application, was tested with the simulated data of the business cases. The input data is written into XML files, according to the defined structure in a schema file.

The diagnostic engine (DE) provides interactive problem-solving aid to users, with recourse to a structured method of case-based reasoning (CBR) to get the required problem-solving information. The module has been implemented in C++, using the function library of the ReCall tool, and connected to the FOKSai system through a CORBA interface. The user utilises the functionality of the DE, and accesses its results through the product support

Figure 6. FOKSai modules

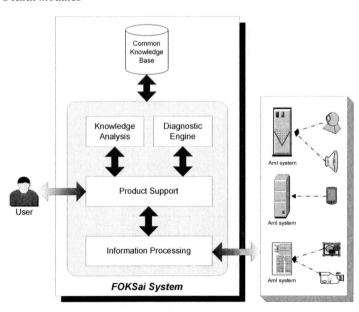

module. The testing of this module was done through the assessment of the product support module, and its functionalities are fully hidden from the system user.

The product support module (PSM) is the central point of interaction between the user and the FOKSai system, that is, it contains the graphical user interface. This module further includes information, documents, and knowledge relevant for product and customer support (e.g., information on new product models, new services, advice on how to apply products and services in order to avoid problems, etc.). The early prototype of the product support module is implemented in Enterprise Java Beans (J2EE 1.4) and available through a Java graphical user interface only.

The knowledge analysis module (KAM) is charged with three main functionalities:

- **Statistical analysis:** FOKSai users can create Pareto charts of most common problems by type and severity using the utility; the users can list all those charted problems using a special utility; this tool is intended to be used for problem identification.

- **Database query tool:** It allows FOKSai users to perform flexible database queries by simply selecting the predefined items available; FOKSai administrator can create and store SQL queries in order to allow other users to use them; the administrator can easily create specific queries for CKB maintenance, according to the necessities.

- **Knowledge analysis:** FOKSai users can use a forum in order to provide statistical analysis reports and send feedback to design staff, create and upload maintenance reports, receive online technical support, and obtain quick fixes for current problems or to get information about new developments on products.

The knowledge analysis module has been developed following the Sun J2EE 1.4 standard. It combines servlets, JSP, and EJB, and has been tested in JBoss 4.0.2 Java Application Server. The module is connected to the PSM and the CKB and is accessible using a Web browser. Basically, this module allows the users to perform *statistical analyses* of the problems stored in the CKB; lists the problems which have been selected; shows any table of the CKB for maintenance purposes; and provides feedback to FOKSai users via a Forum tool. The KAM module uses SSL and form-based authentication, which allows the users to search among all forum elements.

The FOKSai project, promoted within quite conventional SMEs, shows that the existing ICT tools allow high interactivity levels, authorising knowledge-driven reconfiguring of earlier businesses, to be now focussed on the *externalities* of the supply chain. In the upgrading, out of the politico-legal and socio-economic rules discussed in the previous sections, the technical background represents the necessary enabling prerequisite. To that purpose, the ambient intelligence deserves special mention, at different levels of sophistication, and the reference to actual issues is a good signal, when addressing real problems to solve, rather than abstractly looking for clever solutions (out of underlying demands).

Conclusion

The chapter gives a bird's-eye view on the emerging options offered by distributed intelligence tools, to foster competitiveness in the supply chains of industrialised countries. The ICT tools are recognised as the driving aid, basically, on their ability of providing information-intensive tools, in parallel to the traditional trading of manufactured goods. This has falls-off on the value buildup, enhancing direct intangible provisions, and opening indirect opportunities with *product and service* deliveries, on the condition that suitable ICT aids are joined. The new business paradigms are grounded on the availability of the full transparency over the product life cycle, with profit for the manufacturers (according to the economy of scope rules), for the users (for reliable conformance-to-specification management), and for the third parties (for better eco-consistency compliance). The prospected analysis moves from the connections that link product life-cycle management (PLM) and service engineering (SE) to show how these are the information prerequisites to aim at condition monitoring maintenance (CMM) setups, built as knowledge-based systems (KBS) to provide the ambient intelligence (AmI), consistent with the new business paradigms.

The discussion specifically addresses the domain of the ICT cooperative infrastructures, supporting products and services by networked organisations, such as clusters of enterprises that collaborate for given delivery, with benefit of the customers having a unified responsibility over the lifelong exploitation of the purchased goods. This certainly does not means that the manufacturer will remain in charge of the whole activity (even if this seems to be prospected by the EU rules, on the suppliers' responsibilities), rather than outsourcing could establish, on the condition that appropriate PLM/SE tools are provided together with every extended artefact, to make operative the supporting extended enterprises.

The scenario, quite challenging by itself, faces completely new driving demands when considered in the framework of the environmental policy already enacted by the European Council. The situation, it should be said, is a bit puzzling. In the chapter, we have recalled the broad domains, where *voluntary agreements* between the actors of the common market can be exploited to improve a value chain; we have also outlined the demanding *compulsory targets* enacted to deal with resource recovery and eco-impact control. These are not fanciful problems, and manufacturers without a winning solution shall be expelled from the market. Now, the basic *business paradigms* upgrading rules can suitably be stated; the *economic instruments* that modify the existing market are enacted; the *technical prerequisites* can be derived with reliable trust. Still, suitably diffused knowledge on these requests seems to be (at least in some areas) far below the necessities, as if the EU regulations could still be ignored or bypassed. We have recognised in the *networked organisation* ideas the most powerful means to enable the *business paradigms* of the new knowledge-driven entrepreneurship, with efficient exploitation of the EU-enacted *economic instruments*, due to the *technical prerequisites* of, for instance, the ambient intelligence aids. On these facts, this chapter deals with solutions to come, but strictly linked with urgent (and well-posed) problems.

Industrial systems in the future will typically incorporate integrated design and flexible manufacturing for user-oriented extended artefacts and should expand over virtual organisations, with intelligence (mostly in the form of decision support systems [DSS]) covering the life cycle of products and services, using different AI tools, with a certified visibility of environmental impact. The trends show that the main issues are *eco-consistent extended-*

artefacts, with life-cycle visibility supported by virtual organisations. An extended artefact modifies its basic technical properties in such a way to expand suppliers' responsibility up to the point-of-service. Virtual setups emerge as powerful aids due to **e**-functions: Sustainability potentials are expected to enable *method*-innovation, supplying technological consistency to *intelligent* extensions. Now, an extended enterprise answers to the challenge of globalisation, and not to the urgencies of sustainability: The need to remain competitive and the availability of information and communication technologies suggest that, to become "world-class," a company could focus on its core business, group foreign know-how, and resources to achieve extended business scope. The option, although enabled by existing hardware/software instruments, needs to be assessed on a case-to-case basis, to design and develop the targeted cooperation infrastructure, with supporting platform, effective protocols, and exchange rules.

Service aspects are naturally the same for the smallest single organisation and for the most complex extended/virtual enterprise. Services involved may be services provided by the product and/or services necessary for the product. The concept concerns mainly the services joined to special classes of products (EXPIDE, 2003), such as the ones obtained by manufacturing activity. This is in the definition of the extended artefact. Namely:

- **Engineering product:** as defined by EXPIDE (2003), with the following main features: One can make a distinction between products in a narrow sense and a product in a broader sense. By narrow, we consider the product as a tangible entity which is offered in the market, whereas the broader sense (extended artefact) gives an indication about the objective of the product, which means solving a problem of the customer or satisfying a demand. This includes services provided by the product.

- **Engineering service:** Services for the product are a common-sense idea, which means that a lifelong service (maintenance, correction, spare parts, etc.) should accompany all products. This lifelong is some years today (2-10 depending on the product); however, it should be truly lifelong, that is, as long as the product exists. The last steps of the product should be the collection of the product for re-use, and the re-use itself. Such service exists already today for car tires, for example. If the product is produced by a virtual organisation, which by definition does not necessarily live as long as the product itself, lifelong service should be organised somehow. This is quite a new problem, and several organisations are working on the legal and technical solutions.

Acknowledgments

The ideas in this chapter were developed on the some twenty years' long collaboration of the Hungarian and Italian research teams. In Budapest, this work was partially supported by European Research Consortium for Informatics and Mathematics (ERCIM), by the European Union in the frame of the FOKSai project, and by the Hungarian State Eötvös Scholarship. In Genova, this work was mainly established within the Centro Italiano di Eccellenza per la Logistica Integrata (CIELI), funded by the Italian Ministry of Education, University and Research, MIUR, in Genova, along multi-disciplinary tracks, with partners in the business, engineering, and law schools.

References

Abowd, G. D. (2004). *Investigating research issues in ubiquitous computing: The capture, integration, and access problem.* Retrieved from http://www.cc.gatech.edu/fce/c2000/pubs/nsf97/summary.html

Acaccia, G. M., Michelini, R. C., & Qualich, N. (2005, October 24-26). End-of-life vehicles collection and disassembly: Modelling and simulation. In *Proceedings of the Joint ESM-MESM Conference (EUROSIS 05)*, Porto (pp. 34-40).

Ailisto, H., Kotila, A., & Strömmer, E. (2003). *Ubicom applications and technologies.* Presentation slides from ITEA 2003, Oulu, Finland. Retrieved from http://www.vtt.fi/ict/publications/ailisto_et_al_030821.pdf

Ameri, F., & Dutta, D. (2005). *Product life-cycle management needs, concepts, and components* (Tech. Rep.). (pp.1-3). Retrieved from http://plm.engin.umich.edu/PDFs/PLMA-TR3-2004.pdf

Arnaiz, A., Arana, R., Maurtua, I., & Susperregi, L. (2004, May 17-19). Maintenance: Future technologies. In *Proceedings of the International IMS Forum 2004: Vol. 1. Global Challenges in Manufacturing,* Villa-Erba-Cernobbio, Italy (pp. 300-307).

Bengtsson, M. (2004, May 11-13). Condition-based maintenance system technology: Where is development heading? In *Proceedings of the 17th European Maintenance Congress, AMS (Spanish Maintenance Society),* Barcelona, Spain.

Blumberg, D. F. (2004, October). Introduction to management of reverse logistics and closed loop supply chain processes. *CRC Press*, 248.

Camarinha-Matos, L. M., Afsarmanesh, H., Kaletas E. C., Cardoso, T. (2002). Service federation in virtual organisations. In G. Kovacs et al. (Eds.), *Proceedings of the 11th PROLAMAT Conference. Digital Enterprise Challenges,* Budapest (Vol. 205, pp. 305-324). Kluwer Academic Publishers.

Chan, C. K., & Lee, H. W. J. (2005). *Successful strategies in supply chain management* (p. 300). Hershey, PA: IRM Press.

Corafas, D. N. (2001). *Enterprise architecture and new generation information systems: Enterprise architecture and new generation information systems.* CRC-St.Lucie Press.

Dekker, R., Fleischmann, M., Inderfurth, K., & van Wassenhove, L. N. (Eds.). (2004). *Reverse logistics: Quantitative models for closed loop supply chains* (p. 436). Springer.

Directive 2000/53/EC (2000 L 0053). (2000). *Official Journal L 269, 21/10/2000* (p. 0034 – 0043). Retrieved from http://europa.eu.int/eur-lex/pri/en/oj/dat/2000/l_269/l_26920001021en00340042.pdf

Directive 2002/95/EC (2002 L 0095). (2002). *Official Journal L 037, 13/02/2003* (p. 0019 – 0023). Retrieved from http://europa.eu.int/eur-lex/pri/en/oj/dat/2003/l_037/l_03720030213en00190023.pdf

Directive 2002/96/EC (2002 L 0096). (2002). *Official Journal L 037, 13/02/2003* (p. 0024 – 0039). Retrieved from http://europa.eu.int/eur-lex/pri/en/oj/dat/2003/l_037/l_03720030213en00240038.pdf

Directive 2005/32/EC (2005 L 0032). (2005). *Official Journal L 191, 22/07/2005* (p. 0029 - 0058).

Dyckhoff, H., Lackes, R., & Reese, J. (2004). *Supply chain management and reverse logistics* (p. 426). Springer.

EXPIDE. (2003). *Project.* Retrieved from http://www.expide.org (30.4.2003)

FOKSai. (2003). SME focussed KM system to support extended product in ambient intelligence domain. 6th FP, COOP-CT-2003-508637, *Annex: Description of Work,* 2003.

Garetti, M. (2004, May 17-19). PLM: A new business model to foster product innovation. In *Proceedings of the International IMS Forum 2004. Global Challenges in Manufacturing,* Villa-Erba-Cernobbio, Italy (Vol. 2, pp. 917-924).

Gupta, M. (2003, June 17). Ambient intelligence: Unobtrusive technology for the information society. *Pressbox.co.uk.* Retrieved from http://www.pressbox.co.uk/Detailed/7625.html

IMTR. (2000). Retrieved from http://www.imti21.org/Documents/Roadmaps%20Ovrw%20no%20cover.pdf.

ISTAG, IST Advisory Group. (2005). *Advisory Group to the European Community's Information Society Technology Program.* Retrieved from http://www.cordis.lu/ist/istag.htm

Jansson, K., & Thoben, K.-D. (2002). The extended products paradigm. An introduction. In *Proceedings of the 5th International Conference on Design of Information Infrastructure Systems for Manufacturing (DIISM '2002),* Osaka, Japan (pp. 39-48).

Krutwagen, B., & van Kampen, M. (1999, September 24-26). Eco-services for sustainable development. In *Proceedings of the IIIEE Network: The First Global Experience Sharing Conference.*

Lee, J., Qiu, H., Ni, J., & Djurdjanovic, D. (2004, April 5-7). Infotronics technologies and predective tools for next-generation maintenance systems. In *Proceedings at the 11th IFAC Symposium on Information Control Problems in Manufacturing (INCOM 2004),* Salvador, Brazil (pp. 85-90).

Liestmann, V., Gudergan, G., & Gill, C. (2004, May 17-19). Architecture for service engineering: The design and development of industrial services. In *Proceedings of the International IMS Forum 2004. Global Challenges in Manufacturing,* Villa-Erba-Cernobbio, Italy (Vol. 1, pp. 249-256).

Lyytinen, K., & Yoo, Y. J. (2002). Issues and challenges in ubiquitous computing. *Communications of the ACM, 45*(12) 62-70.

Michelini, R. C., Crenna, F., & Rossi, G. B. (2001). Diagnostics for monitoring maintenance and quality manufacturing. In C. T. Leondes (Ed.), *Computer aided design and manufacturing: Techniques and applications* (Vol. I, pp. 5.01-5.66). Boca Raton, FL: CRC Press.

Michelini, R. C., & Kovacs, G. L. (1999). Knowledge organisation and govern-for-flexibility in lean manufacturing. In A. B. Baskin, G. L. Kovacs, & G. Jacucci (Eds.), *Co-operative knowledge processing for engineering design* (pp. 61-82). Norwell, MA: Kluwer Academic Publishers.

Michelini, R. C., & Kovacs, G. L. (2004). Information infrastructures and sustainability. In L. Camarinha-Matos (Ed.) *Emerging solutions for future manufacturing systems* (pp. 347-356). Springer.

Michelini, R. C., & Razzoli, R. P. (2003, June 3-5). Ambienti PLM e gestione della sostenibil-ità tecnologica dei manufatti. In *Proceedings of the XIII ADM & XV INTERGRAPH Conference: Tools and Methods Evolution in Engineering Design*, Cassino-Napoli-Salerno (pp. 301-310).

Michelini, R. C., & Razzoli, R. P. (2005). Collaborative networked organisations for eco-consistent supply-chains. In G. D. Putnik & M. M.Cunha (Eds)., *Virtual enterprise integration: Technological and organisational perspectives* (pp. 45-77). Hershey, PA: Idea Group Publishing.

Mish, F. C., & Morse, J. M. (Eds.). (1999). *Merriam-Webster's collegiate dictionary* (10th ed.). Springfield MA: Merriam-Webster, Inc.

Projetech. (2005). Retrieved from http://www.projetech.com

Riva, G., Vatalaro, F., Davide, F., & Alcañiz, M. (2005). *Ambient intelligence: The evolution of technology, communication, and cognition towards the future of human-computer interaction* (pp. 1-320). IOS Press.

Stahel, W. R. (1989). *The limits to certainty: Facing risks in the new service economy.* Kluwer Academic Publishers Dordrecht.

Stark, J. (2005). *Product life-cycle management.* London: Springer.

Stephanidis, C. (2001, October): Ambient intelligence in the context of universal access. *ERCIM News, 47*, 10-11.

Van Loenen, E. J. (2003, January 10). *Ambient intelligence: Philips' vision.* Presentation at ITEA 2003, Oulu, Finland. Retrieved from http://www.vtt.fi/ele/new/ambience/evert_van_loenen.ppt

Vernadat, F. B. (1996). *Enterprise modelling and integration: Principles and applications.* Chapman & Hall.

Weiser, M. (1991, September). The computer for the 21st century. *Scientific American, 265*(3), 94-104. Retrieved from http://www.ubiq.com/hypertext/weiser/SciAmDraft3.html

Chapter III

Offshoring:
Evolution or Revolution?

Nicholas Beaumont, Monash University, Australia

Abstract

This chapter describes the emergence of offshoring. It defines relevant concepts, and documents its rapid growth. The factors differentiating offshoring from outsourcing are discussed, especially access to markedly lower costs, extra risks, and cultural differences. A methodology for deciding what processes to offshore, and establishing, maintaining, and renewing offshoring projects is proposed. Offshoring is no longer the preserve of organizations; individuals can obtain an increasing variety of services from overseas. Offshoring is contentious because it threatens to replace high-paid jobs in First World countries with less well-paid Third World jobs. Most outsourcing depends on organizations' ability to transfer data instantly, accurately, and at nearly zero marginal cost. This chapter suggests that the ramifications for individuals, organizations, and societies of this technical advance are underestimated. Further research, especially on the ramifications, is suggested. The difficulty of researching offshoring, a sensitive topic for many organizations, is noted.

Introduction

Outsourcing of business processes has become popular among management, management consultants, and governments, although it has been used for centuries. Its recent prominence is attributable to changes in technology—exemplified by the World Wide Web (WWW)—that have made it easy for organizations to share large amounts of data almost instantly, with high fidelity, and at almost zero marginal cost. Outsourcing is perhaps the latest managerial fad (Shapiro, 1995), but has more substance than predecessors such as total quality management, business process re-engineering, and empowerment. The latest manifestation of outsourcing is "offshoring;" organizations have discovered that some costs can be substantially reduced by locating operations in Third World countries. Customers' expectations of constantly improving value for money and competitive pressure will force firms to adopt outsourcing and especially offshoring. Now that techniques such as total quality management and business process re-engineering have been fully exploited, offshoring is the cost reduction method with greatest short-term potential.

This chapter defines relevant terms; describes contemporary offshoring's historical precedents; describes the costs and benefits of outsourcing and offshoring; evidences the growth of offshoring; proposes a methodology for establishing and running offshoring projects, outlines the risks inherent in offshoring; notes the emergence of personal offshoring; and discusses offshoring's social and political implications. Conclusions and suggestions for future research are given.

A Historical Perspective

Modern offshoring is the last of three waves, reminiscent of Krondatief cycles, each driven by access to lower costs and radical technical changes yielding reduced costs, product or service improvement, and/or increases in scope. Increasing scope means operating in more geographic areas; selling to more kinds of customers; and/or selling products and services fulfilling more functions. Offshoring is an aspect of globalization (Business Council of Australia, 2004) that has progressively expanded by including trade in agriculture, manufactures, and services. Globalization's progress has been lubricated by reductions in protection and regulation, and advances in technology exemplified by the World Wide Web.

Agriculture

Agricultural products and minerals have long been obtained by First World countries from overseas. Blainey (1966) points out that, when supplying primary produce (first wool, then meat) to England and Europe, Australia had intrinsic advantages of cheap labor and land. Technical advances (especially to transport) such as railways, refrigeration, and the "stump-jump" plough and cheaper inputs (e.g., of fencing wire) reduced the cost, improved the quality, and increased the scope of Australian products, with disastrous effects on British farmers but beneficial effects for British consumers and downstream industries.

Manufacturing

In the 1970s and 1980s, manufacturing's migration to the Third World caused much First World angst. This migration was caused by improvements in communication (exemplified by the fax machine, cheaper and more reliable international phone calls, and cheaper and better travel), lower wage costs, and lower transport costs (exemplified by the container). Better control systems exemplified by information technology, total quality management, and just-in-time made it easier to specify and monitor manufacturing processes. Increased Third World literacy was perhaps a contributing factor. Bronfenbrenner and Luce (2004) and Bardhan and Kroll (2003) report on the transfer of manufacturing from the United States to countries such as Mexico, China, and India; the rate of transfer increased between 2001 and 2004, and the lower cost of manufacturing in Third World countries offset the extra costs of transport and managing at a distance (Bronfenbrenner & Luce, 2004). Conventional wisdom is that more skilled aspects of manufacturing such as product design and market analysis could be retained in America, but Bardhan and Kroll (2003) note that foreign manufacturers' skills constantly improve.

Services

A wide variety of services is being, or could be, sourced more cheaply from low-wage countries, exemplified by India, than from the First World. Some services commonly offshored are: call centers, software development, product development, and back-office functions such as entering transaction data. The contribution of Indian programmers to Y2K may have been an icebreaker to treating offshoring as a standard business procedure. As shown below, the offshoring market's rapid growth is explained by its benefits to business.

Reasons for Using Outsourcing

Outsourcing is defined as "having work that was formerly done inside the organization performed by an external organization" (Beaumont & Sohal, 2004, p. 689) or "the act of transferring some of a company's recurring internal activities and decision rights to outside providers as set forth in a contract" (Greaver, 1999, p. 3). Perhaps illogically, the term is usually applied to services, not manufacture of components, and to continuing business functions, not projects. Lonsdale and Cox (2000, pp. 445-449) summarize the history of outsourcing, noting that it has supplanted once fashionable enthusiasms for conglomeration, horizontal integration, and vertical integration. *Offshoring* is having business processes performed overseas, primarily to exploit low labor costs; it conventionally includes wholly-owned overseas subsidiaries. The terms *client* and *vendor* are the firms respectively obtaining and supplying services through an outsourcing agreement. In this chapter, the archetypal client and vendor are American and Indian firms respectively (for brevity, the term "firm" encompasses all organizations, profit and non-profit). The client's *customers* may be affected by offshoring.

Coase (1937) asked why, given that the market allocates resources efficiently, do firms exist? There are several answers: Some assets (such as a large oil refinery) are immobile, have high fixed costs and low variable costs, have a narrow range of applications, and have few or no external potential buyers or sellers of inputs and outputs. Such assets are inoperable without a cluster of peripheral assets and high levels of skill and knowledge in the firm and its suppliers. There is no perfect market for such assets; investment in them is only practical in a planned environment that provides a guaranteed market for a high volume of very specific outputs and guaranteed supply of specific components. Information technology has weakened some of these reasons (applicable mostly to physical processes). In particular, immediate, accurate, and convenient transfer of data among organizations at nearly zero marginal cost enables data and information processes (interpreted broadly) to be performed out-of-house.

A related question is: "Why do firms choose to outsource some activities and retain others?" There are myriad reasons (see Table 1 and Table 2), but outsourcing is fundamentally a compromise between vertical integration (associated with cumbersome hierarchies and bureaucratic procedures) and reliance on market mechanisms. The latter entails administrative costs (identifying appropriate vendors and verifying their competence, communicating changing requirements to them, providing feedback, and monitoring their performances), communication costs (transferring data and information between vendor and client), and risks (of vendors failing or being unable to meet specifications, or clients failing to pay).

Deciding whether to outsource depends on comparisons of the long-term costs, benefits, and risks of different modes of supply. A long-term outsourcing relationship with a trusted vendor may be preferable to securing supply by backward integration, or developing or retaining an in-house capacity. An organization will always outsource some activities (the supply of water and electricity), but in-source others such as employee assessment or strategic planning.

Table 1. Reasons for adopting outsourcing

Reason	Comment
Reduce processing costs	By accessing lower input costs, economies of scale, or expertise
Focus	Outsource non-core activities and concentrate on areas of competence. Identifying core activities may not be straightforward (Quinn & Hilmer, 1994).
Access expertise	On taking responsibility for a client's human resource management, a human resource executive consultant opined that she expected to cut costs by between 20% and 50% by using proven systems and applying experience without lessening service quality (personal communication, March 2004). Vendors are advantaged by knowing about their industry's costs and service quality standards. Client function managers may not know that their costs exceed the industry average.
Avoid internal cultural differences	The IT department having anomalous working conditions and compensation (attributable to the need to retain competent staff) may cause resentment among other employees.

Table 1. continued

Financial and cost restructuring	Outsourcing can be used to manipulate cost structures and cash flows. Instead of purchasing delivery vehicles (a capital cost), outsourcing can be used to re-express deliveries as an ongoing expense.
Benchmark internal operations	It is very difficult for top management to determine whether the firm's IT department is as efficient as those of their competitors. Outsourcing some IT functions may give some insight.
Eliminate an unsatisfactory department	Top management may be dissatisfied with the IT department and/or feel unable to control it. Relations between IT and other departments may be so strained that the best course is to close down the department and rely on vendors. The mere threat of outsourcing may improve performance.
Uneven resource requirement	It may be economic to meet base load for call center services or delivery from the firm's own resources and use outsourcing to meet peak or unanticipated demand.
Fractional resource requirement	A small firm without enough demand to employ a lawyer full-time will outsource its legal requirements.
Risk avoidance	Firms can avoid financial uncertainty by using a fixed cost per transaction. If a new computer system is proposed, management may prefer to eliminate risk by accepting an outsider's quote than have the work done in-house and risk time and cost overruns.
Careers	A firm with a small IT department will not be able to offer careers in IT, and may therefore be unable to retain competent IT staff. It may be difficult for managers to assess the performance of the IT department.
Avoid legal constraints	Offshoring, especially to Third World countries, may make it possible to avoid the costs of First World legislation pertaining to pollution, unionization, discrimination, or work practices. This is best exemplified by the U.S.'s rendition of prisoners.
Ideology and fashion	The current Australian government has an ideological commitment to outsourcing, opining that the private sector is intrinsically more efficient than the public sector. Offshoring may be the "flavor of the month" among executives.

Table 2. Reasons for not adopting outsourcing

Reason	Comment
Dependence	Outsourcing a critical business function may make the client uncomfortably dependent on the vendor. The client should ensure that, in extremis, a critical process could be resumed in-house.
Confidentiality	Keep confidential data in-house. The dangers of misuse are multiplied if data is available to two organizations.
Intellectual property	It may be strategically disadvantageous to give other firms access to intellectual property or learning opportunities. An American automotive firm engaged a Japanese firm to manufacture carburetors. The arrangement was satisfactory in the short-run. However, the Japanese firm used this opportunity to develop design and manufacturing expertise, eventually becoming a formidable competitor.

Table 2. continued

Loss of distinctive competencies	Outsourcing may atrophy in-house skills. A firm that outsources stimulating legal work or systems development may not be able to attract or retain creative staff.
Loss of flexibility	A three-year outsourcing contract may reduce the ability to adjust to changes in the client's environment or to exploit new technology.
Personnel and change problems	Staff made redundant by outsourcing may have to be dismissed or redeployed. This may create anxiety among remaining staff.
Information asymmetry	A practiced vendor has the experience to accurately assess the cost of performing an outsourced business process and estimate how technology will affect that cost over time. A less well-informed client may be disadvantaged in negotiation.
Project management risk	Poor methodology (especially in specifying requirements and failure to detect that the proposed vendor is incompetent or unscrupulous), negotiation, or monitoring may result in project failure.
Cultural differences	May create misunderstandings and communication failures
Negotiation difficulties	The operation is so complex that it is impossible to agree on and codify performance criteria.
Complexity	A computer application may be so interwoven with other applications that it cannot be separated out and handed to a vendor.

Tangible Costs and Benefits of Offshoring

The prime motivation for offshoring is lower labor costs. India has a huge pool of graduates, especially IT graduates, for whom a job as a call center operator or programmer compares well with other opportunities. The consensus is that Indian labor costs about 15% of U.S. labor (see Table 3). There is some indication that Third World workers are more motivated, harder working, and more productive than their First World counterparts (Dutta, Lanvin, & Paua, 2003). Costs in India especially may increase in response to demand and because of increased congestion and operating costs, for example, in Bangalore.

McKinsey's (2003) analysis of the effect of offshoring on cost components is summarized in Table 4 and discussed as follows. Although labor savings dominate, offshoring changes other costs.

- **Greater communication and management costs:** Communication costs are dropping precipitously (Edwards, 2004), since optical fiber's enormous capacity and nearly zero intrinsic marginal costs are independent of distance. Telecommunications costs are likely to become negligible within 10 years. Offshoring entails executive travel and accommodation, executives distracted from other duties, and an increased likelihood of illness. When establishing an offshore outsourcing arrangement, the search and transition costs are higher than for onshore outsourcing. However, once a relationship is established with a reputable Indian vendor, the cost of managing and monitoring the relationship may be less than anticipated. Large Indian vendors such as Infosys, Wipro, and Tata are practiced and competent.

Table 3. Comparative costs of different skills ($U.S.)

Reference	Skill or task	Relative costs ($U.S.)
(McKinsey & Company, 2003)	Software development	"$60/hour in the U.S ... $6/hour in India" (p.1)
	Data entry	$20/hour in U.S., $2/hour in India
(Field, 2002)	Programmer	Salaries $63,000 US, India $5,850.
(Overby, 2006)	Programmer	The average salaries of programmers in 26 countries from Asia and the Far East, Europe and Africa, and the Americas are given. Some Asian and ex-communist countries have very low programmer salaries.
(Neelakantan, 2003)	Medical procedures	"Open heart surgery ... (could cost up to) $150,000 in the USA; in India's best hospitals, it could cost between $3,000 and $10,000", "Dental, high and cosmetic surgeries in Western countries cost three to four times as much as in India." (p.54) Citizens can avoid lengthy delays by having procedures performed in India.
(Cronin, Catchpowle, & Hall, 2004, p. 18)	Not specified	" ... low cost labour offshore, typically 20% of UK levels."

- **Consolidation and standardization:** Large organizations, especially those growing through takeovers, often inherit a variety of administrative systems. Different locations and departments tend to resist central office's attempts to impose uniformity. Offshoring a business process may reduce costs by forcing standardization.

- **Training and enhanced skills:** Consolidation and more employees make improved methods of employee selection and monitoring, and specialized training more economical. The outsourcing contract may specify employee selection criteria and skills to be taught.

- **Changes in scope:** Lower processing costs may allow changes in the tasks and the scope of tasks undertaken. For example, it may now be economic to accept orders that were unprofitable when administrative costs were higher, or to pursue small debts formerly written off. A greater range of language skills may allow a call center to service more countries.

- **Process reengineering:** The different costs of labor and different skills available in First and Third World countries may allow different parts of a process to be located in different places so as to exploit cheaper labor or available skills. Lower labor costs may imply less capital-intensive technology. Digital x-ray images taken in First World countries may be transmitted electronically to Third World countries where the analysis is done and recorded, with the reports then being returned electronically to the originating doctor for discussion with the patient. Eyeglasses prescribed in New York may be manufactured in Mexico. Loan applications and insurance claims

Table 4. Offshoring's effect on costs

Component	Increase (+) or reduction (-) in costs
Labor	-60 to 65%
Additional communication	+5 to 10%
Additional management	+5%
Consolidations and standardization	-6 to 10%
Skills and training	-2 to 3%
Task re-engineering	-5 to 7%
Economies of scale	-3 to 5%
Process re-engineering	-15%
Net effect of offshoring	-65 to 70%

originating in New York may be assessed in New Delhi, with reports being returned to consultants for discussion with clients. Architectural concepts developed in Australia were translated into blueprints by Indonesian draftspeople (personal communication, September 2004).

- **Economies of scale:** Offshoring often results in the establishment of large operations in Third World countries. Most business operations, exemplified by the call center, have fixed (communications, selection, and training procedures, design of dialogues, and software) and variable cost components. A 1,000-seat call center is not twice as expensive as a 500-seat center.

- **External:** There are other tangible costs and benefits relevant to offshoring. There may be a difference between the First and Third World in the cost of land, equipment, and premises. Taxes (on property values, labor costs, inputs, and profits), the cost of inputs and services such as electricity, water, and insurance may vary among countries and regions. Some governments may offer inducements such as tax relief to attract foreign business.

Growth of Offshoring

The fundamental reasons for the explosive increase in offshoring are that technology makes India's lower costs accessible from the First World and has removed the barriers that protected internal departments from external competition. For example, payroll data can be transferred to a vendor instantly, accurately, and at a nearly zero marginal cost that is independent of distance. Some evidence for the growth of offshoring is given in Table 5.

Table 5. Evidence of the growth of offshoring

(McKinsey & Company, 2003, p. 5)	"Offshoring is expected to grow at ... 30 to 40% per year over the next five years." "Forrester ... the number of U.S. jobs offshored will grow from 400,000 to 3.3 million by 2015."
(National Computing Center, 2004, p. 3)	"Growth in offshoring has been in the region of 30% in monetary terms ... "
(Dieffenbach, 2003)	"A recent report by TowerGroup... forecasts a 46% annual growth rate in U.S. financial companies' use of offshore outsourcing ... "
EBS (www.ebstrategy.com/outsourcing/trends/statistics.htm) contains quotes from many sources, some of which are repeated here.	"International data Corporation (IDC) has predicted that the global IT-enabled services market will account for revenues of $1.2 trillion by 2006."
	"Meta group predicts that offshore outsourcing will grow by more than 20% annually ... from $7B in 2003 to $10B in 2005."
	"McKinsey and others forecast that the Information Technology and Enterprise Solutions (ITES) market in India will reach $142B by 2009 and that it would cost $532B to provide those services in the USA."
	"According to WR Hambrecht, the offshore PPO market is expected to grow at a CAGR of 79% through 2008. The offshore IT service market is expected to grow at a CAGR of 43%."
(Information Technology Association of America, 2004, p. 1)	"Spending for global sourcing of computer software and services is expected to grow at a compound rate of almost 26% p.a. ... "

An Offshoring Methodology

There are several interrelated decisions that have to be made when deciding to offshore the whole or part of a business process. A fundamental question is what functions should be offshored. Subsequent but related decisions depend on the organization's strategy and objectives (broadly classifiable as lower costs, superior service, or flexibility); the attitude to risk and public criticism; its relationship with its workforce; and the intensity of competition. Intense competition may force the organization to use offshoring to reduce costs regardless of other considerations. We summarize the methodology and describe the steps in detail only where offshoring (as opposed to on-shoring) raises additional issues.

Many writers have proposed overviews, methodologies, checklists, and lists of critical success factors. Some of these are Ho, Torres, and Vu (2004); Keane, Inc. (2004); Ker, Murphy, and Valle (2000); and National Computing Center (2004). Cronin, Catchepowle, and Hall (2004) compare the costs, benefits, and risks of implementing and using offshoring and outsourcing arrangements. Moore (2002) discusses the risks, costs, and rewards of offshoring. Several writers, for example, Overby (2003a) and Ho, Torres, and Vu present successful or unsuccessful examples of offshoring.

The Outsourcing Cycle

The term "outsourcing cycle", mentioned by Beaumont and Sohal (2004) and perhaps implicit in some texts, for example, Sturm, Morris, and Jander (2000), denotes a sequence of stages into which an outsourcing project can be broken; analogous approaches are espoused by Franceschini, Galetto, Pignatelli, and Varetto (2003) and Momme (2002). The concept is often used in industry. In common with other methodologies recommended for change projects (commonly pertaining to quality improvement), and software development projects; outsourcing methodologies tend to emphasize the broader business aspects such as ascertaining business requirements, motivating staff, and monitoring the anticipated performance improvements. Cyclicity is often emphasized: Once a project is completed, other change opportunities should be sought.

The outsourcing cycle presented here is derived primarily from project management methodologies and comprises the following steps:

- Identify a process that might be advantageously offshored.
- Define objectives.
- Choose a vendor.
- Negotiate a service level agreement (SLA).
- Implement the agreement, that is, transfer the process to the vendor.
- Monitor vendor performance.
- Incrementally modify the agreement.
- Renew/cancel the arrangement.

Identify a Process That Might be Advantageously Offshored

Only some kinds of work can be taken offshore but the scope is increasing, especially as overseas workers acquire new skills, communication costs decline, and new technology is deployed. Customer relationship management, telephone selling, and medical tourism (see below) exemplify emerging applications.

Several writers give selection criteria, identify suitable processes suitable for offshoring, and give examples of offshoring (McKinsey & Company, 2003; National Computing Center, 2004; Robinson & Kalakota, 2004). Classic applications are: call centers and help desks; back-office operations that have not been wholly automated (these include processing applications for loans, mortgages, and insurance claims; debt collection, processing employee expenses (Edwards, 2004); data entry, analysis of x-ray images; creating databases of, for example, newspaper articles); architectural or engineering design; and computer programming. It may be appropriate to offshore running legacy IT systems, releasing domestic staff for work on new systems (National Computing Center, 2004).

Edwards (2004) identifies three layers of services. The top layer, comprising services tailored to individual businesses, is unlikely to be outsourced. The bottom layer, comprising processes common to all business, is very likely to be outsourced. The thick middle layer comprises services that are capable of being standardized, then outsourced. Enterprise resource planning (ERP) packages such as SAP, are accelerating standardization and the potential for outsourcing. That standardizing internal processes may facilitate accessing lower costs through offshoring is itself a force for standardization (Gere, 2003).

Karmarkar (2004) notes the huge size, increasing automation of, increasing self-service in, and growth of the global services market, and suggests that certain categories of services can be offshored. A complex service can be expressed as a sequence of services, some of which require face-to-face contact (e.g., doctor and patient), but some of which might be automatable and executable offshore. The potential is enormous; an authority estimates that the world's companies spend about $U.S. 19 trillion on expenses, of which only $U.S. 1.4 trillion is outsourced (Edwards, 2004). ADP (a firm providing payroll services) paying one in six private sector American workers is a harbinger.

There are a number of constraints on what processes should be offshored. Processes such as sales calls or medical consultations that ostensibly require face-to-face contact cannot be offshored. However, many of the back-office processes (such as identifying potential clients or analyzing x-ray images) preceding or following a consultation can be advantageously offshored. Some transactions that used to require face-to-face contact can now be mediated by computers; many sales transactions are consummated on the Web. It is possible for an Indian salesperson to present to an American customer by video link.

Quinn and Hilmer (1994) suggest that non-core processes and common business processes should be outsourced, and that processes giving strategic advantage be retained and improved, although identifying core processes may not be straightforward. Mechanical aspects of business processes can be outsourced provided the client precisely defines the work which vendors do and monitors vendors' performances. Customer relationship management manifest in call center services can be outsourced provided that the client precisely defines and controls the selection criteria and training used and the dialogues that call center staff are to use on its behalf.

Organizations might be reluctant to outsource, let alone offshore, some business processes. Obstacles include concerns about the reduced flexibility inherent in a three-year agreement, and creating dependence on a supplier. Mechanizing processing of individuals' tax returns might conceal opportunities for better service that would be revealed by expertise or first-hand knowledge of a customer's circumstances. A more practical concern is that a large organization's systems might have so many interfaces and entanglements with each other that it is not safe to run one of these systems independent of the others (see Table 2).

Define Objectives

The objectives of an offshoring project should be clarified. The prime objective will probably be to reduce costs; direct and indirect, tangible and intangible costs should all be considered. Offshoring is probably a good way of reducing direct costs, but there may be long-term advantages in using offshoring to access expertise, improve quality, or strip out routine activities, thereby allowing management to concentrate on and exploit expertise (see Table 1).

Choose a Vendor

Robinson and Kalakota (2004) cover this issue thoroughly. The time taken to select and become comfortable with an overseas vendor is longer and more costly than for an onshore vendor. Large Indian vendors have front offices in the USA which may contribute to confidence. Field (2002) describes the pros and cons of using brokers to choose foreign vendors. Overby (2006) compares 26 countries offering offshoring services, noting each country's overall rating, its geopolitical risk, English proficiency, and average programmer salary. Selection processes may be less thorough for "tactical" (mostly short-term) than "strategic" (mostly long-term) relationships (National Computing Center, 2004).

Executives selecting an onshore vendor would probably have access to informal information gleaned from colleagues, the media, and acquaintances. That network will not help when selecting an offshore vendor. The possible delays and misunderstandings caused by differences in culture, time zones, and language mean that an offshore project requires more careful planning than an onshore project.

Negotiate a Service Level Agreement (SLA)

A service level agreement (SLA) is a contract precisely defining the services to be provided by a vendor, and minimum acceptable levels of service; procedures for measuring performance; payments and penalties for underperformance; and procedures for resolving differences and renegotiating the agreement itself. SLAs are "formally negotiated agreements that enable IT organizations (and vendors of other services) and their customers to collaboratively identify, discuss, and manage ... service expectations" (Karten, 1998, p. 1.7).

The contents and negotiation of an SLA are discussed in Beaumont (2006) and elsewhere (Anonymous, 2004; Davies, 2004; Karten, 1998; Kobitzsch, Rombach, & Feldmann, 2001; McLaughlin, 2003; Robinson & Kalakota, 2004; Sturm et al., 2000). Negotiating an SLA is vital and difficult. Only in the SLA are the services to be provided, prices, performance criteria, penalties, and scope precisely defined. Negotiations between parties from different cultures (see *The Effect of Cultural Differences*) and countries can be impeded by:

- **Language differences:** The parties may have different masteries of English and different understandings of important words and technical terms; an oral "yes" may be interpreted as agreement, but intended as an acknowledgment. Ironical or facetious comments may be interpreted literally. English is becoming the universal business language, and non-English-speaking countries may have fewer offshoring opportunities (Karmarkar, 2004; McKinsey & Company, 2003).

- **Misinterpreted body language:** Asians consider Americans staring at a speaker to be rude and aggressive. Indians' body language may wrongly suggest to an American that an audience is uninterested. A nod may be interpreted as agreement whereas "please continue" is intended.

- **Modalities and signals may be misunderstood or misinterpreted:** The other nego-tiating team may not comprise decision-makers but minions who take instruction from decision makers between sessions. The negotiation process may be an entertainment for one party, much more interesting than routine work. Handshakes may signify agreement and commitment in one culture, mere polite acknowledgment in another. Signing a document may signify commitment in one culture, a form of noting progress in another. Americans may be baffled by making no progress for several weeks, then experiencing a sudden breakthrough when an Asian team reaches consensus. Ameri-cans may be frustrated by Asians (perhaps prudently) insisting on a perfect document rather than agreeing on broad principles and letting subordinates and lawyers fill in the gaps. Asians may resist American "man-to-man" approaches, hiding behind formal manners, and attempts to resolve issues behind the scenes.

Transfer the Process to the Vendor

The differences between offshoring and onshoring are not marked, except that the number of employees displaced by offshoring back-office processes or call centers may be larger than usual with less opportunity to move to the vendor's employ or be transferred to other of the client's functions.

Gere (2003) cogently notes that effective exploitation of an offshoring relationship may entail changes to the client's structure, strategy, systems, culture, and staffing. The vendor may require the client to use the vendor's forms, software, and procedures. Outsourcing requires managers to get results through negotiation and co-operation with partners instead of instructing subordinates. New internal skills will be required, for example, in writing and negotiating service level agreements with vendors. If the IT function is outsourced, a small IT group must be retained to monitor and liaise with the vendor, monitor advances in technology, anticipate future IT needs, and negotiate the contract's renewal or the reabsorb-ing of outsourced processes.

Monitor Vendor Performance

There should be no difference between offshoring and onshoring so far as tangible perfor-mance measures are concerned. Because the operation is distant, it may be slightly more difficult to monitor intangible measures such as the recruitment and training processes used that may have a long-term effect on service quality. Different cultures may have very different understandings of, for example, the term "empathy" and how much empathy help call center operators should display.

Modifying, Canceling or Renewing the Agreement

The associated negations may be impeded by distance and the cultural differences affecting negotiation.

Intangible Costs and Risks of Offshoring

Some hidden costs and risks of offshoring, noted by Pinto (2005) and Overby (2003b) are:

Geopolitical

The previously hospitable host country government could be overthrown, introduce hampering legislation, restrict repatriation of profits, or yield to xenophobia directed at foreigners or their "lackeys." Terrorism and crime may be less well controlled and protection money may be extorted. The infrastructure, especially water, electricity, or telecommunications system, may be unreliable, and travel and accommodation may be below Western standards. The social environment may make it difficult to find First World employees willing to stay on-site for long periods. Currency fluctuations may make the whole operation more expensive or cheaper than planned.

The Effect of Cultural Differences

Cultural differences that might impede efficiency and the client's knowledge have often been noted. We list some often cited cultural differences, the effects they may have, and measures that can be taken to minimize their effects. Many Asian organizations are as conscious of cultural differences as their Western counterparts and take their own steps to lessen their effects. Davies (2004) and Kobayashi-Hillary (2005) each devote chapters to Indian culture and living and traveling in India. Brett and Gelfand (2005) illustrate the fruitfulness of culturally-sensitive action. Cultural differences can be discussed using five dimensions identified by Hofstede and Bond (1988):

- **Power distance** measures the degree of inequality between people in the country's society. High Power Distance may imply reluctance to openly disagree with superiors. If disputing a superior's statements is considered rude, progress and status reports may be distorted. Programmers who regard systems analysts as hierarchically superior may be reluctant to dispute or discuss program specifications handed down.

- **Individualism** reflects the balance between individuals' rights and responsibilities (America) and respect for groups (Asia). Asians usually have a greater regard for group processes. It is asserted that a group of Asian workers will not accept a change until it has been accepted by the whole group. Implementation of the change will then proceed rapidly. North Americans, used to allocating responsibility to individual project leaders, may be frustrated with Asian concern for group processes and the apparent lack of progress.

- **Masculinity** is high if the society reinforces traditional models of male achievement, control, and power. Interactions between men and women, especially of men with women in authority, or members of different races, castes, or religions may be especially fraught if masculinity is high. North Americans are conditioned, perhaps even compelled, to frame issues in terms of tangible criteria, especially cash flow. Other cultures may frustrate Americans by treating the well-being and morale of employees and their families as equally important.

- **Uncertainty avoidance** reflects the level of tolerance for uncertainty, risk-taking, and ambiguity.

- **Long or short-term orientation** reflects the degree to which the society habitually uses long or short-term time horizons.

Other cultural differences may arise when socializing with foreigners. Westerners may be unused to blatant corruption or the influence of patriarchs in small organizations.

Security and Confidentiality

The standards pertaining to securing company assets and customer confidentiality, implemented and monitored at home, may not apply or be as well policed in other countries. Even if the procedures are as good as those prevailing in the First World, it takes an effort to verify this. Dieffenbach (2003) notes that potential security, disaster recovery, and privacy risks are greater for offshoring than onshoring.

Information Asymmetry

American clients may be disadvantaged when negotiating with an Indian vendor. The vendor has knowledge of local conditions such as input prices, possible changes in government policies, and infrastructure that the client cannot readily obtain. This may result in the vendor retaining a disproportionate share of cost savings. The client may find monitoring service levels provided to its customers (e.g., by a call center) difficult. The vendor may save money by employing people with less competence than was contracted or compromise the client's data by subcontracting some aspect of the client's task to an unreliable organization. In 2003, a medical transcriber in Pakistan threatened to post patients' records online unless the University of California San Francisco (UCSF) Medical Center paid the wages owed to her by the U.S. subcontractor that had sent the work to her. Most importantly, the client, not plugged into the local network, may not be forewarned by rumor that the vendor is about to go bankrupt.

Intangibles and Offshoring

Some other intangible costs and benefits of offshoring should be noted:

- **The need to retain some backup of data and skills at home:** If the offshoring deal comes unstuck, could the client resume the in-house operation, or have the necessary skills eroded?
- Offshoring may **expose corporations to two sets of laws**.
- **Major customers may be concerned** to find that their sensitive data are stored off-shore.
- The **cost** of dealing with displaced employees (transferred to other departments or dismissed?).
- **Unpopularity** caused by the client "exporting jobs" and possible domestic boy-cotts.

Modes of Offshoring

Deciding whether and how to offshore a business process entails making several interrelated decisions. Assuming that a business process is being considered for offshoring, decisions have to be made on what mode of offshoring should be used. The three dimensions are:

- **Location:** Farshore, nearshore, onshore, or in-house
- **Ownership:** In-house, insource, outsource, or joint venture
- The **degree of control** granted to the vendor

Location and ownership decisions are independent, low labor costs can be exploited by establishing a wholly-owned operation in a foreign country, and a vendor could use the client's premises and/or equipment. We simplify discussion by assuming that the process is currently located in the USA and owned and operated by the client.

Location

Location is the physical location of the operation. *Farshore* signifies a location (classically India) with markedly lower labor costs but potential difficulties exemplified by differences in language, culture, and infrastructure. *Nearshore* means a location exemplified by Canada or Australia with lower labor costs but a similar business culture and language. *Onshore* means that the operation is performed in the home country, obviating cultural and language difficulties. An *in-house* operation is conducted on the client's premises; possibly by a vendor.

Onshore is obviously necessary for processes entailing face-to-face contact with customers and some services such as delivery or physical security.

The National Computing Center (2004) defines offshoring and several terms used in this context. Cronin, Catchpowle, and Hall (2004) suggest a typology and enumerate the differential costs and benefits of onshoring and offshoring. Kennedy and Kolding (2003) discuss the pros and cons of local, farshore, and nearshore sourcing. They usefully distinguish between short-term arrangements (e.g., creating a computer system) and long-term engagements (running a business process). The Business Council of Australia (2004) gives several examples of nearshoring to Australia.

Ownership

Regardless of location, the process may be retained in-house, in-sourced, outsourced, or run as a joint venture. Gere (2003) details different possible commercial arrangements relating the vendor and client and location, and proposes a framework for identifying processes that should be offshored.

General Electric established its own call center in India, subsequently deciding to sell it. By establishing its own software house in China, Microsoft exploited lower labor costs, choosing not to use a vendor with local knowledge as its intermediary. The British companies, Standard Chartered Bank and Prudential, successfully established their own processing centers in India, enjoying control of critical processes, access to abundant skilled labor, and significant cost savings (Preston, 2004). Preston argues that the benefits of "do-it-yourself" are underestimated and that it is unnecessary to share profits with a vendor.

Insourcing is the formalization of a pseudo-commercial supply relationship between two departments of the same organization. The supplying department commits to agreed performance criteria. Payments and penalties are expressed in internal currency and may affect executives' remuneration.

In some cases, a joint venture between the client and vendor is appropriate. The design and installation of a major new computer system may require intense day-to-day cooperation between both parties. It may be impossible to specify the system requirements in advance; they emerge from the vendor's investigation of the client's systems and requirements, and on the client learning from the vendor the potential of new computer systems. Especially if the vendor will gain valuable experience and an enhanced reputation from a new and challenging project, it may be appropriate for the parties to share risks and rewards by creating a joint venture in which they have (usually) equal shares. Industry members might decide to set up their own subsidiary offering common services, most frequently lobbying and defining industry standards.

Degree of Control

Outsourcing comes in a variety of flavors that in part reflect the day-to-day control the vendor retains and the degree of cooperation required. Strassmann (1997) defines *out-tasking* as outsourcing in which the client designs and retains full control over the business process, the vendor simply providing the resources (usually labor or computer resources). Out-tasking is exemplified by a call center operation in which the client defines the scripts which the operators must follow. General Electric's Trading Process Network (TPN) entails putting GE's tender documents on the Web, in effect precisely defining, that is, out-tasking, work that was often offshored. In this case, offshoring was not essentially different from onshoring. When distance, language, and culture are obstacles, out-tasking to a foreign entity may be less demanding.

Contrastingly, a client may "black box"; that is, grant the vendor full control over *how* the operation (delivery, security, back-office) is performed (exploiting the vendor's expertise) and simply monitor the amount and quality of work done.

Personal Offshoring

Offshoring is usually treated as an option only for organizations. However, cheap communications and cheap travel also empower individuals. Banally, computer-literate consumers can purchase an increasingly wide range of goods and services (e.g., gambling and entertainment) non-locally from Amazon.com or E-bay, intensifying competitive pressures on local businesses once protected by distance. Duty-free shops could be construed as examples of offshoring. More controversially, consumers can avoid some of their country's legal restrictions and imposts by using the Web to acquire pharmaceuticals, music, and pornography, and/or facilitate self-diagnosis of real or imagined ailments.

The most striking example of personal offshoring is the recent emergence of "medical tourism" (Bradley & Kim, 1994; Colvin, 2004; Neelakantan, 2003). Customers save money (see Table 3) and avoid lengthy queues by having medical procedures performed overseas. It would be technically possible for customers to enter symptoms at a Web page, have measurements of blood pressure, temperature, and so forth, done locally by paramedics, and receive diagnoses written by Indian doctors. It seems likely that Americans will increasingly obtain otherwise expensive professional services such as legal advice and accountancy from overseas.

Political and Social Implications

Privacy and Security Issues

The U.S. has a number of laws (e.g., the Gramm-Leach-Bliley Act) that allow corporations to share customers' private data, provided certain criteria are met. Most of these laws were written before offshoring became prominent and do not forbid offshoring of individuals' financial or health data. In Ohio, allegations that citizens' birth records had been sent to a facility in Sri Lanka led to the U.S. company that had offshored the work being barred from state contract work for 15 months. A number of U.S. state legislatures have proposed laws preserving employments by restricting offshoring, but few such proposals have been enacted.

"European consumers are afforded considerably greater protection (than U.S. citizens) by a European Union (EU) law that permits personal data to be sent offshore *only* to countries whose privacy laws have been deemed to provide equivalent privacy protections and that have been found to have strong enforcement capabilities. Because most countries cannot meet these 'safe harbour' requirements, European jobs that involve the handling of confidential information have been offshored at a far slower rate than in the United States" (Public Citizen, 2006).

Job Creation and Destruction

The 1970s and 1980s saw a contraction, or "hollowing out," of manufacturing in First World countries (Bronfenbrenner & Luce, 2004). Price differences and data mobility imply that, on the face of it, white-collar jobs will move from First to Third World countries. Not just clerical and call center jobs are threatened. It is reasonable to believe that work such as architectural drafting, product design, legal analysis, financial and market analysis, indexing of newspaper articles, programming, and systems design could be carried out in low-wage countries. Professional work can be loosely defined as transforming and analyzing data, or as obtaining information from data; any work done primarily on a PC can be done in a low-wage country. Some labor markets are now unconstrained by national boundaries; an emerging global market, for example, for English-speaking call center operators, will supplant national markets and reflect converging remuneration for U.S. and Indian workers with identical skills.

Many consultants and interested parties have forecast the effects of offshoring on the First World job markets (Bardhan & Kroll, 2003; Business Council of Australia, 2004; Mann, 2003; McKinsey & Company, 2003). McKinsey argues that offshoring will increase the U.S. standard of living; $1 spent offshore will generate direct and indirect net benefits conservatively estimated at $1.12-$1.14, but the benefits of spending *onshore* are not given.

EBS (2005) cites the following opinions:

- "By 2015, Forrester research estimates that as many as 3.3 million US jobs and $US13 6B in wages could be moved to countries such as India, China, and Russia."
- "According to Deloitte consulting, 2 million jobs will move from the United States and Europe to cheaper locations in the financial services business alone. The exodus of service jobs across all industries could be as high as 4 million." Gartner opines that "500,000 of the 10.3 million U.S. technology jobs could move offshore in 2003-2004."
- The Information Technology Association of America (2004, p. 1) opines that "In the software and services area, the economy is expected to create 516,000 jobs over the next five years in an environment with global sourcing but only 490,000 jobs without it. Of these 516,000 new jobs, 272,000 are expected to go offshore, while 244,000 are expected to remain onshore." The report details essentially beneficial effects on growth, inflation, incomes, job markets, and interest rates.

The effect on job markets can be best understood using narrow and broad perspectives.

Narrow Perspective

This perspective considers the direct effects only. Assume that a firm transfers work from the USA to India, exploiting 80% labor cost reductions. U.S. workers and shareholders in supplanted suppliers lose jobs and income. The benefits are transferred to Indian workers through better working conditions and remuneration and to the clients' customers and shareholders. In competitive markets, customers will enjoy most of the benefit as lower prices and/or better quality. This scenario perhaps characterizes the cutthroat U.S. auto market.

Broad Perspective

The broad perspective considers the indirect as well as the direct effects. Some indirect effects are:

- Stakeholders in Indian vendors spend their increased income. This will have a multiplier effect on the Indian economy, stimulating imports some of which will come from the U.S., increasing employment. For example, more Indians will be able to afford American holidays.

- American consumers will have their quality of life increased by cheaper and better quality services. Clients' shareholders will enjoy increased income, and consumers will spend a high proportion of the time and money saved on other goods and services.

- The extra competition will benefit consumers by limiting inflation and eroding the excess profits and restrictive practices of some industries hitherto protected from foreign competition. The medical and legal professions might suffer most.

The U.S. job market is dynamic. Edwards (2004, pp. 12-13) notes that most new technologies have been perceived as a threat to employment, but that new occupations emerge. " ... Who would have guessed that America ... now has 139,000 psychologists, 104,000 floral designers, and 51,000 manicurists and pedicurists?"

It is important to realize that a serious socio/political problem remains (surfacing in the 2004 U.S. elections). The benefits of offshoring for the U.S., although large, are thinly spread and not immediate. The considerable costs of offshoring are shared among a comparatively few employees who lose well paid and stimulating jobs and may find it difficult to find equally satisfying employment. The adjustment process is likely to be more prolonged in other countries (e.g., Europe) with more protected and rigid labor markets.

Firms have been understandably reluctant to admit that they are offshoring. It is tempting to fudge the issue by outsourcing work to an ostensibly domestic vendor and taking care not to find out where the work is actually performed.

An Australian Case: Qantas

We illustrate some of the complexities of offshoring by summarizing an Australian company's as yet tentative steps.

Qantas is Australia's dominant airline company. To reduce costs, it is threatening to off-shore activities traditionally performed in Australia. Some major offshoring decisions were proposed early in 2005. The company has to evaluate the cost savings, transition costs, the costs of possible strike action, and the possible loss of reputation that would be caused by "exporting" Australian jobs.

Some characteristics of Qantas and its environment are: Qantas does not operate in a perfect market, for example, the Australian government protects Qantas's share of the lucrative Australian-North American market, but insists on Qantas being Australian majority-owned (restricting its ability to raise capital). The company is locked into long-term contracts with pilots and cabin crew who are probably receiving compensation higher than they would in a perfect market. In common with other airlines, Qantas has to cope with air travel becoming commoditized and extremely competitive (there is excess capacity, and the failure of some U.S. airlines is symptomatic). Threats of terrorist activities, airport congestion, and SARS have deterred travelers. Although Qantas dominates the Australian domestic market, it would like to obtain economies of scale by merging with other airlines (e.g., Air New Zealand), but it has been frustrated by governments and regulations enforcing competition.

Qantas has taken some steps. Better information and accounting systems have facilitated better monitoring of costs (accentuating the competition between internal and external suppliers). Partly to circumvent extant agreements with unions, Qantas has established Jetstar, a low-cost airline. A new generation of aircraft will substantially reduce passenger-mile costs.

Offshoring in an airline is less visible than in other domestic businesses. Aircraft receive between-flight maintenance wherever they land, crew must be accommodated overseas, and some food is loaded overseas. In 2002, Qantas's CIO stated that [the] offshoring of tech-nology work to India was "a strategy for survival." (Hayes, 2002, p. 36) In January, 2005, Qantas released plans to move more than 7,000 jobs offshore. These initiatives included proposals to:

- Hire overseas-based cabin crew who would be paid less than their Australian counter-parts. This provoked Australian employees, but it has obvious benefits. The outcome was an agreement with the flight attendants' union for some staff to be based (more cheaply) in London.

- Have non-Australian contractors supply and load more passenger meals. This issue is not yet resolved.

- Have aircraft maintenance performed overseas. The outcome was some consolidation of maintenance operations and an agreement with the union on productivity targets. The union proposed cost savings that contributed to the maintenance being done in Australia.

It is not clear (and scarcely matters) whether management's ostensible intent to offshore was an ambit claim used in negotiations with unions or a firm intention. The issues of offshoring information technology and catering are in abeyance. Qantas recently agreed to outsource $A1.4B worth of Information Technology and data center services to IBM and Telstra (Australia's dominant telecommunications company). The vendors could have some of Qantas's work done overseas. Qantas constantly opines that it will have to continuously reduce costs to stay competitive (a claim belied by its large and growing profits and cash flows), and that offshoring is a way of obtaining drastic rather than incremental cost reduction.

This section was sourced from the Qantas Chairman and CEO's reports at http://www.qantas.com.au/info/about/investors/annualReports, Qantas press releases at http://www.qantas.com.au/regions/dyn/au/publicaffairs/introduction?, and reports from various Australian newspapers.

Conclusion and Suggested Further Research

Summary

The forces (especially access to lower wages) underlying outsourcing and especially offshoring are irresistible. Competition and customers demanding constant improvements in quality and price will force the most squeamish firms' hands. Offshoring is the simplest and quickest way for First World firms to obtain substantial cost savings and improved service quality. Offshoring is an aspect of intensified and globalized competition (Porter, 2003), and services offshoring follows the offshoring of primary production and manufacturing. Because it will affect millions of white-collar workers who are more numerous and articulate than their blue-collar counterparts, offshoring will be a live political topic for several years. Especially pleasant (for some) and painful (for others) will be the emergence of a global market and converging remuneration, for example, for programming skills. There are many choices to be made when offshoring a business process; managerial discipline and adherence to a methodology multiply the chances of success.

This chapter discusses the costs and benefits of offshoring and estimates of the offshoring market's size and growth. The economic and societal effects of offshoring are noted. It suggests an offshoring methodology, and that more care is required when planning and monitoring an offshore relationship. There are several business models incorporating decisions on location, ownership, and degree of control that should be considered. Cultural differences, some cost components, and some risks particular to offshoring should be noted.

Suggested Further Research

Offshoring suggests several research problems. As the bibliography implies, academic research on outsourcing and especially offshoring is not proportionate to its importance to industry. This may be attributable to the research difficulties adumbrated here. Some outstanding research issues are:

- The size and growth of the offshoring market needs to be ascertained. This is difficult and expensive. Executives may be reluctant to admit that they are using offshoring or know that work offshored to an ostensibly local vendor is done overseas. An international research consortium might be appropriate.

- The tangible and intangible costs and benefits of offshoring to participants and broader society need to be ascertained. So too does the interaction between offshoring and organizations' strategies and evolution. Case studies are probably the most appropriate instrument. However, a comprehensive study of one firm would require several interviews in the firm and with its vendors and/or clients; it is likely that some parties would decline participation. Low response rates would limit the generalizability of findings.

- Research determining the success of different methodologies and applications of offshoring is appropriate. Anecdotal evidence suggests that the relationship between vendor and client is often fraught. Typically, euphoria experienced when the contract is signed sometimes sours when unanticipated difficulties emerge; a working relationship emerges after much hard work. These difficulties can be exacerbated by geographic and cultural differences. The influence on business success of the relationship between the two parties (intimate or arms-length) and its contractual basis (especially service level agreements) merits research.

- Statistical studies relating knowledge of a firm's use of offshoring and financial success might be illuminating. For example, iconoclast Strassmann (1997) provides statistical evidence that heavy use of outsourcing presages a firm's failure.

- The socio-political effects of offshoring merit investigation. Will they be as severe as some alarmists anticipate? What government policies would help spread offshoring benefits rapidly and widely? Will public disquiet impede free trade negotiations or fuel xenophobic political movements?

References

Anonymous. (2004). Explaining offshoring/outsourcing in India/What's this India business: Offshore outsourcing and the global services revolution. *Transnational Corporations, 13*(3), 151.

Bardhan, A. D., & Kroll, C. A. (2003). *The new wave of outsourcing.* Berkeley, CA: Fisher Center for Real Estate & Urban Economics.

Beaumont, N. B. (2004). Outsourcing: A multidimensional relationship. *Contract Management in Practice, 1*(8), 84-86.

Beaumont, N. B. (2006). An overview of service level agreements. In H. Kehal & V. Singh (Eds.), *Outsourcing and offshoring in the 21ˢᵗ century: A socio-economic perspective*. Hershey, PA: Idea Group.

Beaumont, N. B., & Sohal, A. (2004). Outsourcing in Australia. *International Journal of Operations and Production Management, 24*(7), 688-700.

Blainey, G. (1966). *The tyranny of distance*. Melbourne, Australia: Sun Books.

Bradley, R., & Kim, E. (1994). Loosening the reins: Autonomy boosts Cuban medical industry. *Harvard International Review, 16*(4), 66.

Brett, J. M., & Gelfand, M. J. (2005, January). Lessons from abroad: When culture affects negotiating style. *Negotiation*, 3-5.

Bronfenbrenner, K., & Luce, S. (2004). Offshoring: The evolving profile of corporate global restructuring. *Multinational Monitor, 25*(12), 26-29.

Business Council of Australia (2004). *Offshoring, global outsourcing and the Australian economy—continuing Australia's integration into the world economy*. Canberra: Business Council of Australia.

Coase, R. H. (1937). The nature of the firm. *Economica N. S., 4*, 386-405.

Colvin, G. (2004, December 13). Think your job can't be sent to India? Just watch. *Fortune, 150*, 80.

Cronin, B., Catchpowle, L., & Hall, D. (2004). Outsourcing and offshoring. *CESifo Forum, 5*(2), 17-21.

Davies, P. (2004). *What's this India business? Offshoring, outsourcing, and the global services revolution*. London: Nicholas Brearley International.

Dieffenbach, J. (2003). *A passport through issues in global outsourcing*. Retrieved November 14, 2006 from http://library.findlaw.com/2003/Jun/30/132840.html

Dutta, S., Lanvin, B., & Paua, F. (Eds.). (2003). *The global information technology report 2002-2003: Readiness for the networked world*. Oxford University Press.

EBS. (2005). *Trends, statistics and perspectives 2005*. Retrieved November 14, 2006 from http://www.ebstrategy.com/outsourcing/trends/statistics.htm

Edwards, B. (2004, November 13). A world of work: A survey of outsourcing. *The Economist*, 1-16.

Field, T. (2002, April 1). The man in the middle. *CIO US, 15*, 70.

Franceschini, F., Galetto, M., Pignatelli, A., & Varetto, M. (2003). Outsourcing: Guidelines for a structured approach. *Benchmarking: An International Journal, 10*(3), 246 - 261.

Gere, T. (2003). *Accessing offshore: Options for strategies and relationships* (No. 29459). International Data Corporation.

Greaver, M. F. (1999). *Strategic outsourcing: A structured approach to outsourcing decisions and initiatives*. New York: Amacom.

Hayes, S. (2002, November 12) Taking an extra step in the airline world. *The Australian*, (p. 36).

Ho, L., Torres, M., & Vu, P. (2004). *The dynamics of outsourcing: Offshoring, insourcing, and a case study: India.*

Hofstede, G., & Bond, M. (1988). The Confucius connection: From cultural roots to economic growth. *Organizational Dynamics, 16*, 5-21.

Information Technology Association of America. (2004). *Executive summary: The comprehensive impact of offshore IT software and services outsourcing on the U.S. economy and the IT industry.* Arlington, VA: Information Technology Association of America.

Karmarkar, U. (2004). Will you survive the services revolution? *Harvard Business Review, 82*(6), 100-107.

Karten, N. (1998). *How to establish service level agreements.* Randolph, MA: Naomi Karten.

Keane Inc. (2004). *A balanced approach to offshore outsourcing: Gain strategic improvements in business performance.* Boston: Keane Inc.

Kennedy, E., & Kolding, M. (2003). *Offshore services: IDC's view* (No. R105K). International Data Corporation.

Ker, S., Murphy, T., & Valle, C. D. (2000). *Mapping offshore: A new competitive landscape* (No. 21645). International Data Corporation.

Kobayashi-Hillary, M. (2005) *Outsourcing to india: The offshore advantage* (2nd ed.) New York: Springer

Kobitzsch, W., Rombach, D., & Feldmann, R. L. (2001). Outsourcing in India (software development). *IEEE Software, 18*(2), 78-86.

Lonsdale, C., & Cox, A. (2000). The historical development of outsourcing: The latest fad? *Industrial Management & Data Systems, 100*(9), 444-450.

Mann, C. (2003). *Globalisation of IT services and white collar jobs: The next wave of productivity growth.* Washington, DC: Institute for International Economics.

McKinsey & Company (2003). *Offshoring: Is it a win-win game?* McKinsey Global Institute.

McLaughlin, L. (2003). An eye on India: Outsourcing debate continues. *IEEE Software, 20*(3), 114-117.

Momme, J. (2002). Framework for outsourcing manufacturing: Strategic and operational implications. *Computers in Industry, 49*(1), 59-76.

Moore, S. (2002). *Critical success factors for offshore outsourcing.* Giga Information Group Inc.

National Computing Center (2004). *Guidelines for IT management: Planning for offshore outsourcing.* London: National Computing Center.

Neelakantan, S. (2003, November 6). India's global ambitions. *Far Eastern Economic Review, 166*, 52-54.

Overby, S. (2003a, July, 2003). Inside outsourcing in India. *CIO 16*(1).

Overby, S. (2003b, September, 2003). The hidden costs of offshore outsourcing. [Electronic version] *CIO*. Retrieved November 14, 2006 from http://www.cio.com/archive/090103/money.html

Overby, S. (2006). 2006 Global outsourcing guide; Risks, rewards, challanges and opportunities, country by country [Electronic version]. *CIO 19*(1). Retrieved November 14, 2006 from http://64.28.79.79/offshoremap/

Pinto, J. A. M. (2005). Swimming against the tide: The hidden costs of offshoring. *The CPA Journal, 75*(1), 9-11.

Porter, M. E. (2003). Strategy and the Internet. *Harvard Business Review, 79*(3), 62-78.

Public Citizen. (2006). *Global trade watch*. Retrieved November 14, 2006 from http://www.citizen.org/trade/offshoring/privacy/index.cfm

Preston, S. (2004). Lost in migration: Offshore need not mean outsourced. *Strategy & Leadership, 32*(6), 32-36.

Quinn, J. B., & Hilmer, F. G. (1994). Strategic outsourcing. *Sloan Management Review, 35*(4), 43-55.

Robinson, M., & Kalakota, R. (2004). *Offshore outsourcing: Business models, ROI, and best practices*. Alpharetta, GA: Mivar Press.

Shapiro, E. C. (1995). *Fad surfing in the boardroom*. Sydney, Australia: Harper Collins.

Strassmann, P. A. (1997). *The squandered computer: Evaluating the business alignment of information technologies*. New Canaan, CT: Information Economics.

Sturm, R., Morris, W., & Jander, M. (2000). *Foundations of service level management*. Indianapolis, IN: SAMS.

Section II

Models and Architectures

Chapter IV

How Should Enterprises Integrate?
From the Need
to the Solution ...

Alexandre Félix-Alves, INOVA+, Portugal

Abstract

While industrial companies have learned to establish added-value relationships and flows with their supply chain satellite companies, when they now face the new challenge of building relationships with other value chains, they suffer from the lack of existing know-how and expertise in meta-value chain operation and management (including methodologies, reference models, case studies, best practices, and business and ICT solution maps). Collaboration only becomes a competitive advantage for a meta-value chain when it leads to meta-value chain agility. While the customisation of the single value proposition has led to the need of mass customisation in productive processes, customising and continuously adapting an extended value preposition (EVP) is mainly achieved by reshaping the composition and geometry of the whole extended enterprise (EE) relying on dynamic and agile business models. This meta-value chain agility needs, in turn, to be based on extended organisational learning. This self and external awareness requires continuous assessment processes and models based on key performance indicators.

Introduction

Globalisation and enhanced national, European, and worldwide competitiveness have promoted the creation and consolidation of the so-called extended enterprises (EE), which transcend the single enterprise domain and builds meta-enterprises.[1] These meta-enterprises can be broadly defined as networks of complementary companies that work jointly to provide more value to their customers and improve their human, knowledge, operational, and structural capitals.

Most existing EE have initially focused on reinforcing the links and flows between companies that are involved in the same value chain. However, the phenomenon has recently shifted towards the creation of EE that cross the barriers of a single value chain, and link different complementary value chains, thus building meta-value chains.

EE face the same customer challenges ever. One straightforward way they have to boost their added-value is to aggregate to their own value proposition those of other complementary value chains, building the so-called extended value proposition (EVP). At mid- and long-term, competitiveness will become more and more based on EVP added-value and agility.

The general perspective of this chapter is to address this new problem and, based on a new methodology and architecture, try to explain the major achievements to the present time, specifically about the new changes in the organisational dimensions, and to discuss future and emerging trends.

The objective of the chapter is to face issues like:

- *Our customers want more and more each day. We can improve and extend our own products and services, but now they request us complementary products and services we have never been involved in and we have no control on.*
- *It is already difficult to plan, manage, and operate our own company, but now we need to plan, manage, and operate also all the other ones that are linked with it!*
- *What's currently the state of this order? Where is the product? Will we supply it on time?*

The idea is to develop in the reader's mind some kind of awareness to the new interorganisational integration.

Background

Growing internationalisation implies that the growth of the market economy has been increasingly relying on the expansion of the world market, rather than on domestic market (Fotopoulos, 2005). Thus, under conditions of growing internationalisation, the economy's increasing growth depends on supply conditions, which in turn determines trade performance.

Figure 1. Extended enterprise

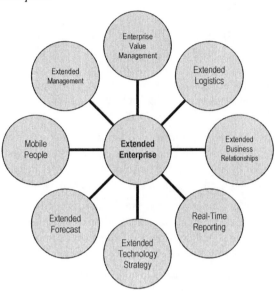

Growing market complexity, continuous organisational change, and increased international competitiveness are key issues of all companies at the present time. The constant challenge is to bring products/services to the market faster, with reduced cost and higher intrinsic quality.

The solution in building and maintaining a highly competitive environment is full integration of business processes across the enterprise and involvement of key suppliers, usually SMEs, throughout the supply chain. This demands the use of new technologies that eliminate traditional information barriers; transportation and information networks have the role of linking the cells into productive agglomerates of networked systems. Enterprise processes, as we know them today (research and development, design engineering, manufacturing, marketing and customer support), are highly integrated and have promoted the consolidation of the so-called EE, which transcend the single enterprise sphere and generate meta-enterprises, defined as networks of complementary companies that work jointly to provide more value to their customers and improve their human, knowledge, operational, and structural capitals.

Extended Value Proposition

In a customer-centred world, companies have to be fully customer-oriented, customer-customised, and customer-governed in order to maintain their competitive advantage. Similarly, at the meta-enterprise level, EE have to face the same customer challenges; they have to boost their added-value by aggregating their own value proposition those of other complementary value chains, building the EVP. Competitiveness will become more and more defined in terms of EVP added-value and agility.

Figure 2. From the single value chain to the meta-value chain

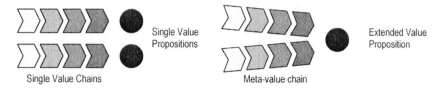

During the last years a livid search for new ways in providing better visibility of supply-chain activities has been endured. Organisations in general started to feel the need to be closer to their partners. This was done mainly through win-lose relations that inevitably led to fusions, acquisitions, or takeovers. This solution was far from being optimal and frequently led to major losses in profit because focus on the core business of the companies got misplaced.

HP believes that manufacturers should collaborate with key members of the supply chain in order to increase revenues, reduce manufacturing costs, speed time to market, and sharpen their competitive edge. In today's economic environment, it is increasingly clear that focusing on core competencies, to satisfy customer demands whatever they are, is critical to success.

The keywords are meta-value chain collaboration. A recent trend in meta-enterprises has begun to transform their traditional master-slave, win-lose, or lose-win business relationship models into fully peer-to-peer, win-win ones. The same collaborative model is required now for meta-value chains.

The starting point of any meta-value chain award-winning approach is consequently collaboration, where the concept inherently implies agility and learn-to-learn capacity. Within a value chain, the downstream supply chain, the so-called selling chain, plays a key role to build and deliver competitive value propositions to customers, as it represents the relation between the value chain and the customer. Similarly, the meta-selling chain, defined as the aggregation of selling chains within a meta-value chain, becomes a key player to build and deliver competitive Extended Value Proposition to customers.

Leading companies show why extended enterprises demand radically new buyer-supplier relationships, why traditional business structures inhibit alliances and partnerships, and how to develop the competencies that companies need (Davis & Spekman, 2003). They are also identifying integration issues head-on, earlier in the meta-value chain sphere. Indeed, companies in general are finding that approaching business processes from an integration perspective is essential in building better added-value.

Moreover, according to Jeffery Perry (2005) from Ernst & Young, successful organisations are now considering integration issues as part of due diligence, to help them understand synergy opportunities, costs and risks, and develop a plan to realise the deal's strategic rationale. Moreover, he says that "taking an early integration perspective enhances a company's ability to analyze a deal's potential," (p.1) that is, understand the challenges and opportunities that lie at the forefront, assess transaction jeopardy, judge costs associated with synergies, and realistically price business integration.

Understanding the Extended Collaborative Enterprise Concept

According to Browne and Zhang (1999) the manufacturing systems today are subject to tremendous pressure of the ever-changing marketing environment. They also conclude that individual companies have to work together to form inter-enterprise networks across the product value chain in order to survive and achieve business success. They denominate those inter-enterprise networks, the extended enterprise. Extended enterprise collaboration can occur between any two or more enterprises across the value chain; and requires a closer integration than traditional supply chain collaboration (Jagdev & Thoben, 2001). The development of a fully integrated extended enterprise can be defined as "the formation of closer co-ordination in the design, development, costing, and the coordination of the respective manufacturing schedules of co-operating independent manufacturing enterprises and related suppliers" (Jagdev & Browne, 1998, pp. 216-229). The key words in this definition are the "co-ordination of respective manufacturing schedules." An efficient extended enterprise requires that production schedules, dispatch, transportation/delivery, and receipt notifications are coordinated within and across company borders.

On the other hand, mass customisation is defined by Zipkin (2001) as: "the capability, realized by a few companies, to offer individually tailored products or services on a larger scale." (p.81)

The concept of mass customisation tries to provide the best of two worlds: mass production that strives for economy of scale by providing uniform products, and customisation that seeks to fulfil customers' individual wishes. In mass customisation, each customer provides unique information so that the product[2] can be tailored to his/her requirements. The production process must be very flexible in order to meet those requirements, and there is no finished goods inventory (Zipkin, 2001).

But we can go even further and try to reach an extended collaborative enterprise (ECE). This is full integration of multi-value chains (or the meta-value chain).

According to Accenture, IT tools are already accelerating the design and delivery of integration-based business capabilities. But is this enough? Do we have methodologies, best practices, guidelines, or business models to make this process efficient? Creating and sustaining high-performance business collaboration is indeed a challenge, waiting to be mastered.

Figure 3. Special focus on dynamic changes along the meta-value chain

Production planning and control

Handling of disturbances and decision support

Logistics and transports

Performance indicators and collaborative forecast

State-of-the-Art

According to Bruce Temkin (2002) from Forrester Research, and despite the current volatility in the B2B sector, initiatives are still being implemented and supply chains are still targets of optimisation efforts; the focus has been on implementing Internet-enabled systems.

Enterprise applications such as enterprise resource planning (ERP) are so common that we will not reference them. From Adonix to Syspro, they basically manage most of the business processes within, and closely related to, the company.

According to Sho Hanaoka (2002), and based on the results of some surveys, business performances will have no clear relevance to the utilisation of B2B information systems. This implies that there is a clear necessity for new innovative Information Systems.

There is a clear lack in the market for extended collaborative IT solutions, and literature to support its implementation, namely concerning extended collaborative enterprise integration and management models.

Understanding the Opportunity

Several years ago, the EE trend started to be detected as a major industrial opportunity. Now, ongoing initiatives, statistics, and surveys confirm its importance and sustained interest for the industrial community during the following years. Similarly, current R&D actions of the Sixth Framework Programme (see www.cordis.lu) confirm the major interest for EE at the European level.

With efficient models, methodologies, and implementation tools to build up an extended collaborative logistics system, end users and industrial partners will be interested in implementing them in their logistic structure in order to improve their customer focusing, and the quality and amount of product-associated services.

Figure 4. Benefits for companies

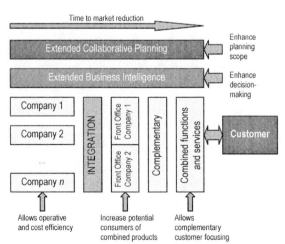

Figure 5. Roadmap from AS-IS to TO-BE: The importance of business models

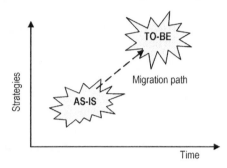

In addition, the added-value proposition that is going to be offered to the final customer, will become, from the combination of logistic activities, coupled to different value chains as complementary product manufacturers from the market point of view.

The Problem

The creation of a successful meta-value chain is certainly a complex and risky endeavour that implies major transformation for a set of industrial companies, especially in terms of dependency of another value chain, cross-enterprise and cross-value chain culture, market strategy, business processes and models, production and demand planning, logistics and integration of materials/management/decision/knowledge flows.

In order to achieve a state of full extended collaborative integration (TO-BE state), companies have to take a complex migration path, changing most of the company's business processes as they are (AS-IS state). In order to successfully accomplish this transformation, the companies have to follow some type of guidelines or strategies tagging along a migration path.

Sharing equipments, ideas, and resources to develop new products over raw materials offers great possibilities for innovation, making it possible to achieve competitive advantages, but has the inconvenience of keeping the industrial secrets close to the competitors. When companies in an extended collaborative selling chain model intend to develop new products, questions like: What kind of product innovation could we offer working together? How must costs/efforts be shared? Can I trust you? come to certainty. This is part of the migration path.

Manufacturing and Production

The increased flexibility of lean manufacturing enables industrial production managers to experiment with ways of improving the assembly and manufacturing process. As companies endeavour in inventory minimisation, they fancy maintaining only a limited stock of finished products.

Just-in-time production techniques have reduced inventory levels, making constant communication among companies even more important. Information systems play an integral part in this coordination. They are also used to provide up-to-date information on inventory, the status of work in progress, and quality standards.

What is the next step? In order to keep competitiveness, companies in general must now start integrating themselves with companies within different value-chains. This *migration path* poses some difficulties, without question.

Logistics

One of the most important issues under extended collaborative selling chains is the logistic dilemma. In order to fully integrate companies under an extended collaborative environment, connecting different value chains, it is necessary to improve the whole cross-value chain demand forecast for complex products and services.

A global and systematic vision of the complex meta-value chain is the solution. Yet, in order to achieve this *holistic* visualisation, improved market knowledge and understanding of customer/consumer demand trends, based on combining the internal forecast with an external one, is necessary.

What at the first sight can be considered easy is, in reality, extremely complex. Even though mathematically this problem is solvable, modelling it can be a long process, yet to be correctly valorised.

Sales and Marketing

Much of the benefits associated with the trend towards identity-preserving marketing, based on individuality, can be surpassed by a greater benefit in joint collaboration. Both marketing and production business processes can systematise their interests through cooperative give-away business models.

The problem could be formulated to develop partnerships with similar groups with the purpose of promoting, fostering, and discussing marketing cooperative operations. But within the companies, as we know them today, this problem can be hazardous or even impractical, which will lead us inevitably to provisions of good faith in negotiations, dispute resolution mechanisms, and enforcement procedures.

The Solution

Complex problems have complex solutions or no solutions at all. In order to achieve the full benefits of collaboration, companies must integrate their business processes. Collaboration comprehends coordination of activities and communication. So, is this the solution?

Globalisation and enhanced competitiveness have increased the enterprise's need for collaboration: link different complementary value chains to offer added-value to the final customers.

Then, enterprises can form collaborative networks of complementary companies that work jointly in order to provide more value to their customers and improve their human, knowledge, operational, and structural capitals, thus offering added-value complementary products (complex made-up products) to customers.

Products and services can provide companies with a competitive advantage, and the end customer with an extended value proposition, through the collaboration among extended selling chains, as seen on previous sub-chapters.

Many industrial companies have been selling and distributing jointly their aggregated products for a long time. Now they face the complete integration of their value chains, defining an extended collaborative selling chain model. This model provides major benefits mainly in terms of:

- **Enhanced overall competitiveness**, innovation, and adaptability in today and tomorrow's enterprise partnership scenario;
- **Cross-country and inter-enterprise interchanges**, building world-wide networked enterprises that are supported by dynamic relationship schemas and innovative cooperation and coordination business paradigms;
- **Higher added-value to customers**, in terms of improved value proposition and better and more accurate customer service;
- **Cost reduction** at the intra-enterprise level (inefficiencies of processes, stocks, flows, plans, etc.) based on new extended models for the value chain; and
- **Human capital improved quality** of work and empowerment, through better knowledge management and integration, better understanding of dynamics and flows, and clearer definition of roles and responsibilities.

The temporal horizon for an optimum extended collaborative integration business model must cover the following objectives:

- **Strategic:** It responds to the question, "What can we offer to the customer in order to increase differentiation with our competitors?"
- **Tactic:** It responds to the question, "What are the models that we must complete in order to achieve our business strategy?"
- **Operative:** It responds to the question, "What are the tools that we need to develop to test the efficiency of the new extended collaborative enterprise model?"

Research and Development in Cooperation

The research and development cooperation proposes to share equipments, ideas, and resources between manufacturers. This cooperation can exist in various levels of the value chain. It could appear in manufactures which compete in the same market, between complementary manufactures and their suppliers or in a cluster.

In order to increase manufacturers' competitive advantage, this model proposes to share manufacturers' technology and know-how to develop all new designs and tests in cooperation. Thus, better communication channels and patent protection politics and rules should be designed to develop this model.

Extended Product Packs Definition

Nowadays, when the supply chain management is highly developed and optimised, the differentiation between an enterprise and its sector's competitors is carried out on the supply of added-value complementary products (complex made-up products, with strong added-value).

The extended collaborative business model is the industrial and commercial environment which allows complementary partners of different selling chains to work in a collaborative manner, in order to offer to the final consumer new added-value packaged products and services. These meta-value products will provide the company with a competitive advantage and the end customer with an extended value proposition, through the collaboration among meta-value chains.

In order to define these products, the below stages must be realised:

- Necessity of firm agreements between partners to avoid industrial secrets dissemination to the competitors
- Definition of the extended value proposition; (pack components and rules for the configuration, prices, etc.)
- Definition of a shared catalogue and its implications
- Business process reengineering
- Analysis of resulting cost reductions
- Logistics network redefinition

To conclude, a differential factor for enterprises of the extended enterprise model is to have know-how of the complex products and all their cycles of order and realisation, in order to increase general quality and profit margins.

Extended Planning

Complementary partners need to work jointly in order to offer greater added-value to the final clients. They need to be coordinated to offer to the customer added-value and an efficient service.

In order to achieve an optimum coordination between complementary partners to serve to the final clients, it is necessary to:

- Manage orders for the product pack between them
- Coordinate their production and distributions plans
- Share knowledge about actual and forecasted demand, that can be useful to plan production and distribution and to know customers' trends
- Share information about available stock materials and/or production capacity (offered by the ATP/CTP extended models)

Then, in order to develop this business model, it will be necessary to establish a strong relationship between complementary manufacturers; that is why good communication channels and agreements should be designed.

However, this business model has the following implications:

- The creation of a shared catalogue of collaborative products offered to the final client
- The development of an extended ATP/CTP model for the principal actors of the complementary value chains; in order to propose to the final client a delivery date in real-time
- Coordinate production and distribution times between complementary manufacturers to deliver the product on time
- Offer data about demand and forecast to other partners

Extended Distribution Models

An important problem that is necessary to analyse is how to update the upstream and downstream distribution models for all actors in the meta-value chain in order to achieve the best global distribution model for the cross-value chain.

A reengineering in the whole cross-value chain can be found necessary to develop the new distribution model. It can also be necessary to develop new work procedures in all affected models in the distribution, and take into account all actors in the cross-value chain.

Following are described some steps in the distribution models that are necessary to analyse and eventually to reengineer:

- Load of individual products development for actors in the cross-value chain
- Transport from manufacturers to a consolidation area
- **Consolidation:** This can include picking, packing, assembly, treatment, and so forth, depending on the product, the market, and the business model to be defined.
- **Product presentation:** how the product is presented to the final customer
- Returns logistics

The Social Problem

Workers have to be knowledge-driven workers rather than machine feeders. In fact, the communication system of a knowledge-based meta-value chain will allow the incorporation of learning and training procedures within the communication system itself, and will create methods for remote transfer of skills, both between different enterprises and inside a single enterprise.

Interpersonal skills must be highly developed, cross-cultural barriers must be greatly reduced, and remaining differences must be assessed for their contributions to innovate manufacturing. Individuals must have a sense of purpose and satisfaction, and be able to clearly see how their skills and intellectual capabilities add value to the enterprise. Information systems and methods for remote transfer of skills will enhance workers' access and usability of information, thus reducing the current gap between individual intellectual capabilities and shared knowledge.

By introducing better modelling methods, partners and users will be able to exploit new styles of cooperation in an optimal way.

We can frequently find the most amazing comparisons between science and economics. Charles Darwin once said that "it is not the strongest of the species that survive, nor the most intelligent, but the ones most responsive to change". This is the key to enterprise integration success.

Future Trends

Information systems will play an important role, where trust will be valorised.

New IT tools and applications will appear to enable the collaboration between industrial partners presenting different profiles (ranging from very small companies to large multinational ones). Leading companies continue, and will continue, to use Internet-based technologies to develop new collaborative relationships with suppliers.

The inherent risk that arises is that enterprises, and especially SMEs, do not manage to fully integrate on time and lose competitive advantage awarded to collaborative value chains and meta-value chains, and remain left aside from tomorrow's competitive productive superstructures. Consequently, there appears to be a clear need to establish a wide-reaching scenario to pose the problem.

Global synergy of business cultures, new business dynamics, knowledge interchange, renewed industrial paradigms and supporting improved regulation policies and laws will be keywords for the success of international industrial policies.

Moreover, close integration and networking of people, organisations, and technologies, will be the crucial input to maintain competitive production. The focus will be on moving more and more towards the collaboration with partners, both within and outside the value chain, seeking an enhanced value proposition.

Added-value products must be achieved and tailored to meet customers' demand.

New organisational structures and work practices are emerging. The change to innovative high performance logistics and distribution systems, with agile collaborative value chains and meta-value chains will be tomorrow's major industrial challenge.

Conclusion

Selling chain management, extended enterprises, and collaborative enterprises are clearly identified as today's and tomorrow's business opportunities.

The competitiveness improvement will come from the greater focus on consumer needs and time to market decrease, through the packaging of products and increase in the amount and quality of associated services to those packaged products, thanks to the collaboration of dynamic re-engineered and integrated complementary value chains.

Benefits for companies come from the reduction in time to market and integration with complementary products value chains and systems. Even more, the possibilities of commercialising not only in their selling points, but in complementary products resellers, can open an expectable increase in sales per year.

Although, manufacturing and commercialising companies compound the initially-targeted market, the potential market can be extended to all industrial and consulting companies involved or willing to be involved in extended collaborative selling chains, focused on packaged complementary products offered to the customer.

It is urgent to increase industry's innovation capacity and adaptability to change to extended collaborative business models, tomorrow's production systems, while enhancing flexibility and capability to respond in real-time to customer needs.

The challenge is especially critical for SMEs, as they are facing the risk of being left aside in tomorrow's competitive industry, but at the same time lacking in required skills, collaborative culture, and power to negotiate.

We have discussed the extended collaborative enterprise Integration model in this chapter as a next stage, in the hope that it will be developed and improved in the future. Hopefully, the reader will end up with more questions upon reaching the end of this chapter than when he or she began.

References

Boyson, S., Corsi, T. M., Dresner, M. E., & Harrington, L. H. (1999). *Logistics and the extended enterprise: Benchmarks and best practices for the manufacturing professional*. New York: John Wiley & Sons, Inc.

Browne, J., & Zhang, J. (1999). Extended and virtual enterprises—similarities and differences. *International Journal of Agile Management Systems, 1*(1), 30-36.

Davis, E. W., & Spekman, R. E. (2003). *The extended enterprise: Gaining competitive advantage through collaborative supply chains*.

European Logistics Association (2000). *Diversity in logistics and the importance of logistics in the extended enterprise*. Paper presented at the Symposium conducted at the Logistics Educators' Conference 2000, Athens, Greece.

Fotopoulos, T. (2005, August). Special Issue: The multidimensional crisis and inclusive democracy. *The International Journal of Inclusive Democracy*. Retrieved January 30, 2006, from http://www.inclusivedemocracy.org/journal/

Hanaoka, S. (2002, June). A study of the B2B progress in Japanese enterprises. *Informing Science*. Retrieved September 2, 2005, from http://proceedings.informingscience.org/

Handfield, R. B., & Nichols, E. L. (2001). *Supply chain redesign: Transforming supply chains into integrated supply systems*. Prentice Hall.

Ireland, R. K. (2005). *Supply chain collaboration: How to implement CPFRR and other best collaborative practices*. J. Ross Publishing.

Jagdev, H. S., & Browne, J. (1998). The extended enterprise—a context for manufacturing. *Production Planning & Control, 9*(3), 216-219.

Jagdev, H. S., & Thoben, K. D. (2001). Anatomy of enterprise collaborations. Production Planning & Control, 12(5), 437-451.

Perry, J. (2005). The integration perspective. *InterChange, 6*. Retrieved September 23, 2005 from http://www.ey.com/global/content.nsf/International/Home

Temkin, B. (2002). Building a collaborative supply chain. *ASCET—Achieving Supply Chain Excellence through Technology, 4*. Retrieved November 25, 2005, from http://www.ascet.com/

Zipkin, P. (2001). The limits of mass customization. *Sloan Management Review, 42*(12), 81-87.

Endnotes

1.   The prefix meta is used here to represent a higher level entity (the EE) formed by a set of lower level entities (the enterprises).

2.   Services are, by nature, customised solutions.

Chapter V

A Generation of Moderators from Single Product to Global E-Supply

Jennifer Anne Harding, Loughborough University, UK

Keith Popplewell, Coventry University, UK

Hsiao-Kang Lin, I-Shou University, Taiwan

Abstract

This chapter presents the concepts and history of moderator research, covering the long journey from the first engineering moderator to recent proposals for an e-supply chains moderator. The main function of a moderator is to support a design group or team by raising individual members' awareness of the needs and experiences of other team members. Moderators are specialist intelligent software systems which support each individual to perform his particular role from a position of strength, using his preferred methods of working while still understanding the needs of other individuals and the total team. This research addresses demanding and complex business requirements by exploiting the increasingly powerful technologies and infrastructures available for business integration.

Introduction:
Setting the Context

The strength and success of a team depends on how well each individual can contribute the maximum benefit of their skills to a consolidated and shared vision of the total group. The different backgrounds, experiences, and environments of the individuals inevitably influence their views and interpretations of the overall objectives. Hence, as soon as people from different disciplines and backgrounds try to work together, there is potential for misunderstanding or lack of awareness of the needs and interdependencies of each individual contributor. This is true even in small, co-located teams where individuals meet regularly to discuss overall project requirements and progress. It is clearly a far greater problem when teams are large and physically located in different companies or even different countries (see Figure 1).

A simple example, taken from the earliest demonstrations of moderators, may serve to illustrate the problem. The earliest specification of a moderator (Harding & Popplewell, 1996) was demonstrated in a case study examining the design of a shaft for an electrical machine. The shaft is initially designed primarily for its function, namely to carry and rotate copper windings rotating at high speed while being supported in bearings at each end. A set of form features are designed into the shaft to attach windings, to rest in bearings, and to transmit rotation into or out of the machine. These features mainly include cylindrical sections, steps, tapers, bearing surfaces, and keyways. The designer was an expert in the functional design of electrical machines, but not in manufacturing technology, and included in his design a step between cylindrical sections. This precisely met his functional needs, but cannot be machined by conventional methods: The transition between the smaller radius and the radial face must itself have a fillet radius of at least the size of the cutting tool used. The designer has thus, through lack of knowledge of the manufacturing issues, designed an impossible, or at least extremely expensive, feature into the product.

The manufacturing engineer subsequently looks at the design and, without full understanding of the functional reasons for the step, plans to simply use the smallest available tool

Figure 1. Awareness is critical to project success

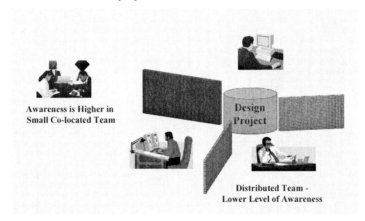

Awareness is Higher in
Small Co-located Team

Design
Project

Distributed Team -
Lower Level of Awareness

to machine the step, thus introducing a fillet to the design. If the precise surface transition was essential to function (e.g., as a thrust-bearing surface), we now have a design which is manufacturable but which either will not work, or will cause rapid wear—again with expensive consequences.

If the functional designer and manufacturing engineer are physically co-located and are constantly communicating, there is a reasonable chance that such design conflicts will be identified as they arise. This does, however, require the two contributors to know when to raise a design issue with the other: Each does not have the other's expertise, but has sufficient knowledge of the broad categories of issues which are critical to the other to know when to consult.

However, if the design team is geographically distributed, and this is increasingly the case, the members have little opportunity for informal communication, and in consequence they rely on formal systems transferring design authority between disciplines. This formalises the points in time when communication occurs, but if a design conflict is introduced a long time before the next formal review point, much expensive work may already have built upon the controversial design decision, and resolution is slow and expensive. The loss of informal communication also reduces the opportunities for team members to gain understanding and knowledge of the kinds of design decisions which can conflict with the interests of other design team members. Thus, the probability of identifying a design conflict quickly and cheaply is greatly reduced.

In this early demonstration, the engineering moderator (EM) was monitoring the design process, by examining each design decision as it was committed to the design database. When the radius step was introduced to the functional design, the EM, using its own knowledge of the issues important to the manufacturing of shafts, recognised that a potential conflict had arisen, and notified the manufacturing engineer that he should examine the design. Subsequently, when he introduced a fillet radius to accommodate the tool, the EM, now

Figure 2. Stages of moderation of shaft design

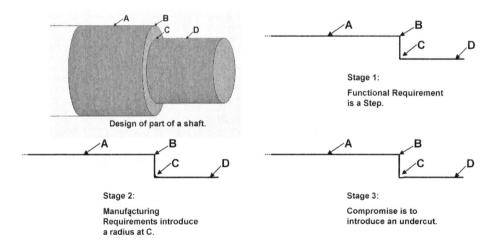

Figure 3. The generic moderation process

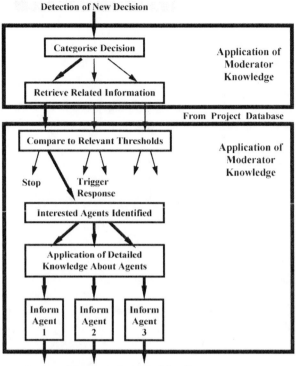

using knowledge of issues important to functional shaft design, recognised the potential for conflict and alerted the functional designer. This dialogue driven by the moderator led to a mutually-acceptable undercut design, as demonstrated in Figure 2.

This is, of course, a fairly trivial example of a moderator application and merely serves to illustrate the principle. It is also specific to the product design process, which, historically, was the domain where a moderator was first developed. An important characteristic demonstrated by this example is that the moderator does not have any design knowledge itself, but it does have knowledge about each contributing designer and knowledge of what is important for the application of their knowledge. In order to have the flexibility to capture knowledge about the knowledge used by a wide range of contributors to the design team, the moderator had to have a generic structure able to apply an evolving base of knowledge from a wide range of disciplines. Subsequent research has investigated the application of the same principles of knowledge structuring and the same generic moderation process, illustrated in Figure 3, in a variety of fields besides product design, including for example, global manufacturing systems (supply chain) design, and operational management of global manufacturing systems.

Inevitably, organisations using a moderator will not have explicit knowledge of the full range of possible issues, and this may lead to decision conflicts at the time of the initial implementation of a moderator. Hence, a newly-implemented moderator cannot be fully populated with knowledge: Indeed we can argue that as the moderator knowledge base is derived from experience, it can never be complete. Manufacturing organisations are constantly changing, as new products are developed addressing new markets and technologies, and so we can also expect that the range of collaborators (and their domains of expertise) will change over time, requiring the moderator knowledge base to constantly evolve. It is therefore essential that any moderator is built around a very flexible knowledge structure, which can be constantly updated by its users, both directly and through the application of knowledge discovery tools.

This chapter will discuss how moderators can support the global organisation and project team to achieve their goals while reducing remoteness arising from distributing the team, and promoting exchange of information between team members at different physical locations. Moderators support individuals to perform their individual roles from positions of strength and understanding, with raised awareness of the needs of other contributors. Moderators also support individuals' preferred methods of working while still understanding the needs of both individuals and the total team.

The technological approaches to implementing effective moderators are also examined. A flexible knowledge structure is necessary to allow moderator knowledge to evolve, and the moderator must be able to support the collaboration of independent enterprises, sharing knowledge where this is of mutual advantage, while maintaining security and confidentiality of knowledge and information as needed. A number of potential moderator application areas in manufacturing industry will be identified, although application areas from outside the manufacturing domain can also benefit from moderator technologies.

Background

History Part 1:
The Birth of an Engineering Moderator

The moderator concept was first proposed in the MOSES research project[1] as a support tool for design project teams. It was coordinating software for concurrent engineering (CE) design, to raise awareness among the inter-working cross-disciplinary participants that exist and need to cooperate in modern-day engineering teams. An important function of the Engineering Moderator was also to support the human designers, but not to attempt to replace them with any sort of automated, artificial intelligence systems.

In the first implementations of the engineering moderator, in the early 1990s, certain assumptions were made about the technology requirements and available environments. Primary among these was the assumption that all contributors would share a design environment, so that the product design would be gradually constructed within a *product model*, (Krause, Kimura, Kjellberg, & Lu, 1993; McKay, Bloor, & de Pennington, 1996), stored in an ob-

Figure 4. Engineering moderator knowledge areas

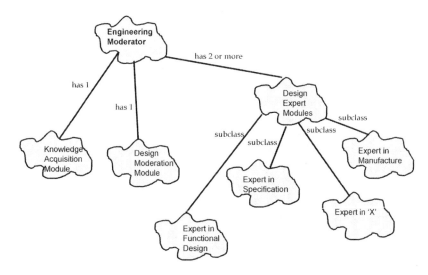

ject-oriented database. It was also assumed that designers would have knowledge of the manufacturing capabilities of their manufacturing facilities and that this would be accessible as information from a second object-oriented database, known as the *manufacturing model* (Molina & Bell, 1999).

To raise awareness between members of the design team, the engineering moderator needed knowledge about the individuals within the team, for example, who they were, what elements of the design they were interested in and could contribute to. It also needed to understand the twin model environment that the team was working in, and have knowledge of how to **moderate** within this environment. The engineering moderator therefore needed to store knowledge in an adaptable format that could potentially work with different databases and applications. The three key areas of moderator knowledge are shown in Figure 4.

A flexible knowledge representation structure was therefore needed to support the implementation of these three knowledge types. The structure that was designed and developed was called the knowledge representation model (KRM) (Harding, 1996). Each element of knowledge, from the simplest expression to the complex expert modules (shown in Figure 4), was designed as an object, which could interact with other knowledge objects. Storing the knowledge as persistent objects within an object-oriented database system enabled the Moderator to operate with a high level of flexibility in different computing environments. By making use of inheritance structures and polymorphism, it was possible for the similarity of behaviour of certain classes of objects to be exploited even when the implementation of particular sub-classes of these objects was significantly different.

The key types of knowledge required by a moderator include the knowledge acquisition module (Figure 5), which provides the moderator with all the knowledge it requires to create, update, and remove knowledge during the course of its operation. Part of the functionality of the knowledge acquisition module is to create new design expert modules when a new

Figure 5. Knowledge acquisition module functionality

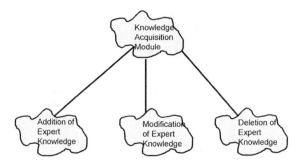

Figure 6. Content of each design expert module

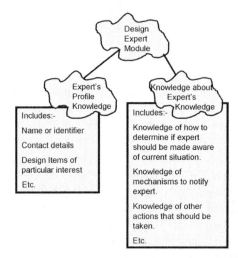

team member joins the design team. The content of any expert module can also be modified at any time as the project progresses. Figure 6 shows the basic content of each different type of design expert module.

The design moderation module operates continuously throughout the design project as each change to the design needs to be examined to assess if any potential problems may be occurring. The types of knowledge required in this moderation process are shown in Figure 7.

The MOSES design environment, which required the contributors to share a single object-oriented project database, restricted the applicability of the engineering moderator, but did enable its feasibility to be demonstrated. Figure 8 shows how the moderator concepts were achieved; the knowledge representation structures and other key models (e.g., product model) were purpose-built using C++ and commercial object-oriented database systems (OODBS).

Figure 7. Content of the design moderation module

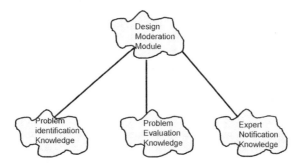

Figure 8. Technology used by engineering moderator

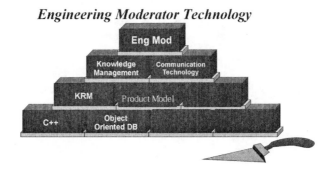

Knowledge management was achieved through the functionality of these databases with the addition of specially-designed KRM objects which were stored within an additional OODBS. The communication technology used in the engineering moderator was limited to message passing between objects in the databases and the engineering moderator applications.

History Part 2:
Moderators Branch Out as Globalisation Becomes Common

In the late 1990s, there were growing demands for core competencies to be moved from large, UK single-company design and manufacture scenarios and be distributed to multiple companies in the logistic chain for product development and production. This approach could exploit smaller, more specialist design and manufacture units and cheaper wage rates that exist worldwide. Manufacturing industry needed to cut its costs and overheads, and there were growing demands for flexible, fast, well-planned manufacturing system design. Manufacturing systems therefore started to move from distributed manufacturing and global manufacturing towards cross-organisation manufacturing, using inter-connected systems.

The process of designing a manufacturing system (MS) requires the application of different areas of expertise, including, for example, functions such as process selection, equipment selection, facility layout, performance prediction (perhaps by simulation), and potentially many others. Additionally, information on the strategic requirements (e.g., what product(s) are to be made in what volumes, to satisfy what market constraints) from the MS must be available, since this effectively forms the design specification for the MS. Large-scale projects rely on inputs from a team of specialist engineers with various different types of expertise who are commonly located in different organisations.

An MSE Moderator

The Mission project[2] addressed these requirements through the provision of appropriate software tools, including simulation and a MSE moderator (see Figure 9).

The developing design is shared between the moderator and project contributors through the MSE integration environment. It was no longer possible to assume that all contributors (team members) could share the same huge object-oriented database of design information. In the mission environment, access was provided through an information manager to all partners' database systems.

In the mission environment, the moderator still uses the KRM within an OODBS, but now the MSE moderator needs more sophisticated knowledge of partners, and more complex relationships with the project manager and other partners. The increase in technology is shown in Figure 10.

Figure 9. The mission modelling platform

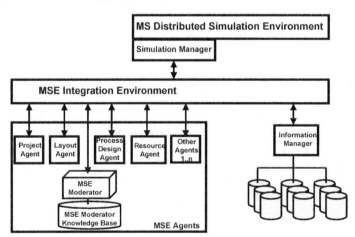

Figure 10. Technology used by MSE moderator

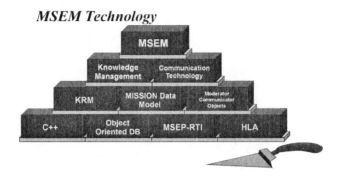

MSEM Technology

Evolving Moderator Knowledge

Moderator knowledge structuring, sharing, and evolution become even more important when teams come together from different companies and locations, and the shared working environments have to become more flexible and diffuse to support the extended or virtual enterprise (VE). In such circumstances, the core functionality of the moderator remains the same, but its knowledge must be extended to provide greater understanding of the extended environment in which it is operating (see Figure 11).

Figure 11 shows a small core of moderator functionality which, as described above, is embedded in the moderator knowledge base and is common to all implementations. Upon this is built a body of general VE knowledge of how any collaboration can be supported by moderation. These two core knowledge bases could be part of the proprietary software for a moderator, and may perhaps include a body of industrial sector knowledge, which can specialise a moderator to operate in a particular industrial domain. For example, knowledge

Figure 11. Evolving moderator knowledge

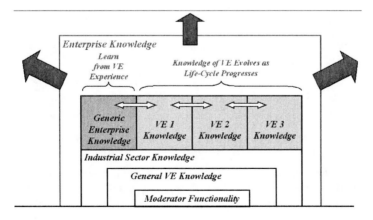

of how collaboration works in the automotive industry and the issues which are critical to successful competition in the industry may be common to all automotive applications of moderators.

Beyond this, the enterprise generates its own knowledge and experience of collaboration, which can be embedded in its moderator knowledge base. This is certainly proprietary knowledge, which is part of the enterprise's strategic competitive armoury. This will include knowledge developed in, and specific to, each VE of which it is currently a member, enabling it to perform effectively in every collaboration, with the ability to identify and respond to developing decision conflicts in the context of the VE. However, the enterprise can also derive a body of generic enterprise knowledge from the VE-specific knowledge, through a process of project reviews to identify experience which can be applied beyond the individual VE. The enterprise knowledge base is thus constantly growing and evolving.

Current Reality:
An E-Supply Chains Moderator on the Semantic Web

The first mission MSE moderator supported the product design and manufacture process by integrating a set of software applications using a single information manager for the information exchange between all the involved MSE agents. Individual design agents do not consider the requirement of the systems in other companies. However, the VE knowledge in the global supply chain design should include partnership and cross-organisation-related information, which should be shared among participants. Organisations in multiple relationships, with different sets of partners, can no longer rely on imposing a single shared information model for any particular project.

The growing complexity of VE knowledge has made it increasingly difficult to share and exchange knowledge and information between companies where inevitably individual partners will have their own terminology and information sources. Problems might arise due to the heterogeneity of the data to be shared and exchanged. The three most general heterogeneity problems within the multi-database community are:

- **Syntax:** data format heterogeneity
- **Structure:** different data organisations (e.g., schema heterogeneity in RDBs and OODBs)
- **Semantic:** conceptual knowledge, where the intended interpretation or meaning of the data is specified in a special context; so, for example, semantic heterogeneity refers to differences or similarity in the meaning of data between the different component databases

Enterprise information integration is, therefore, an important step for VE knowledge sharing and exchange. Along with the rapid progress of online and digitized information, the MSE moderator concepts have had to evolve to apply in this electronic format global supply chain environment context. The adoption of "Semantic Web" technologies, like ontologies, content metadata, and reasoning about conceptual knowledge, have been investigated to support a variety of the essential activities of evolving MSE moderator knowledge management, including knowledge retrieval, storage, sharing, and moderation.

A MSE ontology model that is motivated by the concepts of a moderator has been developed and encoded using the Semantic Web technology. This approach enhances inter-enterprise interoperability and enables the operation of an e-supply chain moderator (E-SCM) within globally-distributed virtual manufacturing enterprises.

MSE Ontology Model

The Semantic Web has been proposed as an ontology-based approach for dealing with heterogeneous data, and in particular for managing semantic heterogeneity. Widely quoted definitions of "ontology" are given in Gruber (1992) and Gruber (1993, pp. 199-220) as "an explicit specification of a conceptualization" and "a specification of a representational vocabulary for a shared domain of discourse—definitions of classes, relations, functions, and other objects—is called an ontology." Ontologies have been widely applied in many areas, such as ontology-based query search (Hyvonen, Saarela, & Viljanen, 2004; Mena & Illarramendi, 2001); ontology-mediated translation service to enable data integration of disparate data sources (Fensel, 2002; Fensel, Ding, Omelayenko, Schulten, Botquin, Brown & Flett, 2001), Web service (Hu, Kruse, & Draws, 2003) and knowledge mining (Priebe & Pernul, 2003).

The MSE ontology model adopts the Semantic Web technology in an ontology-mediated translation function and provides efficient access by a common/mediated schema across all the teams' members within many inter-enterprise collaboration activities, including design and planning. This ontology-based multi-lingual dictionary supports information autonomy for cross-organisation collaboration by allowing the individual enterprises to keep their own individual languages through semantic matching to this mediated schema, rather than by imposing a single shared-information model or requiring them all to adopt standardised terminology.

Ontological engineering is required to define the necessary concepts, in sufficient detail, for all the terminologies that are to be integrated through a shared ontology. Figure 12 illustrates the steps of engineering the MSE ontology model for VE knowledge sharing. It consists of three steps, building, manipulating, and maintaining, which are executed in an iterative process; the individual steps are described in Figure 12.

Building the MSE Ontology Model and Metadata

The initial step in building the MSE ontology is to find common concepts for VE knowledge sharing in the global supply chain design and operational management of the global manufacturing system. This common concept enables a semantic translation to be made from one information source into another; Stuckenschmidt and van Harmelen (2004) call it a bridge concept. They also point out that top-level classifications or taxonomies that subsume every

Figure 12. The steps of engineering the MSE ontology model for VE knowledge sharing

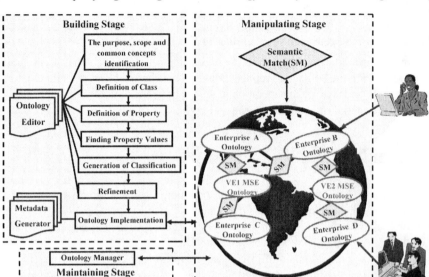

other possible concept are mainly used to find the bridge concept to enable the definition of all terms to be translated. The common concepts of a manufacturing system in the MSE ontology have been well defined, containing the manufacturing taxonomy and axioms of basic manufacturing concepts, properties of concepts, relationships, and constraints between different enterprises' MSE applications. Figure 13 illustrates the basic elements of the MSE abstract classes' structure and the relationships between classes, using the ontology editor tool, Protégé OWL Plugin (http://protege.stanford.edu/plugins/owl/) and its visualization ontology Plugin, Jambalaya (http://www.thechiselgroup.org/~chisel/projects/jambalaya/jambalaya.html).

The top-level taxonomy of the MSE ontology model has been captured in seven key base classes, ***project, flow, virtual enterprise, enterprise, resource, process, and strategy***, using the knowledge and experiences of published manufacturing system information models (Harding & Yu, 1999; Kosanke, Roland, & Nell, 2003; Molina & Bell, 1999).

The *Project class* provides the trigger for the formation and operation of a VE MSE process. The definition of the Project class is used to represent the business objects, that is, documents, contracts, or a program that flows through the manufacturing systems and processes. The relationships of the *Project class*, *Flow class*, and *Process class* for executing a new order flow for a VE project is represented in Figure 13. Each instance of the *Project class* travels along one or more flows (instances of the *Flow class*) that connect independent processes or activities into a system with a purpose.

The MSE ontology model enables the moderator to operate within an E-SCM which has been designed to support manufacturing system collaborative design and engineering within a VE environment. Therefore, the MSE ontology model encompasses several independent companies assembled into a temporary consortium of partners and services for one or a

Figure 13. Top-level taxonomy of manufacturing system in the MSE ontology model

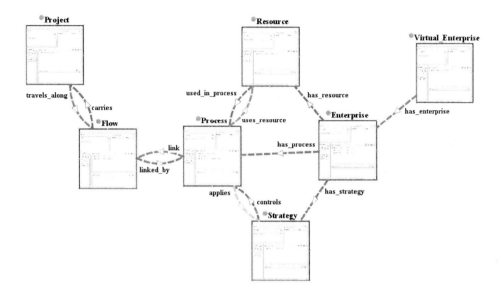

limited number of specific projects in order to pursue a market opportunity and to achieve competitive advantage since individual companies concentrate on their own core competencies (Prahalad & Hamel, 1990)]. Therefore, the *virtual enterprise* class has been defined, and this is an aggregation of *enterprise classes*. Each *enterprise class* object is concerned with the representation of capabilities and information in any specific company within the VE system, since the processes, resources, and strategies are arranged into different enterprises related to their individual business objectives and function.

The relationships between *resource class*, *process class*, and *strategy class* are interacting in the MSE ontology model. The **resource class** describes mechanisms that enable a process to be performed. The *process class* are business functions or activities necessary for the operation of the enterprise. The **strategy class** is used to describe not only the business strategy but also the efficient production or manufacturing strategies. The processes can be measured and controlled through links to strategies, and resources can also be effectively allocated through links from processes to strategies.

The MSE ontology model has been encoded in resource description framework (RDF), RDF schema, and Web Ontology Language (OWL), which is the W3C standard semantic mark-up language for publishing, sharing, and reuse of semantic data on the World Wide Web. The top-level classifications of the MSE metadata shown in Figure 13 are all abstract classes, so each represents a hierarchy of subclasses that are classified according to their main characteristics. Each class has properties that may be thought of as attributes of the class and can also represent relationships between classes. For example, properties such as uses resource, used in process, apply, and controls, and so forth, represent inter-relationships between resource, process, and strategy classes, as shown in Figure 13. Further details of classes, subclasses hierarchy, and properties of the MSE metadata can be found in Lin (2004).

Figure 14. Architecture for the e-supply chains moderator and the functional modules

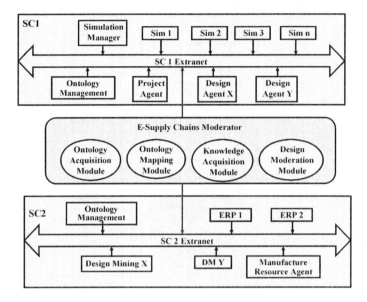

Metadata plays a central role in information processing in general and in information sharing in particular. In addition, the expressiveness of the OWL primitives is made available not only in the taxonomy and axioms to define the classification, but also in the constructions to state equality between classes and between properties. These provide the mediate service for enhancing information integration within an inter-enterprise community; an example of semantic match manipulation using OWL primitives will be illustrated later in the next section.

An E-Supply Chains Moderator

The main objective of developing the MSE OWL metadata is to support the VE information integration and to enable the operation of an E-SCM on the Semantic Web. The proposed design of the new form of E-SCM is operating on an open extranet-based platform and is supporting execution of globally-distributed MSE Web applications on the WWW. The E-SCM includes four major modules: ontology acquisition module, ontology mapping module, knowledge acquisition module, and design moderation module, as shown in Figure 14.

Ontology Acquisition Module

The first step in developing the ontology acquisition module (OAM) is to acquire the common ontology and metadata created by a particular VE team group. Additionally, the common ontology should be extensible so that it can be changed as necessary when the structure of project team in the VEs or supply chains environment is changed. In the proposed architecture, the top-level MSE ontology as described above and further details of the model are available in Lin (2004), where it is used to illustrate the manufacturing system domain and cover all the terminology aspects and needs for an E-SCM. It therefore serves as a core for the complete, extensible, or reorganised structure of the individual VE common model. The common ontology defines the meaning of terms that have to be encoded in OWL language to express the concepts in a metadata context for information repositories and semantic match manipulation in the OAM.

Ontology Mapping Module

Ontology mapping module (OMM) enables all participants' individual terminology to be translated to the mediating metadata created in the OAM. In order to perform the semantic match translation, the initial step of OMM is to solve the syntactical level heterogeneity by transforming all participants' information, presented in the different data formats, into a standard ontology format. For example, in this research, the transformation of free text, Web documents, and legacy database must be normalised into the OWL primitives used Jena (McBride, 2002) and must be mapped to the mediating metadata through OWL built-in equality statements.

Knowledge Acquisition Module

As in the very first moderators, the knowledge acquisition module (KAM) is used to create, delete, or amend knowledge about what is important to any individual design agent. This knowledge is important and must be modified when new design agents join or if existing agents are changed significantly, as the E-SCM uses it to identify potential design conflicts. The knowledge structures repose in an object-oriented knowledge rules database based on the knowledge representation model as in the original engineering moderator and the MIS-SION MSE moderator.

However, the KAM in the E-SCM would be translated into the neutral format for dealing with any syntactic and semantic differences in the terminology that may be used by different project team members. This is achieved through the OAM and the OMM, and then this knowledge about design agents can repose as mapped results in the knowledge rules ontology server, as shown in Figure 15.

Design Moderation Module

The design moderation module (DMM) is used to assist and keep track of changes made to the MSE design documents and identify whether any current design agent may be interested in the change. The change details should therefore also go through the translation process into the neutral format as described above for the KAM, and the mapped result of the change details will be reposed in the VE Ontology server, as shown in Figure 15. Therefore the DMM

Figure 15. The structure of the KAM and DMM in the E-SCM

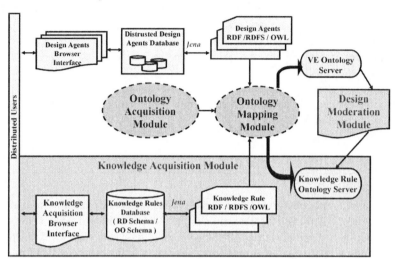

should be activated whenever a change is made to any information that may be related to interests recorded in any design agent module. These changes can then be passed through the translation process, through the OAM and the OMM, and into the VE ontology server. If information changes in the VE ontology server have been identified, the DMM will be notified of the change and also connected to the knowledge rule ontology server which is needed for the moderation process of conflict detection.

An Example of Semantic Match Manipulation

A VE customisation product project study has been used to illustrate the functionality of the E-SCM. CAD drawing documents flow through the customisation product process for building a new model of electrical grinders. LU design and ISU tools and other virtual participators will work together to fulfil this project. A conflict moderation example of an E-SCM operating in a customisation product design and development task is now presented to demonstrate the semantic match manipulation of the "interlingua" process between the project teams' MSE software application.

As part of the VE project, the ISU Tools group determines that there should be a minimum quantities limitation of not less than 3,000 units on their gear order, which is expressed as *Gear* (quantity$\geq$1000). The Moderator needs to have knowledge of this constraint so that it can warn team members during their design or planning activities. Therefore, ISU's engineer adds this important knowledge to the system through the moderator's KAM. Assume now that there is a new design function change at LU design for the flexible shaft. LU personnel decide that the maximum quantity of the new Shaft should be 100 units for the prototype, which is *Shaft* (quantity$\leq$100), and this is recorded through their CAD system. Hence, the

Figure 16. The mediated MSE metadata

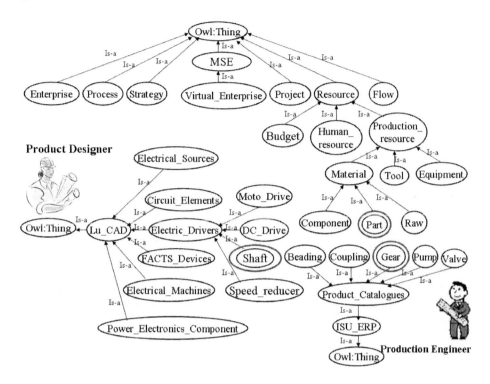

knowledge in the E-SCM's knowledge bases needs to detect that the quantity attribute of Gear has been changed from quantity$\geq$1000 to quantity$\leq$100. The moderator must be able to identify this change in the LU's CAD system in the quantity attribute of the *Shaft* object as this change may cause conflict with ISU's enterprise resource planning (ERP). Hence the Moderator must also be able to communicate the detection of this possible conflict to LU's CAD designers, to ISU's ERP production engineers, and to the users of any other interested MSE applications.

This example shows the importance of knowledge semantic sharing among product designers and production engineers. The designers express their ideas and conceptualisations by access to information related to structure and/or shape of artefacts; however, the production engineers communicate through capturing target devices from functional viewpoint (even behaviour). In this case, the concepts from CAD:Shaft have the same meaning as the concepts from ERP:Gear. Therefore, the common MSE metadata will play a mediated role for ISU's ERP and his partner LU's CAD in this new product introduction VE project as shown in Figure 16.

OWL provides built-in ontology mapping support, that is, a particular class or property in one ontology is the same as a class or property in another ontology (owl:sameClassAs, owl:samePropertyAs): The individuals therefore have the same "identity." Table 1 illustrates how the OWL's equality statements perform the semantic match manipulation between the common MSE metadata, ISU's ERP and LU's CAD systems.

Table 1. Owl:sameAs axioms for semantic match manipulation

ERP:Gear → MSE:Part←CAD:Sheft	ERP:quantity →MSE:quantity←CAD:quantity
<owl:Class rdf:ID="erp.Gear"> <owl:sameAs ref.resource ="#mse.Part"/> </owl:Class> <owl:Class rdf:ID="cad.Shaft"> <owl:sameAs ref.resource ="#mse.Part"/> </owl:Class>	<owl:DatatypeProperty rdf:ID="erp.quantity"> <rdfs:domain rdf:resource="#erp_Gear"> <owl:sameAs rdf:resource="#mse:quantity"/> </owl:DatatypeProperty> <owl:DatatypeProperty rdf:ID="cad.quantity"> <rdfs:domain rdf:resource="#cad_Shaft"> <owl:sameAs rdf:resource="#mse:quantity"/> </owl:DatatypeProperty>

In this case, the concepts from ERP:Gear have the same meaning as the concepts from MSE:Part. Moreover, the concepts from CAD:Shaft also have the same meaning as the concepts from MSE:Part. The axioms should ensure that when someone queries the ISU's ERP for the instances of the *Gear*, the result include all the instances of *Shaft* from the ISU's CAD through mapping to the MSE:Part. Therefore, when the *Shaft* (quantity$\leq$100) information changes, the moderator should identify that ISU's ERP quantity attribute of the *Gear class* will be affected and may cause conflict. Therefore the Moderator should issue an appropriate warning message to the ISU group, for example, by an e-mail saying that the required minimum quantity level 1,000 has been changed by another MSE application.

Where Next?

The proposed MSE ontology approach is extremely flexible and does not constrain or require individual partners to change their existing terminology or practices. There are still, however, time and cost overheads in this method as individual partners need to commit to mapping their vocabularies to the MSE ontology initially. Using the current manual methods, this can be slow and may cause major barriers against the large-scale use of this approach for information integration within global supply chains. However, likely future advances in this area should reduce this overhead. These include semi-automated features for formal mapping representation, such as algorithms and heuristics to identify similarities between two ontologies, machine learning for ontology matching (Doan, Madhavan, Domingos, & Halevy, 2004; Ehrig, Sure, & Staab, 2005), and knowledge discovery (Dhamanka, Lee, Doan, Halevy & Domingos, 2004).

The quality of the support that any moderator can provide is limited by its knowledge of the designer's knowledge, as collected by the KAM and stored in the design expert modules. The E-SCM framework will therefore also be limited to a knowledge-based approach for the extraction of useful information based on the established knowledge in the KAM. This section will therefore discuss future research directions for this work, including the potential for advancing the moderation process and the critical challenges to be addressed.

Moderation Throughout the VE Life Cycle

The concept of a virtual enterprise (VE) was proposed by Onosato and Iwata (1993) in response to a changing industrial environment, where product lines have a significantly shorter lifetime. For example, from the early 1960s for a period of some 30 years, the design of home telephones was virtually unchanged: Companies could be established to manufacture one stable product and know that there was a stable market. However, with the advent of mobile telephones, and their status as fashion accessories, the marketable life of a product line once launched is measured in, at best, months. Indeed, the life cycle from product concept to obsolescence is likely to be less than a year.

To meet this challenge, supply chains take the form of collaborating consortia of specialist partners who come together to provide the expertise necessary to exploit just one product, and it is such a consortium which is termed a virtual enterprise. A number of features distinguish this particular kind of supply chain:

- Collaboration on the selected product is close, well-coordinated, and open, so as to have the agility to maximise the exploitation of the product.
- Partners may not collaborate on any other products. Indeed, it is probable that they will be competitors on other products. This implies a need for confidentiality, mitigating against the need for openness noted above, and complicating collaboration issues.
- The life cycle of a VE is limited to that of the product, as in Figure 17, and partners have no obligation beyond that.
- Partners may be added to the VE or leave it as the product life cycle progresses.
- The VE will include contributors responsible for products and manufacturing engineering in the early stages at least, as these activities must be concurrent with one another and with the formation of the VE consortium. Indeed, selection of VE partners is a major aspect of manufacturing engineering.

We have seen from the above that there is significant potential benefit in applying a moderation in the design phase of the VE life cycle. The same issues are relevant to any subsequent changes to the manufacturing system design during the life of the VE.

However, intelligent moderation has potential application at subsequent stages of the VE life cycle, as suggested in Figure 18. Here we see that the potential for decision conflict remains through the life cycle, both in operations management of the MS to meet current, changing demands, and in terms of planning to respond to the product life cycle. Intelligent moderation uses operational information, together with its knowledge about the distributed, specialist contributors to the VE to identify conflicting decisions where these may be critical to current and future VE performance. Moderation knowledge can also be applied to external information, such as market conditions, to identify where this may conflict with existing or proposed VE activity. These applications, their benefits to industry, and the research issues to be addressed to achieve these benefits may be summarised as follows.

Figure 17. The virtual enterprise life cycle

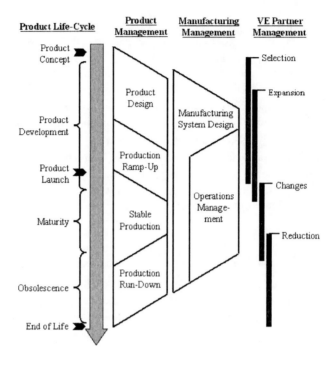

Ramp-Up

In this phase of its life cycle, the VE is expanding from prototype production, up to a launch capacity, and then on to planned full production. Partners collaborate to plan and monitor capacity, selecting additional partners as necessary, and consistently expanding the logistics activity. Potential for introducing inadvertent conflict remains, including, for example, differences in technical capabilities (e.g., tolerances capabilities) in selected new partners, mismatched expansion rates (e.g., component capacity runs ahead of assembly capacity, creating stocks), or transport mode conflicts (e.g., new partner does not have rail access where existing logistics are based on rail transport).

Operation

Although at this stage of the life cycle VE demand is relatively stable, it will normally be subject to seasonal and/or random variability. Partners must collaborate to plan to meet varying demand, but distribution offers the potential for conflicting responses (e.g., assembly is planned to build to stock in a low-demand period while component suppliers plan to reduce output). In a more durable VE, it is possible that partners may need to be replaced during this phase, reintroducing many of the possible conflicts met during ramp-

Figure 18. Moderation in VE ramp-up, operation and run-down

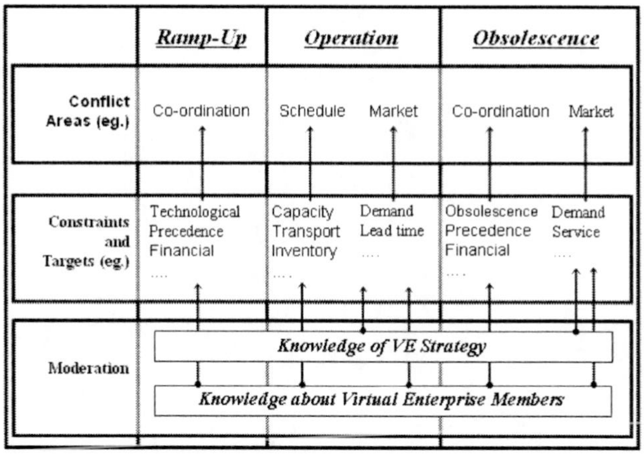

	Ramp-Up	Operation		Obsolescence	
Conflict Areas (eg.)	Co-ordination	Schedule	Market	Co-ordination	Market
Constraints and Targets (eg.)	Technological Precedence Financial	Capacity Transport Inventory	Demand Lead time	Obsolescence Precedence Financial	Demand Service ....
Moderation	*Knowledge of VE Strategy*				
	Knowledge about Virtual Enterprise Members				

up. Changes in transport cost structures are particularly likely to conflict with the basis of earlier logistics planning, and moderation may be applicable in triggering response to such externally-imposed change.

Obsolescence

At this stage, collaboration to maximise exploitation of the product is especially vulnerable as partners plan exit strategies to meet their own business needs with reduced incentive to consider the VE as a whole. Conflicting plans on shutdown timing are probable. At the same time, depending on product, industry, and perhaps regulation, there is a requirement to ensure implementation of a coordinated plan to provide a continuing supply of spares. Conflicting plans in response to a now falling demand are more likely than during operation.

Sharing Knowledge in Collaborative Moderation

The use of moderators to support collaboration in virtual enterprises offers the opportunity for relevant knowledge held by individual partners to be shared in moderating the behaviour of the VE. However, issues of security and value of knowledge and experience which an individual partner may feel contributes to its competitive advantage also arise. In the VE environment, an individual company may be a partner in several distinct VEs at any one time. While collaborating with a partner in one VE, each company may also be collaborating in other VEs which are in direct competition with one another: Indeed, the same company may be a partner in two directly-competing VEs. In this configuration, there is clear advantage to all partners in the network of VEs if a moderator specific to each VE can be populated not only with its own knowledge of how it operates, but with access to relevant subsets of each

Figure 19. Shared access moderator knowledge

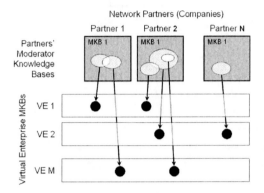

partners' moderator knowledge base, the content of the accessible subset being strictly and clearly controlled by the partner so as to protect confidentiality and competitive advantage. There is also the opportunity for each partner to access VE moderator knowledge and add to its own knowledge base for future use. This is illustrated in Figure 19.

Other Future Research Areas

As highlighted at the start of this section, the quality of support that a moderator can provide is limited by the quality of knowledge gained through its KAM. To date, all knowledge acquired for the moderators has been provided by human experts. However, huge quantities of experience and expertise lie within the databases of manufacturing operations; hence an important future research area is:

- Knowledge discovery for moderation

The following are unconnected with manufacturing, but still considered to have potential moderator applications and therefore should be examined as future research areas:

- Scheduling applications (e.g., air traffic control, railway timetabling [planning and operations])
- Agent moderation in autonomous agent-based systems
- Pharmacology (e.g., identifying conflicts in medication)

Conclusion

This chapter has provided an examination of how moderators, which are specialist intelligent software systems, contribute to Business Integration. It has provided a historical journey through changing and increasingly demanding and complex business requirements and business integration requirements, and has demonstrated how the initial single product, single enterprise-based Moderator concept has developed and exploited the increasingly powerful technologies and infrastructures available for business integration. Significant progress has been made since the early days of the first engineering moderator, but as shown in the "Where Next?"section, the challenges to be addressed in the future could be even more interesting.

References

Dhamankar, R., Lee, Y., Doan, A., Halevy, A., & Domingos, P. (2004). iMAP: Discovering complex semantic matches between database schemas. In *Proceedings of the ACM SIGMOD International Conference on Management of Data (SIGMOD 2004)*(pp. 383-394), Paris, France.

Doan, A., Madhavan, J., Domingos, P., & Halevy, A. (2004). Ontology matching: A machine learning approach. In S. Staab & R. Studer (Eds.), *Handbook on ontologies (International Handbooks on Information Systems)* (pp. 397-416). Berlin; Heidelberg: Springer-Verlag/GmbH & Co.

Ehrig, M., Sure, Y., & Staab, S. (2005). Supervised learning of an ontology alignment process. In *Proceedings of the 3rd Conference on Professional Knowledge Management, Workshop on IT Tools for Knowledge Management Systems: Applicability, Usability, and Benefits (IKMTOOLS 2005)*(pp. 487-492), Kaiserslautern, Germany.

Fensel, D. (Ed.). (2002). *Intelligent information integration in B2B electronic commerce.* Kluwer Academic Publishers.

Fensel, D., Ding, Y., Omelayenko, B., Schulten, E., Botquin, G., Brown, M., & Flett, A. (2001). Product data integration in B2B e-commerce. *IEEE Intelligent Systems, 16*(4), 54-59.

Gruber, T. R. (1992). *Toward principles for the design of ontologies used for knowledge sharing* (Tech. Rep. No. KSL 93-04). Knowledge System Laboratory, Stanford University.

Gruber, T. R. (1993). A translation approach to portable ontology specifications. *Knowledge Acquisition, Elsevier Science, 5*(2), 199-220.

Harding, J. A. (1996). *A knowledge representation model to support concurrent engineering team working.* PhD thesis, Loughborough University, UK.

Harding, J. A., & Popplewell, K. (1996). Driving concurrency in a distributed concurrent engineering project team: A specification for an engineering moderator. *International Journal of Production Research, 34*(3), 841-861.

Harding, J. A., & Yu, B. (1999). Information-centred enterprise design supported by a factory data model and data warehousing. *Computers in Industry, 40*, 23-36.

Hu, Z., Kruse, E., & Draws, L. (2003). Intelligent binding in the engineering of automation systems using ontology and Web services. *IEEE Transactions on Systems, Man, and Cybernetics, Part C, 33*(3), 403 - 412.

Hyvönen, E., Saarela, S., & K. Viljanen, K. (2004). Application of ontology techniques to view-based semantic search and browsing. In *Proceedings of the First European Semantic Web Symposium (ESWS 2004)*(pp. 92-106), Heraklion, Crete, Greece.

Kosanke, K., Roland, J., & Nell, J. G. (Ed.). (2003). Enterprise inter- and intra-organizational integration: Building international consensus (International Federation for Information Processing).In *Proceedings of the International Conference on Enterprise Integration and Modeling Technology (ICEIMT'02)*,Valencia, Spain. Kluwer Academic Publishers.

Krause, F. L., Kimura, F., Kjellberg, T., & Lu, S. C. Y. (1993). Product modelling. *Annals of the CIRP, 42*(2), 695-706.

Lin, H. K. (2004). *Manufacturing system engineering ontology model for global extended projects team*. PhD thesis, Wolfson School of Mechanical and Manufacturing Engineering, Loughborough University, UK.

McKay, A., Bloor, M. S., & de Pennington, A. (1996, October). A framework for product data. *IEE Transactions on Knowledge and Data Engineering, 8*(5), 825-838.

McBride, B. (2002). Jena: A semantic Web toolkit. *IEEE Internet Computing, 6*(6), 55-59.

Mena, E., & Illarramendi, A. (2001). *Ontology-based query processing for global information systems*. Kluwer Academic Publishers.

Molina, A., & Bell, R. (1999). A manufacturing model representation of a flexible manufacturing facility. In *Proceedings of the Institution of Mechanical Engineers: Part B, 213*(3)(pp. 225-246).

Onosato, M., & Iwata, K. (1993). Development of a virtual manufacturing system by integrating product models and factory models. *Annuals of the CIRP, 42*(1), 475-478

Prahalad, C. K., & Hamel, G. (1990, May/June). The core competence of the corporation. *Harvard Business Review, 68*(3), 79-91.

Priebe, T., & Pernul, G. (2003). Ontology-based integration of OLAP and information retrieval. In *Proceedings of the 14th International Conference on Database and Expert Systems Applications (DEXA 2003), Workshop on Web Semantics*, (pp. 610-614) Prague, Czech Republic.

Stuckenschmidt, H., & van Harmelen, F. (2004). *Information sharing on the semantic Web*. Berlin; Heidelberg: Springer-Verlag/GmbH & Co. K.

Endnotes

[1]   MOSES: Model-Oriented Simultaneous Engineering Systems—EPSRC Project Number (GR/H24273), 1992-1995.

[2]   Modelling and Simulation Environments for Design, Planning, and Operation of Globally-Distributed Enterprises (IMS/ESPRIT 29656) 1998 - 2001.

Chapter VI

Integrating Business Processes and Information Systems in an Interorganizational Context

Peter Rittgen, University College Borås, Sweden

Abstract

When organizations engage in close cooperation they usually need to reorganize the business processes that serve the interface between them. This reorganization is often done with the help of business process models. As a result, the underlying information systems have to be adapted, too. The changes to the latter can be supported by information system models which are typically "written" in a different language from that of the business processes. Here we suggest an approach to facilitate the development of information system models based on the models of the respective business processes. This is achieved by mapping a suitable business process language to the Unified Modeling Language. We apply this approach in the context of an interorganizational business process.

Introduction

Today we can witness two seemingly opposed trends in the cooperation between businesses: On the one hand, companies are forced to concentrate on their core competencies and to outsource all activities that lie outside the core. On the other hand, customers demand that a supplier should cover an increasing range of products and services. They want to buy a complete solution from only one supplier instead of buying bits and pieces from many. This latter point seems to suggest an increased amount of "insourcing." The solution to both is that companies have to engage in closer cooperations, each concentrating on its area of expertise, but jointly offering a complete suite of related products and services that are well matched (one face to the customer). But this scenario represents an enormous challenge both in terms of organization and regarding the information system support.

Companies that want to engage in a closer cooperation, for example, a value network, a virtual enterprise, or the like, bring into this cooperation not only their different organizational cultures, but also different, often incompatible, information systems. A successful cooperation therefore requires the alignment or integration of both the business processes and the information systems to a certain degree. In some industries, such as the automotive industry, this can go as far as the customer forcing the suppliers to introduce the ERP system of the customer's choice (e.g., SAP). But on the whole, it is more common that the organizations involved will strive for some kind of mutual adaptation of their business processes and information systems. In a very simple case, this could be the introduction of a file transfer accompanied by suitable import and export functionalities and some organizational measures for providing and handling the new data. In more advanced cases, it will imply substantial reorganization of business processes and changes to existing information systems and/or introduction of new ones.

In order to tackle such a problem, we first need to analyze the interorganizational business process, that is, the process that involves both partners. This process is situated at the interface between the participating organizations and is therefore of a highly communicative nature. This suggests the use of a modeling approach that views organizations as networks of communicating actors. The language-action perspective (LAP) offers precisely this view. It is based on the communicative-action theory by Habermas (1984) and the speech-act theory by Austin (1962) and Searle (1969). According to LAP, each language utterance is an elementary social activity called a speech act. Speech acts often come in action-reaction pairs, such as a request and an ensuing promise (to fulfill the request). These action pairs are used to create commitments in the social world which form the fundamental building blocks of an organization. They are also the simplest conversational pattern.

Patterns of a higher order describe purposeful conversations for achieving results in the real world. An example of such a pattern is the transaction, or action workflow (Denning & Medina-Mora, 1995; Medina-Mora, Winograd, Flores, & Flores, 1992), which embodies the principle of delegation of some action by an initiator (I) to an executor (E). It consists of two conversations and the action. The first conversation is called actagenic. It aims at reaching an agreement regarding the execution of the action. The second conversation is called factagenic, and it has the purpose of coming to an agreement regarding the outcome of the action. The shortest path through the conversational network of a transaction is as follows: I: request (execute action), E: promise (execute action), E: execute action, E: state (action executed), I: accept (action executed). A more general model of the possible communication paths is provided by the so-called conversation-for-action schema (Winograd & Flores, 1986).

A business process is a network of such transactions. Dynamic Essential Modeling of Organization (DEMO) (Dietz, 1999; Dietz & Habing, 2004; Liu, Sun, Barjis, & Dietz, 2003; van Reijswoud & Dietz, 1999) is a language that allows for the analysis of a business process in terms of an organization's communicative structure which lies at the heart of many problems that we encounter in interorganizational contexts. It can be used to analyse and reorganize the business process to improve the cooperation between the involved organizations. DEMO is described in detail in the section, "Background."

But integrating the business processes alone is not enough. We also need to address the issue of heterogeneous information systems. In order to support the changed organizations, we have to adapt these systems accordingly. This will typically involve the development of some new software components or changes to existing software. The Unified Modeling Language (UML) plays an important role in this area. It allows for the specification and design of software with the help of structural and behavioral models such as class and interaction diagrams. The background section gives an overview of the relevant UML diagrams.

To ensure an optimal support of the organization, there should be a tight link between the behavior as described in the business process model and the supporting activities in the software model. To facilitate this, we suggest employing a language-mapping approach that makes use of the language-action models of the business process to create suitable UML models for the design of the information system. Details on this approach can be found in the section, "A Language-Mapping Approach."

The approach that we describe has been used in a project that involved a retail chain and a third-party logistics provider. We started this project by doing a comprehensive analysis of the interorganizational business process. The result was a language-action model of this process that we used to discuss the problems with the current organization of the cooperation and for identifying goals for improvement. A large list of problems and goals was compiled out of which the two most pressing goals were chosen: a tighter integration between the respective information systems (SAP and DISA), and a better fit between reserved logistics capacities and the capacities that are actually used. We have applied the approach described above to the first problem. The section, "An Interorganizational Case Study," gives an account of a part of the problem, and how it was solved.

Background

The current section provides background regarding the two languages that are involved in our approach: DEMO and UML.

Dynamic Essential Modeling of Organization

In the action view, the structure of an organization is understood as a network of commitments. As these commitments are the result of communication, it follows that a model of the organization is essentially a model based on purposeful, communicative acts. In DEMO, all acts that serve the same purpose are collected in a *transaction* in which two roles are engaged: the *initiator* and the *executor*. The definition of a transaction in DEMO is close to that of an action workflow, but it also includes a non-communicative action, namely the agreed action that the executor performs in the object world. Hence each transaction is assumed to follow a certain pattern, which is divided into three sequential phases and three layers. The phases are: *order* (O), *execute* (E), and *result* (R). The layers are: success, discussion, and discourse. On the success layer, the phases are structured as follows. In the order phase the contract is negotiated. This involves typically a *request* being made by the initiator and a *promise* by the executor to carry out the request. In the next phase, the contract is executed which involves factual changes in the object world (as opposed to the inter-subject world of communication). Finally, in the result phase, the executor *states* that the agreed result has been achieved, and the initiator *accepts* this *fact*. If anything goes wrong on the success layer, the participants can decide to move to the discussion or discourse layer. For details on these layers, see van Reijswoud (1996).

Figure 1 gives an overview of the architecture of DEMO. The interaction model shows actors and their relations to transactions, but abstracts from time. The business process model, on the other hand, abstracts from the actors, but refines the transactional logic in two ways: It breaks each transaction into its phases and specifies how they are ordered causally and conditionally. This allows us to determine the order of the communicative acts in time. The fact model describes all information that is created or used by an organization. A fact is the result of a successful transaction and implies that the proposition of the request has become true. The interstriction model (not shown in Figure 1) is similar to the interaction model, but in addition to the communication that is part of the transactions, it also exhibits informative

Figure 1. Architecture of DEMO (simplified)

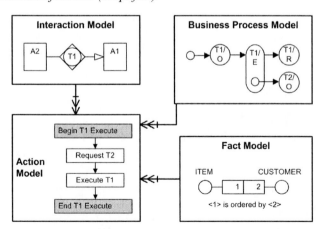

Figure 2. Examples of an interaction model and a business process model

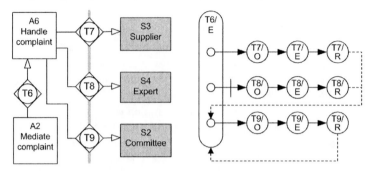

communication. All models are linked to the action model, which gives a detailed account of activities carried out within a transaction phase (which can also involve links to other transactions).

Figure 2 gives examples of an interaction model and a business process model. They are taken from van Reijswoud and Dietz (1999) and show a part of the business process of an organization called SGC, a non-profit organization that mediates consumer complaints in The Netherlands.

The transactions of the example are as follows:

- **T6:** Handling complaint
- **T7:** Defending complaint
- **T8:** Giving advice
- **T9:** Passing judgment

The actor A2, who is responsible for mediating the claim, requests that actor A6 handle the complaint. Both A2 and A6 are internal actors (represented by white boxes). The latter will give the supplier a chance to defend the complaint, ask an expert to give advice, and request that the committee passes a judgment. S2 – S4 are external actors as the grey boxes show. A simple line connects the initiator with the transaction; an arrow points from it to the executor. The grey line represents the system boundary. Observe that Figure 2 shows only a fragment of the model.

The right side of Figure 2 contains a part of the business process model. It shows details of the execution phase of transaction 6: handling complaint. This phase is called T6/E. From inside it, the transactions T7, T8, and T9 are started. This is represented by arrows from the initiation points (small, white circles) to the order phases of the respective transactions. Solid arrows indicate a causal relation; dashed ones indicate a conditional relation. The inside of a phase is viewed as a concurrent region, so all three triggered transactions could start at the same time if it were not for the dashed lines. An arrow that is crossed by a line represents an optional relation. In short: The supplier is asked to defend the complaint in

Figure 3. UML behavioral packages

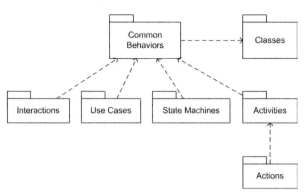

any case, and the expert is possibly consulted. After T7 (and possibly T8) have been completed, the committee is asked to pass judgment. Only when T9/R has been finished can we also terminate T6/E. Observe that this is due to the dashed arrow between them. As a rule, the initiation points inside a phase trigger transactions in an asynchronous manner without waiting for their completion.

The Unified Modeling Language

The Unified Modeling Language (OMG, 2004) defines a number of packages that contain modeling concepts and notations for a specific area. Figure 3 shows the packages that are relevant for our approach (OMG, 2004).

All concepts for structural models are defined in the Classes package. They comprise static aspects of a system such as classes, interfaces, and attributes. Based on the Classes package, the elements of the behavioral (dynamic) models are specified which consist of the packages common behaviors, interactions, use cases, state machines, activities, and actions. An *action* is the fundamental unit of behavior specification. *Activities* allow for the coordination of actions in terms of control flow and object flow. They can also take into account events that are external to the flow. *State machines* are finite state-transition systems that express the internal behavior of model elements such as individual entities (e.g., class instances). They can alternatively also express protocol usage that is associated with interfaces and ports. *Use cases* can be employed to specify the required usage of a system. *Interactions* describe the exchange between different parts of a system.

Each of the packages specifies a graphical representation of each of its elements and a number of diagrams that define how the graphical elements can be arranged in a meaningful way to express a certain aspect of the system. For the purpose of this chapter, the relevant diagrams are: communication diagram (interactions package), state machine diagram (state machines package), activity diagram (activities package) and class diagram (classes package). For a detailed description of these diagrams, refer to OMG (2004).

A Language-Mapping Framework
for DEMO and UML

A General Framework for Mapping Languages

The Object Management Group (OMG) has suggested an architecture for language integration that is called model-driven architecture (MDA) (Miller & Mukerji, 2003). In it a system is specified from three different viewpoints: computation-independent, platform-independent, and platform-specific. Although the scope of MDA is much broader, a typical assumption is that all models (views) can be constructed with the help of only one language, and UML is the preferred candidate for that role. But Evans, Maskeri, Sammut, and Willans (2003, p.1) argue that "a truly flexible model-driven development process should not dictate the language that practitioners should use to construct models, even an extensible one. Instead they should be free to use whichever language is appropriate for their particular domain and application, particularly as many languages cannot be shoe-horned into the UML family". We follow this argument and suggest extending the model mapping of MDA (Caplat & Sourrouille, 2003) to "language mapping."

A general framework for mapping a modeling language to another one is shown in Figure 4. We distinguish between the conceptual level and the instance level. On the conceptual level, we first perform concept mapping. This step involves finding for each concept of the source language a matching one in the target language. A successful match implies that a significant part of the semantics of the source concept can also be expressed by the target concept. Note that concept mapping as defined here does not relate to the one known from empirical social research. For example, the DEMO concept of an action maps to the UML

Figure 4. A framework for language mapping

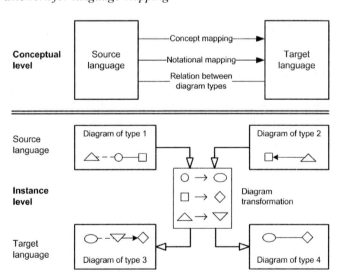

concept of an action. The latter is something that is performed while the system is in a certain state. As this is very general, it encompasses the meaning of action in DEMO for which the same holds, but in addition to that, an action is restricted to being either an objective action in the object world or a communicative action in the inter-subject world (see subsection "Concept Mapping" for more details). Note that such a mapping is not always possible, because the target language might not have a related concept at all, or the "common denominator" between both concepts is not a significant part of the semantics of the source concept (i.e., the two concepts have very little in common). This implies that language mapping cannot be done for any combination of languages, at least not in the way described here. Moreover, we cannot expect that we will always succeed in establishing a one-to-one correspondence between concepts. Sometimes several source concepts jointly map to one target concept, or one source concept maps to a conjunction of target concepts.

The second step consists of a notational mapping. We assume that each concept is associated with a notational element in the respective language, so with concept mapping being done this step is straightforward. The third and last step is about establishing a relation between the diagram types of both languages. This step provides rules for carrying out the actual diagram transformation on the instance level. In the example of Figure 4, this step is trivial: It involves only a slight change in the notation and a rearrangement of the six basic concepts (three node types and three relation types: solid arc, dashed arc, and arrow) into different diagrams. But for realistic modeling languages, the mapping rules can be much more complex. Typical types of transformations include:

1. One element has to be mapped to a number of elements (e.g., a sub graph). This process is called unfolding.

2. Additional elements (of a different type) have to be introduced. This process is called element introduction.

3. Nodes are transformed into arcs (node inversion) or arcs are transformed into nodes (arc inversion).

4. A substructure of the source language is transformed into a different substructure of the target language. This is called graph conversion.

In the following subsections, we apply this framework for DEMO as the source language and UML as the target language.

Concept Mapping

Mapping concepts from one language to another requires an ontological analysis of both languages and a matching of corresponding concepts. The Bunge-Wand-Weber ontology (BWW ontology) is an established tool for analyzing modeling languages. It is based on Mario Bunge's ontology (Bunge 1977, 1979) and was later adapted by Yair Wand and Ron Weber to the information systems field (Wand & Weber, 1989, 1995; Weber, 1997). According to this ontology, the world consists of *things* that possess *properties*. Both exist irrespective of the human observer. An *intrinsic property* belongs to an individual thing, a *mutual property*

Table 1. Interpretation mapping of DEMO and UML constructs

DEMO construct	UML construct	BWW construct
DEMO-actor	UML-actor / UML-object	BWW-thing
DEMO-action	UML-action (in an action state)	BWW-transformation law that describes a single event
DEMO-transaction	UML-sequence of messages (operations) (in a state)	BWW-transformation law that describes a process
DEMO-phase	UML-sub state	BWW-state
DEMO-category	UML-class	BWW-(functional schema for modeling entities that form the corresponding) natural kind

to two or more things. The observer can only witness *attributes* that he takes for the properties of the things he observes. The things themselves are not observable. The attributes are functions over time (*state functions*). A *class* is a set of things that share a property, a *kind* is a set of things sharing two or more properties, and a *natural kind* is a kind where some of the properties are related by laws. A *law* is a relation between properties. A set of attributes used to describe a set of things with common properties is called a *functional schema*. The *state* of a thing is a complete assignment of values to all state functions in the functional schema. A change of state is called an *event*. A *lawful transformation* (or *transformation law*) defines which events in a thing are lawful.

Let us look at five core concepts of DEMO, that is, actor, action, transaction, phase, and category, and how they can be mapped to UML concepts. An analysis of UML based on the BWW ontology has already been performed by Evermann and Wand (2001) and Opdahl and Henderson-Sellers (2002). The interpretation mapping of the respective UML constructs is shown in columns 2 and 3 in Table 1, with that of the DEMO constructs in columns 1 and 3 of the same table. The resulting mappings from DEMO to UML are explained in the following subsections.

Actor → Actor/Object

The concept of an actor in DEMO is mapped both to that of an actor and to that of an object in UML. An actor (in DEMO) is a role that a subject (human being) plays. An actor (in UML) "models a type of role played by an entity that interacts with the subject. (…) Note that an actor does not necessarily represent a specific physical entity, but merely a particular facet (i.e., "role") of some entity that is relevant to the specification of its associated use cases. Thus, a single physical instance may play the role of several different actors and, conversely, a given actor may be played by multiple different instances" (OMG, 2004, p. 643). In UML, an actor can play many roles; in DEMO, it can play only one role (i.e., the actor is the role).

But in UML, actors can only interact with the information system. In DEMO, they interact with each other. As use cases (or a similar notion) are not defined in DEMO, the mapping actor → actor is valid but not helpful. But if we also introduce a mapping actor → object we can at least interpret (or view) the actor as a (re)acting object. This means that we will lose the mind of the actor, but we can still express a significant part of the semantics of an actor: The structure and behavior of the actor are retained in the object.

Action → Action (in an Action State)

The concept of an action in DEMO is mapped to that of the same name in UML. In DEMO, actions are divided into communicative actions and objective actions. Communicative actions take place in the inter-subject world and consist of speech acts. Objective actions are performed in the object world and can be material or immaterial. Communicative actions can lead to changes in the social (inter-subject) world (i.e., creating obligations); objective actions can lead to changes in the object world (i.e., the creation of facts). An action state refers to a state of the system. Upon entering the state, the entry action is triggered. Upon completion of the action, the state is left. As the latter definition does not restrict the type of action, it also encompasses the action concept of the former. In an Activity Diagram, the action is associated with a state during which the action is executed.

Transaction → Sequence of Messages (Operations) (in a State)

The concept of a transaction in DEMO is mapped to that of sequence of messages in UML where each message triggers a corresponding operation. A transaction is a pattern that consists of the conversation for an objective action, the execution of that action, and the conversation for the result of that action. This concept has no direct counterpart in UML. Instead it has to be mapped to a sequence of messages which represent the speech acts. Technically, this is done by unfolding on the instance level (i.e., transformation interaction model → communication diagram). In the state machine diagram, a transaction is represented by a state during which the messages are passed. When the system enters this state, the transaction is initiated. When the transaction is finished, the system leaves the state.

Category → Class

The concept of a category in DEMO is mapped to that of a class in UML. A category is a primal class (derived classes are used to define roles in DEMO). Each object is an instance of exactly one category, but can also be an instance of arbitrarily many derived classes. In UML "(t)he purpose of a class is to specify a classification of objects and to specify the features that characterize the structure and behavior of those objects" (OMG, 2004, p. 48). A category (as a primal class) is a class in the sense of this definition. Categories can have n-ary relations which correspond to association classes in UML. Categories and their relations are used to represent facts about the inter-subject world and the object world.

Figure 5. Mapping DEMO to UML

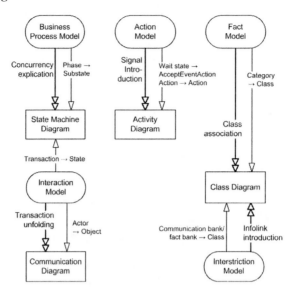

Diagram Transformation

Figure 5 shows the overall framework for the language mapping. The DEMO diagrams are represented by rounded boxes, the UML diagrams by rectangular boxes. The mapping of concepts is visualized by single-headed arrows, the transformation of diagrams by double-headed arrows. Each diagram conversion involves a transformation of the notation, but will also require some more sophisticated transformation process (e.g., transaction unfolding). Concurrency explication and class association are graph conversions, Signal and Infolink introduction are element introductions, and Transaction unfolding is an unfolding in the sense of the general integration framework.

The interaction model introduces actors and transactions. The actors become objects in the communication diagram; the transactions are transformed into sequences of messages (operations) in the same diagram, but they correspond also to states in the state machine diagram. The business process model refines transactions into phases which in turn become substates of the respective transaction state in the state machine diagram. The basic elements of the fact model are the categories. They correspond to classes in UML. The interstriction model introduces fact and communication banks to store records of facts and communication. They also correspond to classes in UML. Actions and wait states in the action model become actions (in action states) and signal receipts, respectively, in the activity diagram.

The interaction model is transformed into the communication diagram. Apart from a notational conversion, this requires an unfolding of the transactions, a concept which has no immediate dynamic counterpart in UML. Each transaction is split into its communicative acts which then are represented by messages in UML. An example of that is given in the next section.

The business process model is transformed into the state machine diagram. Again this involves a change in notation and also an explication of the inherent concurrent behavior of a phase. A phase can have many concurrent initiation points, but each state has only one initial (sub)state. Dividing the state into concurrent regions is not feasible due to the asynchronous nature of the threads triggered by the initiation points. Hence the initial state is forked into as many threads as there are initiation points that have no arrows pointing at them (plus one that leads to the final state if no arrow points to the phase). An arrow pointing at a phase maps to one pointing at the corresponding final state. If more than one arrow points at a phase or initiation point, the respective arrows in the state machine diagram are joined by a synchronization bar. Optional relationships map to guarded transitions. An example for such a transformation is given in the next section.

The action model is transformed into the activity diagram. Apart from the usual notational conversion, this means that an AcceptEventAction has to be introduced into the activity diagram for each wait state that is found in the action model. Likewise, a SendSignalAction is introduced after the activity that corresponds to the action that is waited for.

The fact model is transformed into the class diagram. This involves that each fact (which is an *n*-ary relations between categories) is mapped to an association class that has associations to each of the classes corresponding to the categories. That process is called class association.

The interstriction model introduces further associations into the class Diagram, one for each informational link between an actor and a transaction, fact bank, or communication bank. We call that process infolink introduction.

Examples of Diagram Transformation

Due to the limited space, we give examples for the first two transformations only. Figure 6 shows the communication diagram (upper half) for the interaction model of Figure 2 (left) and also the state machine diagram (lower half) for the business process model of Figure 2 (right). Each system or actor of the interaction model becomes an object (instance) in the communication diagram. A transaction is represented by a communication link that bears the name of the transaction (i.e., its purpose). This link is bidirectional (i.e., it does not have an arrowhead that restricts the navigability) because a transaction involves communication in both directions, from initiator to executor and back. This link can now be used to exchange the messages that correspond to the communicative acts in DEMO. Each executor has also a link to itself which means that the execution phase is self-induced. A request and an accept message are introduced along the link with arrows that point from the initiator to the executor. They represent the first and the last communicative acts of a transaction, respectively. In the same way, a promise and a state message are attached to the link. They are passed from the executor to the initiator and form the second and penultimate speech acts, respectively. Observe that a communication diagram does not require us to specify the order of messages, but we could do so with the help of sequence numbers in front of the message names.

The lower half of Figure 6 shows the state machine diagram that corresponds to the excerpt from the business process model of Figure 2. The execution phase of T6 becomes a state (which itself is a substate of the transaction state T6). Within T6/E, the initial state

Figure 6. Communication diagram and state machine diagram

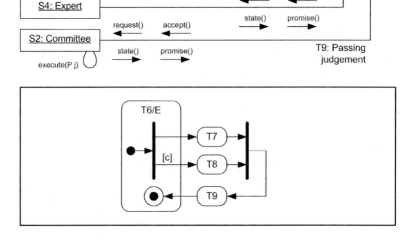

is forked into two concurrent threads to trigger transactions T7: Defending complaint and T8: Giving advice. While T7 is triggered in any case, the transition to T8 is guarded by (c), which means that the expert is asked to give advice under a condition that has not yet been specified; the business process model only indicates that T8 is optional, not under which circumstances it is carried out. On completion of T7 (and possibly T8), T9: Passing judgment is carried out. After that, we enter the terminal state of T6/E, which concludes the execution phase of T6.

An Interorganizational Case Study

The ideas in this chapter were applied in a project which we carried out together with two companies: a logistics provider and a large retail chain. The objective was to model the complex interorganizational business process as a basis for its reorganization. We found that the language-action perspective was successful in that scenario. One of the reasons for this is certainly the highly interactive nature of the process we studied where communication is

Figure 7. Data-flow diagram of receiving goods (excerpt)

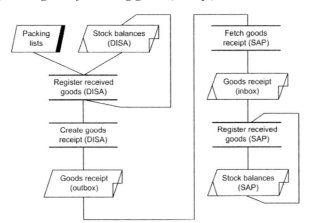

vital and frequent. But LAP also facilitated understanding among people who not only came from different organizations but also worked in different domains: purchase, marketing, inbound and outbound logistics, and so forth. It made a complex process more transparent to all participants (each of whom provided only a small puzzle piece to the overall picture) and it allowed them to discuss in a constructive way possible options for reorganization. As a result, two major areas for improvement were identified: a tighter integration between the different information systems of both companies, and a greater accuracy in the forecasts concerning incoming and outgoing commodity flows.

The framework that we have presented helped us in developing an approach to solve the first problem. The study proceeded in three steps. In the first step, we analyzed from a language-action perspective those parts of the two businesses that require cooperation. As a result, we created detailed models of information flows and information dependencies, problem graphs, and goal graphs, together with a comprehensive, textual description of the businesses and their problems in relation to their cooperation. Figure 7 shows a part of the data flows for receiving goods.

Both companies operate their own warehouse management system. The physical warehouse at the logistics provider is managed with DISA. During the night a file, which details the goods that were dispatched and received during the day, is sent to the retail chain to update their "virtual" warehouse which is managed with SAP. This "double bookkeeping" often leads to inconsistencies between the two databases, for example, if a file is not received in order.

In the second step, we decided to address one of the problems that were elicited in the first step, namely that of integrating the respective information systems. We did so by developing Interaction Models to bring the communicative structure to the surface. A simple example is shown in Figure 8 (top) concerning the inconsistency issue. We thereby identified the respective warehouse managers as the actors who are responsible to negotiate and control the synchronization of the warehouses.

Figure 8. Partial interaction model (top) and communication diagram (bottom)

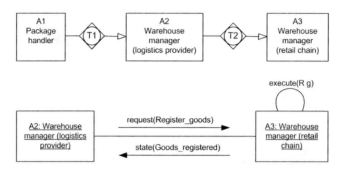

In the third step, we used language mapping to create initial UML models for the design of an appropriate information system support. Figure 8 (bottom) shows the part of the communication diagram for transaction T2: Register goods. The phases "promise" and "accept" can be omitted as they are provided for in a framework contract. In the light of this model, we were able to assess that the "state" phase is not implemented in the current system. As a consequence, a failure in receiving the update file cannot be recognized by the sender, and the file is not resent.

Future Trends

So far we have described an approach for combining interorganizational modeling and information systems modeling in a way that the first can support the second. But this is only a small endeavor that is part of a larger development in research that takes into account the current trend in the (global) economy that leads towards a decentralization of the economy. Contrary to the expectations of a (simplistic) coordination theory, this does not lead to a decrease in coordination effort which would only be true in the case of markets of independent products and services. But organizations rather have to coordinate their processes in order to provide more complex, combined products and services. The hierarchy is in the product or service, not in the company, which requires organizations to cooperate in a way that is less reminiscent of pure market coordination and more like a changing value network of virtual enterprises constantly adapting to the changing needs of customers. But contrary to a conventional, hierarchical organization, the virtual enterprise lacks the direct, explicit power structure to enforce coordination between member companies. Instead members have to negotiate (and renegotiate) contracts that regulate the cooperation between them. In this scenario a number of interesting questions arises that is the subject of ongoing and future research: How do we design the cooperation between organizations? How do we describe interorganizational business processes? How can these be supported by information systems? How do we design coordination contracts? Is the design of such a contract the consequence of process design, or vice versa? Are they designed together (i.e., co-designed)?

In the course of answering these questions, we consider it worthwhile to:

- Develop a coordination theory based on contracts and business processes
- Develop a method to analyse and design interorganizational contracts and processes together with information systems to support them
- Integrate this new method with existing ones for organizational development and development of information systems

Conclusion

The purpose of this chapter is to introduce an approach for supporting the development of information system models based on models of an interorganizational business process. We assume that interorganizational processes involve more interactions than processes within an organization, as the former requires the communication between members of different businesses which cannot rely on a common organizational context that regulates a substantial part of their behavior. We therefore suggest the use of the language-action perspective that views an organization as a network of communicating actors. The DEMO method provides a modeling language that expresses this perspective and is also sufficiently formal to provide support for the development of information systems. For the latter we use the de-facto standard language UML. We then introduce a framework for mapping DEMO to UML that facilitates the design of an information system to support the interorganizational process. We finally describe one of the cases where we used this approach successfully. This research is part of a larger effort to develop a method for analyzing and designing interorganizational contracts and processes and, ultimately, a theory of coordination based on contracts and processes.

References

Austin, J. L. (1962). *How to do things with words*. Oxford, UK: Oxford University Press.

Bunge, M. (1977). *Ontology I: The furniture of the world*. Dordrecht, Holland.

Bunge, M. (1979). *Ontology II: A world of systems*. Dordrecht, Holland.

Caplat, G., & Sourrouille, J. L. (2003). Considerations about model mapping. In J. Bezivin & M. Gogolla (Eds.), *Proceedings of the Workshop in Software Model Engineering WiSME@UML '2003*, (pp. 1-6). Retrieved December 20, 2005, from http://www. metamodel.com/wisme-2003/18.pdf

Denning, P. J., & Medina-Mora, R. (1995). Completing the loops. *Interfaces, 25*(3), 42-57.

Dietz, J. L. G. (1999). Understanding and modeling business processes with DEMO. In J. Akoka, M. Bouzeghoub, I. Comyn-Wattiau, & E. Métais (Eds.), *Proceedings of the 18th International Conference on Conceptual Modeling (ER 1999)* (LNCS 1728, pp. 188-202). Berlin, Germany: Springer.

Dietz, J. L. G., & Habing, N. (2004). The notion of business process revisited. In R. Meersman & Z. Tari (Eds.), *Proceedings of the OTM Confederated International Conferences, CoopIS, DOA, and ODBASE* (LNCS 3290, pp. 85-100). Berlin, Germany: Springer.

Evans, A., Maskeri, G., Sammut, P., & Willans, J. S. (2003). Building families of languages for model-driven system development. In J. Bezivin & M. Gogolla (Eds.), *Proceedings of the Workshop in Software Model Engineering WiSME@UML'2003* (pp. 1-9). Retrieved December 20, 2005, from http://www.metamodel.com/wisme-2003/06.pdf

Evermann, J., & Wand, Y. (2001). Towards ontologically based semantics for UML constructs. In H. S. Kunii, S. Jajodia, & A. Sølvberg (Eds.), *Proceedings of the 20th International Conference on Conceptual Modeling (ER 2001)* (LNCS 2224, pp. 354-367). Berlin, Germany: Springer.

Habermas, J. (1984). *The theory of communicative action 1, Reason and the rationalization of society*. Boston: Beacon Press.

Liu, K., Sun, L., Barjis, J., & Dietz, J. L. G. (2003). Modelling dynamic behaviour of business organisations—extension of DEMO from a semiotic perspective. *Knowledge-Based Systems, 16*(2), 101-111.

Medina-Mora, R., Winograd, T., Flores, R., & Flores, F. (1992). The action workflow approach to workflow management technology. In J. Turner & R. Kraut (Eds.), *Proceedings of the Conference on Computer-Supported Cooperative Work (CSCW'92)* (pp. 281-288). New York: ACM.

Miller, J., & Mukerji, J. (2003). *MDA Guide Version 1.0.1* (pp. i-B2). OMG. Retrieved December 20, 2005, from http://www.omg.org/docs/omg/03-06-01.pdf

OMG (2004). *UML 2.0 Superstructure Specification*. Retrieved December 20, 2005, from http://www.uml.org/

Opdahl, A. L., & Henderson-Sellers, B. (2002). Ontological evaluation of the UML using the Bunge-Wand-Weber model. *Software and Systems Modeling, 1*(1), 43-67.

Searle, J. R. (1969). *Speech acts: An essay in the philosophy of language*. London: Cambridge University Press.

Wand, Y., & Weber, R. (1989). An ontological evaluation of systems analysis and design methods. In E. D. Falkenberg & P. Lindgreen (Eds.), *Information systems concepts: An in-depth analysis* (pp. 79-107). Amsterdam, The Netherlands: North-Holland.

Wand, Y., & Weber, R. (1995). On the deep structure of information systems. *Information Systems Journal, 5*(3), 203-223.

Weber, R. (1997). *Ontological foundations of information systems*. Melbourne, Australia: Coopers & Lybrand and the Accounting Association of Australia and New Zealand.

Winograd, T., & Flores, F. (1986). *Understanding computers and cognition: A new foundation for design*. Norwood, NJ: Ablex.

van Reijswoud, V. E. (1996). *The structure of business communication: Theory, model, and application*. Unpublished doctoral thesis, Technical University Delft, The Netherlands.

van Reijswoud, V. E., & Dietz, J. L. G. (1999). *DEMO modelling handbook* (pp. 1-173). (Technical report). Department of Information Systems, Technical University Delft. Retrieved December 20, 2005, from http://www.demo.nl/documents/handbook.pdf

Section III

Virtual Organization Management

Chapter VII

The Organisation of Performance Measurement in an Extended Enterprise

Paul Folan, National University of Ireland, Ireland

Harinder Jagdev, University of Manchester, UK

Jimmie Browne, National University of Ireland, Ireland

Abstract

This chapter discusses the administrative requirements for business integration between partnering companies in the extended enterprise who operate a performance measurement (PM) system. It argues that, while on the one hand, interorganisational performance measurement is expected to become increasingly significant in the research literature, it is currently difficult to legislate and coordinate the various PM activities that must be taken into account so as to overcome the disparity in geographical location and culture of extended enterprise nodes. Furthermore, while Extended enterprise performance measurement concepts are increasingly being promulgated, the complex nature of these models has made business integration of the firms involved a difficult task: There are problems with regulating the policies and behaviour of those who participate in the system, as well as assessing their understanding of the process itself. These problems are tackled here by the development of a series of questionnaires and assessment checklists, and by their application in an empirical study in an extended enterprise of the automotive industry.

Introduction

Performance measurement (PM) is undergoing a transformation in today's business environment. Analysis is currently being performed to bring PM into line with interorganisational concepts, such as the virtual enterprise (Chalmeta & Grangel, 2005), the extended enterprise (EE) (Bititci, Mendibil, Martinez, & Albores, 2005; Folan & Browne, 2005a; Folan, Higgins, & Browne, in press), and supply chain management (Basu, 2001; Beamon, 1999; Brewer & Speh, 2000; Chan & Qi, 2003; Dreyer, 2000; Gunasekaran, Patel, & Tirtiroglu, 2001; van Hoek, 1998). In these attempts, however, a crucial circumstance that is assumed to already exist is that of efficient business integration between enterprise nodes; that is, that legislative and contractual agreements have been discussed and considered, and subsequently been signed-up to by all participating partners. Nothing could be further from the truth, however: Efforts to align the concept of PM under the umbrella of interorganisational paradigms are suffering from a lack of groundwork in areas that emphasise the need for efficient PM administration and management *between* nodal partners; there is a current lack of literature analysing the requirements of business integration that allows for clear and efficient guidelines towards PM legislation and administration in the supply chain, EE, and virtual enterprise paradigms.

In the coming years, there is expected to be a significant increase in interorganisational PM, with the resulting requirement that peripheral interorganisational PM initiatives will increasingly have to be coordinated, integrated and, generally, legislated for. With the development of new concepts in the arena of PM—such as those in the interorganisational arena—comes the requirement that the associated and larger arena of *performance management* is updated to reflect these developments; management both precedes and follows measurement, and in doing so creates the context for its existence (Lebas, 1995). Internally, performance management is set at the company-wide level; externally, however, issues are more difficult: For example, legislation and coordination of PM activities must take into account the disparity in geographical location and culture of supply chain or EE nodes. There is a need for research into ways to efficiently solve this interorganisational performance management dilemma.

This chapter analyses the problem of business integration with regard to interorganisational PM, by using an EE viewpoint to develop a number of administrative assessments and questionnaires. The developed assessments and questionnaires may be seen as a complimentary approach to that found in the research of Folan and Browne (2005a), who attempt to formulate an EE PM system via the use of an EE node leader, termed the *EE host*, the EE node that controls the administrative and legislative features of the interorganisational PM system for the EE partners. In the next section, the background research examines both EE and PM concepts individually and in conjunction with each other; this is followed by new proposals towards increased EE PM integration and collaboration via a set of administrative questionnaires and assessment checklists. These are subsequently tested in an empirical study of the automotive industry; and finally, the chapter is rounded off by conclusions.

Background Research

Research on the EE is a well-established subject, as is PM. The combination of these concepts, however, is a relatively recent development, and so the background literature has been divided into the following four sections: The first section analyses the EE and the level of integration that the paradigm stipulates; the second section outlines the recent interorganisational literature on PM; the third section examines PM under the umbrella of the EE, the relationships developed, and so forth; while the last section summarises the requirements that have become evident, and uses this to suggest the way forward.

Integration and the Extended Enterprise

With an increasing focus on core competences within organisations, there has been a correspondingly increased amount of focus on closer links with suppliers, and the management of supplier relationships, such that suppliers have effectively becoming an extension of the firm (Childe, 1998). The traditional view of manufacturing companies with clear boundaries, limited relationships with other companies, and a focus on internal efficiency and effectiveness is no longer adequate (Browne & Zhang, 1999). The core concept of the EE is that the extended enterprise can no longer treat suppliers and customers as *them*; they are all now part of a larger *us* (Browne, Sackett, & Wortmann, 1995). The concept of the EE arises partly from attempts of manufacturers, situated at geographically-dispersed locations, to build formal partnerships to gain competitive advantage. The crux of this logic is to embrace external resources and services without owning them (Jagdev & Browne, 1998). Whicker and Walton (1996) suggest that the EE concept differs from the virtual enterprise concept insomuch as it consists of a dominant trader that is associated with all, or some, of its suppliers; the boundary of any particular EE an organisation belongs to can be defined by how far the influence of its internal value chain reaches throughout its suppliers and partners. It is probable and desirable that an organisation will belong to a number of EEs within different industry sectors (Clegg, 2003). Table 1 outlines the main characteristics of the EE as seen by Jagdev and Thoben (2001). EEs are concepts that emphasise extreme business integration at the interorganisational level.

With an increasing business focus on core activities has come a reliance on subcontracted work, continued outsourcing of non-core competencies, and increased control over supplier networks (Browne et al., 1995). This has resulted in enterprises buying items that they might previously have manufactured for themselves, with the intention of focusing their own activities in those particular areas in which they have a critical core competence (Prahalad & Hamel, 1990). The result has been that individual enterprises have become part of enterprise networks of independent core competencies in order to produce marketable products. However, the realisation of these networks in practice requires reintegration of those areas that have been outsourced if they are to succeed: The EE, for example, is facilitated by the availability of new communications and information technology tools, plus the emergence of global telecomputing, intranets, and the Internet (Browne, 1996; Jagdev & Thoben, 2001). Interorganisational networking evolves from intensive information system integration; the EE is a paradigm that reflects the extent to which the information systems

Table 1. Characteristics of EEs (Adapted from Jagdev & Thoben, 2001)

Factor	Characteristic
Duration	Long-term relationships: Treat each other as business partners, with understanding and acceptance of other partner's requirements and priorities.
Collaboration	Within the scope of collaboration, partners share vision and work towards a shared goal.
Advanced technologies	Participating enterprises must have sufficiently sophisticated IT and decision support tools and mechanisms to make EE integration possible. It is also important to have the maximum degree of compatibility among partners' IT systems.
Drivers	The efficiency of the EE is greatly determined by the speed and efficiency with which information can be exchanged and managed among business partners.
Information sharing	The primary mode of communication and sharing of information between collaborating enterprises will always be through telecomputing. It is, therefore, important to have available advanced ICT tools to support the EE. Day-to-day communications between the respective IT systems of two enterprises will always be real-time and online and without human intervention.
Structure	Technology permitting, EE can take the form of a complex enterprise network where each enterprise can be seen as a node.
Decision-making	Decisions are jointly arrived at by making best use of the competencies among the partners.
Size	EEs can occur between any two enterprises across the value chain of any product or service; the whole value chain is not a necessary precondition to its formation.
Node relationship	The nodes in an EE may be hierarchical or non-hierarchical.

of the collaborating enterprises are integrated with one another and the way they actually communicate and collaborate with one another (Jagdev & Thoben, 2001).

What is presupposed, however, in the paradigm of the EE is a sufficiently integrated vision of what the EE is, and where each EE node fits into the pattern; a problem, for example, that each individual manufacturer faces is that of developing a manufacturing strategy that accounts for the business environment and allows for the manufacturer's position in the EE (Browne et al., 1995). Currently, despite the great advances in the information technology that facilitates the EE concept, not enough research has been performed on large-scale collaboration between large numbers of partners in the EE. The difficulty faced by the manufacturer is not the development of an internally-oriented strategy, but the development of an EE-wide strategy for the future; despite the existence of collaborative tools, the manufacturer is still unable to decipher what is in the minds of his EE partners. This problem is unfortunately characteristic of the EE where collaboration is assumed to exist already: Integrating the collaborative environment for the EE must be built as solutions to individual problems are developed. Further, the situation is exacerbated by existing competition laws that frown on extensive collaboration; as Cullen (2000) points out, these laws are underpinned by presumptions that strategic collaborations are anti-competitive and therefore not in the public interest. Thus, researchers working with the EE paradigm face a situation where they must try to solve the problem of EE partner collaboration, while keeping a close eye on anti-competitive laws. So far, there has been a relative absence of literature in this area.

Figure 1. Performance measurement reference model

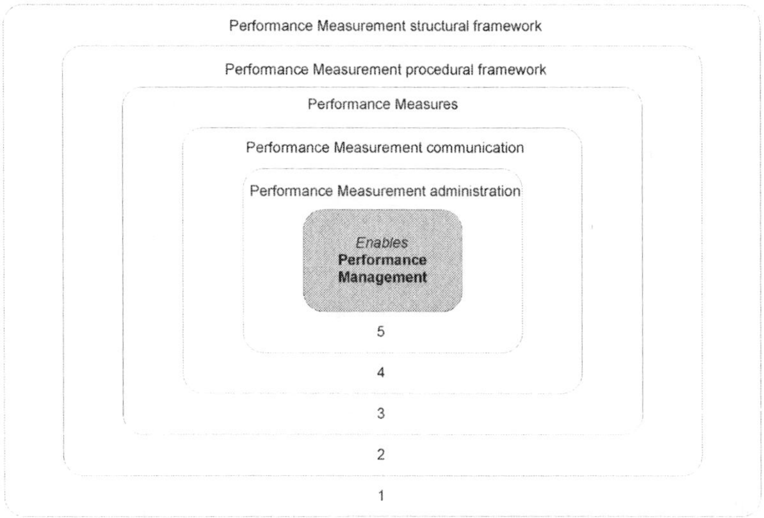

Integration in Interorganisational Performance Measurement

Integration within the concept of interorganisational PM literature depends on a number of entities working successfully together. The existing interorganisational PM literature can be accommodated in the performance measurement reference model presented in Figure 1, which is segregated into five sections of decreasing importance that together enable performance management. The PM structural framework, the most important section, specifies a typology for performance measure management (Folan & Browne, 2005b), which enables top management to visualise performance measures under various headings and sub-headings; typical examples of these frameworks include those by Beamon (1999), Brewer and Speh (2000), Lapide (2000), Gunasekaran et al. (2001), Bullinger, Kuhner, and van Hoof (2002), Chan and Qi (2003), Gunasekaran, Patel, and McGaughey (2004), and Folan and Browne (2005a). The second most important section is the development of a PM procedural framework that allows top management a step-by-step process for developing performance measures from strategy; this has been relatively neglected by the literature, with studies by Dreyer (2000), Basu (2001), and Folan and Browne (2005a) being the only ones noted so far. There is a relative absence of performance measures (third section) in the literature, with the SCOR model being the most widely known approach; the development of predefined lists of performance measures help to reduce the amount of subjectivity required in the PM system process; however, they may result in a certain loss of flexibility of the methodology; and are apt to become old, due to the fact that no process for updating them is usually stipulated.

PM communication (fourth section) examines the problems of effective interorganisational sharing of measurement information. Holmberg (2000) has suggested the use of a systems thinking approach to overcome communication issues, a postulation upheld by the research of Backhouse and Burns (1999), who emphasise that communication methods to ensure measure visibility at the level of the EE requires further investigation, while Bititci, Martinez, Albores, and Mendibil (2003) stipulate that the flow of individual EE node performance management information (such as performance objectives and targets) via a specialised meta-manage process should be considered. Kleijnen and Smits (2003) suggest that communication and coordination within the supply chain should be applied in such a manner so as to overcome the obstacles created by an independent balanced scorecard development process, and Chalmeta and Grangel (2005) have tackled virtual enterprise PM system development via a computer infrastructure based on an extranet design as, in a similar manner, does Folan and Browne (2005a) and Folan et al. (in press). Alongside PM administration in the fifth section, which is the scope of this chapter, each of these entities, when brought together, enable not only PM system development, but performance management.

In terms of performance management, there is little on the subject of interorganisational PM administration and integration, with the exception of isolated proposals from Dreyer (2000) who suggested a three-step supply chain PM framework to develop a successful supply chain PM system, and advice from Basu (2001), who proposes a six-step cycle framework in order to implement and sustain the benefits of a performance management system with new measures (i.e., measures for the extended supply chain). In other areas of measurement, however, integration is more commonplace. The Deming Prize and the Malcolm Baldridge National Quality Award (MBNQA) are just two of the best known quality-related competitions in the world. The Deming Prize has been awarded since the early 1950s (Zairi, 1994), and the MBNQA was established in the USA in 1987, to counteract the increasing concern about a lack of quality, productivity, and competitiveness in today's dynamic world (Wongrassamee, Gardiner, & Simmons, 2003). The central legislative concept by which these awards function is the use made of assessment procedures; the quality-related performance factors of the participating companies are measured using self-assessment and external assessment processes.

Extended Enterprise Performance Measurement

Recently, Folan and Browne (2005a) have introduced an EE PM system concept which attempts to tackle the legislative problem by the introduction of what is termed an EE host. The EE host is the member of the EE with responsibilities for formulating, detailing and distributing information concerning the EE direction and requirements to the other nodes of the EE; and for controlling the aggregated EE-perspective of the EE balanced scorecard. The recommended EE host was a first-tier supplier of the EE (not an original equipment manufacturer)—a choice dictated by the need to avoid coercive practices in the EE from the introduction of a large-scale PM system that crosses a number of company boundaries. By introducing the EE host, the concept of integrating the disparate factors associated with interorganisational PM is centralised in one node leader. The integrative core of the EE PM part of the solution lies in the development of a structural EE balanced scorecard with four perspectives (see Figure 2): supplier, internal, customer, and EE.

Figure 2. The extended enterprise balanced scorecard framework

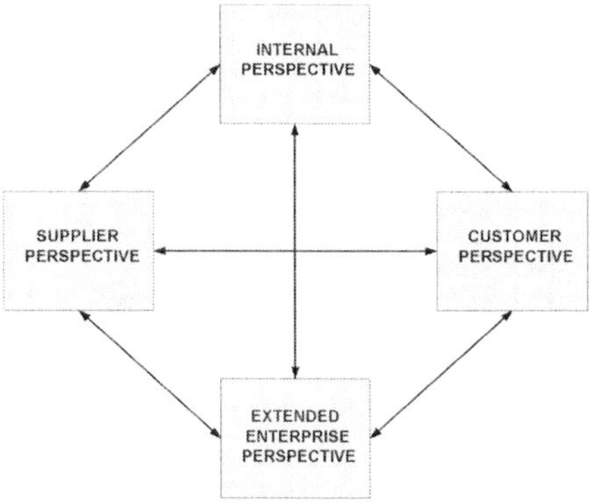

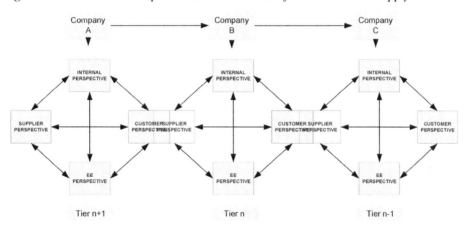

Figure 3. The extended enterprise balanced scorecard framework in the supply chain

The EE balanced scorecard framework depicted in Figure 2 is, as Zimmermann (2001) suggests, "balanced" by external perspectives and internal perspectives; the external interface perspectives of supplier-, customer- and EE-perspective against the internal perspective. When the EE Balanced Scorecard in Figure 2 is extended and depicted at each node of the supply chain, a situation as shown in Figure 3 is obtainable; the Figure presents a linear representation of the supply chain for simplicities' sake. Note the overlapping of the customer- and supplier- perspectives between succeeding supply chain nodes in Figure 3. This represents the fact that the *supplier-perspective* of a company in the nth tier and the *customer-perspective* of a supplier in the $(n+1)^{th}$ tier may be virtually equivalent in make-up in a one-to-one relationship.

The relationship difference comes more as a matter of *viewpoint* than anything else. To the company of the nth tier, the supplier in the $(n+1)^{th}$ tier *is* a supplier, which requires certain supplier-orientated measures to be held between them. The situation is reversed from the

Figure 4. One-to-one supply chain relationship with extended enterprise balanced scorecard framework: Integrated measures

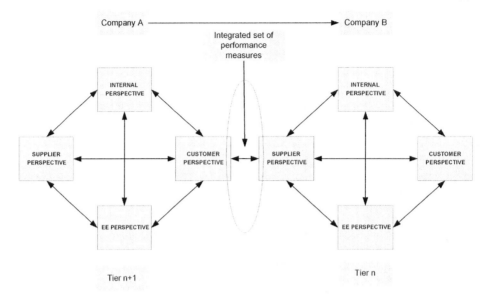

$(n+1)^{th}$ supplier's perspective: The nth tier company is a *customer* and therefore certain customer-oriented measures have to be agreed. Thus, a performance measure such as "delivery time" is a business-integrated measure between the supply chain nodes: It is held in common, and measures virtually the same thing from both companies' perspectives (see Figure 4).

In reality, of course, an EE usually holds more than one-to-one relationships between suppliers. Thus, as in the many-to-many relationship shown in Figure 5, the *supplier-perspective* of the company in the nth tier is comprised of all of the measures held between the group of suppliers in the $(n+1)^{th}$ tier and itself; similarly with its customer measures in the $(n-1)^{th}$ tier. Thus, while succeeding supply chain nodes may overlap in their respective interface measures, it is unlikely that they will succeed in being exactly integrated. This mismatch is usually caused by many-to-many relationships within and without the EE; the presence of outside influences on the framework should not be totally neglected as it may introduce other, foreign measures to the EE node.

The main points of the EE balanced scorecard have been advocated from a supply chain viewpoint in the paragraphs above. The key to turning this framework into an EE PM framework lies in the systems thinking concept proposed by Holmberg (2000). The EE-perspective should consist of local (that is node-level) performance measures that must be aggregated up into EE-level measures. The methodology requires the integration of the EE perspective of each EE node's EE balanced scorecard; this allows for the development of an EE-wide PM system, as in Figure 6.

Figure 5. Many-to-many relationship in the supply chain with extended enterprise balanced scorecard framework

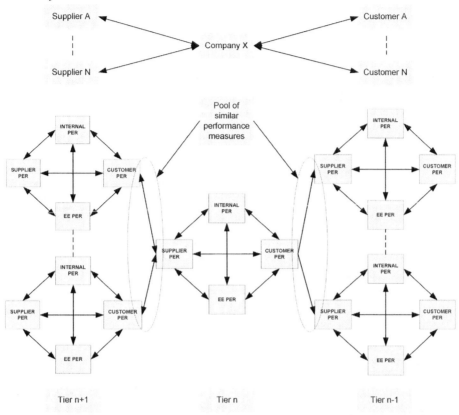

Figure 6. Extended enterprise wide performance measurement system

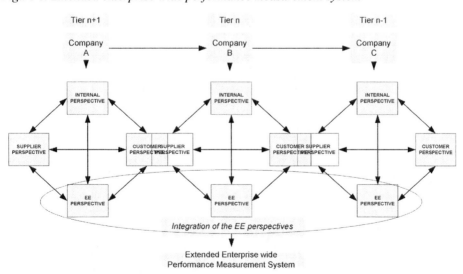

This section will finish with some elucidatory notes on each of the four perspectives:

- **Internal perspective:** The internal-perspective of the EE balanced scorecard represents, at each node of the EE, the intra-organisational PM system used by that node. Performance measures are chosen from a list of measures that is a standard in the EE; however, internally EE nodes are free to use and display performance measures as they see fit. This standardisation proviso allows individual nodes to express their independence at the intra-organisational level, while still ensuring that the measures selected are taken from the standard measure list; thus participation in the EE of the internal-perspective still remains despite the fact that at various nodes of the EE, different PM frameworks may be used to develop intra-organisational PM systems.

- **Supplier perspective:** The supplier-perspective of the EE balanced scorecard represents, at each node of the EE, the integrated *supplier interface* PM system used by that node. The supplier interface performance measures are the sum of the measures between the respective node and *all* of its suppliers in the EE; measures are drawn

Figure 7. Supplier interface performance measurement system

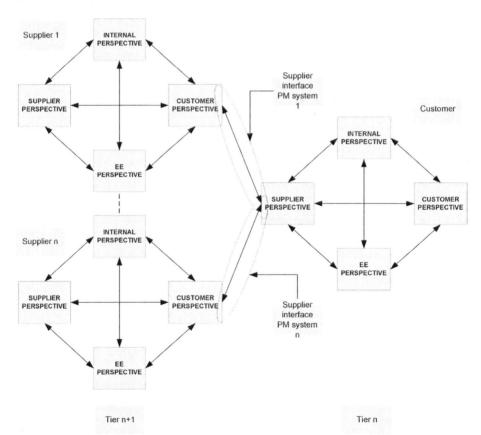

Figure 8. Customer interface performance measurement system

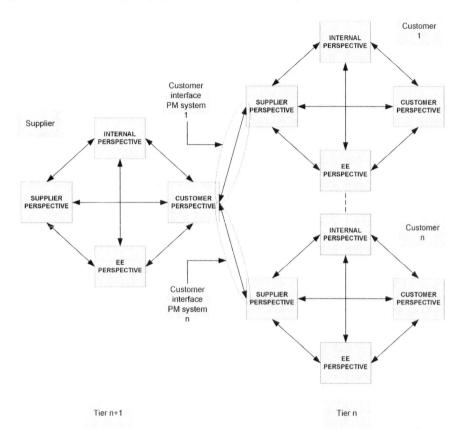

from the standard EE performance measure list. The *supplier interface PM system* may be seen as a small system of performance measures that are held jointly between the node and each of its suppliers; the more suppliers a node has, the more supplier interface PM systems it has (this is depicted in Figure 7). Much of the raw data for the shared measures is found in the documentation that passes back and forth in the supplier-customer relationship (e.g., request for quotations, orders, etc.).

- **Customer perspective:** The customer-perspective of the EE balanced scorecard represents, at each node of the EE, the integrated *customer interface* PM system used by that node. The customer interface performance measures are the sum of the measures between the respective node and *all* of its customers in the EE; measures are drawn from the standard EE performance measure list. The *customer interface PM system* may be seen as a small system of performance measures that are held jointly between the node and each of its customers; the more customers a node has, the more customer interface PM systems it has (this is depicted in Figure 8). Much of the raw data for the shared measures is found in the documentation that passes back and forth in the supplier-customer relationship (e.g., request for quotations, orders, etc.).

Figure 9. Summary of the EE balanced scorecard in the EE

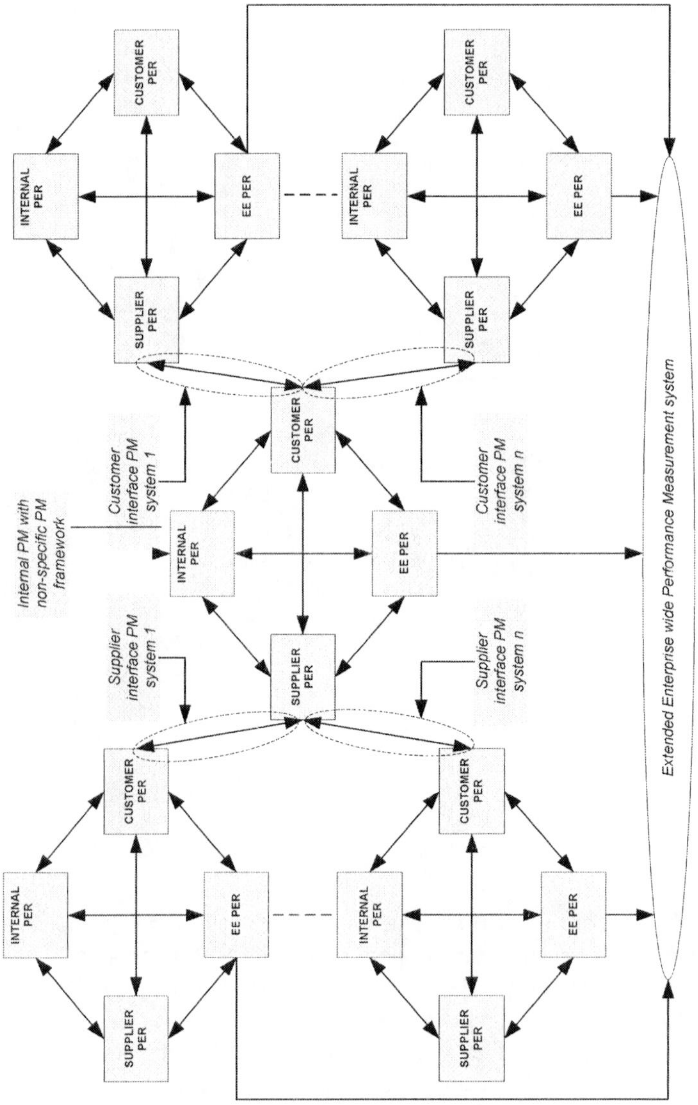

- **Extended enterprise perspective:** The EE-perspective of the EE balanced scorecard represents, at each node of the EE, the EE PM system used by that node. The EE performance measures represent measures held by a particular node that will ultimately be aggregated on an EE level; performance measures are drawn from the standard EE performance measure list. The *EE PM system* may therefore be seen as a series of node systems of measures that are combined to form the EE PM system; the more nodes an EE has, the larger the EE PM system may become, depending on how many nodes wish to participate in the EE PM system.

Summary of Extended Enterprise Balanced Scorecard Perspectives

The above notes may be summarised by Figure 9, which demonstrates that each node is expected to organise its own internal PM system, while integrating supplier and customer PM systems that consist of shared performance measures, and providing information for the aggregation of performance measures at the EE perspective.

Summary

Clearly, there is a requirement for further business integration of such a complex EE PM structure; as it stands, it is attempting to cross company boundaries, and trying to introduce specific initiatives across a range of firms that may be geographically, as well as culturally, diverse. This situation, if not managed properly, may give rise to a number of specific problems; Lohman, Fortuin, and Wouters (2004), for example, specify:

- Decentralised reporting leading to inconsistencies
- Deficient insight in cohesion between measures
- Uncertainty about what to measure
- Poor communication between reporters and users
- Dispersed information technology infrastructure

There is a need for a set of standardised administrative policies to regulate the EE at the high EE-level, and at the local, node level. These issues will be addressed here with the development of a standard rulebook, questionnaire, and checklist. Here, this document can only be developed in generic form; for an actual EE, specific rules may be drawn up using this generic format as a basis for rule development.

Extended Enterprise
Performance Measurement Questionnaire

To facilitate the role of the EE host as the member of the EE with responsibilities for formulating, detailing, and distributing information concerning the EE direction and requirements to the other nodes of the EE, and for controlling the general integration of the EE PM system, an extended enterprise performance measurement questionnaire should be developed. Although dealing with intra-organisational issues and focusing on the uses that management and teams make of PM systems, the work of Meyer (1994) shows a striking resemblance to the problems faced by practitioners at the interorganisational level. Table 2 shows a set of the most generic propositions made by Meyer (1994).

Table 2. Propositions for team and management interaction (Adapted from Meyer, 1994)

Participant	The Measurement system should allow:
Top Management	A means to intervene if the team runs into problems which it cannot solve by itself
	To ensure that the resulting measurement system is consistent with the company's strategy
	Must require the teams to decide which measures will best help them perform their jobs
	Must define the problem and decide what corrective action to take (with teams)
	Negotiate contracts if necessary
Teams	To use the measurement system for corrective action purposes
	To create a structure, the team, that is responsible for a complete value-delivery process
	To create measures that support their mission, or they will not fully exploit their ability to perform the process faster and in a way that is more responsive to customer demands
	To ensure that ownership of and accountability for performance remains with the teams
	To know at the outset that it will have to review the measures it has selected with top managers to ensure consistency with strategic goals
	To know at the outset that it may have to adjust its measures
	To promise to renegotiate with managers any major changes in the measures made during the course of the project
	To, during an "out-of-bounds" review, allow teams and managers to define the problem and decide what corrective action to take
	To retain responsibility for calling and running the review and executing any decisions

Many of these intra-organisational points retain their validity when transferred to the inter-organisational arena, especially when we consider the individual EE node in the role of the "team," and the EE host representing the role of "top management." The following paragraphs represent a subjective elucidation of these points from an interorganisational perspective.

The EE PM system, as a concept, should help both the EE node and EE host gauge progress. Just as with teams, EE PM at the local node level uses the PM system for corrective action purposes. Corrective action may come in two forms: corrective action required for internal errors, and corrective action required for external errors; the former being the property of the local level intra-organisational PM system—this form of corrective action is the property of the individual EE node; while the latter corrective action type may be the property of more than one node in the EE. If the corrective action is required between two EE nodes (i.e., a supplier and a customer), it has occurred at the interfaces of the company. Corrective action may result from a change in EE direction, whereby the corrective action is owned by the entire EE. The EE node, however, may, at times, experience difficulties in using/developing the EE PM system, whereby the EE host may be asked for help; this is left to the discretion of the EE node, however. The use of the first-tier supplier as the EE host should help to reduce the amount of political use of the EE PM system, as has been mentioned before. The EE host should not seek to *force* certain internal-, supplier-, or customer-perspective measures on EE nodes; individual EE nodes decide these for themselves. The EE host does have the ability to insist on certain EE-perspective measures, as these lie under its jurisdiction.

The EE node must play the lead role in designing its own EE PM system, a point borne out in Folan and Browne's (2005a) EE PM system model. The EE node designs its intra-organisational PM system itself, and chooses measures for internal-, supplier-, and customer-perspectives; the EE-perspective is, however, supplied by the EE host who is better informed for making the measure selection for this perspective. Thus the EE node has an EE PM system that is consistent with their own company strategy while, through the EE perspective designed by the EE host, taking into account the holistic, EE-perspective.

An EE node is responsible for a value-delivery process; it must create measures to track that process. The EE node is, through its internal-perspective, given the opportunity to track the value-delivery process through its own company. The interface perspectives (i.e., supplier and customer) track the value-delivery process *between* succeeding suppliers in the EE, while the EE-perspective provides an overview of the *whole* value-delivery process. While a negative value-delivery process at the EE-perspective may not be noticeable at the level of the other three perspectives, the EE-perspective, by providing a holistic overview, will still indicate its existence. The value-delivery excellence of each EE node is a requirement for holistic EE excellence, although compromises between nodes may be sought to avoid local optimisation at the expense of EE performance.

An EE node should adopt only a handful of measures. An EE node should adopt measures for the four perspectives of the EE Balanced Scorecard framework. For the internal-, supplier-, and customer-perspectives, 15 to 20 measures (Kaplan & Norton, 1993) may be ideal. The number of measures assigned to each EE node by the EE host for the EE-perspective may change over time; however, four measures may be sufficient here.

EE host dictates EE direction and requirements and ensures that each node understands how it fits into the EE, and provides training so that they can devise their own measures. The EE host *is* responsible for providing the EE direction and requirements plan to the EE nodes; it *is not* responsible for developing each EE node's company strategy. The EE host should provide clear guidelines on *all* aspects of EE PM development in the EE to the EE nodes. Training manuals may be one solution for those companies that may be unsure of themselves when it comes to developing measures, for example, for small- to medium-sized enterprises (SMEs).

The EE host and EE node should jointly establish rules about when or under what circumstances reviews of the node's performance and its PM system will take place. This should be done clearly and in writing. Periodic review intervals should be specified between the EE host and the EE node(s), and maintained. The right to ask for *emergency* reviews should also be insisted on by the EE host, in case the EE-perspective is unexpectedly altered significantly, requiring changes elsewhere in the EE. EE hosts must also insist that:

- Outdated measures be deleted from the EE node's PM system
- New measures (particularly from the EE-perspective) are accepted
- Supplier- and customer-perspective measures are negotiated (and not forced) between the interested parties

EE host and EE node should also set boundaries, which, if crossed, will signal that the node has run into trouble serious enough to trigger an "out-of-bounds" EE review. Targets

Table 3. Extended enterprise performance measurement questionnaire

No.	Question
1.	*Participation in the EE PM by EE nodes*
	A.	How many EE nodes wish to participate?
	B.	Are they linked?
	C.	How many EE nodes do not wish to participate?
	D.	What are the reasons why not?
	E.	Have enough EE nodes expressed interest in the EE PM project to proceed?
	F.	Do we have a viable system of EE nodes to proceed?
	G.	Having decided to proceed, is there full agreement within the participating EE nodes on the terms and conditions required for EE PM?
2.	*Dissemination of EE PM system information to those who wish to participate*
	A.	Have participating EE nodes been supplied with all relevant EE PM frameworks, guidelines, and PM recommendations?
	B.	Is each EE node satisfied with the material which was supplied?
	C.	If not, why not?
	D.	Has additional information been required/provided?
	E.	Does each participating EE node access to the EE PM system decision support system?
	F.	Is each participating EE node able to use the decision support system which was provided?
3.	*Obligatory acceptance questions for EE nodes—General acceptance*
	A.	Do you accept all of the EE PM frameworks, recommendations, and guidelines which were provided to you by the EE host?
	B.	Do you accept that updates may occur to these materials at any time, and will you implement them?
	C.	Do you agree to use only the most current versions of all EE PM frameworks, recommendations, and guidelines, as they are made available to you by the EE host?
	D.	Will you undertake to hold and measure (and subsequently disseminate the results using the EE PM system decision support system) EE measures supplied to you by the EE host, although they may have no immediate relevance use to you?
	E.	Do you agree to present all measures used in your EE PM system in the decision support system which was provided?
	F.	Do you, as a participating EE node in the EE PM system, undertake to guarantee that the information shared in the EE PM system will remain the property of the participating EE nodes, and that, under no circumstances, will the information found there be released in any format to outside interests?
4.	*Obligatory acceptance questions for EE nodes—Interaction*
	A.	Do you agree to share all relevant information with those other EE nodes (such as suppliers and customers) who require it?
	B.	Do you agree to jointly develop both supplier and customer measures with those affected suppliers and customers?
	C.	Do you agree to interact fully with the EE host, and use and supply information concerning EE-perspective measures?
	D.	Do you agree to present all measures used in your EE PM system in the decision support system which was provided?

Table 3. continued

5.		*Obligatory acceptance questions for EE nodes—Audits and reviews*
	A.	Do you agree to audit, at periodic intervals set between the EE host and respective EE node, the EE measure template list, and agree to transmit the results of this to the EE host for continual updating of the EE measure list?
	B.	Do you agree to "emergency" audits of the EE measure list, as requested by the EE host, if they are deemed as a requirement?
	C.	Do you agree to perform periodic reviews of the EE node's strategy?
	D.	Additionally, do you agree to perform periodic reviews of the EE node's strategy if specific requests are made to do so by the EE host?
	E.	Do you agree to take part in an "out-of-bounds" review if your respective EE node does not reach certain target performance levels?
6.		*Obligatory acceptance questions for EE nodes—Miscellaneous*
	A.	Do you accept the Performance Measure record sheet (Neely et al., 1997) as the standard for record-keeping in the EE PM system?
	B.	Do you agree to use the EE measure list and associated formulas as they are provided (i.e., as part of the EE PM system)?
7.		*Additional questions to determine EE node responses*
	A.	In your opinion: • At what interval period should the audit of the EE measure list be set to? • At what interval period should the respective EE node's company strategy be reviewed? • At what target performance failure level should an "out-of-bounds" review be set at?
	B.	What internal-perspective PM framework do you intend to use?
	C.	Do you intend to disseminate this EE PM system concept outside the EE?
	D.	Do you intend to disseminate this EE PM system concept inside the EE to those not already participating?

should be set for all measures used in this EE PM system (note that as a standard, Neely, Richards, Mills, Platts, & Bourne's [1997] record sheet is recommended). If individual EE nodes are consistently falling below the targeted performance levels on EE measures (how many "failures" that will be allowed needs to be set), then an "out-of-bounds" review of the *whole* EE PM system, as applied by that node, should take place. In particular, if individual nodes are causing major logistics backlogs (i.e., inventory problems, such as stockpiling, etc.), the internal-, supplier-, and customer-perspectives of that node's PM system need to be examined in detail. The "out-of-bounds" review is not a fault-finding exercise; rather it is an attempt at fixing serious problems that are affecting the whole EE.

Based on these points, the EE PM questionnaire that regulates the policies and behaviour of both the EE host and EE nodes may be derived (see Table 3). As can be seen from the generic questionnaire, the issue of communication and rule-setting between the EE host and the EE nodes is of paramount importance. This questionnaire is of use to the EE host when setting-up an EE PM system, asking some basic questions of participating EE nodes that require positive answers. Notice the issue of "choice": For an EE PM system to be truly successful, a non-broken linkage of EE nodes is a necessity, or else EE PM cannot be accurately measured. The key point, however, is that the questionnaire attempts to achieve an integrated and coherent vision of what PM at the EE level is; the use of legal devices, such as contracts and agreements, may be required to strengthen the issues outlined here.

In practical terms, the questionnaire in Table 3 should be seen as a free-lance tool used by EE hosts as part of the initial EE PM system set-up, and as such its use, and the use made of the results derived from its questions, will differ for each EE implementation. An example of one particular use, from the perspective of one EE host, will be given later in the section outlining the case study.

Extended Enterprise Performance Measurement Self Assessment Checklist

The concept of using self-assessment procedures, as outlined in the quality-related arena above, may be shifted to meet the requirements of assessing EE PM. Based on an adaptation of the Deming Prize criteria, as depicted by Zairi (1994), Table 4 presents the extended enterprise performance measurement self assessment checklist. In this case, self-assessment becomes vital for individual EE nodes to enable them to analyse their success in adapting to established EE PM practices; it is suggested that each node of the EE be required to complete this self-assessment checklist (or a variant tailored to the EE requirements) on a regular basis, with the results to be collected and displayed by the EE host. This self-assessment procedure helps to maintain individual EE node commitment and integration to the EE PM system, while ensuring that procedures and processes connected to it are fully understood and used at each node.

The self-assessment checklist is in eleven sections. Section one asks whether the EE node has implemented a structured, coherent EE PM policy and a set of well-defined objectives: It is important that EE PM is considered as a serious management function by all participating EE nodes; to this end, assessing the appropriateness, consistency, utilisation, deployment, and dissemination (both internally and externally) of policies allows EE nodes to analyse their EE PM policies and objectives to ensure that they are obtaining the maximum benefit, in terms of performance management, from the implemented EE PM system. Section two analyses the organisation's delegation of control over the EE PM system: The functions of PM committees (for internal and supplier/customer interfaces), the appropriateness of who holds what responsibilities in the management of the system, the cooperation between internal functions and with interface partners, and the utilisation of the EE PM tools and audits are assessed. Section three examines the organisation's educational structures for EE PM: It is supposed that an educational PM plan is implemented, and that this should result in an increased awareness among employees of the existence and usage of EE PM in the organisation; outside of the organisation, the benefits of EE PM may also be impressed on suppliers, customers, and subcontractors. Section four handles the assembly and distributing of PM information, both via a specialised decision support system developed for the EE PM

Table 4. Extended enterprise performance measurement self assessment checklist

No.		Question
1.		*EE PM policy and objectives*
	A.	Policy with regard to performance management, PM, and control
	B.	Are the methods advocated for determining EE PM policy and objectives followed?
	C.	Appropriateness and consistency of the contents of the EE PM objectives as related to by the individual company
	D.	Utilisation of standard EE PM frameworks
	E.	Deployment, dissemination, and permeation of EE PM objectives internally/ externally
	F.	Checking of EE PM objectives and their implementation
	G.	Relationships between EE PM long-range plans and company-wide short-range PM plans
2.		*Organisation and its operation*
	A.	A clear-cut line of responsibilities to develop, manage, and deal with EE PM (within the company) has been established.
	B.	Appropriateness of delegation and power
	C.	Cooperation between divisions (internal-perspective), and suppliers and customers (supplier-, customer-perspectives)
	D.	Activities of PM committees
	E.	Utilisation of the PM tools
	F.	EE PM control audits
3.		*Education and its extension*
	A.	PM education plan (internally) and actual accomplishment
	B.	Consciousness of PM, understanding of PM
	C.	Education concerning PM concepts and tools, and degree of permeation
	D.	Ability to understand the effects of good PM at internal and EE levels
	E.	Education of those outside the EE PM system: suppliers, subcontractors, and so forth
	F.	PM training activities
	G.	PM suggestion system and its implementation
4.		*Assembling and disseminating PM information and its utilisation*
	A.	Assembling outside information: supplier-, customer-, EE-perspective information, for inclusion in the EE PM system
	B.	Disseminating information with other EE nodes
	C.	Speed of disseminating information
	D.	Use of the decision support system for EE PM assembling/disseminating information requirements
	E.	Use of other devices for EE PM assembling/disseminating information requirements
	F.	Analysis of the information available on the EE PM system decision support system

Table 4. continued

5.	Analysis	
	A.	Selection of important performance measures for the four perspectives
	B.	Correct utilisation of the EE PM tools and techniques
	C.	Utilisation of other methods outside of the EE PM technique
	D.	Fit of existing (in-house) techniques with EE PM techniques
	E.	PM analysis, and use made of this analysis
	F.	Positiveness of suggestions for PM improvement
6.	Standardisation	
	A.	System used by the node to standardise the EE PM system within the company
	B.	Methods of establishing, revising, and withdrawing standards
	C.	Actual records in establishing, revising, and withdrawing standards
	D.	Contents of EE PM standards
	E.	Utilisation of EE PM standards in the company
7.	Control	
	A.	Control systems (internal) for PM and in related areas
	B.	Actual conditions of the control activity
8.	Performance Measurement—Operational	
	A.	Measurement and inspection facilities
	B.	Control of facilities/equipment, subcontracting, purchasing, services, and so forth
	C.	Operational PM system and its audit
9.	Performance Measurement—Strategic	
	A.	Feedback of performance measures into new strategy development
	B.	Use of EE PM techniques to distill company strategy into performance measures
	C.	Development of new performance measures outside of the EE performance measure list
10.	Effects	
	A.	PM effects
	B.	Visible effects, such as quality, cost, time, and so forth, monitoring effectiveness
	C.	Invisible effects
	D.	Compatibility between prediction of effects and actual records
11.	Future plans	
	A.	Understanding of the EE PM status quo and concreteness
	B.	Policies adopted to solve PM shortcomings
	C.	Plans for the promotion of EE PM for the future
	D.	EE PM, and its relationship with the company's long-range plans

system, and via the use of other devices (for example, via email, the Internet, by post, etc.); while section five analyses the use made of the provided EE PM tools, in particular the EE PM frameworks to develop performances measures suitable for both the EE and internal levels: Here there is also an opportunity to document improvements and suggestions to the EE PM system.

Section six examines whether the organisation has taken steps to ensure the standardisation of EE PM within the company: This is performed by setting down standards in terms of benchmarking results from the EE PM system; settling the question of ownership of individual performance measures; and setting concrete dates for frequency of measuring, audits, and reviews. The establishment of records and the ability of being able to revise, clarify, and withdraw these (when appropriate) are also examined here. Section seven asks whether a control activity, which enables the organisation to tell whether their inputs into the EE PM system are consistent and valid, is in place and is actually being used, as opposed to a situation whereby only lip service is being paid to it. Section eight questions whether operational measures are being regularly monitored, especially in "hard-to-reach" areas, such as with services, purchasing, and subcontractors, and whether the whole is being audited regularly. Section nine queries the strategic use of the results from the EE PM system: Is effective use being made of the feedback for updated strategy formulation? Are there requirements for new performance measures? Section ten explores the overall good and bad effects of the implemented system: Effects may be either visible (for example, improvements in the measuring of quality, cost, time, etc.) or invisible (the political implications of the implementation); it also asks whether existing PM policies reflect these effects of the EE PM system. Finally, section eleven points to the fact that EE PM is not a stable entity; organisations need to understand that EE PM moves on, and requires both long-term EE PM plans, and immediate internally-oriented short-term solutions to succeed.

A specific ranking and weighting of the areas in the self-assessment checklist has not been outlined here in the generic version of the checklist; however, an example of its usage is given in the section outlining the case study.

Extended Enterprise Performance Measurement External Assessment Checklist

The concept of using external assessment procedures may also be shifted to meet the requirements of assessing EE PM. Based on an adaptation of the Malcolm Baldridge Award criteria, as depicted by Zairi (1994), Table 5 presents the extended enterprise performance measurement external assessment checklist. It is suggested that for each node of the EE PM system this assessment checklist (or a variant tailored to the EE requirements) be completed by the EE host for each EE node on a regular basis, with the results to be collected and displayed by the EE host. This external assessment procedure helps the EE host gain a wider perception of individual EE node commitment and integration to the EE PM system.

Table 5. Extended enterprise performance measurement external assessment checklist

No.	Question	
1.	*PM Leadership for each EE node*	
	A.	Senior executive leadership
	B.	Management for PM
	C.	Responsibility for PM and shared EE PM system ideology
2.	*PM Information and analysis*	
	A.	Scope and management of EE PM and associated information
	B.	Competitive comparisons and benchmarking
	C.	Analysis and uses made of internal-perspective measures
3.	*Strategic PM planning*	
	A.	Strategic PM planning process used
	B.	PM plans
4.	*Human resources within PM*	
	A.	Employee involvement in PM
	B.	Employee education and training in PM
	C.	Employee performance and recognition systems in PM
	D.	Employee well-being and satisfaction with PM in company
5.	*Management of the PM system*	
	A.	Design and introduction of PM into production and service functions
	B.	Process measurement: product and service production and delivery processes
	C.	Process measurement: business processes and support services
	D.	Internal measurement
	E.	Supplier measurement
	F.	Maintenance of EE measures
	G.	Frequency of audits
6.	*PM and operational results*	
	A.	Product and service measurement results
	B.	Company operational results
	C.	Business process and support service results
	D.	Internal results
	E.	Supplier results
7.	*EE PM*	
	A.	EE-perspective measures actively measured?
	B.	EE-perspective measures actively used?
	C.	EE-perspective measures actively disseminated?

Table 5. continued

8.		Customer focus
	A.	Customer-perspective: current and future
	B.	Customer relationship measurement
	C.	Customer satisfaction determination
	D.	Customer satisfaction results
	E.	Customer satisfaction comparison

In order to clearly understand the function of this assessment checklist, it must be remembered that it represents the EE node as seen from the *external* EE host's viewpoint. For example, the EE host, when looking at the EE PM system as applied by an individual EE node, will be looking for clear signs of PM leadership (section one), at senior executive level that cascades down towards the operational level, with a shared sense of responsibility for the success of the EE PM initiative as a whole. The scope of the management of the EE PM system (section two), and its use of benchmarking and comparative procedures may also be expected as an assessment priority; while the use made of strategic planning (section three), with the appropriate EE PM tools, and strategic PM plans of implementation may also be deemed a necessity. The issue of spreading the message of EE PM beyond management to include employees (section four) is a must for successful EE PM; consequently, the EE host may look for the signs of employee education, training, and satisfaction within the node's EE PM system.

The EE PM system functions in a number of areas, in particular the production and service departments of the EE node's organisation (section five); the EE host wishes to ensure the smooth operation of the EE, and so particular attention must be paid to process measurements (as opposed to measures simply devoted to the product); this may result in a concentration on the EE node's measures to regulate delivery, service, and production processes, as they impact on the internal and supplier perspectives. Further, an examination of operational measures and results may be expected (section six) in these areas also. At the EE level, the EE host will wish to be satisfied that EE-perspective measures are actively measured, used, and disseminated (section seven). The original emphasis for EE PM comes from a desire to satisfy the customer, so a focus on the EE node's customer-perspective (section eight) should also be expected. The relationship which the node has with its customers, in terms of the interaction between them to develop customer-oriented measures, and the results of this interaction and the subsequent satisfaction of customers with their supplier, may also be analysed.

Note that, as with the self-assessment checklist, a specific ranking and weighting of the areas in the external checklist has not been outlined here in the generic version; however, an example of its usage is given in the following section outlining the case study.

Case Study

Company Application

The identity of the company discussed in this case study, plus its associated EE partners, has been protected. The company, which in this case study acts as the EE host of the EE, is a first-tier supplier of component products to leading automotive companies in the European automotive industry, and to a lesser extent to other industrial sectors. Products are manufactured by the company to suit the requirements of seven main customers, at separate locations in Europe; the company has over fifty suppliers, which are grouped into specific subsets of suppliers according to product-type, in order to allow the company to build its business around custom-designed solutions that can either be engineered-to-order or made-to-order. Indeed, the most valuable competitive advantage of the company is the competence to create new materials adjusted to meet the required technical and functional specifications of the end product as demanded by their customers. Currently, the company wishes to expand its existing markets and wants to enhance existing relationships, as well as establish new ones, particularly those of a collaboratively intense nature, so as to leverage a range of recently implemented tools and differentiated expertise. As part of a package of tools, the three questionnaires and checklists were tested by the company, whose overall objective was to improve the company's performance in controlling its supply chain, from suppliers, through specific component inventories, different assembly stations, and finished goods dispatches, to their customers. The main objective was to utilise the three question-naires and checklists so as to increase visibility throughout the value chain to allow for the conceptualising, design, implementation, and testing of an EE-wide PM system.

Communications Framework for Business Integration in Extended Enterprise Performance Measurement

In order to facilitate the improvement of business integration via EE PM procedures, a dedi-cated communications framework with a front-end dashboard infrastructure was designed and implemented at the company. While the communications framework employed is out-side the scope of this chapter (the interested reader is referred to Folan et al. (in press) for more details), it can be summarised as an intranet/extranet system model with a Web-based user interface that contains the dashboard itself. The dashboard represents the front-end of each EE node's respective EE PM intranet, which, when integrated with the intranets at other EE nodes, produces the EE PM extranet. In terms of the three questionnaires and checklists for EE PM administration outlined above, these are represented in a standard format in the dashboard interface, as in Figure 10, which depicts the layout of the external assessment checklist. As can be seen from the screenshot, the assessment questions are laid out in descending order, giving the user the option to add a specific identifying name and description at the top; for each question, the user must select a specific weighting from the drop-down list, and supply an answer by selecting one of the radio buttons on the right of the screenshot. The user is obliged to provide answers for each question to enable the

Figure 10. Questionnaire and assessment layout in the EE PM dashboard

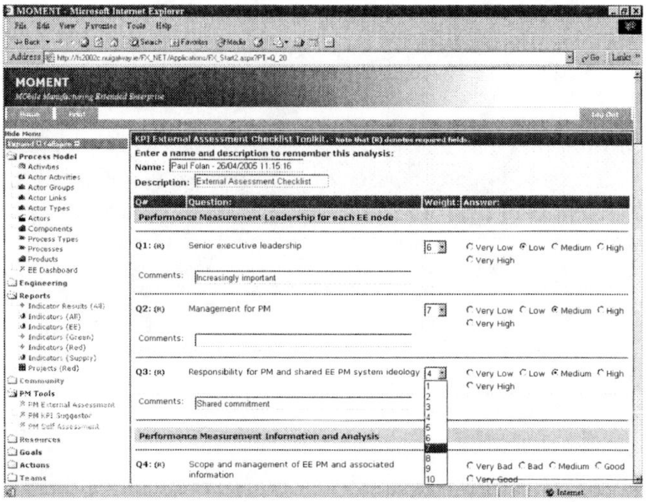

calculation of a weighted "score" at the end for each assessment; the weighting procedure used here will be described more fully in the next subsection.

Note that Figure 10 outlines the generic format that was used to represent both the questionnaire and the two assessment checklists; by using the same standard interface for each, the user can quickly move from one to another. Further, by using an integrated communications infrastructure to promote the EE PM system throughout the participating enterprises in the EE, the problem of disseminating the three questionnaires and checklists for EE PM administration outlined above is solved. The dashboard infrastructure allows the three questionnaires and checklists to be seen by all, and acted on by all in the EE; also, the ease of functionality and user-friendliness of the dashboard design makes the mundane questionnaire and checklists, as they are represented above in Tables 3, 4, and 5, more colourful and visually attractive. Further, the EE PM system can save the results of the questionnaire and checklists as they are used, enabling detailed analysis to be performed as previous results are compared against recent results. The EE PM system also has the ability to display these results graphically (see as follows).

Weighting Procedure Used on the Questionnaire and Checklists

Both the self-assessment and external assessment checklists are designed so that performance measurement practices in EE nodes can be assessed as to their currency and effectiveness. If they are effectively plotted upon a regular basis, a company's evolution in terms of performance measurement can become readily available to the user. The proviso, of course, is that an effective weighting procedure has been agreed upon for use in conjunction with the three questionnaires and checklists; this standard weighting procedure should be integrated into the dashboard infrastructure.

The weighting procedure in the dashboard for this empirical investigation consisted of two main elements (see Figure 10):

1. **A drop-down weight list:** This list lets the user select a weight for the question under consideration; as performance measurement is an ongoing evolutionary practice, question weightings will change as time passes to reflect the growing importance of some aspects of the company's environment, while others will correspondingly decrease in importance; thus, weightings may change over time. The focal company here has decided to allow a weight selection from 1 to 10, where 1 is very low and 10 is very high.

2. **A five-point Likert scale:** This Likert scale (represented as radio buttons in Figure 10) allows the user to select an appropriate description of the question under consideration to show its adoption level in the company. Behind each of the descriptions of the Likert scales, there is a number from one to five, reflecting the five-point scale used. For example, for Likert scale descriptions, "very low" (or "very bad"), the number is one; and for Likert scale description, "very high," the number is five. These numbers will be used to calculate the results of the assessment.

Hence, the two main weighting elements for each question (Q) as outlined above are, in shorthand:

Current Importance of Q vs. Current Description of Q

That is, for each question in the assessment checklists, the company wishes to know its contemporary importance to itself and its business environment, and the actual status of the company upon this parameter. Once an assessment is completed in the dashboard interface, the user submits the results for analysis. The analysis develops a simple evaluative figure (X) for each question in the assessment by multiplying the current importance of the question by the current description of the question; thus:

Current Importance of Q_n x Current Description of $Q_n = X_n$

Then for each assessment, the sum of the evaluative figures of each question is derived to determine the "final score" of the assessment; thus:

$X_1 + X_2 + \ldots + X_n = $ Final Score

This simple weighting mechanism allows the user to derive weighted scores, not only for individual questions in the assessments, but also for a total score for the assessment itself.

This is useful for comparative purposes against other, previously completed assessments; the final scores of one assessment can be compared against another to enable a generic comparison of the assessment's performance, as well as a more detailed question-by-question comparison.

Now that the weighting mechanism used for this empirical study has been outlined, we can move forward to a consideration of how the three questionnaires and checklists were used by the focal company in the next subsection.

Application of the Questionnaire and Checklists

Since the focal company has over fifty suppliers, it decided only to empirically evaluate a subgroup of these with both the self-assessment and external assessment checklists. The questionnaire, meanwhile, was applied in a more free-lance manner, which allowed the focal company to gain a deeper perspective of the requirements for closer business integration via EE PM procedures.

Using the family product level as a basis for selecting a subgroup of suppliers allowed the focal company to apply the self-assessment checklist. They considered that since the different product families they produce have substantially similar characteristics, the results would not be reduced in their validity by being applied to only a small number of suppliers. Therefore, in considering a subset of three suppliers, with a further sub-string of six second-tier suppliers behind and directly influencing these, the following results were obtained for the self-assessment checklist, as applied by the focal company (see Figure 11, a screenshot from the dashboard which contains a generic bar-graph of the result). Figure 11 was developed by applying the self-assessment checklist and using the weighting procedure outlined above.

Figure 11. Dashboard screenshot of self-assessment checklist results

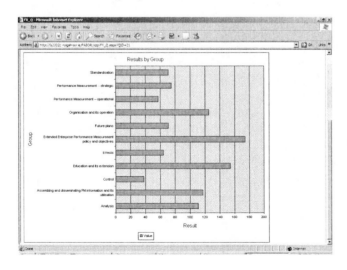

In detail, the graph results of the self-assessment provide a visual list of specific EE PM administrative areas which require particular attention for the focal company; these are (with comments added, derived from the question-level results inputted by the user):

- **Standardisation (medium improvement required):** The focal company feels that standards for EE PM could be improved inside the company walls, from the actual record-keeping involved to the utilisation of these in the company, and the continued improvement of the uses made of these standards.

- **Performance measurement: Strategic (medium improvement required):** The focal company currently feels that, with regard to the strategic utilisation of the results of the PM system in place, it could improve. This improvement could cover how performance measure results are being fed into the strategy development process, and how the EE PM techniques are being used.

- **Organisation and its operation (high level improvement required):** The focal company in general feels that they have not done enough to ensure clear responsibilities for PM in terms of: ensuring personnel with the appropriate responsibilities for PM are in position, with proper delegation and power hierarchies in place; and the development and operation of PM committees is ongoing.

- **Future plans (medium improvement required):** The focal company feels that their current PM is rather blind to the future and needs to take into account future trends more seriously.

- **Extended enterprise performance measurement policy and objectives (extremely high level improvement required):** The focal company are very concerned at their present level on this parameter. There is currently a dearth of official PM policies and objectives in the focal company, and so the employment and utilisation of these is practically non-existent. EE PM policies and objectives have to be put in place so this can change.

- **PM effects (medium improvement required):** The focal company would like to be clearer on how PM affects its operations, and what all the visible and invisible effects involved are.

- **Education and its extension (very high level improvement required):** The focal company is concerned that the message of EE PM is not filtering sufficiently far down the organisational hierarchy; operational personnel do not seem to have a good understanding of PM.

- **Assembling and disseminating PM information and its utilisation (high level improvement required):** The focal company feels that its three main suppliers are not cognisant enough of the EE PM information that it supplies. Further, they fear these suppliers may not be taking the information supplied seriously.

- **Analysis (high level improvement required):** The focal company is aware that it must improve its ability and the use it makes of the EE PM tools and techniques available.

Figure 12. Dashboard screenshot of external assessment checklist results

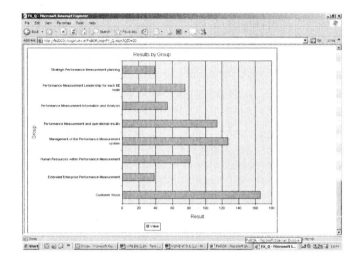

Other areas in the self-assessment checklist are deemed to be under control. From the above comments, it becomes clear that there are a number of sectors in which the focal company can improve its position in terms of EE PM, in particular in the setting of EE PM policy and objectives, which will probably have a beneficial impact upon other parameters when in place.

If we turn to an examination of the external assessment checklist, the following results have been obtained (see Figure 12) as part of the examination of the focal company upon these parameters. Figure 12 was developed by applying the external assessment checklist and using the weighting procedure outlined previously.

In detail, the graph results of the external assessment provide a visual list of specific EE PM administrative areas which require particular attention for the focal company; these are (with comments added, derived from the question-level results inputted by the user):

- **Performance measurement leadership for each EE node (medium improvement required):** Senior executive leadership and continual management and responsibility for the implemented PM could be improved further in the focal company.

- **Performance measurement and operational results (high level improvement required):** The focal company is worried that the results being produced from the PM system in such areas as products, processes, and services, and operational results in general are not being developed to sufficiently refined levels, and need further enhancement.

- **Management of the performance measurement system (very high level improvement required):** The focal company is very worried about their current performance management levels: in particular, process and supplier measurement and the continued maintenance of EE measures are of heightened concern.

- **Human resources within performance measurement (medium improvement required):** The human touch, particularly at the lower levels of the organisation, must be improved within the focal company.

- **Customer focus (extremely high level improvement required):** All aspects of the customer perspective, from the measures utilised for today and those needed for tomorrow, to satisfaction and relationship measures, must be kept under active maintenance for the focal company.

Other areas in the external assessment checklist are deemed to be under control. From the above comments, it becomes clear that there are a number of sectors in which the focal company can improve its position in terms of EE PM, in particular in the active monitoring of the customer focus, a prime parameter of interest to parties outside the company that view the company's operations, which will probably have a beneficial impact upon some of the other parameters in place.

This case study will conclude with some of the comments of the focal company on the EE PM questionnaire outlined above in Table 3. Note that in the dashboard the EE PM questionnaire does not have any weighting procedures attached to its question parameters as in the case of the self-assessment and external assessment checklists dealt with above; rather, these functionalities of the questionnaire template have been disabled in the case of the EE PM questionnaire, in order that it can be used as a free-lance tool for the examination and analysis of only those areas of the questionnaire that are deemed to be of practical interest to the focal company. In general, the comments suggest that while the EE PM questionnaire is at its most useful when setting-up EE PM at first, it can be used as a valuable tool for prompting the user to think more about the whole idea of a holistic PM system and of the idea of integrating independent businesses; in other words, it promotes outside-of-the-four-walls-of-the-company thinking in its user, to consider, for example, the impact of the focal company upon its near neighbours in the value chain, or the negative effect that local optimisation may have upon other nodes, and the EE as a whole. Further, the tool was found to be of interest to those considering the strategic direction of the focal company: For many users, one of the most difficult aspects to imagine and to satisfactorily promulgate, is those factors that impinge upon the company from outside the company, that is, from the external environment; the EE PM questionnaire, it was found, helped in this direction by orientating the user to those areas of the external environment that would have a direct impact upon the company and its associated partners.

In general, the tool was found to supply a natural deficit in the knowledge of the general user, by quickly allowing them to orientate themselves to the concept of EE PM, its aims and priorities, and those of business integration, by supplying the related background thinking that, in many ways, explains the need for PM at the EE level; the questions themselves supply a latent background knowledge to the unfamiliar user. This effect was only heightened by the use of the questionnaire in the dashboard, which, with its user-friendly interface and colourful design, helped to maintain the user's interest, while not displaying too much information at one time. Most interesting of all was the unintended use made of the questionnaire by the focal company, who allowed *different* users to answer the questionnaire in their own way, and subsequently analysed the results of this exercise. It was found that the questionnaire was useful in bringing out not only differences of opinion among those who answered the questionnaire, but even very different core ideas as to what EE PM is and should mean to the company; without the questionnaire, these differences would not be known and therefore could not be resolved. Once they were brought to light, the personnel in the focal company could air their differences and a consensus could be reached.

Summary of the Case Study

The case study was performed at a focal company that is a first-tier supplier of component products to leading automotive companies in the European automotive industry, and was operating an interorganisational PM system. This made them ideal candidates to test the EE PM questionnaire, the EE PM self-assessment checklist, and the EE PM external checklist in their immediate value chain. Having performed the empirical evaluation, the focal company was surprised to find that the administrative tools very quickly outlined areas of their management policies, in relation to EE PM, that needed rethinking or redevelopment. In particular, four key areas were:

1.   The implementation of more concrete EE PM policies and objectives that span the value chain

2.   The need to continually monitor the needs and wishes of their customers, and to more efficiently capture these needs via performance measures

3.   The need for further education of EE PM to all relevant personnel in the company

4.   The need to improve current management levels of the implemented PM system at both the internal level and the EE level

Asked to rate the questionnaire and assessment checklist as part of an EE PM system, the focal company was, in general, very favourable, a reaction that was probably improved because the tools were embedded in a user-friendly and colourful dashboard system dedicated to EE PM. General concerns that were expressed, however, included:

•   A difficulty in determining the appropriate weights for the parameters of the self-assessment and external assessment checklists

•   A difficulty in determining the appropriate status on the Likert scales for the parameters of the self-assessment and external assessment checklists

•   Not possible to omit questions in the self-assessment and external assessment checklists if required

•   Assumptions sometimes taken with the tools, where necessary, of the thoughts and ideas of external parties

In selected implementations in other empirical cases, the benefits and limitations of the EE PM questionnaire, the EE PM self-assessment checklist, and the EE PM external checklist outlined in this case study, were broadly endorsed.

Conclusion

While there are signs that interorganisational PM activities are on the increase, the need for further research into the integration of PM legislation and administration into these initiatives is a neglected facet of the literature. Current attempts to depict EE PM activities are resulting in the setting-up of integrated relationships up and down the supply chain, while use of specialised decision support systems enables the development of EE-wide PM systems that are viable, flexible, and open to future enlargement. With these developments, however, comes the need for tighter integration of administration and legislation services for the PM system in the EE: A set of standardised administrative policies to allow efficient regulation, coordination, and monitoring of the EE PM system are a necessity if the initiative is to survive beyond the conceptual phase. In Folan and Browne's (2005a) approach, an EE host, with specialist powers to hold the administrative powers outlined above, is specified; this chapter has outlined a set of administrative PM questionnaires and assessments to facilitate the role of the EE host, as it attempts to control the PM integration issues that affect efficient EE operation. Three distinct tools were introduced: the extended enterprise performance measurement questionnaire; the extended enterprise performance measurement self assessment checklist; and the extended enterprise performance measurement external assessment checklist.

The use of these checklists and questionnaire in conjunction with Folan and Browne's (2005a) EE PM system may be imagined. Initially, the EE host prepares the background information for the EE PM system; the information may be tailored to the requirements of individual EE nodes. This information is then disseminated to the interested EE nodes where feedback (through the use of the EE PM questionnaire) may be obtained. This feedback may be instrumental in changing certain aspects of the EE PM system to suit the EE nodes. Once consensus has been reached on an EE PM system vision, the EE host may proceed to select those EE nodes that are required for participation; the external assessment checklist is useful for this purpose. Once selected, the EE nodes proceed to familiarise themselves with the EE PM system itself; when the EE nodes are satisfied that they have this at their command, they proceed to develop their EE PM systems at the internal-, supplier-, and customer-perspectives. Meanwhile, the EE host develops the EE measures for the EE-perspective and sends the various unaggregated measures to the individual node's EE-perspective. In situations where change is required to the EE PM system, the EE host may request an *assessment* of an individual EE node (for "out-of-bounds" reasons, etc.). Using the self-assessment checklist, the individual EE node performs a check of itself, and the results are fed back to the EE host. Ultimately, the final assessment (using the external assessment checklist) is performed on feedback from the EE node, and this analysis is, in turn, returned to the EE node involved, for corrective action (if required).

The empirical case study of the operation of the questionnaire and assessment checklists was found to broadly endorse their usefulness for the administrative purpose for which they were developed; however, this is not to say that the implementation was completely free from problems. These problems, which mainly lie in the area of trying to ensure precision in the answering of the questionnaire and assessment checklists, lies in the region of future work for these tools of EE PM business integration.

The concept of interorganisational PM allows practitioners to envisage integrated measurement interaction with any number of supply chain or EE nodes. However, while internally intra-organisational performance management is set at the company-wide level, externally issues are more difficult to legislate for. The use of checklists and questionnaires, such as those outlined above, help to limit the scope and administrative size of any EE PM system developed; they provide limits to the measures that may be selected and methods to update these; and they also provide idealised rules, regulations, and guidelines, as well as assessments for EE PM system development. There is a need for a continual development of EE PM tools that promote business integration in the long term.

References

Backhouse, C., & Burns, N. (1999). Agile value chains for manufacturing—implications for performance measures. *International Journal of Agile Management Systems, 1*(2), 76-82.

Basu, R. (2001). New criteria of performance management: A transition from enterprise to collaborative supply chain. *Measuring Business Excellence, 5*(4), 7-12.

Beamon, B. M. (1999). Measuring supply chain performance. *International Journal of Operations & Production Management, 19*(3), 275-292.

Bititci, U., Mendibil, K., Martinez, V., & Albores, P. (2005). Measuring and managing performance in extended enterprises. *International Journal of Operations & Production Management, 25*(4), 333-353.

Bititci, U. S., Martinez, V., Albores, P., & Mendibil, K. (2003). Creating and sustaining competitive advantage in collaborative systems: The what and the how. *Production Planning and Control, 14*(5), 410-424.

Brewer, P., & Speh, T. (2000). Using the balanced scorecard to measure supply chain performance. *Journal of Business Logistics, 21*(1), 75-93.

Browne, J. (1996). Extended enterprises, INTRANET, and SMEs. *Production Planning and Control, 8*(3), 207.

Browne, J., Sackett, P., & Wortmann, J. C. (1995). Future manufacturing systems—towards the extended enterprise. *Computers in Industry, 25*(3), 235-254.

Browne, J., & Zhang, J. (1999). Extended and virtual enterprises—similarities and differences. *International Journal of Agile Management Systems, 1*(1), 30-36.

Bullinger, H. J., Kuhner, M., & van Hoof, A. (2002). Analysing supply chain performance using a balanced measurement method. *International Journal of Production Research, 40*(15), 3533-3543.

Chalmeta, R., & Grangel, R. (2005). Performance measurement systems for virtual enterprise integration. *International Journal of Computer Integrated Manufacturing, 18*(1), 73-84.

Chan, F., & Qi, H. (2003). Feasibility of performance measurement system for supply chain: A process-based approach and measures. *Integrated Manufacturing Systems, 14*(3), 179-190.

Childe, S. J. (1998). The extended enterprise—a concept of co-operation. *Production Planning and Control, 9*(4), 320-327.

Clegg, B. (2003). The extended enterprise: A matrix framework for effective strategic operations management. In *Proceedings of the 20ᵗʰ International Manufacturing Conference, IMC 20*, Cork, Ireland (pp. 739-746).

Cullen, P. A. (2000). Contracting, co-operative relations, and extended enterprises. *Technovation, 20*(7), 363-372.

Dreyer, D. (2000). Performance measurement: A practitioner's perspective. *Supply Chain Management Review,* (September-October), 62-68.

Folan, P., & Browne, J. (2005a). Development of an extended enterprise performance measurement system. *Production Planning and Control, 16*(6), 531-544.

Folan, P., & Browne, J. (2005b). A review of performance measurement: Towards performance management. *Computers in Industry, 56*(7), 663-680.

Folan, P., Higgins, P., & Browne, J. (2006). A communications framework for extended enterprise performance measurement. *International Journal of Computer Integrated Manufacturing 19*(4), 301-314.

Gunasekaran, A., Patel, C., & McGaughey, R. E. (2004). A framework for supply chain performance measurement. *International Journal of Production Economics, 87*(3), 333-347.

Gunasekaran, A., Patel, C., & Tirtiroglu, E. (2001). Performance measures and metrics in a supply chain environment. *International Journal of Operations & Production Management, 21*(1/2), 71-87.

Holmberg, S. (2000). A systems perspective on supply chain measurements. *International Journal of Physical Distribution & Logistics, 30*(10), 847-868.

Jagdev, H., & Browne, J. (1998). The extended enterprise—a context for manufacturing. *Production Planning and Control, 9*(3), 216-229.

Jagdev, H., & Thoben, K. (2001). Anatomy of enterprise collaborations. *Production Planning and Control, 12*(3), 437-451.

Kaplan, R., & Norton, D. (1993, September-October). Putting the balanced scorecard to work. *Harvard Business Review, 71*(5), 134-147.

Kleijnen, J., & Smits, M. (2003). Performance metrics in supply chain management. *Journal of the Operational Research Society, 54*(5), 507-514.

Lapide, L. (2000, July-August). True measures of supply chain performance. *Supply Chain Management Review, 4*(3), 25-28.

Lebas, M. (1995). Performance measurement and performance management. *International Journal of Production Economics, 41*(1-3), 23-25.

Lohman, C., Fortuin, L., & Wouters, M. (2004). Designing a performance measurement system: A case study. *European Journal of Operational Research, 156*(2), 267-286.

Meyer, C. (1994, May-June). How the right measures help teams excel. *Harvard Business Review, 72*(3), 95-103.

Neely, A., Richards, H., Mills, J., Platts, K., & Bourne, M. (1997). Designing performance measures: A structured approach. *International Journal of Operations & Production Management, 17*(11), 1131-1152.

Prahalad, C. K., & Hamel, G. (1990, May-June). The core competence of the corporation. *Harvard Business Review, 68*(3), 79-91.

van Hoek, R. (1998). Measuring the unmeasureable—measuring and improving performance in the supply chain. *Supply Chain Management, 3*(4), 187-192.

Whicker, L., & Walton, J. (1996). Logistics and the virtual enterprise. *Logistics Focus, 4*(8), 7-10.

Wongrassamee, S., Gardiner, P., & Simmons, J. (2003). Performance measurement tools: The balanced scorecard and the EFQM excellence model. *Measuring Business Excellence, 7*(1), 14-29.

Zairi, M. (1994). *Measuring performance for business results*. London: Chapman & Hall.

Zimmermann, K. (2001). Using the balanced scorecard for interorganisational performance management of supply chains—a case study. In S. Seuring & M. Goldbach (Eds.), *Cost management in supply chains* (pp. 399-415). Heidelberg: Physica.

Chapter VIII

Process-Driven Business Integration Management for Collaboration Networks

Dominik Vanderhaeghen, Institute for Information Systems (IWi)
at the German Research Center for Artificial Intelligence (DFKI), Germany

Anja Hofer, Institute for Information Systems (IWi)
at the German Research Center for Artificial Intelligence (DFKI), Germany

Florian Kupsch, Institute for Information Systems (IWi)
at the German Research Center for Artificial Intelligence (DFKI), Germany

Abstract

In the chapter, a framework for cross-enterprise business integration management addressing the organizational and technical dimension is developed. Firstly, the authors identify basic characteristics of cross-organizational business processes whose complexity results in the need for an efficient and effective business integration management. Therefore, a holistic framework is focused, consisting of a view concept for knowledge management in collaboration networks, a three-tier architecture, and a process-oriented life-cycle model. The framework for business integration management offers the required methods to set up enterprise processes and ICT-support in collaboration networks. It proposes a management guideline for collaboration participants defining what, why, when, and how they might manage their business integration intra- and cross-organizationally.

Business Integration in the Value-Added Chain

Regarding the value-added chain of enterprises, a transition from an intra-organizational perspective, keeping value-creation within its own borders, towards a cross- or inter-organizational view, value-creation within a network of specialized firms, can be observed (Kanter, 1991). The growing importance of cooperation is a result of globalization in combination with the disappearance of political borders and, above all, technological advances caused mainly by the Internet (Scheer, Erbach, & Thomas, 2000; Scheer, Grieble, Hans & Zang, 2002). Thus, enterprises have to react to the raised innovation pressure and facilitate flexible collaboration on a global scale by aligning their business processes.

The borderless enterprise has been the subject of scientific discussion for years (Naisbitt, 1982; Picot, Wigand, & Reichwald, 1997). Current approaches addressing solutions to specific problems of dynamically interacting organizations are summarized under the term "*collaborative business (c-business)*" (Röhricht & Schlögel, 2001). It describes the Internet-based, interlinked collaboration of all participants in a value-added network, from the raw material supplier to the end-consumer (Scheer, Grieble, & Zang, 2003). Unlike former concepts regarding only small parts of the value chain, as for example, e-procurement, c-business incorporates all stages of added value (Scheer, Feld, & Zang, 2003).

The ability to network enterprises turns out to be a key success factor in c-business. As a consequence, *business integration* (Scheer et al., 2002) with a holistic view on networking solutions and their business value concerns both, economic-driven as well as information technology-driven aspects of collaboration networking. The link between evolving economic requirements towards the implementation with technology especially gains importance within collaborative environments with a growing heterogeneity of participating partners. Cross-organizational processes have to be designed, implemented, and managed sustainably. While, for example, the technological implementation (Linthicum, 2003) on the one hand, or the life cycle of cooperations (Liebhart, 2002) on the other hand, have already been intensively researched, too little consideration has been given to interconnecting, complexity-reducing management concepts. A rethinking from a pure technology-driven implementation or profit-driven business model discussion to an integrated view spanning from the conceptual level to the system blueprint is needed in order to reduce the inherent complexity and required efforts of business integration in cross-organizational business processes.

A management framework meeting these requirements provides a basis for a holistic and systematic Business Integration. This includes planning, design, and controlling of cross-organizational processes. A proposal for such a framework is being developed by the research projects "ArKoS—Architecture for Collaborative Scenarios" (Adam, Hofer, Zang, Hammer, Jerrentrup, & Levenbach, 2004) and "P2E2—Peer-to-Peer Enterprise Environment" (Kupsch & Werth, 2005). Existing business process management (BPM) methods and cooperation phase models are used as a foundation in the framework, regarding all necessary requirements for business integration from a business process-oriented view with state-of-the art implementation technology.

For a purpose-driven definition of requirements towards a process-oriented management of business integration, central objectives must be identified in order to specify efficient and effective management and implementation instruments. Due to its elementary importance in business networks, the *cross-organizational business process* may be seen as the initial point considering business integration issues. Hence, the authors exemplarily point out the basic characteristics of such processes motivating business integration management in the next section. The authors stress the need for appropriate management instruments on both an *organizational* as well as a *technical* dimension. The complexity which is emphasized by these upcoming examples, managing and implementing business integration through the management and implementation of cross-organizational processes, requires a business-driven reduction. The execution of business integration management activities has to be simplified within the scope of their intra- and cross-organizational application in an effective and efficient manner. Therefore, an appropriate framework which addresses the organizational as well as technical dimensions of business integration is developed in the following sections. The chapter ends with a conclusion and an outlook on future work.

Cross-Enterprise Business Process Integration

As the most characterizing part of c-business resp. collaboration networks, processes among two or more enterprise departments, branches, and also business partners are integrated (Schmitt, 2000). However, only subprocesses have been supported by business process management (BPM) in the past. Single subprocesses of collaborating enterprises have to be integrated on different layers. Process characteristics indicating differences between ordinary, *intra-* and *inter-*organizational business processes mainly base on two pillars:

- **Interorganizational business process flows** as tangible objects describing static and dynamic process elements and characteristics on the one hand;
- **Security and trust** as a fuzzy necessity for collaboration network design, implementation, and controlling

Both classes of characteristics are coexisting interdependently and complementarily. They are explained in the following.

Characteristics of Interorganizational Business Processes

Business Process Flows

Business processes include different flows as continuous, directed movements of data or information; goods and services; or currency between process objects as well as a determination of an underlying processing logic. These flows remain inside an enterprise, for instance, as a data flow between departments (e.g., internal transfer of bills). But they also cross enterprise borders and address external stakeholders (Hirschmann, 1998; Leimstoll, 2003; Thaler, 2001). A complex mesh of connections among the flows of individual and distributed process steps characterizes those inter- or cross-organizational flows. From an organisation's perspective, internal process steps are initiated with well-defined *interfaces* by external process events. Thus, the authors will have a closer look at interfaces implying flowing objects between different sending and receiving participants of different organizations in a collaborative business process.

Decentralization leads to high coordination efforts of cross-enterprise business processes. The circumstance results in an increasing number of organizational and IT-related (process) interfaces (Schmitt, 2000). Interfaces interlink activity-executing process objects as application systems or databases, but also employees via, for instance, data exchange. Such interfaces may be identified both internally (intra-organizationally) and externally (interorganizationally, e.g., between one enterprise and its business partners or customers) (Schubert, 2003). These *process interfaces* cause friction losses. They result from long lead times caused by redundant work, high coordination efforts, and competence breaks (Thaler, 2001). In the following, the authors focus on external interfaces only. They are divided into two main interface classes: process interfaces on an *organizational, human layer,* and on a *technical, machine-oriented layer.*

Organizational Interfaces

Enterprise-spanning business processes are characterized by interfaces concerning the organizational units involved in process executions (Hirschmann, 1998). Depending on cooperation forms, value-adding partners, which participate in cooperation, have different roles: Central cooperation instances, as they exist, for example, in supply chain management, define *organizational requirements* for cross-enterprise process design and execution, whereas electronic markets grant equal roles and autonomy to their value-adding participants (Wölfle, 2003). The existence of organizational interfaces has numerous impacts on the type of process execution and on the involved organizational control instances. From an organizational point of view, explicit responsibilities concerning "power structures" and explicit "control instances" have to be defined in enterprise-spanning business processes. They ensure a smooth process flow even across the borders of a single enterprise (Scheer et al., 2002). However, this turns out to be particularly complicated in cross-enterprise processes as these responsibilities are mostly non-existent or even unintentional due to the kind of cooperation. A lack of organizational regulations leads to increasing coordination efforts concerning the process execution (Hirschmann, 1998).

Technical Interfaces

Cross-enterprise integration and optimization of business processes aim at a minimization of interruptions in process flows caused by information and communication technology (Wölfle, 2003). In a cooperation scenario, the compatibility of application or information systems is required for a smooth cross-enterprise data and information exchange (Hirschmann, 1998). The benefits concerning an increase in efficiency and effectiveness is only achieved with a vast implementation of processes over different application systems (Wölfle, 2003). Thus, the technical layer of process execution considering IT interfaces as relevant process interfaces are described in the following in detail:

- **Heterogeneous IT infrastructures** may be identified as one central problem causing ineffective and inefficient process hurdles: Predefined standards for IT interfaces have to ensure that IT systems used can be integrated (Scheer, Grieble, Hans, & Zang, 2002). As various application systems of different software engineers are applied in different enterprises for heterogeneous purposes, the complexity of the process integration increases as a result of the heterogeneity of IT landscapes. However, systems have to be interlinked through suitable mechanisms to reach business objectives (Wölfle, 2003). Integration of heterogeneous application systems is addressed within the field of enterprise application integration (EAI) (Linthicum, 2003) on a rather technical layer.

- The number of existing **format mismatches**, which describes the frequency of changed communication media for the transmission of relevant information, may be seen as one resulting problem of IT heterogeneity. The manual transfer of information from a fax document (an order, for instance) to an online form of an ERP system may serve as an example. In the context of interorganizational business process controlling, the number of format mismatches can be used as a value for the analysis of the process as a whole (Bullinger, Lebender, Otto, & Weisbecker, 2003).

- The **use of different standards** may be identified as another relevant technical aspect within interorganizational business processes. The integration of IT systems requires standardized methods for the connection of different communication end points and IT interfaces respectively. With interface heterogeneity, integration efforts increase (Wölfle, 2003). Inefficiencies concerning the electronic exchange of data and information can be eliminated by the definition of central semantic and syntactic standards for exchange objects (for example, business documents) as well as transfer methods (e.g., transmission medium, or exchange protocols) (Müller-Lankenau, 2003). The complexity of a holistic process integration, caused by the multiplicity of potential business partners and IT systems to be integrated, is intensified by the existence of numerous specific and differently sophisticated standardization approaches (Wölfle, 2003). This has negative impacts on process integration efforts. Adequate measures reducing the complexity are required.

- Finally, **automation** of process steps is addressed with IT support as a primary objective in a cross-enterprise collaboration. A reduction of format mismatches is intended. With regard to process efficiency and effectiveness, improvements concerning process performance can be realized by the removal of manual process executions (Scheer Grieble, Hans, & Zang, 2002). Moreover, by defining automation as a valuable characteristic (key performance indicators) (Scheer & Jost, 2002), interorganizational processes can be analysed in a measurable manner (Bullinger, Lebender, Otto, & Weisbecker, 2003).

Security and Trust

Exchange of information between employees is complicated. Employees receive information willingly, but they only reveal them under individual circumstances (Wölfle, 2003). This aspect is even worse at a level of collaboration and interorganizational business processes. This information exchange is much more complicated due to cultural and mental aspects.

Collaborations are characterized by insecurities during many phases of the collaboration life cycle (Wehner, 2001). With the Internet as the central medium for information exchange and transfer, the network economy turns out to be more impersonal and insecure in practice. The electronic exchange of information is a weak point for hacker attacks. A disturbance of interorganizational partner relationships may result. Hence, *security and trust* can be regarded as particularly critical for an interorganizational process integration. Trust has to be regarded as an essential basis for an effective and efficient information exchange. It enables communication between business partners. The aspects described have to be regarded as key success factors for the realization of collaborative networks (Ratnasingam, 2003).

Regarding the design of cross-enterprise processes, enterprises rely on negotiations for the coordination and the discussion or avoidance of potential partner conflicts. As the communication among partners plays a major role in this context, *cultural* and *social discrepancies* have to be taken into account as well (Hirschmann, 1998). Thereby, organizations are characterized considerably by cultural imprints because of organizational behavior patterns and values (Scholz, 1997). Within international cooperations, the problem to find common agreements due to cultural (e.g., language, terminology, and understanding barriers, mental imprinting, legal distinctions) and temporal barriers (different time zones) by cooperating with acceptable coordination efforts is even aggravated (Wölfle, 2003).

Impacts on Collaboration Networks

From a high number of interfaces and resulting efforts concerning process coordination, explicit and purpose-driven description instruments are derived. From a conceptual point of view, an adequate graphical and model-based visualization of problems, requirements, and possible solutions is required.

To derive appropriate and relevant information for the design of integrated but heterogeneous IT landscapes, business process models have to be extended considering IT-related information. The crucial information of which system covers which part of a subprocess has to be specified explicitly, similarly to the description of organizational responsibilities. Moreover, interfaces have to be described in detail with special attributes marking heterogeneous systems (e.g., syntactical description of exchange formats as individual XML structures or supported standards) (Lebender, Ondrusch, Otto, & Renner, 2003) or necessary associations to related detail descriptions as sequence specification with UML sequence diagrams (Jeckle, Rupp, Hahn, Zengler, & Quiens, 2004).

Modeling and model exchange aiming at partner coordination have to be applied with reasonable efforts. Existing knowledge, cast in models, should be reused in order to save former investments (Vanderhaeghen, Zang, & Scheer, 2005) of, for example, business process reengineering (BPR), or software engineering (SE)-tasks (Vanderhaeghen, Zang, & Scheer, 2005). Furthermore, global information sharing with process models requires model integration and security mechanisms. Any flexible exchange of process data with heterogeneous description formats needs support in business integration. Process information has to be secured, and mechanisms to hide critical information in models towards business partners are required (Vanderhaeghen, Zang, & Scheer, 2005). Finally, adaptation mechanisms for the translation of business process data should be provided regarding a low-effort implementation.

Thus, all possible weak points disturbing cross-organizational business process flows ought to be analyzed in the design phase of a process, monitored during its implementation, as well as measured during process execution of enterprise-spanning business processes. A framework for business integration management requires necessary measures and instruments for a holistic solution based on business processes.

Framework for Business Integration Management

The presented framework, which is described in the following section, consists of three basic elements: a view concepts for knowledge management in collaboration networks, a three-tier architecture which defines the necessary instruments and tools for the management of business integration, and a dynamic life-cycle model for a process-oriented planning and implementation of business integration in collaboration networks.

Knowledge Views

As a foundation of the framework, existing business process management (BPM) methods and phase models are used. However, they have to be adapted to the specifications of collaborative scenarios. Especially because of its completeness of vision and its proven practicability, both in the scientific as well as the economic context, the *ARIS House* (Scheer, 1994) is accepted as a generic framework for business process management and serves as a basis for further considerations. The ARIS House describes a business process, assigning equal importance to the questions of organization, functionality, and the required documentation. First, it isolates these questions for separate treatment, in order to reduce the complexity of the field of description, but then all the relationships are restored using the control view introduced for this purpose.

The framework is based on the ARIS House. The approach divides it into a vertical axis of global knowledge of all collaboration partners and a horizontal axis of local knowledge of single participants (see Figure 1). The organization view and the output view are global knowledge, because a goal-oriented collaboration is impossible without them. At the time the interaction occurs between two partners, local knowledge is shared (bilaterally) in collaboration networks between the partners, that is, additional information, like data structures and semantics, are exchanged. Updates of the local knowledge do not influence the network, as network knowledge has to be available for all partners. This information is stored in the description of interfaces between the process modules of the partners (see further the following sections). Changes in the global network knowledge, and as a consequence, changes in the output and organization view have to be accessible to all partners immediately, for example, if a company leaves the network or if a product or service is no longer available within the network.

Global and local knowledge merge gradually in the step-by-step development of business integration process engineering. Following the distinction between global and local knowledge, a language is needed for the exchange of these knowledge fragments. Because the necessary

Figure 1. Global and local knowledge in value-added networks

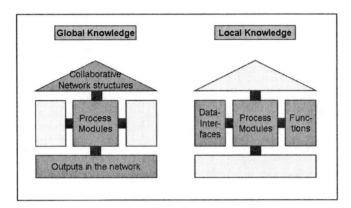

detail functions and data schemes of the respective enterprise are determined in the data and the function view, these are treated from a micro perspective. They are characterized by an intensive internal interdependence, whereas externally a standardized encapsulation has to be provided. Interfaces of the data and function views to other network participants become visible in the process view in the form of attribute correlations to process modules, and concern the technological field of the cooperation during the realization much more intensely than the conceptual one.

This technique enables the generation of *public* (visible to network partners) and *private* (enterprise-internal) *views* and levels of detail for management, process owner, and IT-experts out of a c-business model.

Architecture for Business Integration Management

The three-tier architecture is composed of three levels affiliated with each other (see Figure 7):

1. **Business integration strategy:** On a first *business integration strategy* level, strategic management activities concerning business integration in collaboration networks are considered. The question of core enterprise competences is directly associated with the question, "Which process remains in the enterprise, and which is supposed to be assigned to partner enterprises?" (Jost & Scheer, 2002, p. 37). Hence, partner definitions must be specified on a strategic collaboration level. From here, the need for specific business integration solutions evolves for the first time. It characterizes the scope of business integration solutions sustainably: Collaborative business processes are not planned in detail at the strategic level, but are designed as concentrated, high-level process modules. They combine a public knowledge about the collaborative processes that is shared by all participants. As a basic instrument, business process models for

Figure 2. Example of a c-business scenario

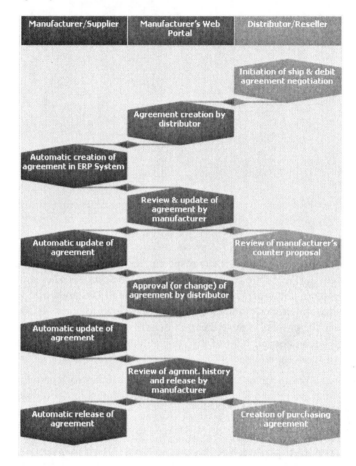

collaborative scenarios at the strategic level no longer act on the assumption of a chronological view of the process exclusively. They rather rely on a more role-based view to discover new value-added potentials in collaboration networks. As an example of an instrument for the business integration strategy management, c-business scenario-diagrams used by SAP for the description of mySAP.com collaboration scenarios may be mentioned. This practical notation aims at the representation of a collaboration of different enterprises and participants by means of an easily understandable method and the documentation of the value-added potentials resulting from ICT (Hack, 2000). This method can be integrated into the ARIS concept and combined with methods of classical business process and data modeling. Individual, intra-corporate views and levels of detail for the management, different departments, and IT experts can thereby be derived from a c-business model.

Figure 3. Generic process module chain

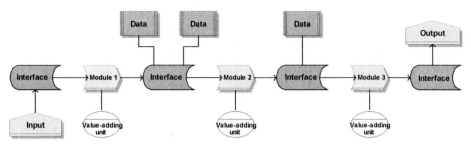

2.   **Business integration process engineering:** Detailed global and local processes have to be planned, designed, implemented, and controlled cross-organizationally on a second *business integration process engineering* level, considering the organizational and technical dimension. A global view on the collaborative process is generated in order to manage common processes and to reduce the complexity of integrating participating organizations into one virtual unit. In doing so, it is important that the partners provide access to all relevant information described as global knowledge, and at the same time are able to hide their business secrets. The so-called process module chain (PMC) (Grieble, Klein, & Scheer, 2002) facilitates appropriate modeling on a global, cross-organizational level, considering private business process definitions as, for example, event-driven process chain (EPC) or business process modeling notation (BPMN) models in the "back-end" of business integration management. The process module chain illustrates the whole global process over the complete cooperation, thus providing knowledge about the process to all organizational units involved in the process. Special importance should be attached to the editing and systematization of process information so that, on the one hand, only relevant data are extracted out of the mass of information and, on the other hand, private corporate data are hidden from other partners.

Figure 3 exemplarily shows a process module chain which is used for the extended illustration of cross-organizational processes, according to Klein, Kupsch, and Scheer (2004).

This process module chain at the highest abstraction level consists of individual process modules or building blocks, which again can contain deposited process module chains. Moreover, the single process modules are connected by magenta symbols which form the interfaces between the modules. They represent the output of the previous module and the input of the following module. The interface can thereby contain products/ services or information/data which are necessary for the process continuation.

The value-added chain diagram (VACD) serves as a representation of highly aggregated processes (Rosemann & Schwegmann, 2002). The value-added chain links illustrate the value-adding functions of an enterprise in a highly abstracted way. Furthermore, organizational units can be annotated to the links as executing subjects of the functions (McMichael, 2003). Both services and application systems can additionally be

Figure 4. Value-added chain diagram at different hierarchy levels

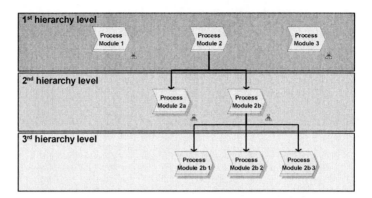

represented. The hierarchization of chain links and whole chains is symbolized by directed arrows.

Key performance-indicators are defined based on records, log files, time stamps, and so forth, which afterwards can be measured and analyzed by means of intelligent tools (Jost & Scheer, 2002) within the scope of business integration process engineering.

3.   **Business integration execution:** Instead of closed systems which have been used so far in an entrepreneurial environment, business integration requires the integration of different applications in a business network with a business-oriented view to execute collaboration activities. Cross-organizational business process models serve as the elementary initial point to implement cross-enterprise ICT solutions. Such technology-driven issues are addressed at the last layer called *business integration execution.*

Component-based, process-driven architectures which rely on fully-developed standards and interfaces can be seen as a state-of-the-art approach to overcome integration problems (McMichael, 2003). The term *process-driven* emphasizes the importance of process models created on the preliminary layer as the foundation for implementation. In this context, approaches such as the model-driven architecture (MDA) (Object Management Group, 2003) of the Object Management Group (OMG) are developed. On the execution layer, process models are used, for example, for the orchestration of Web services. Orchestration describes the composition of business objects in a process flow. In detail, it defines the complex interaction between business objects, including the business logic and execution order of the interactions and the exchange of messages between them. Based on predefined processes of the second architecture layer, business process models have to be translated into corresponding, execution-driven workflow models. After the mapping of the business process layer onto workflow-dimensions, the final process execution can be performed. To ensure interoperability between heterogeneous application systems, different approaches have to be considered with their strengths and shortcomings: middleware architectures, enterprise application integration (EAI), as well as service-oriented architectures with Web services.

Depending on strategic arrangements, an explicit engineering of business processes is obtained aiming at a high-value business integration. So, on the one hand, the design and implementation of intra- and cross-organizational business processes closely depends on the design of a collaboration network. On the other hand, executable processes cast in ICT implementations determine business process engineering. As a consequence, the different dimensions of the architecture for business integration management are connected through control loops, expressing interdependencies.

An integration of the core IT-systems is essential to guarantee a frictionless handling of business processes. In an optimal scenario, the result would be a seamless IT infrastructure that is completely transparent for all participants: It appears as one single system, supporting a service-oriented interaction of all relevant business processes. So far, the efforts to manage this integration are pooled with the keyword enterprise application integration (EAI). They contain a set of technologies and concepts such as middleware; extract, transform, load (ETL)-tools; and EAI-software that focus on a central planning and control of business application data in real-time. In Figure 5, an example for embedding an EAI server into the enterprise architecture is shown.

In the scenario in Figure 5, a central EAI-server manages the coordination of both control and data flow between the attached systems. In this manner, the number of required interfaces can be reduced, as there is only one bidirectional connection from each system to the server.

Figure 5. Intra-enterprise-integration

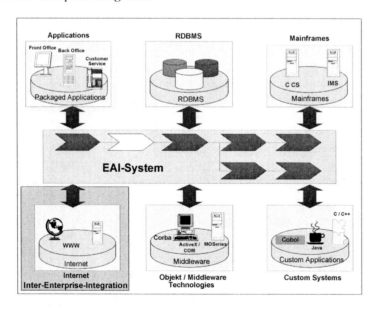

Because of the central component (ordinarily called *information hub*), these approaches cause several problems that complicate a reliable integration of numerous systems. Major well-reported problems are the following:

- **Single point of failure:** The Information Hub is the central node between the different applications. In case of a breakdown, all business processes are affected, possibly even inoperable.
- **Bottleneck:** All network traffic has to be forwarded through the information hub. This results in an extremely high load of data that has to be handled. In a situation of peak load, the system performance will crash down dramatically.
- **Configuration icebergs:** The EAI application must contain all relevant business transactions: The distribution of information has to be represented by formal rules for transformation and routing. Because of its complexity, interdependencies, and lots of exceptions, the number of configuration rules increases exponentially. This may cause insufficient and fault-prone integration solutions.

We consider EAI systems as mission critical applications whose blackout is associated with a substantial business risk. In recent years, awareness of cost-intensive administration and insufficient management of complex business application systems by centralistic approaches has arisen. New fields of research such as *Autonomic Computing* gave thought-provoking impulses to find better alternatives for an efficient management of business integration.

Assigning the *peer-to-peer paradigm* to the context of business integration means that all systems and components of an enterprise work in a self-organizing manner. This allows a flexible and dynamic coupling of applications and processes. Thereby, administration and integration costs can be reduced (Leymann, 2003). A basis for this approach is the non-centralized architecture of a peer-to-peer system which offers the following advantages:

- **Non-central topology:** The complete IT-infrastructure is defined by a variable number of flat (non-hierarchical) peers. Every peer offers (and receives) at least one service (e.g., generate an order, create an invoice, check consistency of data, dispose payment, etc.), where several peers may contain the same services.
- **Reliability:** There is no central component that may cause problems. If a peer breaks down, another peer with similar functionality can replace the broken peer. If a peer with unique services crashes, only those business process instances are affected that require that service.
- **Scalable performance:** The performance of the network can be enhanced nearly unlimited by appending additional peers. Already existing components do not have to be replaced.
- **Easy configuration:** It is no longer necessary to customize the whole EAI system by central transformation rules. Every peer only contains the business knowledge it requires to accomplish its functionality. The configuration of the complete architecture results from the sum of the configuration of the single peers.

- **Adaptive self-configuration:** By implementing intelligent search mechanisms, a peer can find the next service in the process chain by a broadcast into the network. If another peer is able to offer the desired service, it responds. From now on, this peer is part of the process chain and can accept tasks from other peers as well as delegating services to any peers.

While the advantages mentioned above are mainly of a technical nature, these features will not be sufficient to manage the complete field of business integration execution. There is also a high demand of adequate logical representations of business processes to provide an essential process-oriented view that focuses also economical aspects. The vision of both, distributed business processes that are associated with distributed IT-systems, allows an optimization of business processes as well as improving IT applications without interacting each other. In the following Figure, a P2P scenario is shown that gives a first impression:

Every application system (AS) that participates in the whole business process is encapsulated by a P2P-adapter. Every adapter enhances the functionality offered by the single components with additional Web services (WS) that allow a composition of very complex services by a dynamic interaction of different adapters. A peer can initiate business processes, embed local processes in the application flow, and even get embedded by other peers. It only has its own *local business knowledge*, but can also acquire *global business knowledge* by interacting with other peers. In this way, a comprehensive management of meta-data can be achieved without requiring centralistic client/server architectures.

The problem faced above is complex and versatile. Therefore, a highly structured and planned proceeding will be necessary. In contrast to other approaches, we follow a *meet in the middle* strategy, analysing the problem space and creating solving concepts both from the

Figure 6. Peer-to-peer approach towards business integration execution

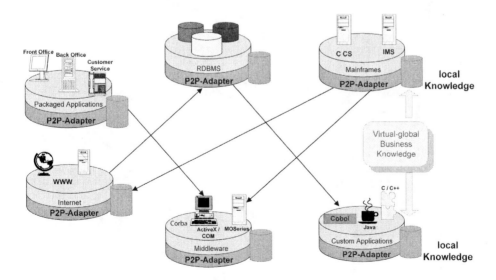

business-oriented as well as from the IT-oriented direction. This ensures that the conceptual solutions are suitable for the business problems targeted and that they are realizable with today's state-of-the-art technologies.

The business-oriented approach will evaluate the requirements of enterprises within internal or collaborative business integration scenarios. The main reference object here is the abstract business process that has to be supported. Thus, the business-oriented conceptual solution has to provide mechanisms and techniques on how to interconnect independent business processes using the P2P paradigm. The main challenge is the lack of a central coordination instance. As a logical consequence, appropriate business process negotiation techniques have to be developed.

Looking at the system-oriented problems, the main question is how to find a mapping between heterogeneous application systems in conformity with the business processes and rules to be supported. This does not only mean to connect interfaces, but also requires to find *reasonable matches* within concrete contexts, as well as to handle a reliable control of the interaction.

Peer-to-peer technologies have been proven to be very flexible and robust. From the authors' point of view, they seem to be an appropriate approach. Hence, new methods and algorithms for a distributed interface and interaction management will be created using the P2P paradigm. The idea is to enable an auto-configuration of the interaction between two independent application systems that succeeds to predefined business processes and that is also compliant to existing, constraining business rules.

Figure 7. Three-tier business integration management architecture

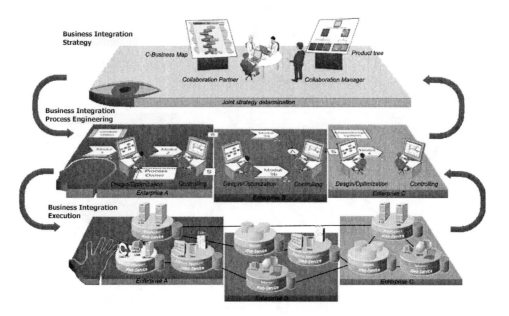

Finally, only developing the two solving concepts described above is not sufficient, as there are strong interdependencies between the business- and system-layer. The formation of business process chains within business integration use cases is always limited by the capabilities of the existing applications supporting the business processes. On the other hand, applications themselves can only be interconnected in a way that the combination of systems is realizing a predefined business process.

Hence, a relationship between the two partial solutions has to be found and specified. The combination of these three concepts will be a conceptual methodology for a dynamic binding of business processes to the behavior of the distributed environment via a semi-automatic reconfiguration in case of need. Figure 7 depicts the three-tier architecture for business integration management.

Life Cycle for Business Integration Management

The third element of the business integration management framework is addressed in a dynamic, time-centric perception. The life-cycle model serves as a manual for the process-oriented setting-up and operation of collaboration networks. Using a consistent phase model and standardized modeling methods increases transparency and structuring of collaborations and creates a basis for communication between participants, including management that lays down strategies, process-owners in the departments, and IT-experts that integrate the different application systems. Thus, the organizational and technical dimension of business integration is considered in one common life cycle. The model is a fusion of classic phase, models with life-cycle models of virtual enterprises (Mertens & Faisst, 1995). The resulting dynamic model is consistent with the structure-oriented business integration management architecture and represents a cyclical approach.

Prior to the use of the architecture is an *awareness* (pre-phase) of one or more enterprises that they can profit by collaboration with complementary core competence partners. *Exploring* partner competences and suitable collaboration compositions (pre-phase) precedes the first main phase *strategy partner analysis* or formation phase. This is also referred to as initiation and agreement of the enterprise network. The collaboration partners are determined by the shared goals of the collaboration and the aspired win-win situation of all partners. The joint aims of the collaboration have to be defined as synthesis of individual economic objectives. To facilitate a collaborative service or product delivery, graphical notations, like product models, are used in this stage for the determination of a common service or product bundle. Having completed the strategy finding, in the second main phase, *local to-be-concept*, an existing or a new local as-is model and the global to-be concepts of business processes are compared. According to predefined conditions about collective product creation, feasible cross-organizational business processes are derived. Each partner considers their part in the inter-enterprise process. Starting with process modeling and optimization over process controlling up to implementation, the processes involved are aligned with the requirements of the collaborative scenario agreed on in the former phase. In the third main phase *global to-be-concept*, coordinated public parts are allocated over the network, establishing a collective to-be concept. Every partner is able to connect their own private model with every other public process model. Every partner gains their partial view of the collaborative process or, in

Figure 8. Life-cycle model

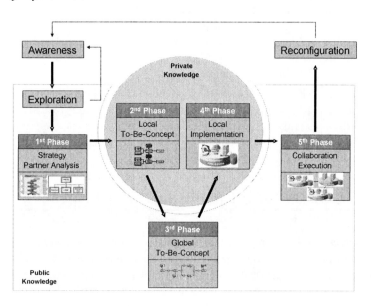

other words, a virtual process chain of the whole collaboration is designed. Global knowledge is described in a public interface, which can be provided by a standardized representation as, for instance, BPMN. The public processes as well as the message formats and contents can be formally defined by B2B protocols as RosettaNet or ebXML. Furthermore, the semantic combination of models of the different partners is necessary. The integrated collaborative business process model enables all partners to configure their application systems locally in a fourth main phase called *local implementation*. Reference systems for interfaces are provided by interface definitions of the collective to-be concept. Now every partner is prepared for the execution of interactions within the collaborative framework. That is the transition to the fifth main phase *collaboration execution*. Based on bilateral coordination, interacting information systems are able to communicate by using standardized protocols and interfaces. Transactions are arranged and executed. The aim of this phase is to support collaboration through the appropriate use of ICT. That requires primarily the configuration of interfaces and the implementation of cross-organizational workflows; at the same time, a permanent monitoring and adaption of the collaboration, based on business ratio defined in the conception phase, must be assured (Scheer, Grieble, & Zang, 2003). In order to automate cross-organizational processes the conceptual models are transformed into formal models applied as configuration data for the orchestration of business objects. The applications of the partners have to communicate bilaterally to negotiate the interface specifications based on the formal models (see Figure 8)

After the collaboration project ends, companies regroup or split and *reconfigurate* themselves. Hence, the life cycle returns to its starting position, *awareness* (pre-/post-phase).

Conclusion

The outlined framework for business integration management offers the necessary instruments to set up enterprise processes and ICT-support in collaboration networks. It proposes a management guideline for collaborating enterprises defining *what, why, when,* and *how* they might manage their *business integration* in collaboration networks. With the different approaches, especially the static three-tier architecture and the dynamic life cycle, the authors aim at a holistic and sustainable treatment for managing business integration intra- and cross-organizationally. In the chapter, the authors have presented basic framework elements which are based on the characteristics of cross-organizational business processes. As a result of high complexity in handling such processes in collaboration networks, the need for business integration originally arises. Appropriate solutions are necessarily needed in order to address the properties of collaboration processes in an organizational and technical dimension. With the framework for business integration management, the authors address both, people and machines, acting operational as well as for planning purposes. A few basic examples emphasizing the scope of requirements and solutions were given throughout all sections.

The presented framework has been developed within the scope of the research projects *ArKoS* and *P2E2,* funded by the Federal Department for Education and Research (BMBF). The competence centre business integration (CCBI) at the Institute for Information Systems (IWi) at DFKI facilitates synergies concerning coherent research of different research projects. By clustering national and international research projects, current research problems are addressed in a holistic view on economical and IT-related topics. Accordingly, the outlined framework results from research merged from both projects aiming at a completeness of vision.

References

Adam, O., Hofer, A., Zang, S., Hammer, C., Jerrentrup, M., & Leinenbach, S. (2004). *Architecture for collaborative business process management—enabling dynamic collaboration.* Paper presented at the European Conference on Product and Process Modeling (ECPPM 2004), Balkema, Istanbul, Turkey.

Bullinger, H. J., Lebender, M., Otto, B., & Weisbecker, A. (2003). Unternehmensübergreifende Prozessintegration für den elektronischen Geschäftsverkehr. In Kersten, W. (Ed.), *E-Collaboration—Prozessoptimierung in der Wertschöpfungsketten* (pp. 59-82, p. 61, pp. 66-78, p. 68). Wiesbaden: Dt. Univ.-Verl.

Grieble, O., Klein, R., & Scheer, A.-W. (2002). Modellbasiertes Dienstleistungsmanagement (p. 22). In A. –W. Scheer (Ed.), *Veröffentlichungen des Instituts für Wirtschaftsinformatik,* No. 171, Saarbrücken.

Hack, S. (2000). Collaborative business scenarios – Wertschöpfung in der Internetökonomie. In A. –W. Scheer (Ed.), *E-business—Wer geht? Wer bleibt? Wer kommt?* (pp. 85-100, p. 88 et seq.). 21. Saarbrücker Arbeitstagung für Industrie, Dienstleistung und Verwaltung. Heidelberg: Physica-Verlag.

Hirschmann, P. (1998). *Kooperative Gestaltung unternehmensübergreifender Geschäftsprozesse* (p. 39, p. 66, pp. 69-70, pp. 77-80). Wiesbaden: Gabler.

Jeckle, M., Rupp,C., Hahn, J., Zengler, B., & Queins, S. (2004). *UML 2 glasklar* (p. 323 et seq.). München: Hanser.

Jost, W., & Scheer, A. -W. (2002). Geschäftsprozessmanagement: Kernaufgabe einer jeden Unternehmensorganisation. In W. Jost & A. -W. Scheer (Eds.), *ARIS in der Praxis: Gestaltung, Implementierung und Optimierung von Geschäftsprozessen* (pp. 33-44). Berlin: Springer.

Kanter, R. M. (1991). Transcending business boundaries: 12,000 world managers view change. *Harvard Business Review, 69*(3), 151-164.

Klein, R., Kupsch, F., & Scheer, A. -W. (2004). Modellierung inter-organisationaler Prozesse mit Ereignisgesteuerten Prozessketten. In A. -W. Scheer (Ed.), *Veröffentlichungen des Instituts für Wirtschaftsinformatik*, No. 178, Saarbrücken.

Kupsch, F., & Werth, D. (2005). Integrating business processes with peer-to-peer technology. In *Proceedings of the First International Conference on Interoperability*, Geneva, Switzerland (pp. 277-289). London: Springer.

Lebender, M., Ondrusch, N., Otto, B., & Renner, T. (2003). *Business integration software: Werkzeuge Anbieter, Lösungen*. Fraunhofer-Institut für Arbeitswirtschaft und Organisation IAO (Ed.). Stuttgart: Fraunhofer IRB Verlag.

Leimstoll, U. (2003). Kaved AG (Informing AG)—Elektroindustrie. In P. Schubert, R. Wöfle, & W. Dettling (Eds.), *E-business integration: Fallstudien zur Optimierung elektronischer Geschäftsprozesse* (pp. 67-80, p. 73). München et al: Hanser.

Leymann, F. (2003). Web services: Distributed applications without limits. In G. Weikum, H. Schöning, & E. Rahm, (Eds.), *Proceedings of the 10th Conference of Databases for Business, Technology und Web (BTW 2003)* (LNI 26). Bonn: Gesellschaft für Informatik.

Liebhart, U. E. (2002). *Strategische Kooperationsnetzwerke: Entwicklung, Gestaltung und Steuerung.* Wiesbaden: Dt. Univ.-Verl.

Linthicum, D. S. (2003). *Enterprise application integration* (4th ed.). Boston: Addison-Wesley.

McMichael, C. (2003). Business process integration may eclipse EDI, EAI. *HP Chronicle, 17*(6), p. 1, p. 6.

Mertens, P., & Faisst, W. (1995). Virtuelle Unternehmen—eine Organisationsstruktur für die Zukunft? *Technologie & Mangement, 44*(2), pp. 61-68.

Müller-Lankenau, C. (2003). Interessengemeinschaft Datenverbund für die Haustechnik IGH. In P. Schubert, R. Wöfle, & W. Dettling (Eds.), *E-business integration: Fallstudien zur Optimierung elektronischer Geschäftsprozesse* (pp. 123-136, p. 128). München: Hanser.

Naisbitt, J. (1982). *Megatrends: Ten new directions transforming our lives* (6th ed.). New York: Warner Books.

Object Management Group. (2005). *OMG model driven architecture*. Retrieved December 12, 2005, from http://www.omg.org/mda/

Picot, A., Wigand, R., & Reichwald, R. (1997). *Information, organization, and management—expanding markets and corporate boundaries*. Chichester: Wiley.

Ratnasingam, P. (2003). *Inter-organizational trust for business-to-business e-commerce* (pp. 2-4, p. 3). Hershey: IBM Press.

Röhricht, J., & Schlögel, C. (2001). *C-business: Erfolgreiche Internetstrategien durch collaborative business am Beispiel mySAP.com*. München: Addison-Wesley.

Rosemann, M., & Schwegmann, A. (2002). Vorbereitung der Prozessmodellierung. In J. Becker, M. Kugeler, & M. Rosemann (Eds.), *Prozessmanagement: Ein Leitfaden zur prozessorientierten Organisationsgestaltung.* (3rd ed., pp. 47-94). Berlin: Springer.

Scheer, A. -W. (1994). *Business process engineering: Reference models for industrial enterprises* (2nd ed.). Berlin: Springer.

Scheer, A. -W., Grieble, O., Hans, S., & Zang, S. (2002). Geschäftsprozessmanagement—the 2nd wave. *IM Information Management & Consulting, 17*(special issue), pp. 9-15, p. 11, p. 12.

Scheer, A. -W., & Jost, W. (2002). Geschäftsprozessmanagement: Kernaufgabe einer jeden Unternehmensorganisation. In A. -W. Scheer & W. Jost (Eds.), *ARIS in der Praxis: Gestaltung, Implementierung und Optimierung von Geschäftsprozessen* (pp. 33-44, p. 43). Berlin: Springer.

Scheer, A. -W., Erbach, F., & Thomas, O. (2000). E-Business—Wer geht? Wer bleibt? Wer kommt? In A. -W. Scheer (Ed.), *E-business—Wer geht? Wer bleibt? Wer kommt?* (pp. 3-45). 21. Saarbrücker Arbeitstagung 2000 für Industrie, Dienstleistung und Verwaltung. Heidelberg: Physica-Verlag.

Scheer, A. -W., Feld, T., & Zang, S. (2003). Vitamin C für Unternehmen—Collaborative business. In K. Küting, & H. -C. Noack (Eds.), *Der große BWL-Führer: Die 50 wichtigsten Strategien und Instrumente zur Unternehmensführung*. Frankfurt am Main: Frankfurter Allg. Buch im FAZ-Inst.

Scheer, A. -W., Grieble, O., & Zang, S. (2003). Collaborative business management. In W. Kersten (Ed.), *E-collaboration—Prozessoptimierung in der Wertschöpfungskette* (p. 30 et seq.). Wiesbaden: Dt. Univ.-Verl.

Scheer, A. -W., Herrmann, K., & Klein, R. (2004). Modellgestütztes service engineering—Entwicklung und Design neuer Dienstleistungen. In M. Bruhn & B. Stauss (Eds.), *Dienstleistungsinnovationen: Dienstleistungsmanagement Jahrbuch 2004.* Wiesbaden: Gabler.

Schmitt, R. (2000). *Unternehmensübergreifender Engineering Workflow: Verteilte Produktentwicklung auf der Grundlage eines parameterbasierten Daten- und Prozessmanagements*. TU Clausthal.

Scholz, C. (1997). *Strategische Organisation: Prinzipien zur Vitalisierung und Virtualisierung* (pp. 225-229). Landsberg/Lech: Moderne Industrie.

Schubert, P. (2003). E-business integration. In P. Schubert, R. Wölfle, & W. Dettling (Eds.), *E-business integration: Fallstudien zur Optimierung elektronischer Geschäftsprozesse* (pp. 1-22, p. 5, p. 7). München: Hanser.

Thaler, K. (2001). *Supply chain management: Prozessoptimierung in der logistischen Kette* (3rd ed., pp. 43-44, p. 46, p. 49, p. 76, p. 95, p. 117). Köln: Fortis Verlag.

Vanderhaeghen, D. et al. (2005). XML-based transformation of business process models—enabler for collaborative business process management. In M. Nüttgens & J. Mendling (Eds.), *XML4BPM 2005, Proceedings of the 2nd GI Workshop XML4BPM—XML for Business Process Management at 11th Conference Business, Technology, and Web (BTW 2005)* (pp. 81-94). Karlsruhe: SUN Site Central Europe (CEUR).

Vanderhaeghen, D., Zang, S., & Scheer, A.-W. (2005). Interorganisationales Geschäftsprozessmanagement durch Modelltransformation. In A.-W. Scheer (Ed.), *Veröffentlichungen des Instituts für Wirtschaftsinformatik*, Saarbrücken (Vol. 182, pp. 6-7).

Wehner, J. (2001). Projektnetzwerke—Neue Unternehmensstrukturen und neue Qualifizierungen. In M. Rohde, W. Rittenbruch, & V. Wulf (Eds.), *Auf dem Weg zur virtuellen Organisation: Fallstudien, Problembeschreibungen, Lösungskonzepte* (pp. 33-54, p. 41). Heidelberg: Physica-Verlag.

Wölfle, R. (2003). Stellenwert von E-Business-Integrationsprojekten in Unternehmen. In P. Schubert, R. Wölfle, & W. Dettling (Eds.), *E-business integration: Fallstudien zur Optimierung elektronischer Geschäftsprozesse* (pp. 22-38, p. 27, p. 29, p.34, p. 37). München: Hanser.

Chapter IX

The Role of Ambiguity in the Transfer of Knowledge within Organizational Networks

Jennifer Priestley, Kennesaw State University, USA

Subhashish Samaddar, Georgia State University, USA

Abstract

Organizations join multi-organizational networks in part to mitigate environmental uncertainties and to access knowledge. However, the transfer of knowledge cannot be assumed simply as a function of network membership. Researchers in the area of knowledge management have identified several factors that have been found to affect the transfer of knowledge within, between, and among organizations. This chapter investigates specifically how organizational ambiguity impacts the transfer of knowledge within multi-organizational networks. The authors explore the effects of causal ambiguity, defined as the ambiguity related to inputs and factors, in a multi-organizational context, and discuss the existence of a previously undefined ambiguity, the ambiguity related to outcomes or "outcome ambiguity." The authors provide a discussion on why outcome ambiguity is particularly relevant when multiple organizations are engaged in a network, where the objective is access to knowledge.

Introduction

Firms engaged in *multi-organizational networks* have been found to benefit from network-wide *knowledge transfer* and sharing which may not be available to a non-networked firm operating independently (Argote, 1999; Darr, Argote, & Epple, 1995; Dyer, 1997). However, membership alone does not guarantee the transfer of knowledge among networked entities. The degree to which transfer occurs can be contingent upon member organizations' ability to remove or abate systemic constraints (Argote, 1999) or *isolating mechanisms* (Knott, 2002). One of these constraints is represented by the *ambiguities* or uncertainties that can be present when multiple organizations become involved in knowledge transfer. Ambiguities can make the transfer of knowledge difficult (Knott, 2002; Mosakowski, 1997), thereby mitigating some of the expected benefits of network participation.

It should be noted that a multi-organizational network is more complex to study than is an intra-organizational or dyadic setting. Simmel (1950), who studied social relationships, found that social triads (and relationships involving more than three entities) had fundamentally different characteristics than did dyads. First, there is no majority in a dyadic relationship. In any group of three or more, an individual organization can be pressured by the others to suppress their individual interests for the interests of the larger group, making the manifestation of the governance structure and internal competitiveness of such networks complex and their influences on knowledge transfer interesting but difficult to understand. The fact that organizations have more bargaining power in a dyad than in a network, and the fact that a network can offer more gaming possibilities, can confound such difficulty. If one member withdraws from a dyad, the dyad disappears; this is not true in a network. Finally, third parties represent alternative and moderating perspectives when disagreements arise. As a result of these differences, multi-organizational networks are more complex, and relevant ambiguities in knowledge transfer may play out differently at the network level than at an intra-organizational or dyadic level.

Informed by the knowledge management and organizational management literature regarding ambiguity, this chapter will begin with a discussion of *causal ambiguity* and how it has been shown to affect knowledge transfer in an intra-organizational context. Based upon this discussion, logical extensions will be made regarding how causal ambiguity would be expected to affect knowledge transfer within an interorganizational network context. This chapter will then make the argument that general discussions on ambiguity, including specific discussions on causal ambiguity, still leave a conceptual gap regarding the ambiguities related to ultimate outcomes that networked organizations would be expected to experience as a result of transferring knowledge outside of their boundaries. In response, the factor of *outcome ambiguity* will be described in an effort to address this gap in the extant literature. Finally, the developments in this chapter are discussed, with an emphasis on raising issues of interest to both researchers engaged in organizational learning and knowledge management, as well as to practitioners engaged in human resources and in management of entities within multi-organizational networks.

Ambiguity and Knowledge Transfer

Economic perspectives such as the knowledge-based view of the firm (Grant, 1997; Kogut & Zander, 1992, 1996) treat knowledge as an asset that will move unencumbered and without cost within and among organizations; although knowledge is recognized as an asset, unlike other assets, its transferability is considered to have no associated costs (von Hippel, 1994). As von Hippel went on to describe, this may not be the case. Knowledge, like most organizational resources, has been found to be "sticky," and its transfer is difficult (Szulanski, 1996). There is a lot that is unknown regarding what makes interorganizational knowledge transfer difficult. What is known, however, is that this process is most generally constrained by ambiguities. Simonin (1999) determined that when the degree of ambiguity is high, the difficulties associated with "repatriating and absorbing competencies" are limited. However, Simonin's work addressed ambiguity in its most general form, and did not differentiate among different forms of ambiguity or how these forms ultimately impact interorganizational knowledge transfer. As will be demonstrated in this chapter, two specific forms of ambiguity can be isolated and better understood within the context of interorganizational knowledge transfer, thereby focusing Simonin's more general treatment of ambiguity.

- **Causal ambiguity:** When knowledge is causally ambiguous, transfer is difficult if not impossible. Causal ambiguity has been used to explain the ambiguity related to the inputs and factors used to generate a known outcome. Here, the outcome is known but the causes are ambiguous, increasing the difficulty associated with knowledge transfer. The conclusion that a firm cannot transfer knowledge of ambiguous inputs or factors that generate a known outcome is well established in an intra-organizational context (Mosakowski, 1997; Szulanski, 1996). At the network level, when causes of an outcome are not clear but the outcome itself is repeatable (i.e., knowledge is causally ambiguous) by the source firm(s), the situation is analogous to what is known as "asset specificity" in transaction costs economics. Asset specificity refers to the relative lack of transferability of assets intended for use in a given transaction to other uses. Knowledge, when causally ambiguous but already known to be useful to the source, will tend to be specified to the source, thereby contributing to the difficulties associated with interorganizational knowledge transfer within a network.

- **Outcome ambiguity:** Causal ambiguity represents an uncertainty about the *causal factors* or *inputs* that generate known *outcome(s)*. However, what if the uncertainty rests with the outcome(s) rather than with the inputs or factors? Specifically, what if the eventual outcome is unknown or unknowable to the knowledge source? The ambiguity surrounding this scenario has not yet been addressed by the extant literature.

Where uncertainty has been addressed, researchers have treated the operating environment exogenous to the firm as highly generalized, without concern for the specific sources of uncertainty (Gerloff, Kanoff, & Bodensteiner, 1991; Milliken, 1987). And although organizations join large-scale multi-organizational networks, in part to satisfy their need to cope with environmental uncertainty (Gulati & Gargiulo, 1999), participation in a network produces unintended consequences of an increased uncertainty related to the very relationships within the network developed to mitigate uncertainty.

The existing gap is characterized by a lack of understanding of the uncertainties regarding how the behavior of one organization will affect the perspectives of another organization, which are both members of the same multi-organizational network, and specific constituents within an environment. In an effort to develop a clearer understanding of how ambiguity ultimately affects multi-organizational knowledge transfer, this chapter attempts to isolate the specific uncertainty that is present in a multi-organizational domain, "outcome ambiguity."

The concept of outcome ambiguity is a factor that influences the transfer of knowledge within a multi-organizational network. It is important to note that because the knowledge of the factors or inputs is considered to be known, the degree to which this knowledge is observable (i.e., tacit or explicit) is less relevant. The focus here is on the difficulty associated with the transfer of knowledge, rather than on the knowledge itself, as a function of the ambiguity associated with the unknown (or unknowable) outcome. In addition, the focus here is not on outcomes not associated with the transfer of knowledge, although it is acknowledged that ambiguous outcomes not related to interorganizational knowledge transfer would exist. This chapter will distinguish between two sources of outcome ambiguity, which may exist separately or in combination.

The first source of outcome ambiguity is the "known-ness" of the knowledge in question. Szulanski (1996) develops the concept of "*unproven-ness*" or unknown-ness in his work examining the factors related to intra-organizational knowledge transfer difficulty. Unproven-ness is explained to be present when the knowledge in question has no previous record of past usefulness (i.e., the outcomes are unknowable). For example, knowledge of a well-established operational best practice would be considered to be proven, with a finite or bounded set of possible applications. Alternatively, the discovery of a new chemical compound, for example, would be considered to be unproven knowledge, with an infinite or unbounded set of possible applications. When knowledge is unproven and the set of possible applications is unbounded, a higher degree of outcome ambiguity, and therefore of knowledge transfer difficulty, would be expected.

The second source of outcome ambiguity is the uncertainty embedded within the relationship between the source organization and the recipient organization(s), and is particularly relevant in the multi-organizational context. The basic premise is that the recipient organization(s) can put the received knowledge to more than one use. That is, it (they) can choose from multiple possible actions to follow once the knowledge has been received. There are two primary concepts that contribute to the manifestation of uncertainty in this relationship: *partner protectiveness* and *trust*.

Partner protectiveness, as described by Simonin (1999), is defined as the degree of protectiveness a knowledge source assigns to its knowledge base, including patents, contracts, and rules for sharing. Hamel (1991) explains that some partners in alliances (and networks) make their knowledge less transparent than others, creating situations dominated by asymmetry. Similarly, Szulanski (1996) found that lack of motivation due to fear of losing ownership, inadequate incentives, or a lack of willingness to allocate appropriate resources, all contributed to knowledge transfer difficulty. Where competition or potential for competition may exist, a similar lack of enthusiasm for knowledge transfer may exist for a fear of opportunistic behavior. Although it may initially appear to be counterintuitive for organizations to engage in networks where opportunistic behavior could exist, consider the VISA network where highly competitive banks voluntarily network for the purposes of lower transaction costs and mitigated risks associated with research and development. In this type of environment, where the possibility of opportunistic behavior exists, the number of elements in the knowledge application set increases and potentially becomes unbounded. This is true because, unlike a situation defined by no competition or a limited probability of opportunism, the knowledge source cannot limit the possible outcomes associated with knowledge transfer, thereby contributing to increased outcome ambiguity.

Trust represents the second component of the relationship between the knowledge source and the recipient. Across the many definitions of trust, the common themes of risk, expectations, and a concept of voluntary vulnerability are consistently present:

> ... the willingness of a party to be vulnerable to the actions of another party based upon the expectation that the other will perform a particular action important to the trustor, irrespective of the ability to monitor or control that other party. (Mayer, Davis, & Schoorman, 1995, p. 712)

Trust deals with the source's present beliefs about the recipient(s) upon which it will then base its future actions with the recipient (Hosmer, 1995; Zucker, 1986). Researchers have suggested that trust is a functional prerequisite for knowledge exchange (Allee, 2002; Lewis & Weigert, 1985). And trust, relative to price and authority, is the most effective mechanism to facilitate the transfer of knowledge resources within and between organizations, in part because the presence of trust decreases situational uncertainty (Adler, 2001). However, Ford (2002) points out that cooperation can (and does) occur without trust, provided that the risk of an undesirable outcome is low. Korczynki (1996) found in a study of the UK construction industry, that "low trust network forms" enabled cost improvements, but not knowledge transfer. Alternatively, "high trust network forms" have been found to excel at transferring knowledge (Adler, 2001). Facing opportunistic threats, which contribute to an unbounded set of possible actions of the recipients, as might be expected in the former, firms will prefer to retain their knowledge at the expense of the network, rather than risk engagement in unknown scenarios where their shared knowledge could be used to their detriment (Walker, 1995).

Figure 1. Typology of outcome ambiguity

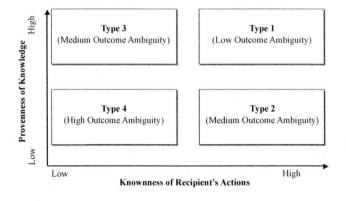

Figure 1 provides a framework based on the two sources of outcome ambiguity discussed above: the proven-ness of the knowledge in question and the certainty with which the knowledge source understands the actions of the knowledge recipient.

In a scenario where knowledge is proven and the actions of the knowledge recipient can be considered to be known, the scenario is one of Type 1, or low outcome ambiguity. An example of Type 1 outcome ambiguity could be represented by a network of hotel franchises who share well-documented check-in procedures. In this scenario, the knowledge in question is proven, creating a bounded knowledge application set. In addition, through limited partner protectiveness practices, the duration of the relationship(s) and/or through trust (or trust-like behaviors facilitated by a strong centralized governance structure with the authority to punish opportunistic behavior), the actions of the recipient would be relatively well understood. Consequently, the overall set of outcomes is considered to be bounded, creating the least amount of outcome ambiguity (Type 1).

On the other extreme, if the knowledge in question is unproven and the actions of the knowledge recipient are unknown and not mitigated by the threat of a strong central governance structure, the scenario is considered to be one of Type 4, or high outcome ambiguity. Where the two element sets are both unbounded, the overall set of outcomes is also considered to be unbounded. And, where the possible outcomes are infinite and unknown, outcome ambiguity is considered to be high. An example of Type 4 outcome ambiguity could be represented by a newly-organized network of pharmaceutical firms who co-discover a compound that inhibits the growth of certain types of cancer cells. In this scenario, the set of knowledge applications is unbounded because the finding is new and unproven. In addition, the actions of the players could be unbounded, in part because the network is new (duration of relationships is limited), partner protectiveness may not be fully understood (especially if the firms are in competition), and trust may exist only as far as contracts or a network governing authority will punish for opportunistic actions.

In scenarios where one element set is bounded and one is unbounded, outcome ambiguity will fall somewhere between low (Type 1) and high (Type 4). However, the scenario where the knowledge in question is unproven and the actions of the recipient(s) is (are) known (Type 2) is not the same as the scenario where the knowledge in question is proven and the actions of the recipient(s) is (are) unknown (Type 3); the contributors of their uncertainties are quite different. Type 2 outcome ambiguity is characterized by unbounded applications of the knowledge, but also characterized by a bounded set of actions by the recipient. Because the actions of the knowledge recipient are considered to be understood, outcomes associated with negative serendipity due to opportunistic action on the part of the recipient can be eliminated. Alternatively, Type 3 outcome ambiguity is characterized by the opposite scenario. In a Type 3 scenario, the knowledge in question is proven, but the actions of the recipient are unknown and the eventual overall set of outcomes is unbounded because outcomes associated with opportunistic behavior cannot be eliminated.

Consequently, the concept of outcome ambiguity is particularly relevant when more than one firm is involved. For example, in a multi-organizational network, the knowledge source would be required to consider the actions for multiple knowledge recipients, increasing the complications related to the decision to share. This is the rationale for why Type 3 outcome ambiguity contributes to a higher level of knowledge transfer difficulty than Type 2 outcome ambiguity; the uncertainties related to the actions of the knowledge recipient(s) make the eventual set of outcomes less stable than uncertainties related to the applications of the knowledge. This is also why the issue of network size is paradoxical; as the size of the network increases, the potential base of accessible knowledge increases. Consequently, the decision to share knowledge becomes more complex because the knowledge source must consider more recipients, translating into greater outcome ambiguity and greater knowledge transfer difficulty. However, multi-organizational networks can mitigate the uncertainties related to initially unbounded recipient actions through governance policies and controls, and positively influence the issues of partner protectiveness, duration, and trust.

Future Trends

This chapter discussed the issues related to ambiguity as a constraint or isolating mechanism of knowledge transfer within multi-organizational networks, with particular emphasis placed on the theoretical gap which exists when causal ambiguity is the only form of ambiguity considered. The concept of outcome ambiguity was introduced and developed in an effort to close this gap. However, the theoretical guidance regarding how ambiguity affects the transfer of knowledge within multi-organizational networks remains incomplete. Specifically, it is still not clear *how* multi-organizational networks should be configured to avoid knowledge transfer ambiguities. Availability of such guidance can be critical since there is more than one type of multi-organizational network in practice, and organizational decision-makers can have a choice in the way they structure and manage, or at least how they operate within, their knowledge networks. For example, how would a highly-structured network of similar organizations such as a franchise experience these ambiguities (and the transfer of knowledge) differently than would a loosely-structured network of different organizations such as an R&D consortium? The organizational experiences would most likely differ between the two networks, but how? Since most extant work on knowledge-related ambiguity is limited to treating it as intra-organizational concepts or, at best, as dyadic, an understanding of how these two factors of ambiguity unfold in different multi-organizational networks is still lacking. This theoretical gap represents an opportunity for investigation, of which the results could provide importance guidance for both researchers engaged in knowledge and organizational management as well as for practitioners of the same.

Conclusion

Organizations engaged in multi-organizational networks are expected to benefit from network-wide knowledge transfer and sharing that may not be available to a non-networked firm operating independently (Argote, 1999; Darr, Argote, & Epple, 1995; Dyer, 1997). However, as was discussed in this chapter, the effectiveness of multi-organizational knowledge transfer can be contingent upon member organizations' ability to remove or abate systemic constraints (Argote, 1999) or isolating mechanisms (Knott, 2002), such as the ambiguities which may exist when multiple organizations interact. The concept of causal ambiguity, present when an organization does not know what combination of inputs and process factors cause a known outcome, has been well established and accepted as an isolating mechanism of the transfer of knowledge within, between, and among organizations. However, causal ambiguity does not address the unintended consequences of the increased uncertainty related to the relationships within the network. Specifically, no concept in the existing literature addresses the issues related to the uncertainties associated with the outcomes precipitated by the application of knowledge. In response, this chapter attempted to isolate this specific uncertainty and its unique role in the multi-organizational domain through the development of the concept of outcome ambiguity and its associated typology. The development of this concept is intended to provide additional theoretical guidance to both researchers and practitioners in this domain.

References

Adler, P. (2001). Market, hierarchy, and trust: The knowledge economy and the future of capitalism. *Organization Science, 12*(2), 215-234.

Allee, V. (2002). Value networks and evolving business models for the knowledge economy. In C. W. Holsapple (Ed.), *Handbook on knowledge management* (pp. 605-621). Berlin: Springer Verlag.

Argote, L. (1999). *Organizational learning. Creating, retaining, and transferring knowledge.* Norwell, MA: Kluwer Academic Publishers.

Darr, E. P., Argote, L., & Epple, D. (1995). The acquisition, transfer, and depreciation of knowledge in service organizations: Productivity in franchises. *Management Science, 41*(11), 1750-1762.

Dyer, J. H. (1997). Effective interfirm collaboration: How firms minimize transaction costs and maximize transaction value. *Strategic Management Journal, 18*(7), 535-556.

Ford, D. P. (2002). Trust and knowledge management: The seeds of success. In C. W. Holsapple (Ed.), *The handbook on knowledge management* (pp. 545-575). Berlin: Springer Verlag.

Gerloff, E. A., Kanoff, N., & Bodensteiner, W. D. (1991). Three components of perceived environmental uncertainty: An exploratory analysis of the effects of aggregation. *Journal of Management, 17*(4), 749-769.

Grant, R. M. (1997). The knowledge-based view of the firm; Implications for management practice. *Long Range Planning, 30*(3), 450-454.

Gulati, R., & Gargiulo, M. (1999). Where do interorganizational networks come from? *American Journal of Sociology, 104*(5), 1439-1493.

Hamel, G. (1991). Competition for competence and inter-partner sharing within international strategic alliances. *Strategic Management Journal, 12*(4), 83-104.

Hosmer, L. T. (1995). Trust: The connecting link between organizational theory and philosophical ethics. *Academy of Management Review, 20*(2), 379-404.

Knott, A. (2003). The organizational routines factor market paradox. *Strategic Management Journal, 24*, 929-943.

Kogut, B., & Zander, U. (1992). Knowledge of the firm, combinative capabilities and the replication of technology. *Organization Science, 3*(3), 383-398.

Kogut, B., & Zander, U. (1996). What firms do? Coordination, identity, and learning. *Organization Science, 7*(5), 502-519.

Korczynski, M. (1996). The low trust route to economic development: Interfirm relations in the UK engineering construction industry in the 1980s and 1990s. *Journal of Management Studies, 33*(6), 787-808.

Lewis, D. J., & Wiegert, A. (1985). Trust as a social reality. *Social Forces, 63*(4), 967-985.

Madhavan, R., Koka, B. R., & Prescott, J. E. (1998). Networks in transition: How industry events (re)shape interfirm relationships. *Strategic Management Journal, 19*(5), 439-459.

Mayer, R., Davis, J., & Schoorman, F. (1995). An integrative model of organizational trust. *Academy of Management Review, 20*(3), 709-734.

Milliken, F. (1987). Three types of perceived uncertainty about the environment: State, effect, and response uncertainty. *Academy of Management Review, 12*(1), 133-144.

Mosakowski, E. (1997). Strategy making under causal ambiguity: Conceptual issues and empirical evidence. *Organization Science, 8*(4), 414-442.

Simmel, G. (1950). Individual and society. In K. H. Wolff (Ed.), *The sociology of Georg Simmel,* (pp. 188-269). New York: Free Press.

Simon, H. (1991). Bounded rationality and organizational learning. *Organization Science, 2*(1), 125-135.

Simonin, B. (1999). Ambiguity and the process of knowledge transfer in strategic alliances. *Strategic Management Journal, 20*(7), 595-624.

Szulanski, G. (1996). Exploring internal stickiness: Impediments to the transfer of best practice within the firm. *Strategic Management Journal, 17*(Winter Special Issue), 27-43.

von Hippel, E. (1994). "Sticky information" and the locus of problem solving: Implications for innovation. *Management Science, 40*(4), 429-438.

Walker, W. (1995). *Technological innovation, corporate R&D alliances, and organizational learning.* Unpublished doctoral dissertation, RAND, Santa Monica, CA. Retrieved November 10, 2006, from http://www.rand.org/pubs/rgs_dissertations/RGSD118/

Zucker, L. (1986). Production of trust: Institutional sources of economic structure, 1840-1920. In B. Straw & L. Cummings (Eds.), *Research in organizational behavior*, (pp. 53-111). Greenwich, CT: JAI Press.

Chapter X

Systemic Innovation Capability:
The Case Study of Embraer, the Brazilian Aircraft Manufacturer

Marcelo A. Machado, Prefeitura de Manaus,
Secretaria Municipal de Ciência e Tecnologia da Informação, Brazil

Abstract

Targeting at an uncovered intersection of the fields of management of technology (MOT), knowledge management, and strategic alliances, we propose the concept of systemic innovation capability, which is the ability to effectively combine knowledge from a variety of internal and external sources into innovative products, services, efficient business processes, and valuable new combinations of knowledge, holistically taking into consideration business, marketing, operations, and technological aspects. Additionally, we validate the concept by presenting the case of Embraer, a Brazilian commercial aircraft manufacturer successfully competing in the global marketplace. Based on an extensive literature review with support from Embraer's case, we also propose the knowledge partnership model. In developing the model, we coined the concept of "new product development effectiveness." Furthermore, we proposed the concept of "knowledge relevance," which is roughly a mutually attractive force between partners' knowledge pools. Finally, we made practical considerations about concepts and models proposed in the chapter.

Introduction

Regarding innovation as the successful combination of existent knowledge, we argue that it is increasingly less likely that all knowledge, proprietary technologies included, necessary to develop a successful product can be found within the boundaries of a specific firm. Thus, hi-tech firms pursuing an early follower strategy can at the same time develop innovative products, but neither do they need to pay for the ever-rising costs of developing cutting-edge technologies nor do they have to face the risks involved in the process, particularly if they are in the pursuit of a coherent strategy to collaborate with partners who own proprietary technologies. In such cases, hi-tech companies have more potential for profitability. Still, a key issue for the development of innovative products based on updated technology, not necessarily developed in-house, is a very effective (i.e., efficiency, efficacy, and productivity combined) new product development process.

Due to the above, co-development and collaborative research and development (R&D) are frequent strategies pursued by high-tech companies. Either in the case of co-development or collaborative R&D, among the most important issues to be dealt with are knowledge issues.

Targeting at an uncovered intersection of the fields of management of technology (MOT), knowledge management, and strategic alliances, we propose the concept of systemic innovation capability as the ability to effectively combine knowledge from a variety of internal and external sources into innovative products, services, efficient business processes, and valuable new combinations of knowledge, holistically taking into consideration business, marketing, operations, and technological aspects. In addition to that, we validate the concept by presenting Embraer's case, a Brazilian aircraft manufacturer successfully competing in the global marketplace. We argue that systemic innovation capability is one of Embraer's core competences and one which is largely associated to the outstanding performance.

Based on an extensive literature review with support from Embraer's case, we also propose "the knowledge partnership model," which is a model of systemic innovation and a model of systemic knowledge creation. In developing the model, we coined the concept of "new product development effectiveness." We also provided a more general explanation of the enabling conditions of an interorganizational *ba* (i.e., shared purpose and trust).

Furthermore, we proposed the concept of "knowledge relevance," which is roughly a mutually attractive force between partners' knowledge pools.

As for the chapter organization, we first review previous research notably on innovation, new product development (NPD), R&D collaboration, and knowledge management (KM) in order to support case analysis and our argumentation. We then describe Embraer's case with emphasis on new product development from the viewpoint of knowledge management. Moreover, in regard of future trends, drawing on the literature review and findings from the case study, we propose the model of knowledge partnership and the model's general aspects and dynamics. Finally, we summarize and discuss the main argument of this chapter.

Background

Theoretical Background

As the first part of the background section, we review key-concepts on innovation. In the early 1930s, Schumpeter (1934) proposed innovation as a new combination of existing knowledge. Moreover, when proposing the concept of combinative capabilities, Kogut and Zander (1992) argued that innovation is the combination of current capabilities and future opportunities. Dodgson (1993) proposed a concept of innovation as the combination of exploration (i.e., developing and finding new alternatives) and exploitation (i.e., using and refining current technologies). According to Ettlie (2000), innovation is invention plus exploitation. Johnson (2002), otherwise, argued that innovation is the result of empirical exploitation, based on goal specificity or intent, and environmental scanning. For Afuah (2003), innovation is invention plus commercialization, which is basically to use new knowledge to provide what customers want. Leonard-Barton (1995) argued that innovation occurs at the boundaries of disciplines and specializations while Hargadon (2002) stated that innovation occurs when ideas in one domain are valuable and unknown in others.

Synthesizing the above, we proposed a definition of innovation as follows: "Innovation is, based on core capabilities and environmental constraints, to match invention (generated either through empirical exploitation or combination of existent knowledge) with future market opportunities to develop new products or services, which enable an organization or group of organizations to capture economic value."

Regarding the strategic intent towards innovation, there are three different paths a firm can follow: (1) *innovation leader*, a firm that succeeds in bringing technological innovation to the market, generally building a dominant design; (2) *early follower*, a company that introduces new products based on dominant design, but differentiates itself by offering superior market concepts, technological modifications, and better after-sales service, or cost reduction due to economies of scale; and (3) *late follower*, mainly competing in mature markets through cost leadership (Boutelier et al., 2000). When following each of those paths, firms tend to generate specific types of innovation. In that manner, we review widely-accepted categorizations of innovation. Henderson and Clark (1990) proposed the idea of modular and architectural innovations. The first category is related to changes in the way components operate internally, within certain architecture (e.g., a more powerful car engine). The second is related to changes in the way components relate to each other (e.g., a new car design). Kogut and Zander (1992), instead, proposed two other categories: incremental and radical innovations. Incremental innovation can be explained as a path-dependent innovation, based on what has been done, and it is basically an improvement of current products or technologies. Radical innovation is the creation of an entirely new solution through experimentation and development of a new set of heuristics. Hargadon (2002), in fact, acknowledges the existence of several dichotomies aiming at categorizing innovation (i.e., revolutionary vs. evolutionary, radical vs. incremental, and discontinuous vs. continuous). Using Table 1, we summarized some of them.

In the text, we are going to use innovation in a broad sense covering all categories of innovation mentioned above.

Table 1. Categories of innovation

Source			
Henderson and Clark (1990)	**Kogut and Zander (1992)**	**Miller and Morris (1999)**	**Christensen et al. (2004)**
Modular (change components' inner functions)	Incremental (path dependent, attached to what has been done)	Continuous (incremental, convergent thinking)	Sustainable (improvement of current products, same value proposition)
Architectural (change how components interact)	Radical (experimental, new heuristics).	Discontinuous (divergent thinking, new knowledge, significant improve in features, benefits or costs)	Disruptive (bring to the market non-customers, create new markets, new to the world products or significantly more cost-effective products).

(left margin label: Categories)

We started reviewing new product development theory with both a general and a classic approach. Wheelwright and Clark (1992) proposed development imperatives and correspondent implications that ultimately result in the development of outstanding products. Those implications consisted of shorter development cycles, better target products, and improved leverage of critical resources (engineering labor included), creativity, and product quality. Moreover, as a result of the development of outstanding products, a firm may open new markets, attract new customers, leverage existing assets, build new competences, and improve the firm's reputation.

A modern approach to the relationship between product development and corporate performance is provided by Cagan and Vogel (2002), who associated the creation of breakthrough products to competitive advantage. In that manner, outstanding products increase sales, improve profitability and brand value, and consequently improve stock performance. Operational and stock performances are essential for a sustainable competitive advantage. Ultimately, the development and the launch of outstanding products contribute to build sustainable competitive advantages. In brief, Cagan and Vogel (2002) successfully linked the development of outstanding products and competitive advantage, and Wheelwright and Clark (1992) provided a referential on what to consider when developing outstanding products. We combined the concepts of Wheelwright and Clark, and Cagan and Vogel (2002), into the concept of NPD effectiveness (see Figure 1).

Wheelwright and Clark's development imperatives were grouped into efficacy performance indicators (e.g., better targeted products), efficiency performance indicators (i.e., shorter development cycles), and productivity performance indicators (i.e., number of successful projects per engineer). Cagan and Vogel's work proposes that outstanding products increase sales, improve profitability and brand value, and consequently improve stock performance. Conclusively, NPD effectiveness means a product development that enables sustainable competitive advantage.

As a complementary approach to product development, we review research on R&D collaboration beginning with Snow et al. (1992), who more than a decade ago argued that due

Figure 1. New product development effectiveness

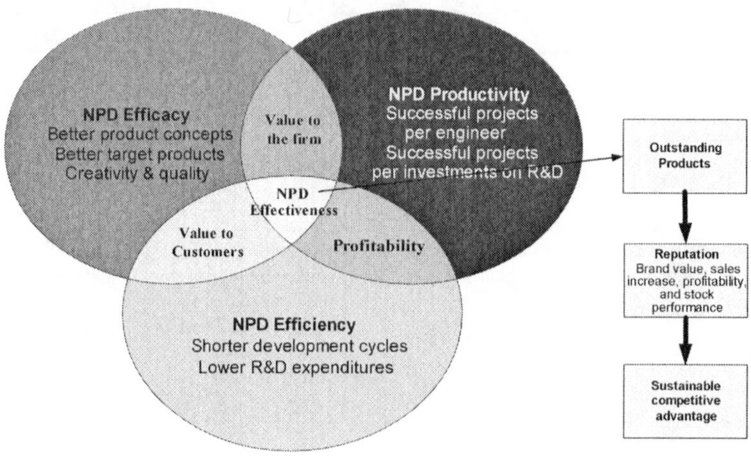

to the rapid pace of technological changes, innovations are transferring from one industry to another and are moving across international borders at an increasing speed. Ohmae (1993) added that no single firm can have the whole set of technological solutions necessary to launch competitive products, the so-called idea of dispersion of technology. Rothwell (1994) proposed a fifth generation of the innovation process, which is characterized as being a networked process of know-how accumulation including, among others, the science and technology infrastructure, competitors, leading-edge customers, strategic partners, and key-suppliers. Accordingly, Duysters et al. (1999), Seufert et al. (1999), Brusoni (2001), Parise and Henderson (2004), and Verspagen and Duysters (2004) acknowledge the embeddedness of the innovation process in a network of external relationships.

Gulati et al. (2000) then summarized: "The image of atomistic actors competing for profits against each other in an impersonal marketplace is increasingly inadequate in a world in which firms are embedded in networks of social, professional, and exchange relationships with other organizational actors" (p. 203). Additionally, Miles et al. (2000) stated that "the ability to collaborate is meta-capacity for innovation" (p. 301).

The global scale of such networks and, therefore, the global dimension of the R&D collaboration, were discussed by a number of scholars, such as Rutten (2003), Taylor and Osland (2003), Blomqvist et al. (2004), Santos et al. (2004), and Von Zedwitz et al. (2004). Chesbrough (2003a) and Birkinshaw (2004) recognized the idea of accessing sources of knowledge other than inside company borders. According to Feinberg and Gupta (2004), the greater dispersion of the R&D effort across firms, the greater the potential relevance of outsourced technology. Afuah (2003) and Santos et al. (2004) extended the concept by saying that the likelihood of an innovation's success is determined by the weakness of the weakest source knowledge. Hence, the wider and more diverse a firm's sources of knowledge are, the more likely an innovation will succeed. Collaborating firms can access their partner's knowledge and indirectly their partner's network's knowledge (Verspagen & Duysters, 2004).

Because knowledge is a quintessential issue in R&D collaboration, we further the subject by reviewing works on knowledge management (KM). A series of dichotomies can be used to clarify what KM is about. For instance, codification versus personification strategies (Hansen et al., 1999), integrative versus interactive (Zack, 1999b), cognitive versus community approach (Newell et al., 2002), object versus process (Figallo & Rhine, 2002), and commodity versus community view (McMahon et al., 2004). Such dichotomies commonly explore the idea of two opposite approaches to KM: (1) to codify, store, and make knowledge available to those who are in need; and (2) to nurture an environment in which people feel free to share hard-to-codify knowledge. In brief, a codification strategy commonly focuses on the technological side of knowledge management, and a personalization strategy focuses on the people side. Seufert et al. (1999) proposed a holistic view on knowledge management, but the first concrete development on that line of thought was proposed by Umemoto, Endo, and Machado (2004), who, based on the case of Fuji-Xerox, coined the term "Hybridization Strategy," which can be easily understood as a balance between codification and personalization KM strategies. In other words, an organization in the pursuit of hybridization strategy will try to balance a technological and a people's approach to KM.

In its evolution as a management discipline, knowledge management also faces a dilemma related to whether KM should be institutionalized and become a function (i.e., finance, marketing, R&D) or should be made part of the way firms do business. Originally, the theory of knowledge creation (Nonaka, 1991; Nonaka & Takeuchi, 1995) did not even mention the idea of managing knowledge, because Japanese companies, used as a reference to build the theory, were naturally knowledge-creating companies, managing knowledge as they operate. Actually, knowledge managers were project managers and team leaders doing their daily jobs. Davenport and Prusak (2000), instead, have given mixed signals by saying that: " ... knowledge management process has to be baked into key knowledge work process. How companies create, gather, store, share, and apply knowledge must blend well with how market researchers, scientists, consultants, engineers, and managers work on a daily basis" (p. xi). Davenport and Prusak later stated that knowledge workers[1] do not necessarily have the expertise or time to manage knowledge, and therefore KM should be the task of knowledge professionals.[2] Hansen et al. (1999) instead argued that despite a relative success of companies that created a structure to manage knowledge, to insolate knowledge management is not a good idea because KM will promote much more benefits to a given firm if it is integrated with human resources and information technology.

Regardless of whether the KM strategy (codification, personalization, or hybridization) is embedded into business process or departmentalized, a complementary and essential approach to KM is provided by the theory of knowledge creation (Nonaka & Takeuchi, 1995). The knowledge-creating process takes a spiral form. In the knowledge spiral, the interaction between tacit and explicit knowledge is amplified through the four modes of knowledge conversion: socialization, externalization, combination, and internalization. In socialization, individuals acquire skills by sharing experiences with others simultaneously as they perform a certain activity. Mental models get integrated into a group's mental model. In externalization, a group's mental model is articulated into explicit concepts. A number of techniques can be used in the process. For instance, Peter Checkland's soft system methodology, as proposed by Machado, Yoshida, and Umemoto (2003). In combination, new explicit concepts are combined with existing explicit knowledge at the organizational level. And in internalization, again, individuals accumulate tacit knowledge as they work.

The whole theory of knowledge creation was developed under an organizational level of analysis; however, Nonaka and Takeuchi (1995) have long pointed out that the process of knowledge creation is not a closed loop. Accordingly, Ahmadjian (2004) proposed the framework of interorganizational knowledge creation. The framework was developed based on examples of Toyota and the Silicon Valley. The former represents a vertical pattern within which a major company leads the process of knowledge creation; the latter is a set of small and medium enterprises in a horizontal, almost informal fashion. As a prerequisite condition for the process to occur, the author proposed the creation of an interorganizational "*Ba*."[3] The concept of *ba* represents not only the physical environment, but also the cognitive, affective, and social contexts in which knowledge creation occurs. There are, in fact, three types of *ba*: physical, virtual, and mental. An office is an example of physical *ba*, an online discussion group is an example of a virtual *ba*, and a shared corporate vision is an example of a mental *ba*.

In summary, our definition of innovation synthesizes previous definitions and emphasizes the importance of combining knowledge from a variety of sources. We identify the NPD process as a key process in the pursuit of successful innovations, and we define parameters to measure NPD effectiveness. In this section we also learn that R&D collaboration is a recommended strategy for hi-tech companies competing in global markets. Furthermore, we learn that knowledge is an essential and complex issue for a successful collaboration process. Finally, we review mainstream theories on knowledge management. Yet, to our best knowledge there is a lack of studies combining theoretical approaches mentioned above, and more importantly there are a lack of real cases combining innovation, NPD, R&D, and knowledge management.

The Case Company

Embraer is the fruition of a successful long-term strategy of the Brazilian government in developing a domestic aircraft industry. The company was created in 1969 and privatized in 1994. Embraer's history can be divided in two periods: before and after privatization. The former is characterized by an entrepreneurial and engineering-driven and entrepreneurial logic, and the latter is characterized by a preponderance of a market and economic oriented logic. During the first period, Embraer built, from scratch, fully-developed technological capabilities mainly through a series of collaborative R&D projects with foreign partners and with strong support from government (i.e., direct investment in R&D, military procurement, and offsets). During the second period, the company remarkably improved its position in the market and its financial performance without giving up in-house development and own brand.

Embraer is the world's fourth largest commercial aircraft manufacturer in terms of sales after Airbus, Boeing, and Bombardier. The company has 40% of the world's market share of aircrafts with 20 to 120 seats. Today, the company has complete control over a new aircraft development cycle, from product concept to customer service.

Furthermore, despite being much smaller than the other three (i.e., Airbus, Boeing, and Bombardier) and located in a semi-developed economy such as Brazil, Embraer has been attracting the attention of scholars because it has the best overall performance among the four companies. The company has proportionally the most profitable operation, the best stock performance in the last five years, and consequently the highest market value among the world's four largest commercial aircraft manufacturers. Embraer has launched a new family of aircrafts, and as a result in 2004, broke its record of net sales and net income. Considering the fact that the aircraft business is high-tech, oligopolistic, with high R&D costs and long return curves, Embraer's achievements are remarkable.

Embraer's Case

NPD Process

Embraer employs a strategy of being an early technological follower launching innovative products, based on updated technology, into specific market niche. The company emphasizes product development rather than basic research, and despite the fact that Embraer has complete control over a new aircraft's development cycle, it neither tries to develop programs alone nor completely outsources development. Rather, Embraer's option is for co-development. Employing 16 risk partners, mostly in charge of major subsystems, the company has a unique and remarkably horizontal partnering strategy.

NPD is organized in a matrix-like structure. In particular, the company employs an integrated approach to product development based on a concurrent engineering philosophy. Furthermore, Embraer employs a dense IT infrastructure interconnecting all functions directly and indirectly involved in the R&D process, as well as interconnecting Embraer's, partners', and customers' operations. Employing an integrated product development, all aspects of the product (i.e., design, engineering, logistics, manufacturing, and customer service) are considered throughout the process with active participation of risk partners and suppliers.

Taking as reference the development of Embraer's new family of aircrafts, the ERJ-170/190 program, one of its unique features is the fact that Embraer and risk partners work collocated during a critical phase of the development process, the Joint Definitions Phase, when an aircraft's main systems are specified. Also, the company nurtures groups for a periodical face-to-face interaction among professionals (Embraer's, partners', and leading customers') who either never had or do not have the chance to work collocated anymore. As an example of such groups, the Steering Groups of Development (SG) are formed of specialists from Embraer, partners, and leading users. Each of those SG was intended to discuss specific aspects of the aircraft development. Regarding the development of ERJ-170/190 family, five different SG were created: (1) payload system, (2) performance & operation, (3) propulsion, (4) mechanical systems, and (5) electric and avionic systems.

Embraer employs IT-based technologies which provide both an alternative and complementary environment for interaction among Embraer, Embraer's partners, and customers. For instance, the company's virtual reality center (VRC) is an interactive design tool, based on stereoscopic applications, using computer aided three-dimensional interactive application (CATIA) drawings. The system can be used in two instances: semi-immersive and fully-interactive. The former uses special goggles and a big screen allowing 3D detailed view of the drawings. The latter employs helmets, gloves, and movement sensors for a more accurate simulation. Both instances can be shared by multiple users.

Another set of the company's IT technologies aims at codifying and reutilizing explicit knowledge. A good example is Embraer's knowledge-based engineering system. Embraer employs a system with the objective to conduct rapid prototyping. Embraer's KBE system integrates information, rules, norms, and restrictions, used to develop projects. In other words, all restrictions necessary for decision-making can be retrieved in future projects. By manipulating functional inputs (e.g., larger range, more passengers, or larger engines), a team can produce a new airframe design in much less of the time that it would normally do, so that engineers and designers can spend more time in creative thinking than in repetitive tasks.

In summary, Embraer is typically in the pursuit of an early-follower strategy, targeting specific niches, and has complete control over a new aircraft's development cycle. The company has a genuinely horizontal partnering strategy and extensively employs collaboration environments (i.e., face-to-face and virtual), notably the Joint Definitions Phase, and complementarily IT-based tools to support the development process, such as the KBE. Additionally, Embraer employs a concurrent engineering philosophy combined with matrix-like structure.

NPD Performance

In this section, we will critically evaluate Embraer's R&D according to the concept of NPD effectiveness, found in the literature review. More specifically, we provide evidence of NPD efficiency, efficacy, and productivity, taking as reference the ERJ-170/190 program. To begin with, we look at the efficiency aspect, and to do so we will use the actual development cycle as a reference (see Table 2). Considering the whole development cycle from June of 1999, when the program was launched, to the certification in February 2004, the process took 56 months, much more than initially planned (i.e., 38 months), because the certification process with the American authority (i.e., FAA) was extremely complicated. The company's new aircrafts embedded technologies which were new for the manufacturer and even technologies that were new to the civil aircraft market (e.g., Honeywell's new avionic system).

Nevertheless, contemplating only engineering aspects of the program and skipping the certification process, the program's first flight occurred 32 months after the program launch, which means it was shorter than average of the sector, indicating high efficiency. Additionally, the company was actually simultaneously developing three other aircrafts: ERJ-175, ERJ-190, and ERJ-195, which is a sign of an even higher NPD efficiency. All three have already flown for the first time and are now in process of certification.

The certification process for the three new members of the ERJ-170/190 is expected to be much easier than the process of certification of the ERJ-170, once the novelty factor is not an issue anymore. If the other three first flights were added to the equation, the productivity over time of Embraer's NPD would be also high (i.e., four aircrafts developed in a period of five years). Furthermore, the company also developed these four aircrafts while counting on a much smaller labor force than the other three largest commercial aircraft manufacturers. In 2003, Embraer had 11,264 employees, while Airbus had 46,000, Boeing had 166,000, and Bombardier had 70,000. In terms of productivity of R&D investments, Embraer invested U.S. $850 million, including U.S. $250 million from risk partners, and developed a program of four different aircrafts. In the aircraft business, the average R&D expenditures is over U.S. $1 billion to develop an aircraft the size of the ERJ-195. For instance, Bombardier

Table 2. ERJ-170/190 development cycle

Program Milestones	Completion	Source
Preliminary studies	May 1999	ERJ-170/190 Progress Report No.1
Product launch	June 1999	ERJ-170/190 Progress Report No.8
Selection of risk partners	July 1999	Embraer 2000 Annual Report
Preliminary Design	March 2000	ERJ-170/190 Progress Report No.2
Joint definitions phase	April 2000	ERJ-170/190 Progress Report No.6
Preliminary design review	April 2000	Ibid
Roll-out	October 2001	Embraer 2001 Annual Report
Detailed definition and certification	February 2004	Press Release 19-20/02/2004
Prototyping	February 2002	Embraer 2002 Annual Report
Final assembly	October 2001	ERJ-170/190 Progress Report No.8
First flight	February 2002	Embraer 2002 Annual Report
Certification (CTA, FAA, JAA and EASA)	February 2004	Press Release 19-20/02/2004
Flight test program starts	February 2002	ERJ-170/190 Progress Report No.10
CTA provisional certification	November 2003	Embraer 2003 Annual Report
FAA provisional certification	December 2003	Ibid
Serial production first flight	April 2003	ERJ-170/190 Progress Report No.13
First serial production completion	March 2003	Ibid
Serial production starts	July 2002	ERJ-170/190 Progress Report No.10
First large sub-assemble	November 2002	ERJ-170/190 Progress Report No.11
First delivery	March 2004	Press Release 10/03/2004

announced its plans to invest U.S. $2 billion to develop a new family of middle-sized aircrafts. Regarding time, labor, and investments, it is possible to argue that Embraer's NPD has high productivity.

Indicators of NPD efficacy are indicators of how well a product fits market requirements. To begin with, we review the program's sales performance to date. Notwithstanding the fact that the ERJ-170 first delivery occurred in March 2004, the new product line was responsible for about 40% of the company's net sales in 2004. Moreover, in 2004, net sales and net profits reached the highest level in Embraer's history. Looking for evidence that 2004 results were a tendency for the years to come, we reviewed Embraer's 2005 first quarter deliveries and delivery forecast. It was found that they were consistent with the 2004 results. More than that, the company's orders backlog showed 301 firm orders and 387 options for the ERJ-170/190, including 60 firm orders from Air Canada, Bombardier's domestic market. Considering the engineering aspects of the program, efficiency, efficacy, and productivity combined point to a high NPD effectiveness.

Embraer's Core Competence

Embraer's main core competence is a "systemic innovation capability." Systemic innovation capability (SIC) is proposed as "the ability to effectively combine knowledge from a variety of internal and external sources into competitive products, services, efficient business processes, and valuable new combinations of knowledge, holistically taking into consideration business, marketing, operations, and technological aspects." SIC is a complex, a multifaceted, and a path-dependent capability (see Figure 2).

Starting from the bottom of the figure, Embraer's and partners' knowledge pools are kept together by knowledge relevance, roughly an attraction force based on complementarity and relative value of two knowledge pools. Complementarity comes from the fact that Embraer knows how to design, develop, market, and service a middle-sized aircraft, and partners are world-leaders in key-aerospace technologies such as avionics, engines, and composites. The process taps into Embraer's and partner's knowledge pools, mostly larger than Embraer's. It is worth noting that partners have their networks, which include other aircraft manufacturers. Hence, Embraer's NPD process starts with much bigger knowledge pool than a single company of Embraer's size would ever hold within its boundaries. Knowledge starts moving up on the pyramid.

The company accesses partner's knowledge because it is able to generate an interorganizational *ba*. An interorganizational *ba* represents the means (i.e., face-to-face environment and virtual collaboration environments) and willingness to share knowledge (i.e., trust and shared purpose). For instance, the joint definitions phase and steering groups are typically face-to-face environments, and the CATIA system is naturally a virtual collaboration en-

Figure 2. Systemic innovation capability and Embraer's performance

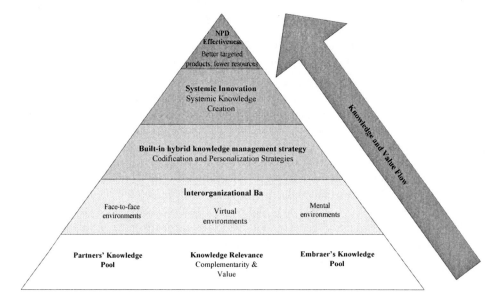

vironment. Trust is the result of Embraer's collaborative know-how built over almost 40 years of collaborative projects with foreign partners, and trust is also the fruition of the company's reputation of market and technology leadership. Shared purpose comes directly from the idea of risk-partnership. For every aircraft sold, Embraer's partners benefit not only at the moment of the sale, but during the whole product life cycle, particularly with reposition-parts. The unique feature of Embraer's interorganizational *ba* is complementarity between physical (i.e., face-to-face and virtual) and mental *ba*. Through interorganizational *ba*, Embraer and partners share, transfer, and create knowledge.

At the organizational level, knowledge transferred from or created with partners has to be internalized into products, services, business processes, and other combinations of knowledge. For that matter, we argue that Embraer employs a built-in hybrid KM strategy (i.e., person-alization and codification strategies combined and embedded into business processes). The company combines a concurrent engineering philosophy with matrix organization, which means teams with professionals from different specialties and even different companies and countries working together, increasing the richness of knowledge sharing while keeping a functional line of command that improves peer support and efficiency in the communica-tion process. Furthermore, the company extensively provides opportunities for people to exchange; Joint Definitions Phase and Steering Groups are examples of that, and Embraer additionally employs IT-based tools (e.g., CATIA) to provide a collaborative environment for those who either never had a chance or do not work collocated anymore. Concurrent engineering, matrix organization, and the emphasis given by the company to the interac-tion among professionals supports the argument of personalization KM strategy. The use of knowledge-based engineering is normally evidence of a codification KM strategy. The fact that elements of both codification and personalization strategies are found embedded into the company's development processes validate the argument that Embraer employs a built-in hybrid KM strategy.[4]

Because of its built-in hybrid KM strategy, Embraer effectively converts tacit knowledge into explicit and vice-versa, resulting in competitive products and services, efficient business processes, and valuable new combinations of knowledge. The process holism comes from the concurrent engineering philosophy, which considers business, marketing, operations, and technological aspects simultaneously during all phases of development. The matrix organization of NPD reinforces the principles of concurrent engineering by putting professionals from different specialties to work together. During the development of the ERJ-170/190, partners and suppliers were parts of the matrix, increasing even more the richness of knowledge sharing. Professionals from different specialties, organizations, and countries naturally have diverse tacit and explicit knowledge. At the same time, the matrix organization of the development effort keeps a functional line of command. Tacit and explicit knowledge is shared rather easier among a team of professionals with the same background than in the case of a cross-functional team. Hence, a matrix organization helps to increase the efficiency of knowledge conversion. Not only knowledge flows up, but most importantly there is a value flow.

Embraer develops better target products because its NPD process integrates knowledge, including proprietary technologies and perspectives, from partners, suppliers, customers, and even competitors. The company employs fewer resources because it can access resources from partners and suppliers, and also because it develops its products taking into consideration all relevant perspectives for product development (e.g., design, engineering, manufacturing, and logistics). Such holistic approach reduces significantly the development cycle and consequently R&D expenditures. Better target products and competitive prices result in strong sales and profitability. Strong sales and profitability improve brand value and therefore improve stock performance.

Future Trends

Based on findings from Embraer's case and in the light of the literature review, we developed the *knowledge partnership model* which is both a model of systemic innovation and model of systemic knowledge creation (see Figure 3).

Figure 3. The knowledge partnership model

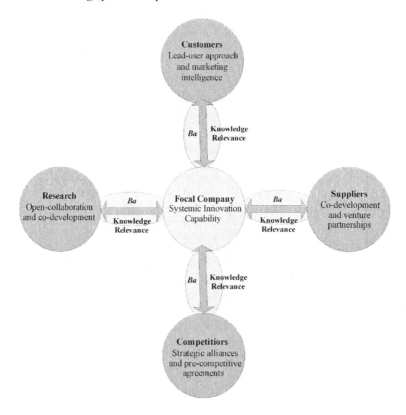

With regard to general aspects and dynamics of the model we propose the following eight insights:

1. **The focal company is a high-tech firm seeking complementary knowledge to enhance its innovative capabilities:** Unlike a risk partnership within which partners share the costs and risks of development, within a knowledge partnership the focal company and partners (i.e., research institutions, customers, suppliers, and competitors) share the knowledge pool necessary to generate innovation and evenly benefit from the process.

2. **To deal with each category of partners, specific strategies should be employed:** Open collaboration and co-development with research institutions grants access to a wide network of researchers, thus granting access to newly-created knowledge. A close relationship with lead-users grants access to their tacit knowledge, and therefore their tacit needs, while market intelligence techniques help to identify overall market trends. Co-development with suppliers grants access to their knowledge pools, in particular proprietary technologies and managerial knowledge. Strategic R&D alliances with competitors enable sharing of overlapping but different knowledge pools, while pre-competitive agreements reduce risks of unilateral development.

3. **What keeps the focal organization and the arrangement of partners together is what we call "knowledge relevance":** Knowledge relevance is determined by two attributes: complementarity and value of knowledge. The more complementary are the knowledge pools of a partner and the focal company, the more the attraction between them. The greater the value of those knowledge pools, the greater the attraction as well. For example, a leading firm in designing and manufacturing personal computers would have a high attraction for a leading firm in memory chips and vice-versa.

4. **The focal company's core competence is a systemic innovation capability:** Systemic innovation capability is defined as the ability to effectively combine knowledge from a variety of internal and external sources into competitive products and services, efficient business processes, and valuable new combinations of knowledge, holistically taking into consideration business, marketing, operations, and technological aspects.

5. **The main feature of the focal company's systemic innovation capability is the ability to build an interorganizational ba:** The interorganization *ba*, built upon shared purpose and trust, generates an environment where partners are willing to share knowledge. The interorganizational *ba* complementarily includes the means, face-to-face or virtual, through which actual knowledge sharing occurs.

6. **To be able to employ a built-in hybrid knowledge management strategy is a complementary feature of the focal company's systemic innovation capability:** Employing such KM strategy, a company has embedded into its processes codification and personalization knowledge management practices.

7. **A concurrent engineering philosophy combined with a matrix-like organization increases the richness and efficiency of the knowledge creation process:** Employing concurrent engineering, a firm considers all relevant aspects of product development during all phases of development. In a matrix-like organization, professionals from different specialties and consequently diverse tacit and explicit knowledge work

together, increasing the richness of the knowledge creation process. Additionally, in a matrix-like organization, a functional line of command and peer support is kept, which increases the efficiency of knowledge creation.

8.   **The focal company's systemic innovation capability optimizes the value creation potential of its R&D:** On the one hand, the interorganizational *ba* grants access to a world-wide pool of knowledge (e.g., new discoveries and inventions from research institutions, proprietary technologies from suppliers, tacit needs from customers, and alternative solutions from partners). On the other hand, the focal company's built-in hybrid KM strategy ensures that knowledge acquired from or created with partners is effectively (value creation) integrated into products, services, business processes, and new combinations of knowledge.

Conclusion

In the light of the literature review, we proposed the concept of systemic innovation capability. We validated the concept with Embraer's case-study, and additionally we proposed the *knowledge partnership model*, which is both a model of systemic innovation and model of systemic knowledge creation. In order to develop the model, we provided a more cogent definition of innovation and the concept of NPD effectiveness. We explored the effects which a concurrent engineering philosophy combined to a matrix-like organization can have on NPD knowledge creation. We also provided a more general explanation of the enabling conditions of an interorganizational ba. Furthermore, we coined the concept of knowledge relevance.

Despite a clear emphasis on theoretical aspects, this chapter is also practical-oriented. The practical side comes from the idea of providing a reference for high-tech companies seeking to build competitive advantage through R&D collaboration. In particular, this chapter will serve companies with strong design and engineering capability but depending on key-technologies or skills from external sources. This chapter can also provide a reference for companies seeking to compete in the global marketplace. Such companies could tap into valuable local knowledge, if the adequate enabling mechanisms were developed.

Embraer's case study suggests that a systemic innovation capability can improve R&D effectiveness and therefore a firm's overall performance, particularly in the case of high-tech companies relying on fewer in-house resources. Benefiting from technological partnerships, however, is not an easy task. Systemic innovation capability is an essential enabling condition of a fruitful partnership. A history of collaborative R&D projects and specifically investing in partnering development (e.g., developing specialists in partnering) might help. The employment of a built-in hybrid KM strategy combined with an integrated approach to product development in a matrix-like organization reinforces systemic innovation capabilities. A hybrid KM strategy is built not only investing in collaborative environments (i.e., both face-to-face and IT-based), but most importantly creating an environment where people feel free to share knowledge. In order to embed a hybrid KM strategy into business process, depending on the stage of awareness to knowledge management, a firm should start with a pilot project or task force leading the efforts during a transition phase until the KM strategy is fully internalized, like quality assurance is part of today's way of doing business, especially in manufacturing.

References

Ahmadjian, C. (2004). Interorganizational knowledge-creation: Knowledge and networks. In I. Nonaka, & H. Takeuchi (Eds.), *Hitotsubashi on knowledge management*. Singapore: John Wiley & Sons.

Boutellier, R. et al. (2000). *Managing global innovation: Uncovering the secrets of future competitiveness*. Berlin: Springer.

Burgelman, R. A., & Sayles, L. R. (2004). Transforming invention into innovation: The conceptualization stage. In R. A. Burgelman et al. (Eds.), *Strategic management of technology and innovation* (4th ed.). New York: McGraw-Hill Irwin.

Cagan, J., & Vogel, C. M. (2002). *Creating breakthrough products: Innovation from production planning to program approval*. Upper Saddle River, NJ: Prentice Hall.

Christensen, C. M. et al. (2004). *Seeing what's next: Using the theories of innovation to predict industrial change*. Boston: Harvard Business School Press.

Clark, K. B. (1989). What strategy can do for technology. In K. B. Clark & S. C. Wheelwright (Eds.), *The product development challenge: Competing through speed, quality, and creativity*. Boston: Harvard Business Review.

Clark, K. B., & Wheelwright, S. C. (1995). *The product development challenge: Competing through speed, quality, and creativity*. Boston: Harvard Business Review.

Cohen, W.M., & Levinthal, D.A.(1990). Absorptive capacity: A new perspective in learning and innovation. *Administrative Science Quarterly, 35*(2), 128-152.

Contractor, F. J., & Lorange, P. (2002). *Cooperative strategies and alliances*. New York: Pergamon.

Contractor, F. J., & Lorange, P. (2003). Why should firms cooperate? The strategy and economics basis for cooperative ventures. In J. J. Reuer (Ed.), *Strategic alliances: Theory and evidences*. New York: Oxford University Press.

Cummings, J. L., & Teng, B. -S. (2003). Transferring R&D knowledge: The key factors affecting knowledge transfer success. *Journal of Engineering and Technology Management, 20*(1), 39-68.

Davenport, T. H., & Prusak, L. (2000). *Working knowledge: How organizations management what they know* (paperback ed.). Boston: Harvard Business School Press.

Doz, Y. L., & Hamel, G. (1998). *Alliance advantage: The art of creating value through partnering*. Boston: Harvard Business School Publishing.

Doz, Y. L. et al. (2000). Formation process of R&D consortia: Which path to take? Where does it lead? *Strategic Management Journal, 21*(2), 239-266.

Duysters, G. et al. (1999). Crafting successful technology partnerships. *R&D Management, 29*(4), 343-351.

Dyer, J. H., & Nabeoka, K. (2000). Creating and managing a high performance knowledge sharing network: The Toyota case. *Strategic Management Journal, 21*(3), 345-367.

Dyer, J. H., & Singh, H. (2004). The relational view: Cooperative strategy and sources of interorganizational competitive advantage. In J. J. Reuer (Ed.), *Strategic alliances: Theory and evidences*. New York: Oxford University Press.

Ettlie, J. E. (2000). *Managing innovation technology*. New York: John Wiley & Sons, Inc.

Farrukh, C. et al. (2004, July-August). Developing an integrated technology management process. How Glaxo Wellcome took up the challenge to develop a company-specific technology management system. *Research Technology Management*, 39-46.

Fayard, P. -M. (2003). Strategic communities for knowledge creation: A western proposal for the Japanese concept of ba. *Journal of Knowledge Management, 7*(5).

Gerwin, D., & Ferris, J. S. (2004). Organizing new product development projects in strategic alliances. *Organization Science, 15*(1), 22-37.

Guemawat, P. et al. (2000). *Embraer: The global leader in regional jets*. Working paper, Harvard Business School.

Hansen, M. T. et al. (1999). What's your strategy for managing knowledge? *Harvard Business Review, 77*(2), 106-116.

Hansen, M. T., & Nohria, N. (2004). How to build collaborative advantage. *MIT Sloan Management Review, 46*(1), 22-31.

Hargadon, A. B. (2002). Brokering knowledge: Linking learning and innovation. *Research and Organizational Behavior, 24*(1), 41-85.

Henderson, R. M., & Clark, K. B. (1990). Architectural innovation: The reconfiguration of existing product technologies and the failure of established firms. *Administrative Science Quarterly, 35*(1), 9–30.

Huotari, M. -L., & Livonen, M. (2004). *Trust in knowledge management and systems in organizations*. Hershey, PA: Idea Group Publishing.

Huxham, C., & Vangen, S. (2001). What make practitioners tick? Understanding collaboration practice and practicing collaboration understanding. In J. Genefke & F. McDonald (Ed.) *Effective collaboration: Managing obstacles to success*. Basingstoke: Palgrave.

Inkpen, A. C. (1996). Creating knowledge through collaboration. In Mintzberg et al. (Ed.), *The strategy process: Concepts, contexts, cases*. Harlow: Pearson Education Limited.

Kogut, B., & Zander, U. (1992). Knowledge of the firm, combinative capabilities, and the replication of technology. *Organizational Science, 3*(3), 383-397.

Koruna, S. (2004). Leveraging knowledge assets: Combinative capabilities-Theory and practice. *R&D Management, 34*(5), 505-516.

Lane, H. W. et al. (2004). Barriers and bonds to knowledge transfer in global alliances and mergers. In H. W. Lane et al. (Eds.), *The Blackwell handbook of global management: A guide to managing complexity*. Oxford: Blackwell Publishing.

Lane, P. J., & Lubatkin, M. (1998). Relative absorptive capacity and interorganizational learning. *Strategic Management Journal, 19*(4), 461-477.

Leonard, D. (2000). Tacit knowledge, unarticulated needs, and emphatic design in new product development. In Morey et al. (Eds.), *Knowledge management: Classic and contemporary works*. Cambridge, MA: MIT Press.

Leonard-Barton, D. (1995). *Wellsprings of knowledge*. Boston: Harvard Business School Publishing.

Leonard-Barton et al. (1994). How to integrate work and deepen expertise. In K. B. Clark & S. C. Wheelwright (Eds.), *The product development challenge: Competing through speed, quality, and creativity*. Boston: Harvard Business Review.

Lichtenthaler, E. (2004). Technology intelligence in leading European and North American multinationals. *R&D Management, 34*(2),121-135.

Lubit, R. (2001). Tacit knowledge and knowledge management: The keys to sustainable competitive advantage. *Organizational Dynamics, 29*(4), 164-178.

Lui, S. S., & Ngo, H. (2004). The role of trust and contractual safeguards on cooperation in non-equity alliances. *Journal of Management, 34*(4), 471-485.

Machado, M. (2003, October 4-5). *Concurrent new product development: From efficiency to creativity*. Paper presented at the Annual Research Conference of the Japan Creativity Society, Tokyo, Japan.

Machado, M. (2005). Global knowledge networking for innovation: A case study of Embraer. *Knowledge Management Professional Society Journal, 2*(1), 22-30.

Machado, M., Yoshida, T., & Umemoto, K. (2003). *System thinking as a tool for externalization*. Paper presented at the Annual Research Conference of the Information Processing Society Japan (IPSJ SIG), Ishikawa, Japan, 7-8 November.

McMahon, C. et al. (2004). Knowledge management in engineering and design: Personalization and codification. *Journal of Engineering Design, 15*(4), 307-325.

Miles, R. E. et al. (2000). The future.org. *Long Range Planning, 33*(3), 300-321.

Miller, W. L., & Morris, L. (1999). *Fourth generation R&D: Managing knowledge, technology, and innovation*. New York: John Wiley & Sons, Inc.

Moir, I., & Seabridge, A. (2004). *Design and implement of aircraft systems: An introduction*. London: Professional Engineering Publishing.

Newell, S., et al. (2002). *Managing knowledge work*. New York: Palgrave.

Nonaka, I. (1991, November-December). The knowledge creating company. *Harvard Business Review*, 96-104.

Nonaka, I., & Takeuchi, H. (1995). *The knowledge-creating company: How Japanese companies create the dynamics of innovation*. Oxford: Oxford University Press.

Nonaka, I., & Takeuchi, H. (2004). *Hitotsubashi on knowledge management*. Singapore: John Wiley & Sons.

Nonaka, I. et al. (2000). SECI, ba, and leadership: A unified model of dynamic knowledge creation. *Long Range Planning, 33*(1), 5-34.

Nonaka, I. et al. (2001). A theory of knowledge creation: Understanding the dynamic process of creating knowledge. In M. Dierkes et al. (Ed.), *Handbook of organizational learning and knowledge*. New York: Oxford University Press.

Nooteboom, B. (2004). *Inter-firm collaboration learning and networks: An integrated approach*. London: Routledge.

Ohmae, K. (1993). The global logic of strategic alliances. In J. Bleeke & D. Ernst (Eds.), *Collaborating to compete: Using strategic alliances and acquisitions in the global marketplace*. New York: John Wiley & Sons, Inc.

Polanyi, K. (1966). *The tacit dimension*. London: Routledge and Kegan Paul.

Reuer, J. J. (2004). *Strategic alliances: Theory and evidences*. New York: Oxford University Press.

Ring, P. S. (1997). Processes facilitating reliance on trust in inter-organizational networks. In M. Ebers (Ed.), *The formation of inter-organizational networks*. New York: Oxford University Press.

Rothwell, R. (1994). Industrial innovation: Success, strategy, trends. In M. Dodgson & R. Rothwell (Eds.), *The handbook of industrial innovation*. Cheltenham: Edward Elgar.

Salk,, J. E., & Simonin, B. L. (2003). Beyond alliances: Towards a meta-theory of collaborative learning. In M. Easterby-Smith & M. Lyles (Ed.), *The Blackwell handbook of organizational learning and knowledge management*. Oxford: Blackwell Publishing.

Sandholtz, W., & Love, W. (2001). Dogfight over Asia: Airbus vs. Boeing. *Business and Politics, 3*(2), 135-156.

Santos, J. et al. (2004). Is your innovation process global? *MIT Sloan Management Review. 45*(4), 31-37.

Snow, C. C. et al. (1992). Managing 21st century network organizations. *Organization Dynamics,.20*(3), 5-21.

Savioz, P. (2004). *Technology intelligence: Concept design and implementation in technology-based SMEs*. New York: Palgrave Macmillan.

Seufert, A. et al. (1999). Towards knowledge networking. *Journal of Knowledge Management, 3*(3), 180-190.

Schumpeter, J. (1934). *The theory of economic development*. Cambridge, MA: Harvard University.

Takeuchi, H., & Nonaka, I. (1986). The new new product development game. *Harvard Business Review*, (Jan-Feb), 137-146.

Taylor, S., & Osland, J. S. (2003). The impact of intercultural communication on global organizational learning. In M. Easterby-Smith & M. Lyles (Eds.), *The Blackwell handbook of organizational learning and knowledge management*. Oxford: Blackwell Publishing.

Teece, D. et al. (1997). Dynamic capabilities and strategic management. *Strategic Management Journal, 18*(7), 509–533.

Tennenhouse, D. (2004). Intel's open collaborative model of industry-university. *Research Technology Management. 47*(4), 19-26.

Umemoto, K. (2002). Managing existent knowledge is not enough: Knowledge management theory and practice in Japan. In N. Bontis & C. W. Choo (Eds.), *The strategic management of intellectual capital and organizational knowledge*. New York: Oxford University Press.

Umemoto, K., Endo, A., & Machado, M. (2004). From Sashimi to Zen-in: The evolution of concurrent engineering at Fuji-Xerox. *Journal of Knowledge of Knowledge Management, 8*(4), 89-99.

Verspagen, B., & Duysters, G. (2004). The small worlds of strategic technology alliances. *Technnovation, 24*(4), 563-571.

Von Zedwitz, M. (2002). Organizational learning through post-project reviews in R&D. *R&D Management, 32*(3), 255-268.

Von Zedwitz, M. et al. (2003). *Management of technology: Growth through business innovation and entrepreneurship*. Oxford: Elsevier.

Von Zedwitz, M. et al. (2004). Organizing global R&D: Challenges and dilemmas. *Journal of International Management, 10*(1), 21-49.

Wheelwright, S. C., & Clark, K. B. (1992). *Revolutionizing new product development*. New York: The Free Press.

Endnotes

[1]   Knowledge workers are professionals whose activities depend mostly on knowledge. Lawyers, medicine doctors, designers, engineers are among them.

[2]   Knowledge professionals are people whose primary task is to manage knowledge.

[3]   The concept of Ba was first proposed by Nonaka and Konno (1998) and was further developed by Nonaka et al. (2000) and Umemoto (2002). Ba is a Japanese word that is commonly translated as place or space, but as proposed by Nonaka and colleagues, it includes a wider range of meanings.

[4]   The concept of built-in hybrid knowledge management strategy was first proposed by Machado (2005).

Chapter XI

I-Accounting:
An Adaptive Approach (Method + Practices) to Account for Intangibles

Adamantios Koumpis, ALTEC S. A., Greece

Bob Roberts, Kingston University, UK

Abstract

This chapter introduces the core aspects of an approach facilitating the valuation of intangible assets created by virtual organisations. The approach we present relies on established simple unified procedures which can drastically reduce problems caused by handling each situation individually, especially if there is no previous experience of similar cases. At the same time, the volume, value, and visibility of transactions between the various stakeholders and involved parties is increased. We conclude with an example case analysis related to the reality faced in collaborative research projects; these are carried out by diverse partners operating as a virtual organisation whose different intellectual assets (IAs) and the value thereof need to be recognised in order to prepare the ground for successful project completion.

Introduction

At the heart of our thinking is a growing body of evidence revealing that reliance on financial measures alone will critically undermine the strategies that leading-edge companies must pursue to survive and thrive long term. As Baruch Lev, professor of Accounting and Finance at New York University's Stern School of Business, argues: "To claim that tangible assets should be measured and valued, while intangibles should not—or could not—is like stating that *things* are valuable, while *ideas* are not" (Ernst & Young, 1996, p. 27).

The comments and finding above and also from others, for example, Sveiby and Lloyd (1988), Sveiby (1997), and Edvinsson and Malone (1997), indicate that there is a linkage between intellectual capital performance and business performance. The International Federation of Accountants define an intellectual capital framework, based on the work of Edvinsson, St. Onge, Armstrong, and Petrash that comprises of human, customer, and organisational components (IFAC, 1998).

Work carried out by Ernst and Young has two major connotations, namely: " ... non-financial indicators can be used as leading indicators of future financial performance" and that " ... all non-financial criteria are fed by performance, and in turn, feed the perception of performance" (Ernst & Young, 1996, p. 35). Thus, traditional ways of "measuring" a company do not necessarily prove future performance; the non-financial (or intangible) indicators provide more reliable information into the future health of the organisation.

Furthermore, the changing economy, in particular, the impact of the Internet and acceleration of timescales, has led to the need for correspondingly enhanced and more reliable financial reporting approaches. Companies are now evolving ever faster as they become enmeshed in an ever more complex network of alliances, virtual networks, joint ventures, partnerships, and other related entities. Furthermore, they increasingly extract their value and growth primarily from intangible assets such as innovative organisational forms, brands, know-how, patents, and so forth, in a way that was previously only vaguely understood. This holds for small and medium sized enterprises as well as for big players, though especially in the latter case, the inefficiencies that they face grow in proportion to their size, thus limiting their growth.

The terms intangibles, intangible assets, knowledge assets, and intellectual capital are all used by different groups of professionals to describe basically the same thing, that is, the knowledge and corporate relationships that are so important for success, indeed more important today in many cases than physical assets. However, the elementary linkage between intangibles and the focus on knowledge is still often overlooked, as is the role of the learning process in value creation. In fact, a surprising number of experts within the accounting discipline ignore the elementary linkage between intangibles and the focus on knowledge, missing also the importance of the basic operation that helps value creation, namely the learning process.

The Current Context

Currently, we face a paradoxical situation:

- On the one hand, accountants are desperate to develop approaches to valuing intangibles to increase their relevance.
- While on the other hand, we note the speed by which the regulators want to introduce ungrounded approaches to intangibles.

In the research literature, three generations of intellectual capital (IC) practices can be identified (Andriessen, 2003; Andriessen, 2004):

- The first generation mainly concerns scorecards, such as Skandia (Edvinsson, 2002).
- The second generation employs IC indexes which focus on resources as well as transformations.
- The third generation focuses on a holistic value-added (HVA) approach.

The field of IC management is now headed towards a fourth generation, aiming to contain clear and easy-to-use linkages to shareholder value.

It is easy to understand that the requirements and benefits of IC management differ for a global enterprise compared to a smaller start-up with a few dozen people. There are several dimensions to this situation:

- There is a scale issue. A smaller organisation works differently than a large organisation. This normally means that the dependency on tacit knowledge as opposed to systems and processes is higher in smaller firms then in larger firms. This in turn means that the managerial issues are completely different, since managing knowledge embodied in people is fundamentally different to managing systems and processes.
- There is a growth issue. A larger firm tends to settle into a pattern that remains sustainable with further growth, whereas most patterns used by smaller firms must be changed in order to become sustainable on a larger scale. This is the well-known growth problem facing start ups, and a lot is written about the different phases that firms go through during this growth and the challenges that exist at each stage. In simplified IC terms, it is about reducing the dependency on individuals and increasing the dependency on processes, systems, brands, information, and so forth.
- IC management allows for the explicit identification of the effectiveness by which any organisation has deployed its intangible (and tangible) resources and the improvements that can be done given the strategic logic of the firm as well as its size. IC management further allows for tracking and improvement of the efficiency by which actual value is extracted from this, by now, effective deployment system.

- IC management allows for understanding of the sources of coordination costs, consequently facilitating their subsequent reduction.

- IC management allows for an understanding of which intangible attributes are drivers of value in the eyes of different stakeholders and therefore which attribute should be focused on to generate more value in the eyes of these stakeholders (the "what" question), and the effectiveness approach allows for an understanding of how this should be done (the "who" question).

- IC management allows for identification of suitable disclosure structures to minimise uncertainty in the eyes of investors without reducing or risking the existing competitive advantages.

- IC management allows for the valuation in a transparent and assurable way of any intangible, or set of intangibles, up through the whole structure of a firm.

Generally speaking, IC management offers many beneficial opportunities, as can be testified by the firms that have deployed it in a professional way.

We also see that organisations err in the way they conceptualise and implement ICM. Three of the most common mistakes companies make are:

- To focus on the presence of resources ("how much of something do we have?") rather then the transformation of resources ("for what are we using that which we have and how well are we extracting value from this use?")[1];

- To employ tools and techniques that do not ensure that the items identified are complete (i.e., tools that miss something important to the firm) and preference independent (i.e., tools that use attributes that impact each other or overlap); falling into this trap means that the outcome is unreliable and does not have any predictive power.

- To assume that everybody values the same thing; this is most obvious when management assumes that investors share their view on what should be done to improve the firm's value. An insightful approach here makes it possible for management to balance the need to communicate (by persuading investors to change their views) with the need to perform (giving investors what they want).[2]

Plausibility of the Approach

The entire edifice of financial reporting and audit of publicly-listed companies is a pragmatic creation, born of political economy. It is a residual legal artefact of the historical opposition between corporations who do not want to disclose, and shareholders who require degrees of disclosure. As such, this statutory reporting edifice has no reliable compass and is arbitrary (nobody is going around deconstructing the two-column trial balance, or questioning its accuracy as a model of commerce). What we are really modelling (to use the "classic" notion of an accounting system) is a sequence of transactions in terms of a historical trail of events.

Having closer experiences with the domain of accounting software, we have identified the following. In the same way that a company uses a specific model for reporting its activities and for documenting its transactions with trading partners (namely that of classic double-entry accounting[3]), there is an equal need to identify a system that describes decision making activities, the majority of which build on (elementary) information management transactions.

Intangibles accounting, and all forms of directly-related business processes, really may be viewed as a representation or a set of symbols for some underlying reality. Obviously one has to consider terms like "alternative," "choice," "option," and names of certain actions throughout the system, for which meanings are not ambiguous. One also has a lot of structures representing relationships and hierarchies, which are more subtle.

Like all systems of notation and semantics, accounting of intangibles can never be anything but a model. It is a map to a territory, whose validity may be evaluated by reference to that underlying reality in the "real world." A basic argument we face is to reconsider the intangibles accounting process from a new perspective. Companies traditionally use classic double-entry accounting as their basic operational mode for their bookkeeping operations, and this now currently faces serious limitations due to the highly networked nature of the economy in general and the business-to-business transactions among trading parties in particular. Similarly, there is a well-identified need to reconsider the reporting foundations for intangibles accounting as well as the related business decision-making process.

Expected Impact

What we shall henceforth call *i-accounting* shall have impact in the area of company asset-management transformation, thus leading to a huge new burst of trading in intangible resources. Its timing is ideal due to the introduction of the International Accounting Standards within the European Union. The needs are real, well-identified, and existing, and employment on a trans-European scale is the most cost-efficient instrument to cope with this need.

Furthermore, i-accounting shall significantly contribute to the rationalisation of the inefficiencies currently faced due to the pressure for more disclosure in corporate reporting. There is no denying the importance of intangible assets, however. Since 1980, the average ratio of market capitalisation to book value for companies has swelled from just over 1 to more than 5, even after the recent fall in stock prices. In this respect, differences in market and book value are rough estimates of the value of intangibles. But, on average, intangible assets now represent about 80 percent of the market value of public companies. One possible explanation for the growth is that irrational exuberance has inflated corporate stock prices far beyond the value of the assets that the shares have claim to. The more likely explanation, however, is that financial statements prepared according to the particular accounting practices that exist fail to reflect the true value of a company's assets and operating performance. It is exactly at this point where the unique contribution of i-accounting can fill the knowledge and asset gaps.

A growing number of academics, consultants, and regulators see the absence of most intangible assets from the books as a major deficiency in the existing accounting "regime." They argue that those assets increasingly drive the value of corporations, and yet currently receive next to no recognition in financial disclosures. In an increasingly competitive, knowledge-based economy, intangible assets, such as brand awareness, innovation, and employee productivity, have become the key determinants of corporate success. Given that the investments which companies make to build those intangible assets, such things as corporate infrastructures for knowledge management, employee training, and R&D, have real costs and real impacts; the fact that they are "flushed" through the balance sheets means that the books increasingly become a poor reflection of the true value of companies' businesses.

Corporate executives, however, see more to lose than gain from increased transparency. Intangible assets essentially represent the secrets of a business enterprise, the key resources and factors that enable it to compete effectively in the marketplace. If the company shares those secrets with investors (and with competitors), it could hasten the erosion of the value of those very intangibles. Furthermore, the added transparency could open up a whole new avenue of attack for plaintiff's lawyers. If corporate disclosures of intangible values prove wrong, and it is easy to be wrong about intangible values, shareholders will have plenty of ammunition for lawsuits.

The major problems of managing heterogeneous corporate information sources in organisations in which i-accounting is implemented, can be summarised as:

- **Insufficient modelling and understanding** of the source data located in various sites across the organisation, due to lack of a common terminology and documentation, differing implementations of reporting infrastructures, and source data not being placed in the context of the dynamic aspects of the organisation;
- **Difficulty in organising ad hoc processing of such information**, making users (corporate management, shareholders, internal and external auditors, etc.) dependent for their information needs on, for example, information resource management departments with the usual shortcomings of this approach (relatively limited reliability of the provided information, need for authentication, etc.); and
- **Lack of facilities for maintaining these resources**, thus making more difficult the task of keeping the various systems in step with the ever increasing rate of change in modern business organisations.

These problems are particularly difficult in small and medium sized enterprises, which have variable access to distinct and heterogeneous information suppliers. The bigger barrier to sharing information about intangibles, however, is the lack of workable reporting standards. The internal metrics currently used to evaluate intangible assets and capabilities fall far short of fitting the overall accounting practices and frameworks currently under use. Part of the problem derives from confusion in distinguishing between the investments made to develop intangible assets and the value resulting from those investments. The same difficulties apply to accounting for internally-developed intangibles. In fact, attempting to isolate and directly value the intangible assets of companies may be counterproductive; the value of an intangible asset comes from its interplay with other assets, both physical and intangible, and attempting to value it on a stand-alone basis is pointless.

For these, i-accounting shall provide a solution in terms of an adaptive approach to the issue of sharing, reporting, auditing, and valuation.

An Example:
The Case of Collaborative European Research Projects

Instead of examining the case of a single company and how this should deal with i-accounting practices, we consider the case of a networked constellation, namely a set of collaborating companies that constitutes a consortium aiming to undertake a special type of a research project.

Research is a special case of business activity that involves high risks, bigger levels of uncertainty, increased demands for investments of all types (financial, technology, and human), with extremely intense volatility and lack of stability. To a great extent, success of a research action cannot be planned for success, and the success is a profoundly subjective matter. For all these reasons, we consider that the case of a research project that is carried out by a set of collaborating companies appears as an ideal case for going deeper in the investigation of i-accounting matters.

European Framework research projects, cofinanced by the European Commission, are carried out by partners operating as an extended enterprise, whose different intellectual assets (IAs) and the value thereof need to be recognised in order to successfully prepare the ground for the completion of the project.

Taking this into account, there is a need to manage the project as a "business" (even if this involves adopting a business attitude research), in the sense that it must be approached as a specific endeavour to achieve certain defined goals.

Based on the experience established from the authors' involvement in several projects, there is clear evidence that a considerable majority of projects fail because they do not succeed in identifying their individual purpose in terms of the knowledge produced and the excellence achieved.

This derives mainly as a result of the actual areas of research and their particular contributions being ill-defined, and the area under focus being insufficiently researched (such as who the competitors are, who the other relevant research actors are, and the nature of international trends in the area).

To avoid this, an obvious remedy for any company, and therefore any project, is to know at each distinct moment:

- Its assets (both tangible and intangible—especially the latter), its competitors, and (of course) the market
- How to express them with the most accurate figures possible

It is not uncommon to find projects which fail to have even a fairly realistic estimation of the global situation regarding the application of the project's intended outputs in the real world and the related market conditions.

Methods for the valuation or measurement of Intellectual Assets can be characterised as "solutions in search of a problem," and although there seems to be confusion about the distinction between valuation and measurement, the distinction is fundamental yet not fully recognised in the field (Andriessen, 2003).

The aim and the motivation of our approach is rather simple and straightforward: to come to a quantitative overview of the monetary value of all types of intangible assets that are to be created by the project in order to be able to exploit these assets, on two levels:

- For the entire consortium cumulatively
- For each individual partner separately

From the plethora of methodologies and practices which have been built variously on the schools of thought or "communities" of, amongst others, intellectual capital management, accounting, performance measurement, and valuation, we built our approach on an adapted version of the Weightless Wealth Toolkit by Andriessen (Andriessen, 2004). We have successfully employed this approach in past work as well as in currently-ongoing projects.

Facts of Life in the Research and Business World: Myths and Most Common Misconceptions

1. An institution able to show a record of efficient involvement in projects and research activities in a specific area in the past is able to set up a similarly adequately skilled research team in any new project.

2. A company active in the area addressed by a research project with a successful record of sales (products or services) will be similarly willing to sell the products or services, resulting from the research project in which it participates.

3. A company or institution participates in a research project in order to develop know-how necessary for its future operations, to cope with future challenges, and to establish strategic alliances.

In many cases, regarding the above, there is a huge discrepancy between what is put forward in a proposal or a review and the daily routine of a project. In certain other cases, intentions need to be supported by actions. In all cases, the everyday financial pressure, in periods of economic uncertainties in particular, affect the initial commitment to a project, under the surging demand for cash-flow and better economic indexes of the organisation.

A research institution might truly wish to enter a new research area, but has to operate under the tremendous pressure to bring in money, which makes researchers grasp at any opportunity that appears on the street corner. In the event of a proposal being successful, they will lose time and momentum because they will have to organise an ad hoc team, either by asking people who might be interested, or by hiring new people to get on board. This kills the potential of a good head start to a project.

A company might truly wish to bring new products in the market, if the project infrastructures were better and followed more closely the market realities and actual market demands, which is a difficult task for research projects; the demand side in a market builds on and pays for tangible items, things that you can see and immediately judge their actual utility and value.

Participation in a research and technological development (RTD) project allows an organisation to gain additional cash flow, national matching funds (for public research or academic institutes), and opportunities for press releases and company promotion. Sometimes organisations join research consortia just because they cannot stay out of them. Organisations tend to look for ready-made consortia to join. In very few cases, a proposal is written by more than three people, while most of the partners limit their contribution to curriculum vitaes (CVs) and lists of previous project participations.

While the other side, namely the project supply-side, usually shows ambivalence towards speculative opportunism (yesterday we were selling information brokerage systems, today we sell Semantic Web, tomorrow we will be selling grids and grid computing), it is not uncommon to have such a concept drift taking place continuously; this happens in the economy and in the market.

As the above may seem apocryphal, here are some examples:

- In a recently completed project, we had taken the responsibility to prepare a business plan. We collaborated closely with the manager. From the very start we had expressed our commitment to support this plan even after the completion of the project. We organised a set of communications and contacts with external consultants and spent much time on it, most of which did not come from the project budget as it involved several people from other departments of our institutions. The result was not positive as the manager's interest faded after the "successful" completion of the project. To our regret, what we know is that they keep on investing in the platform they developed in that project, and they do have a longer-term research plan for their work.

- In another recently completed project, we had taken the responsibility to prepare a business plan. We developed a fully developed draft which we circulated to the consortium, but there was no response or reaction to this. As this project has again terminated "successfully" by submitting also its e-TIP, why bother with such things like a business plan? It is obvious that the completion of the project meant the termination of partners' interest to the subject.

What is a lesson learned from the above stories from the front line is that there is an urgent need to examine our value chains: those that we have and which we need to improve, and those that we do not have and therefore need to create from scratch.

How to Institutionalise Practical Thinking and Business Culture in RTD Projects

An easy way to remedy this is to make the submission of a business plan part of the contractual obligations of a project, but we can imagine the malpractices that could be developed if this should become a requirement.

Figure 1. Research and (its) exploitation are bound together

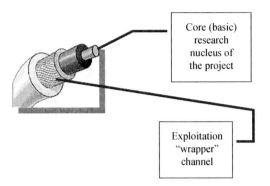

One way to cope with this is to make the business plan and, in general, the exploitation work, part of R&D activities.

Instead of the case of having them running sequentially, or in parallel, currently exploitation is rather regarded as a less important part of a project's scope; the centre of gravity lies in the R&D and technical tasks. The rest is viewed as more part of the administrative duties and paper work.

Actually, a radical approach is to couple these two activities together, as we insulate a channel by a second one to form a coaxial cable. This metaphor helps us to visualise the tight coupling that should exist between the two activities. If we think of the project as a business, then a marketing working group should be established and examine from day one the business potential as well as the business paths the consortium should follow.

To achieve this, a possible approach is to connect them right from the beginning, that is, from the proposal stage. A usual misconception regarding business plans is that they actually have to talk about a ready-to-ship product or service; this is simply not true. A research proposal is a special type of business plan; people prepare one in order to get funding for achieving their goals. One idiosyncratic aspect of the RTD proposals is that they actually form a class of meta-business plans (or business meta-plans) as they ask for funding which, if appropriately used, enables the creation of new businesses or the sustainment and improvement of existing ones.

For this, consortium members need to be able to answer some simple questions, including:

- What explicitly is it that we are proposing?
- How are we going to use it? Or sell it? For this last, we have to check whether the products we intend to use or sell really make sense from a business point of view. This has to do with issues such as not reinventing the wheel, or in the event that we are ambitious enough to introduce some new type of a wheel, we have to provide some evidence to the outside world (and in the case of the commission that cofinances

Table 1. Proposed vs. existing measures

Currently:	Our approach—what we propose:
Submission of one single part encompassing many different aspects, from technology to theology	Submission of a research proposal in two parts: • the research plan • the business plan
Reviews carried out by teams combined by academic/research staff and corporate practitioners doing everything: • Checking the scientific and research quality of the project work; • Assessing the validity of the technical decisions made and of the technological developments; and • Judging the appropriateness of the applications, the potential to the market, and the overall business potential of the project.	Splitting the two tasks in two different reviews, which may not necessarily need to take place in the usual high–cost way of a collocated meeting; thus we have: • A research review • A business review A project may do well in both or only one or none of these two aspects. Appropriate measures may take place to improve any of the weaknesses or shortcomings faced. One open issue is whether the teams of both review boards should or should not have interaction with each other, or whether the only link should be the commission through the project officer; we leave this for others to judge.
End comes with the TIP / e-TIP and Final Report submission	Consortia and coordinators are subject to a five-year period of investigation for the type and degree of usage if the project results. Of course, this may vary: Aspects like the creation of an improved know-how basis *that can be proven* is an important result of such a project. But it is a different thing if a company promises "new products" and ends up with the claim for an "increase of know-how in agent technologies." To conclude: The main item we gain is an increased transparency that shall shed light and fresh air to the Byzantine reality of EU-funded research projects.
Everyone comes with good faith and own quasi-mystic quasi-known repository of capabilities and know-how.	An explicit recognition of each partner's contributions is made by the time of submission, similar to a new business formation where all parties need to state their assets and also the responsibilities they will take in the new scheme. We can call this something like a project's intangible assets chart. This would facilitate the next item below.
Everyone leaves with good faith and virtually all-or-nothing from the board: like being in a party that you are able to leave without any further commitments or responsibilities, and without caring for cleaning up.	After termination of the project, a chart is formed that states explicitly the rights of the partners in regard to each of the assets created by the project. In this should be included anything that was created during the project lifetime and with resources owned: from software code and deliverables to components and systems or other reports and material.

the project, it is a matter of honesty and integrity to our investor) that it will really sell/contribute to the economy. And also:

•   Who is going to use it? Or sell it? For this last, we have to check whether the entities to perform these tasks are actually capable of performing them or are just pretending that they are.

All three of these questions are a matter of basic common sense. They are simple questions that anyone would like to ask but would not feel comfortable to do so, and this brings us to the situation we are facing today: Nobody asks for the business bottom line, and nobody wants to talk on that level either.

However, it is our belief that now is the right time and place to do so: The recent enlargement of EU with ten new countries, and the recession and slowdown in many of the member state economies rings the last warning bell that the new research framework programme must not repeat the mistakes of the previous. To make a clear statement here: especially the first framework programmes reflected a different reality that existed in the campuses of the universities and the research centres as well as in the corporate world. Since those years, the world has changed at many different levels.

Employing the Proposed Approach

Our approach builds on a five-step operation:

- **Step 1:** Identification of core competences of the organisation under consideration
- **Step 2:** Stress tests on each of them
  - o   Added-value test
  - o   Competitiveness test
  - o   Potentiality test
  - o   Sustainability test
  - o   Robustness test
- **Step 3:** Calculation of the contribution margins (monetary estimates) for each organisation
- **Step 4:** Identification of those core competences that are affected by the project
- **Step 5:** Valuation exercise

Going a few steps further from the original methodology (Andriessen, 2004), we have conducted a set of adaptations which are schematically presented in the chapter. For example, in our approach, the valuation is carried out with respect to the contribution of each particular core competence of the current and foreseen business of each partner individually.

Instead of saving on resources, which are usually scarce if not a rarity in technology-driven projects for business development, our goal was to find and apply a model that allows the estimation of the non-financial intangible assets for use in the project (i.e., in a non-accounting format), which would help us in the market valuation of different project results. According to Baruch Lev (2001, p. 68), "an intangible asset is a claim to future benefits that does not have a physical or financial (a stock or a bond) embodiment. A patent, a brand, and a unique organisational structure (for example, an Internet-based supply chain) that generate cost savings are intangible assets."

Table 2. Exemplary recognition of core competences affected within a collaborative research project

Core competence	Related with intangible assets	Contribution margin
Extensive domain know-how on ontologies, Web services, Semantic and Web domain knowledge	Many publications, conferences and research activities	Not yet quantified
Expertise in ERP systems	Highly qualified and domain- (legacy systems) experienced personnel	Not yet quantified
Innovative solutions	Highly qualified R&D department	Not yet quantified

Table 3. Value assessment stress tests for the 1ˢᵗ core competence

Added-value checklist	
Added-value	**Score (1=yes, 0=no)**
The core competence offers a substantial benefit for your customers or a substantial cost saving for your company.	1
Customers demand this specific benefit or cost saving.	0
This benefit is important for a large number of customers; it goes further than just "nice to have."	0
Customers will continue expecting this benefit in the near future; it is not simply a passing fancy.	1
Leadership in this core competence makes customers think you are different from the competition, rather than just better.	1
Total score added-value	3
Competitiveness checklist	
Competitiveness	**Score (1=yes, 0=no)**
Fewer than five of your competitors share this particular competence.	1
You are superior to your competitors in most aspects of this particular competence.	1
You invest substantially more time and money in this competence than your competitors.	1
Your customers choose your products or services largely because you have this competence.	0
Your leadership in this competence is generally recognised and can be illustrated by articles in trade journals, patents, and so on.	1
Total score competitiveness	4

Table 3. continued

Potential checklist	
Potential	**Score (1=yes, 0=no)**
There is an increasing demand for products/services that can be provided thanks to this core competence.	1
The core competence allows the development of new products and services in the future.	1
The core competence allows new markets to be entered in the future.	1
There are no economic threats (customers, suppliers, competitors) that will adversely affect the use of this competence.	1
There are no social threats (regulatory and social) that will adversely affect the use of this competence.	1
Total score potential	5
Sustainability checklist	
Sustainability	**Score (1=yes, 0=no)**
This core competence is scarce in your branch.	1
It would require considerable investments in time and/or money for competitors to master this competence.	1
Patents, trademarks, and other legal measures protect components of the competence.	0
This competence is a combination of a number of intangibles such as skills, knowledge, processes, and corporate culture, thus making it difficult to copy.	1
This competence cannot be obtained through acquisition or from other outside sources.	0
Total score sustainability	3
Robustness checklist	
Robustness	**Score (1=yes, 0=no)**
The group of people that possesses the skills and knowledge crucial for this competence is vulnerable.	0
The values and norms on which this competence is built are under pressure.	0
The technology and information technology systems that form part of this competence are vulnerable.	0
The primary and management processes that this competence uses are unreliable.	0
The endowments on which this core competence depends (like the corporate image or the installed client base) are vulnerable.	0
Total = A	0
Total score robustness = 5 – A	5

Table 4. Valuation table

Competence	CM	G	S	t=1	t=2	t=3	t=4	t=5	R	Value
1. Extensive domain know-how on ontologies, WS, Semantic and Web domain knowledge	Not yet quantified	12	3				—	—	5	Not yet quantified
2. Expertise in ERP systems	Not yet quantified	14	5						5	Not yet quantified
3. Innovative solutions	Not yet quantified	12	4					—	4	Not yet quantified
Total:		—	—						—	

Notes:

- *CM stands for* Contribution Margin in Euro.
- *G stands for* Growth *expressed as a percentage (%) that comes as the sum of:*

    Added Value + Competitiveness + Potential.

    Figures for the latter are taken from the stress tests of Table 3.
- *S stands for* Sustainability.
- *t1, t2, ... :* Monetary returns *for year 1, year 2, ...*
- *R stands for* Robustness *expressed as a percentage (%).*
- *Value stands for the* Gross Monetary Value *of the particular intangible asset created in the project and is expressed in Euro.*

The need to evaluate the intangible assets of a project is apparent, especially in the context of the Europe Union; since 1994, the European Commission has launched a series of studies, actions, and projects which aim to understand better the knowledge economy and the importance of intangibles as competitiveness factors (European Commission, 2000).

Though there is no standard and consistent method to evaluate intangible assets in a research project, we decided to use the Weightless Wealth method developed by Andriessen for a number of reasons:

- **It is up-to-date:** Although this is not a virtue in itself, we believe that the method reflects current trends and concerns in the business and research community; and

- **It is complete**, in that Andriessen took into account a set of 25 competing or competitive methods and approaches, and it is with respect to this that we decided that weightless wealth is an appropriate method to use.

As part of the work in collaborative research projects, we have defined a set of representations for organising the description of the above approach in tabular form that would help both the quantification and the visualisation of the exploitation work. Below, we present in three consecutive tables the aforementioned steps.

Conclusion and an Afterword on Intangibles

How we plan our research is essential and overall resource-critical for the impact this may have on our core business. Even for universities that are not considered as "straight money-making" entities, involvement in research activities without a plan other than gaining access to funds may seriously disorient them from their original mission.

Our experience from several projects shows that good intentions are not sufficient for ensuring the exploitation of results. Many of the existing patterns reflect an earlier situation when research was not as strictly monitored for its short-term results and its financial contributions to outcomes.

Currently, and due to the recession and slowdown in all of the member state economies, *all* organisations, both profit-making and non-profit-making (like universities) are trying to increase their opportunities to access Community funds, while on the other hand they are putting much greater emphasis on cutting costs and limiting their investments. This, as it is currently practiced, implies less-skilled (cheaper) research personnel and an attempt to introduce economies of scale *in any possible way*.

It is our firm belief that by better organising the field of exploitation reporting and planning, as well as by introducing a methodology like that presented in the chapter, major improvements can be achieved in the European research domain.

In this direction, we are working towards the formulation of an analytical scheme that would be able to support the described functionality in terms of a combined methodology and software system and in direct linkage with a project intangibles accounting infrastructure. The goal of such an implementation is the convergence to a cross-entry accounting practice in European RTD projects.

References

Andriessen, D. (2003, October 1-3). IC valuation and measurement: Why and how? In *Proceedings of the First Performance Management Association Intellectual Capital (PMA IC) Research Symposium,* Cranfield School of Management, UK.

Andriessen, D. (2004). *Making sense of intellectual capital: Designing a method for the valuation of intangibles* (pp. 441-464). Butterworth; Heinemann.

Edvinsson, L. (2002). *Corporate longitude: What you need to know to navigate the knowledge economy.* Financial Times Prentice Hall.

Edvinsson, L., & Malone, M. S. (1997). *Intellectual capital: The proven way to establish your company's real value by measuring its hidden brainpower.* London: HarperBusiness.

Ernst & Young. (1996). *Measures that matter.* Center for Business Innovation. Cambridge, MA: Ernst and Young, LLP.

European Commission (2000). *The intangible economy impact and policy issues.* Report of the European High Level Expert Group on the Intangible Economy, Brussels, Belgium.

IFAC—International Federation of Accountants. (Oct 1998). The measurement and management of intellectual capital. In *Professional accountants in business series, study 7* © International Federation of Accountants.

Lev, B. (2001) *Intangibles management, measurement, and reporting.* New York: Brookings Institute.

Sveiby, K. E. (1997). *The new organizational wealth. Managing and measuring knowledge-based assets.* San Francisco: Berret-Koehler Publishers Inc.

Sveiby, K. E., & Lloyd, T. (1988). *Managing knowhow. Increase profits by harnessing the creativity in your company.* London: Bloomsbury.

Endnotes

[1]   This is one of the traps inherent in the traditional balanced scorecard approach.

[2]   The trends in the way ICM is implemented across different sectors are fairly obvious. They are linked to the strategic logic of the firm and therefore to the type of resources and transformations that are fundamental for the value creation of the enterprise. For example, in pharmaceuticals, it is about increasing the effectiveness and efficiency of R&D; in retail, it is about increasing the effectiveness and efficiency of relational resources and organisational resources. For a supermarket or a department store, it is about increasing also the effectiveness and efficiency of competence; this is one of the reasons why department stores have problems if one manages them in terms of resource deployment structure, the same way as one manages a supermarket. In manufacturing, it is about tangible resources, so IC management adds relatively little in standardised subcontracting manufacturing. In telecom, on the operator side, it is about understanding the consequences of being a value network and deploying relational and organisational resources within this framework.

[3]   Under "classic" double entry accounting, a transaction is a collection of two or more rows whose debits equal credits. Each row of a journal entry has attributes that everybody can agree on (date, account code, description, etc.) and a long list of other attributes that begins with everybody agreeing, and descends into progressively less consensus, around the 10th or 15th attribute. In this respect, one can come to the conclusion that classic double entry accounting is both (providing) a methodology and a metadata framework capable of representing every kind of business transaction and financial state change that can exist in the business problem space.

Section IV

Technologies and Infrastructures

Chapter XII

Enabling the Virtual Organization with Agent Technology

Tor Guimaraes, Tennessee Tech University, USA

Abstract

Emerging agent-based systems offer new means of effectively addressing complex decision processes and enabling solutions to business requirements associated with virtual organizations. Intelligent agents can provide more flexible intelligence/expertise and help the smooth integration of a variety of system types (i.e., Internet applications, customer relationship management, supplier network management, enterprise resources management, expert systems). This chapter presents an overview of expert systems as the most widely-used approach for domain knowledge management today as well as agent technology, and shows the latter as a superior systems development vehicle providing flexible intelligence/expertise and the integration of a variety of system types. To illustrate, a system developed first by using an expert system approach and then by an agent-based approach is used to identify the strengths and weaknesses of the agent-based approach. Last, the practical implications of a company adoption of agent-based technology for systems development are addressed.

Introduction

As we enter the 21st century, organizations are faced with extremely difficult challenges in a hyper-competitive world. As posited by Khalil and Wang (2002), to remain competitive they must simultaneously be efficient on a global scale, be responsive to local needs and wants, and continuously learn and adapt to changes in their environment. To accomplish such daunting requirements, organizations must focus on what they do best and find reliable partners to do the rest. Thus, Donlon (1997) stated that being virtual is about having allies to bolster an organization's weaknesses. According to Carlsson (2002), there are a number of reasons for the emergence of the virtual organization, including: (1) to make products and services available at the moment of need, at the right place, tailored and built according to quality standards, and at a competitive price; (2) to enable customers to help design and produce their own products; and (3) to enable suppliers to plan and execute their own part of the production process. The most effective way to eliminate the oscillating variations of demand in the supply chain was to build a good interface for the actors of the supply chain to share their planning.

Rahman and Bhattachryya (2002) propose that virtual organizations provide an effective vehicle to integrate a company's operations with those of other enterprises, to work with customers and create a better product or service, to achieve a faster time to market, and to acquire a higher degree of product customization. Further, these authors observed that virtual organizations seem to have five main characteristics in common: (1) They have a shared vision and goal with their partners and a common protocol of cooperation; (2) they cluster activities around their core competencies; (3) they work jointly in teams of core competence groups, to implement their activities in a holistic approach throughout the value chain; (4) they process and distribute information in real-time throughout the entire network, which allows them to make decisions and coordinate actions quickly; and (5) they tend to delegate from the bottom up whenever economies of scale can be achieved, new conditions arise, or a specific competence is required for serving the needs of the whole group.

According to Khalil and Wang (2002), the management of a virtual organization involves essential functions that are unique when compared to the traditional management practices: (1) much greater need for mechanisms useful for information filtering and knowledge acquisition to assist managers with information overload, a common problem in the new environment; (2) increased need to generate and use knowledge faster and more effectively; further, organizational knowledge needs to be captured, stored, and made available where it is needed; thus, organizations will have to treat human knowledge as a key component of their asset base, and create knowledge bases or repositories that enable workers to shorten learning curves by sharing each other's experience; and (3) management has to be based on trust and minimal supervision since it is very difficult to supervise and control in geographically-dispersed units; managers and workers who are comfortable in a traditional workplace may find the new environment difficult to live with.

The Importance of IT for Virtual Organizations

Needless to say, the price of "virtuality" is also paid as an increased need for intelligence and communication. Indeed, Carlsson (2002) recognized that a virtual organization could not exist without an effective information exchange between all the actors and stakeholders. Over the years, organizations have used a wide variety of mechanisms to keep in contact with their partners, from couriers to the telegraph and telephone, to today's electronic communication systems such as electronic data interchange (EDI), imaging systems, and the Internet. As competition and business globalization increases, so does the need for creating more virtual organizations, for more effective communication systems, and for more intelligent information systems as essential enablers. As discussed in more detail later, expert systems and agent technology are the most important tools to enable the increasing levels of system intelligence required by today's virtual organizations. Besides the more traditional information systems, the Internet provides the ubiquitous global communications infrastructure required, and Martin (1999) observed that the Internet would enable business processes to change in dramatic ways: (1) New ways of buying and selling will create a new breed of online consumer, who will expect faster delivery, easier transactions, and more fact-based information; (2) the intranet will put more information in employees' hands and create virtual work communities; (3) boundaries between the corporation and the outside world, including suppliers and customers, will be erased; (4) new interactive dynamics will change how value is established for products; real-time, flexible pricing as value is established moment-by-moment; (5) new technologies for analyzing and predicting customer behavior in real-time will require companies to organize differently in order to move to a new Internet-version of customer-centric; (6) people will harness instant global communications, aggregating knowledge in real-time; collective experience will play a larger role in collecting information and in decision-making; and (7) the new means of networking will create a new generation of empowered and independent learners.

Khalil and Wang (2002) have proposed ways for IT to enable the management of virtual organizations by providing: (1) Web-based information systems, which enable uniform coupling of transactions within the organization for business-to-business (B2B) and business-to-consumer (B2C) applications; (2) sophisticated customer databases, which enable data mining to inform individual customers when new products become available and to create customized products and services; the main goal is to identify trends and turn consumer statistics into long-term customer relationships; (3) support for organizational learning by storing both structured and unstructured documents; this IT capability integrates, supports, and automates the acquisition, retention, maintenance, and sharing of information/expertise in a multimedia environment; and (4) groupware-supported coordination and decision-making so people from diverse cultures can work together effectively.

The Need for More Flexible and Integrative Intelligence

Carlsson (2002), while discussing the cyber trends proposed by Martin (1999) as the drivers for business in the Internet era, has prescribed the following focus points for IT: (1) intelligent transactions and logistics support, and providing customers with intelligent fact-finding methods and tools "on the run"; (2) intelligent support for virtual teams in planning, problem solving, and decision-making; (3) effective, interactive, and intelligent human-computer interaction; (4) support for products and services customization, continuous scanning of competitors with intelligent fact-finding and comparisons, and intelligent support for dynamic pricing decisions; (5) intelligent analysis and interpretation of customer data in online mode; (6) instant summarizing and synthesis of customer experience and feedback, and effective distribution and sharing of key insights; and (7) collecting, evaluating, and synthesizing insights for new value-adding products and services. Khalil and Wang (2002) confirm the importance of greater system intelligence when proposing that knowledge management support systems can help meet the managerial challenges posed by virtual organizations in the areas of system coordination and decision support for ill-structured tasks in a more loosely-structured organization. Besides the need for greater intelligence, Kishore and McLean (2002) have identified the integration of new information systems and technologies with the existing ones as more critical than ever before, as newer and newer pervasive and mobile information technologies are implemented.

Expert systems (ES) became the most important Artificial Intelligence technology since the early 1980's. Today, ES applications are found widely in business and government as ES development techniques and tool kits have multiplied. ES technology provides a software representation of organizational expertise dealing with specific problems, and it will remain a useful mechanism to accomplish the knowledge management. However, as an enabler of virtual organizations, which require a more flexible and integrative type of intelligence, traditional ES technology has several shortcomings: (1) ES are typically brittle, dealing poorly with situations that "bend" the rules; ES components typically are not intelligent enough to learn from their experiences while interacting directly with users; thus, the rules encoded initially do not evolve on their own but must be modified directly by developers to reflect changes in the environment; (2) ES are typically isolated, self-contained software entities; very little emphasis is placed on tool kits that support interaction with other ES or external software components; (3) as the ES develops, functionality increases are accompanied by an ever-growing knowledge base in which inconsistencies and redundancies are difficult to avoid; and (4) over time, portions of the process that initially required human intervention become well understood and could be totally automated, but there is no mechanism in place to support the transition from human-activated objects to autonomous objects.

These are exactly the types of shortcomings agent technology (AT) was developed to address. According to Carlsson (2002), ES technology is now being replaced by intelligent systems built to provide two key functions: (1) the screening, sifting and filtering of a growing overflow of data, information and knowledge, and (2) the effective decision support. When discussing the evolution of the Internet as a world where humans are quickly becoming a minority overwhelmed by intense communication between devices and services, Waldo (2002) suggests that the very evolution of Internet usage is exacerbating the need for more intelligent systems: "Humans are quickly becoming a minority on the Internet, and the majority stakeholders are computational entities that are interacting with other computational entities without human intervention. When services must be recognized and used by other computational entities, no such assumption can be made. Traditional techniques used in the development of distributed systems can be combined with agent technologies to produce networks that are self-administering and allow the kinds of rapid change and evolution that will be required if the Internet is to continue to grow and thrive as a business vehicle" (p.

9). The objective of this study is to identify AT's characteristics which will make it the most powerful enabler for managing the knowledge flows and system integration required by virtual organizations. To accomplish that we first discuss what distinguishes it from widely-implemented ES technology, and its strengths and weaknesses in systems development. The discussion is further illustrated through a case study in which the specific tradeoffs between these technologies are explored.

Using Agent Technology

While no standard definition of an agent has yet emerged, most definitions agree that agents are software systems that carry out tasks on behalf of human users. Intelligent agents generally possess the three properties: autonomy, sociability, and adaptability.

Autonomy means that an agent operates without the direct intervention of humans and has some control over its own actions and internal state. It is capable of independent action (Wooldridge & Jennings, 1995). An agent does not simply act in response to its environment; it is able to exhibit goal-directed behavior by taking the initiative.

Sociability refers to an agent's ability to cooperate and collaborate with other agents and possibly human users to solve problems. Agents share information, knowledge, and tasks among themselves and cooperate with each other to achieve common goals. The capability of an agent system is not only reflected by the intelligence of individual agents but also by the emergent behavior of the entire agent community. The infrastructure for cooperation and collaboration includes a common agent communication language like the Knowledge Query Manipulation Language (KQML) (Finin, Labrou, & Mayfield, 1998) or the Foundation for Intelligent Physical Agent (FIPA) (FIPA, 2000).

Finally, *adaptability* refers to an agent's ability to modify its own behavior as environmental circumstances change. An agent learns from experience to improve its performance in a dynamic environment. That learning can be centralized, as performed by a single agent without interaction with other agents, or decentralized, as accomplished through the interaction of several agents that cooperate to achieve the learning goal (Cantu, 2000).

Agent technology represents a new and exciting means of decomposing, abstracting, and organizing large complex problems. Agents, as autonomous, cooperating entities, represent a more powerful and flexible alternative for conceptualizing complex problems. As attention is increasingly placed on distributed applications like mobile and Web-based systems, applications will not necessarily run from a central location. Communications can be costly in such environments. Direct routing of data to the recipient must be fast and efficient to make additional bandwidth available to others. Agent architectures provide a template for a distributed architecture that lends itself to many of these emerging applications. Agents can be used as mediators between heterogeneous data sources, providing the means to interoperate, using ontologies for describing the data contained in their information sources, and communicating with the others via an agent communication language (Broome, Gangopadhyay, & Yoon, 2002).

For problems characterized by dynamic knowledge, it is infeasible to predict and analyze all possible interactions among modules at design time. Flexible interaction among agents at run-time enables an agent-based system to effectively handle dynamic, unpredictable knowledge. Although knowledge of some problems is dynamic, the change is often local, affecting a subset of requirements. Therefore, some agents can be designated to deal with the dynamic knowledge of a problem, and the functionality of those agents can evolve, reflecting the changes which are encountered.

The inherent autonomy of agents enables the agent-based system to perform its tasks without direct external intervention. Agents can not only react to specific events but can also be proactive, polling the environment for events to determine the proper action in a given circumstance. Despite the increased level of autonomy in an agent-based system, however, the system itself may not be able to automate all levels of intelligent activity. Human users may be required to perform higher-level intelligent tasks. An intelligent distributed agent architecture that allows flexible interactions among participating agents maps well to applications, like expert systems, that require seamless integration with humans. Further, agent technology offers mechanisms for knowledge sharing and interoperability between autonomous software and hardware systems characterized by heterogeneous languages and platforms. Agents can be used as mediators between these various systems, facilitating interoperability.

Enhancing Expert Systems with Agent-Based Systems

One way to better understand AT is to compare it with the more widely-used expert systems. This does not imply that ES technology is obsolete or that ES development has nothing in common with agent-based system development. Nevertheless, in general there are some important distinctions between ES and agent-based systems, which make the latter ideal for integrating individual ES with other ES and other system types. Probably the most important distinction is that expert systems rely on the user to initiate the reasoning process and to accomplish any action associated with the recommendations provided by the system (Yannis, Finin, & Peng, 1999). The integration of human interaction, then, is assumed and has been greatly facilitated by development tool kits and environments. Agents, on the other hand, are inherently autonomous. That does not mean that the integration of human interaction is necessarily complex. The human is simply another agent in the society of agents. While the user roles vary dramatically between the two paradigms, both readily accommodate human interaction.

Another important distinction is that expert systems have a fixed set of rules that clearly define their reasoning process, while agents interact with their environment and adapt to new conditions. Thus, an application that characteristically incorporates dynamic changes in its data and rules is more naturally accommodated by agent-based techniques. Further, the expert system's knowledge base impacts the modularity and scalability of the system. As new functions are introduced into the system, the central knowledge base grows increasingly large. New rules risk conflicts with old, and changed rules potentially impact more functions than the developer may have planned. Agents, on the other hand, are extremely modular, like self-contained programs that can readily be reused across applications.

Finally, the social interaction inherent in agents facilitates mobile and distributed systems, with formal standards in place outlining interfaces between agents assumed to be heterogeneous in design. Expert systems, on the other hand, are fundamentally built as a cohesive product with a single overarching goal. Despite early emphasis on linking knowledge bases and integrating expertise, those goals are rarely achieved, perhaps because of the issues of combining knowledge bases without the benefit of a standard interface technique. Further, the system components are rarely reused outside the system for which they were built. In fact, it is quite common to throw away one prototype and completely rebuild the next version from scratch. Thus, tools are built with an emphasis on rapid prototyping rather than on facilitating component reuse.

AT Weaknesses

Most AT weaknesses can be traced back to its lack of maturity. While agent concepts were under discussion as far back as 1985 (Minsky, 1985), applications have been slow to develop, due in part to a lack of mature system development tool kits that enable agents to represent and reason about their actions. A number of systems are now available or under development (Barbaceanu, 2001; Traverse, 2001), but they still suffer from a general immaturity. A second weakness is the lack of software engineering techniques specifically tailored to agent-based systems. Although there are software development techniques such as object-oriented analysis and design, the existing approaches fail to adequately capture an agent's flexible, autonomous problem-solving behavior, the richness of an agent's interactions, and the complexity of an agent system's organizational structures; thus they are unsuitable for agent-based systems. If agents are to realize their potential, it is necessary to develop software engineering methods appropriate for developing such systems (Wooldridge, Jennings, & Kinny, 2003). A third weakness is the general difficulty associated with decomposing goals and tasks in ways that balance the computation and communication requirements, avoid or reconcile conflicts, and still achieve the initial objective. Finally, the issue of privacy is particularly relevant for a system in which software components act independently across a distributed environment. While standards are under development for insuring that agents are locked out of systems where they are unwelcome, such standards generally require cooperative agents that do not intentionally attack an unreceptive host.

As discussed by other authors, (Lu & Guimaraes, 1989) whether or not to use ES technology in systems development is one major consideration. Once that decision has been made, various ES development approaches must also be considered (Yoon & Guimaraes, 1993).

Last, as the previous discussion indicates, the software developer must consider numerous issues in determining whether an agent-based approach is appropriate for a given application. In the final analysis, the system requirements must drive these choices. To illustrate the choice of using an agent-based approach over a strictly ES-based approach, a case study is presented next.

The Reverse Mortgage Advisor (Rema) Case Study

REMA Background

A reverse mortgage is a special type of home loan that allows a homeowner to convert the equity in his or her home into retirement income. The equity, built up over years of home mortgage payments, can be paid to the homeowner in a lump sum, in a stream of payments, or a combination of the two. Unlike a traditional home equity loan or second mortgage, repayment is not required as long as the borrowers continue to use the home as their principal residence (HUD, 2001). While reverse mortgages have long been seen as a means of increasing the income of the poor or elderly, they have more recently been proposed as a mechanism for tapping home equity for a variety of options and at various stages in the life cycle (Rassmussen, Megbolugbe, & Morgan, 1997). In either case, "because each reverse mortgage plan has different strengths—and because fees and fraud can catch unsuspecting customers—experts say seniors should either shop smart with these tricky loans or not shop at all" (Larson, 1999, p.12). The Internet already plays an important role in supporting the dissemination of information about reverse mortgages. In an effort to increase public awareness of this unique loan opportunity, federal regulators, consumer advocates, and loan companies have all developed Web sites (AARP, 2001; FannieMae, 2001; HUD, 2001; Reverse, 2001) to supplement the publications and training currently available through more traditional media. Such Web sites provide information on mortgage options and sources, answers to frequently-asked questions, and even "calculator" functions to help "shoppers" estimate the amount of loan for which they are eligible. The use of Web sites, however, can be quite daunting, particularly for the potential reverse mortgage client who is over 62 and of limited income. The REMA project was initiated to increase the accessibility of reverse mortgage information.

REMA I, A Traditional Expert System Approach

REMA I is an expert system designed to provide a structured approach to determining whether an individual qualifies for a reverse mortgage. Unlike the traditional Web site, users are not left to their own devices as they sort through information to better understand their loan options. Instead, REMA I provides advice on Web sites to visit and recommended loan types. It is meant to supplement the Web-based technologies that precede it.

- **System architecture:** REMA I was developed using Multilogic's Resolver® and Netrunner® tools. Resolver® is a knowledge-based system development tool that combines a powerful rule editor with a flexible visual decision tree interface and inference engine. While it supports backward and forward chaining, linear programming, fuzzy logic, and neural net reasoning, REMA used the default goal-driven backward chaining technique. Resolver® greatly facilitated the coding process, supporting not only the encoding of the initial logic representation, but the debug process as well. Once REMA was developed, the executable was ported to Netrunner®, the engine that supports Web-top publication of Resolver® applications. Figure 1 provides a conceptual illustration of the final application, though, in fact, the knowledge base and inference engine are located in Resolver® and their output is located in Netrunner® at the time the application runs.

The decision process was initially represented as a decision tree. The decision tree was then converted into a series of 34 "if-then" statements. Each of the 34 rules resulted in the recommendation of one or more of 16 possible outcomes. The knowledge base represents the 34 rules the experts follow when providing advice to potential reverse mortgage consumers. Queries provide links to local Hypertext Markup Language (HTML) files that provide reverse mortgage training. Those files may, in turn, reference additional information in HTML files at other sites provided by government agencies, consumer advocates, or loan companies. Those links are provided to the Web server through Netrunner®.

- **System interface:** In addition to providing answers to fixed questions, the user may choose to view hypertext about home ownership issues, view the rules associated with the question (by clicking on "Why are you asking this question?"), or return to a previous state by undoing the last answer. The UNDO option is useful if, for example, users find they are not old enough to qualify for a loan but would still like to continue the analysis. The user must backtrack and modify the age answer to continue.

- **REMA I shortcomings:** As is common in the life cycle of an expert system, upon completing REMA I, the current system's shortcomings were identified for improvement in future iterations. The current version is clearly at an early stage of development, so it was expected that the developer would want to "grow the system" by incorporating more than the initial three loan companies selected for Phase 1. However, several of the problems identified indicate that the expert system design may not be best for

Figure 1. REMA architecture

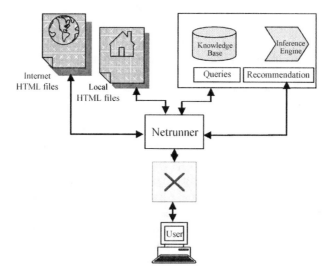

meeting overall project objectives. The "build a little, test a little" approach associated with expert systems was quite useful in facilitating discussions with experts, but the outcome of those discussions indicates an alternative design option should at least be considered before moving to the next development phase.

First, beyond the original assessment of loan qualifications, a cost-benefit analysis is the primary basis for selecting the optimal loan type. While many of the rules for determining whether a user qualifies for a given loan are easily expressed in symbolic terms, the cost-benefit analysis is a computational rather than symbolic algorithm. In order to take full advantage of the Resolver® tools, the cost-benefit analysis was replaced with a number of rules-of-thumb. For example, if the applicant's home is very expensive, the Freedom plan is usually best. Otherwise, the HUD and FannieMae options are best. One problem is that the concept of "expensive" varies from state to state. The REMA I rules were stated crisply (with "expensive" arbitrarily set to $400,000, for example), and at a minimum should be replaced with fuzzy rules. Ideally, however, the exact loan size, interest rates, application fees, and so forth, should be used to provide accurate assessments. These inaccuracies must be avoided in future developments. In some cases, systems (like FannieMae's MorNet) are available to compute exact costs and benefits. While the original objective of the project was not to replace these previously developed computational systems but to augment them with a training system, the longer term objective should most assuredly move toward a combination of the two types of systems. Otherwise, the advice portion of REMA will be inaccurate, which could have adverse legal implications. An agent-based design would more naturally accommodate the seamless integration of other software packages, while expert systems have very little support for interfacing with other expert systems.

Next, in generating REMA I, the developers discovered that both the rules for providing recommendations and the Web sites used for training users were extremely dynamic. A complete redesign of the decision tree and training files was required between building the baseline system, based on books and Web site information, and the current iteration, based on discussions with the experts. It was not just because tables of costs and benefits changed, though that did cause some system reconfiguration. Additionally, over a very brief period, Congress passed new regulations regarding applicant qualification requirements; companies opted out of the list of reverse mortgage providers; other companies restructured their programs to focus on different target audiences; and, as always, Web pages appeared and disappeared across the Internet without notice to the sites that referenced them. Again, expert systems technology was not meant to accommodate such a dynamic environment.

Finally, the training aspect of the system was not as powerful as one might hope. This is due, in part, to the fact that the training simply took the form of instructional text. It certainly was an improvement over the baseline, in which users were on their own to wander the Web looking for relevant documentation. Instead, REMA I focused the Web searches addressing those specific issues of which a prospective applicant should be aware. An online system of this sort, however, has the potential of being a tutor, keeping up with the users' previous searches and expressed preferences to even further tailor the training process. It has a potential for notifying the user as better options arise in this dynamic loan environment. But reaching this potential requires greater autonomy than is typical of expert systems.

The easiest choice for Phase II of system development would be to continue building the next iteration of the current expert system. The next iteration would require: (1) an update of references to outside Web sites; (2) current system assessments from experts; (3) correction of any recently modified data for the HUD, FannieMae, and Freedom Plan options currently represented; (4) incorporation of at least one new loan source; (5) fuzzification of current crisp rules-of-thumb for loan source selection; and (6) incorporation of the MorNet expert system for calculating costs and benefits for those companies it covers. The general system architecture would continue as depicted in Figure 1. However, for the reasons outlined above, instead of enhancing the current ES-based REMA, a decision was made to first explore the use of an agent-based approach to the problem.

REMA II, an Agent-Based Approach

System Architecture: Agents are specific, goal-oriented abstractions of task requirements in systems. From the discussion of the current REMA I system presented in this chapter, we derive a set of system requirements that agents must implement. These are:

1.   **Mediating** between multiple external agencies including HUD and Fannie Mae, to ensure that external information contained in the system remains current

2.   **Translating** between external information collected by the mediation with the external agencies (above) and the internal information on user characteristics and goals

3.   **Recommending** the appropriate course of action to the user based on rules and expertise contained in the system

4.   **Interfacing** with the user to guide them through collection of user characteristics and present the system recommendations to them

5.   **Supervision** of the entire process to ensure that the asynchronous collection of information from external agencies is assimilated and incorporated in the recommendations of the system and the information presented to the user

The above system requirements, as derived from the design of the existing system, form the basis for an agent-based approach. The agent-based approach to REMA consists of multiple mediator agents, tutor agent, user interface agent, recommender agent, and supervisor agent, as shown in Figure 2.

Individual *mediator agents* are responsible for maintaining the most current information for calculating the costs and benefits of an individual company's reverse mortgage plan. These agents are responsible for interfacing with the external agencies that provide critical information about the programs available for REMA users and ensure that such information is available to the users of REMA. *User interface agents* collect and maintain information on the user's goals and personal characteristics, required for a reverse mortgage application. They are responsible for interaction with the user and provide guided input of user goals and characteristics in addition to presenting users with the final results and recommendations

Figure 2. Agent architecture for REMA

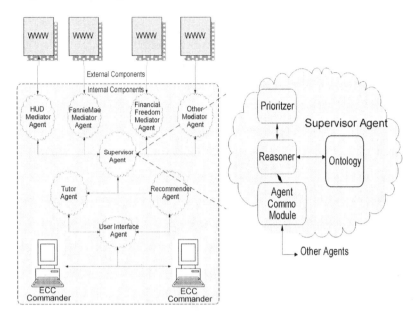

of the REMA system. The user agent receives information from the user, through the user interface, and presents user characteristics and goals to the *tutor agent* to determine which internal and external information is most required to teach the principles of reverse mortgages. A *recommender agent* incorporates user characteristics and the most recent loan company information in performing a cost-benefit analysis to determine the best loan source of those available. This information is passed back to the user interface agent with information on options that are available to the user given their characteristics and goals. Finally, a *supervisor agent* is responsible for the overall function of the agent system and performs critical meta-functions to prioritize data requests, supply the most recent loan company data, and interpret terminology from heterogeneous sources to consistent internal agents by providing and interpreting a shared ontology of concepts contained in the REMA system.

- **System interface:** REMA II is initialized with the user being assigned representation in the system through a user interface agent. This agent interacts with the user and collects information about the user through an interactive questionnaire. Information about the user is passed to the tutor agent who is responsible for matching the goals and characteristics of the user with information from the mediator agents to find the appropriate agency that may fulfill user needs. The mediator agents, under supervision of the supervisor agent, constantly and asynchronously, update their information of the most current programs that are available from the various agencies they interface with. Upon performing the matching, the tutor agent generates a match between the internal information provided by the user and the external information available from the financial agencies, through the mediator agents. These results are transferred to the

Figure 3. Use case diagram for agent-based REMA

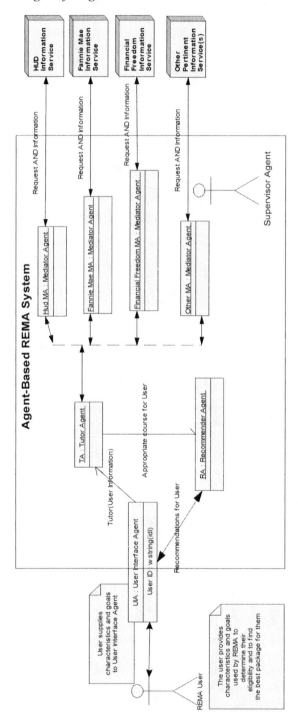

recommender agent, which maintains the knowledge about courses of action based on specific information received by the tutor agent. The recommender agent maintains an active, in-memory representation of the decision tree illustrated in Figure 2. Upon receiving user-specific information, it can select the rules that are fired and present those rules and the associated explanations for the recommendations as the action-specific knowledge that is pertinent given the users' characteristics and goals. The recommender agent sends this knowledge, as specific recommendations for the user, to the user interface agent who is responsible for presenting the recommended course of action(s) to the user.

The overall flow of information and user-system interaction is presented in the use-case diagram in Figure 3. The diagram shows the boundaries of the system and its interactions with external agencies, in addition to the oversight role of the supervisory agent.

Figure 4 shows a sample screen generated for the REMA II user. The top panel shows the rules that are part of REMA II, allowing the user to gain more knowledge about the explanations offered. Each rule, as illustrated in Figure 5, contains a set of conditions and a matching result, or decision value, for the REMA application. Each rule also contains a user-friendly explanation to provide textual explanation of the rule to the user in a human-interpretable manner. The user agent interface takes input from the user on various attributes, in terms of the parameters that are acceptable to REMA. For example, in answer to the question "*Do you own your own home?*" the user can only reply "Yes" or "No". After input of all required parameters, the user asks the system to advise them by clicking the decide button; then the rule space is searched and the result is displayed to the user.

Figure 4. Sample interface screen of agent-based REMA

Figure 5. REMA II Rule in eXtended Markup Language (XML) format

Assessment of ES vs. Agent-Based Approaches

ES Approach

- **Strengths and opportunities:** As outlined in Table 1, the enhanced expert system approach is best when meeting quick turnaround requirements. Multilogic's Resolver® and Netrunner® tools greatly facilitate the system development process, and the consistency of design further insures efficiency. The resulting system will most certainly continue to support faster decision-making and improved consistency, less demand on experts, and improved public understanding of the reverse mortgage process. Further, it will continue to support direct access local HTML files or inserting new ones. Because of its Web emphasis, the system continues to broaden the audience for reverse mortgage training over previous brochure and booklet techniques. Finally, its "build a little, test a little" techniques have been shown to make effective use of the limited time of experts in the field, while essentially serving to formally document a process that is not currently well documented.

- **Weaknesses and threats:** The major shortcoming of this approach, however, is that it fails to resolve the three problem issues identified in developing REMA I. While a link to MorNet will improve the computational component of system recommendations as new loan companies are added, those insertions will continue to be computational,

Table 1. Analysis of the strengths, weaknesses, opportunities, and threats

	Strengths	Weaknesses	Opportunities	Threats
Agent-Based Approach	Faster decision-making; Improved consistency; Less demand on experts; Improved reverse mortgage understanding; Supports better focused Web searches; Rules reflect changes in the environment; Other ES work more easily incorporated; and Recommendations/ training adapt to user.	Limited sites with XML/ontology standard; and Limited agent development tool kits.	Access information directly from source; Easily incorporate new training topics; Reach a broader audience; Formalize expert's process; and Autonomous recommendations.	Web sites volatile, with distributed control; Changing interface standards; and Insufficient training data.
Enhanced ES Approach	Effective development tools; Faster decision-making; Improved consistency; Less demand on experts; Improved reverse mortgage understanding; and Supports better focused Web searches.	Accurately addressing the cost-benefit analysis will render the expert system tools less effective; Dynamic data and rules, controlled outside; Training limited to informational text; Knowledge base isolated from Web data; and Does not incorporate other ES work.	Access information directly from source; Easily incorporate new training topics; Reach a broader audience; Rapid prototype effective use of experts; and Formalize expert's process.	Inaccurate recommendations costly; and Potential legal impact from misinformation.

rather than symbolic, in nature. The value of the more established tool sets associated with expert systems will be less noticeable than if the entire task were heavily symbolic in nature. Further, while this approach will incorporate changes to the current data and rules, bringing the system up-to-date, it does not address the fact that the rules and data will change again. The static nature of the expert system limits its ability to adapt to the dynamic reverse mortgage process it represents or the dynamic Web environment in which it resides. Its lack of advanced communication or interoperability tools limits its ability to incorporate the functionality of other expert systems or Web sites into its knowledge base. As a result, the system will require frequent manual updates or risk providing inaccurate information that could cost its users money. Such losses may, in turn, carry negative legal implications. Finally, its lack of autonomy restricts the training function to the display of informational text rather than a full-blown tutor that learns about the user as it progresses or, on its own initiative, notifies the user of changes in loan options.

Agent-Based Approach

- **Strengths and opportunities:** Possessing the properties of autonomy, social ability, and adaptability, agent technology provides the potential for greatly enhancing the capabilities of the REMA system. As illustrated in Table 1, the strengths and opportunities of an agent-based system parallel in many ways those of the expert system approach. The system will most certainly continue to support faster decision-making, improved consistency, less demand on experts, and improved public understanding of the reverse mortgage process. Further, it will continue to support direct access to a variety of loan sources by linking into their Web sites. Because of its Web emphasis, it continues to broaden the audience for reverse mortgage training over previous brochure and booklet techniques. The agent-based approach, however, has several additional strengths. First, it more specifically addresses the three problem areas identified at the end of Phase I: (1) Agent-based systems deal equally well with problems of a computational or symbolic nature; (2) it better addresses the dynamic nature of the reverse mortgage process; rather than establishing fixed rules that must be intentionally modified by the developer at regular intervals, information agents are established to seek and substitute relevant parameters from regulated websites as appropriate; and (3) the learning component of agent-based systems supports incorporating a well-designed tutoring system that is both diagnostic, discovering the nature and extent of the user's knowledge, and strategic, planning its responses based on its findings about the learner. Also, while the three alternative loan sources are, in fact, representative of the available alternatives, future work must incorporate more companies. The agent-based approach provides a natural mechanism for incorporating new loan companies with minimal impact on previous software components. The ontology component of the supervisor agent would require updates as new loan sites are added, but it minimizes the effort in mediating between heterogeneous data sources. Finally, the autonomous nature of the agent facilitates an ongoing search for the best possible loan. Thus, the agent can provide information about a new or improved loan source without waiting for the user to think of querying for improvements.

- **Weaknesses and threats:** While agent development environments are available, they are generally not as mature as those for expert systems, so system development will generally be more time-consuming. The interface to remote Web sites could be facilitated by the use of the XML standard and an ontology to resolve varied terminology across heterogeneous formats; however, these standards are relatively new, and most of the sites of interest are HTML-based instead. It will, therefore, be important to establish a working relationship with sites across which data is shared; otherwise, the volatility of the data and the distribution of control will render the project ineffectual. Since the standards are relatively new and not widely in force, the developer risks having a new standard move in and replace the one on which the system is based. Finally, while the agent-based approach supports the development of an adaptive tutor/advisor, most learning algorithms require large amounts of data, which may be initially difficult to obtain.

Recommendation for Next Phase of Development

Because of the dramatic increases in functionality associated with the agent-based approach, it is recommended that the fully functional system be built on the agent-based prototype, REMA II, rather than on the REMA I expert system. The only reason for selecting to an expert system approach would be to support a fast turnaround incremental improvement on the current system. Given current availability of a prototype system for immediate use, the plan that best incorporates the dynamic and heavily computational components of the advisor and the user-adaptive, self-initiating components of the tutor is preferred.

Practical Implications

A critical question for system development managers is, Under what circumstances would it likely be better to use AT instead of the presently more widely-used ES technology for the development of specific applications? AT is extremely promising, and it behooves all system development managers to understand its potential and limitations and perhaps begin to experiment with AT for possible adoption in the future. However, there are limitations. There are situations where the use of AT will not be efficient in terms of system development cost and implementation time. Systems development managers must remember that presently AT is still at a relatively early stage of adoption in industry at large. The availability of systems developers competent with the technology is relatively scarce. Also, there is a lack of systems development tool kits and shells, which today are commonly found for the development of ES. As discussed previously in the chapter, the fact that AT is useful for addressing relatively more complex application requirements makes the systems development analysis and design tasks correspondingly more complex and requiring software engineering methods that are still under development. In a similar fashion, the ability of AT to bridge the gap between distributed application components may raise questions about user privacy, data integrity, and human control over the agent-based system. Nevertheless, increasingly there are applications which will require the use of AT. The following conditions are likely to call for the use of AT in system development: (1) applications requiring flexible decision-making beyond fuzzy logic and/or the relatively strict rules required by ES; (2) applications which require enough intelligence for direct system interaction with end users and for system learning from the experience itself, whereby the rules will evolve on their own without the need for modification by systems developers; and (3) applications that require a flexible and complex integration of two or more ES and/or systems of other types.

As the business community puts greater importance on the role of knowledge management in capturing collective expertise and distributing it in a manner that produces a payoff, the use of agent-based technology will have increasingly significant business implications. With the dramatic increase in Internet activity over the past five years, agents can play an important role in monitoring, filtering, and recommending information, using user profiles to personalize their support. Agent mediators can facilitate the exchange of data among heterogeneous sites, maintaining an ongoing record of variable site formats and mapping information seamlessly into a format more easily understood by their users. Network management agents can focus on increasing throughput and minimizing delay by adapting protocols to the current hardware and workload environment. In general, complex problems can be decomposed into smaller, segmented problems that can be more easily resolved. All of these advances open decision support and e-commerce opportunities to a wider community and facilitate tapping more widely-distributed knowledge bases to improve quality. Such advances are already within reach for many application areas. However, the ability to reach the full potential of these advances relies on continued development of software engineering methods specifically tailored to agent-based systems, software development tools, and security mechanisms that accommodate a widely-distributed, mobile computing environment.

The effective use of agent technology enables developers to gain significant advantages over existing technologies in achieving their knowledge management goals. An increased level of software system autonomy limits the user burden for direct intervention and can relieve communication requirements in a bandwidth-limited environment. The distributed decision-making process can increase robustness and, because tasks are performed in parallel, overall system efficiency increases. The approach facilitates developing mediators that can integrate heterogeneous and legacy systems without requiring a single data representation structure. Further, the techniques support incremental development of complex systems via independent reusable components.

The REMA case illustrates some of the many powerful enhancements achieved by using agent techniques where expert systems were originally envisioned. To system designers/developers, one of the most compelling arguments for using only ES is the ready availability of software development tools to support this more mature development technique. Although there are many issues to be addressed for agent technology to realize its full potential, the technology has advanced at a fast rate due to the significant research effort in both academia and industry. Many of the components to build effective agents are moving beyond research communities and coming into common use in the immediate future. With their arrival, we now have a powerful integrator for Web-based systems with the more traditional types of systems (including ES), thus providing a strong infrastructure for managing corporate knowledge.

Acknowledgments

The author is grateful to the Fannie Mae Foundation for the grant that supported the development of the REMA I prototype, to Dr. J. Liebowitz who led that prototype development effort, to Mr. Ed Szymanoski for his constructive review and comments on the REMA I effort, and to Ms. Judy Hees for her assistance with this project.

References

AARP. (2001). Reverse mortgage. Retrieved 2001, from http://www.aarp.org

Barbaceanu, M. (2001). *The agent building shell: Programming cooperative enterprise agents.* Retrieved 2001 from http://www.eil.utoronto.ca/ABS-page/ABS-overview.html

Broome, B., Gangopadhyay, A., & Yoon, V. (2002). *CAER: An ontology-based community of agents for emergency relief.* Paper presented at the 6th World Multi-Conference on Systemics, Cybernetics, and Informatics, July, Orlando, FL.

Cantu, F. (2000). *Reinforcement and Bayesian learning in multiagent systems: The MACS project* (Tech.Rep.No. CIA-RI-042). Center for Artificial Intelligence, ITESM

Carlsson, C. (2002). Decisions support in virtual organizations: The case for multi-agent support. *Group Decision and Negotiation, 11*(3), 185-221.

Donlon, J. P. (1997, July). The virtual organization. *Chief Executive,* (125), 58-66.

FannieMae (2001). *Our business is the American dream.* Retrieved 2001, from: http://www.fanniemae.com

Finin, T., Labrou, Y., & Mayfield, J. (1998). KQML as an agent communication language. In J. M. Bradshaw (Ed.), *Software agents* (p. 28). Boston: MIT Press.

FIPA. (2000). *FIPA specification repository.* Retrieved 2001, from www.fipa.org/repository

HUD. (2001). *Homes and communities.* Retrieved 2001, from http://www.hud.gov

Khalil, O., & Wang, S. (2002). Information technology enabled meta-management for virtual organizations. *International Journal of Production Economics, 75*(1), 127-134.

Kishore, R., & McLean, E. (2002). The next generation enterprise: A CIO perspective on the

vision, its impacts, and implementation challenges. *Information Systems Frontiers, 4*(1), 121.

Larson, M. (1999). *Shopping for a reverse mortgage: Few products, lots of tricky choices.* Retrieved 2001, from http://www.bankrate.com/brm/news/loan

Lu, M., & Guimaraes, T. (1989). A guide to selecting expert systems applications. *Journal of Information Systems Management,* (Spring), *6*(2), 8-15.

Martin, C. (1999). *Net future.* New York: McGraw-Hill.

Minsky, M. (1985). *The society of mind.* New York: Simon and Schuster.

Rahman, Z., & Bhattachryya, S. K. (2002). Virtual organisation: A stratagem. *Singapore Management Review, 24*(2), 29-45.

Rassmussen, D., Megbolugbe, I., & Morgan, B. (1997). The reverse mortgage as an asset management tool. *Housing Policy Debate, 8*(1), 173-194.

Reverse. (2001). *Independent information on reverse mortgages for consumers, their families, professional advisors, and nonprofit counselors.* Retrieved 2001, from http://www.reverse.org

Traverse, M. (2001). *Agent-based programming environments.* Retrieved 2001, from http://xenia.media.mit.edu/~mt/childs-play-pp.html

Waldo, J. (2002). Virtual organizations, pervasive computing, and an infrastructure for networking at the edge. *Information Systems Frontiers, 4*(1), 9.

Wooldridge, M., & Jennings, N. R. (1995). Intelligent agents: Theory and practice. *The Knowledge Engineering Review, 10*(2), 115-152.

Wooldridge, M., Jennings, N. R., & Kinny, D. (2000). The Gaia methodology for agent-oriented analysis and design. *International Journal of Autonomous Agents and Multi-Agent Systems, 3.3*(28), 285.

Yannis, L., Finin, T., & Peng, Y. (1999). Agent communication languages: The current landscape. *IEEE Intelligent Systems and Their Applications, 14*(2).

Yoon, Y., & Guimaraes, T. (1993). Selecting expert system development techniques. *Information and Management, (24),* 209-223.

Chapter XIII

Enterprise Organisational Structure Integration and Service-Oriented Architectures

Nicolaos Protogeros, University of Macedonia, Greece

Abstract

This chapter examines the service-oriented architectures (SOA) in conjunction with the enterprise organisational structure integration problem, applied to innovative organisation schemes such as virtual enterprises (VE). The evolution of software architectures from traditional to SOA is presented, along with the characteristics, advantages and disadvantages, and problems and difficulties in applying the SOA, while also focusing on the compatibility between SOA and modern organisational structures. The new standard in the service orchestration level, BPEL, is considered as a language for business process modelling, and its impact to the integration problem is examined. New messaging protocols and frameworks such as the enterprise service bus (ESB) or messaging service bus are also examined. The main focus is on the SOA technology trends of modern organisational structures, with regards to their formation and integration. The comparison between SOA and traditional architectures provides a clear path to their adoption in various cases.

Introduction

Service-oriented architecture was first introduced by Gartner in 1996. Since then, SOA has excited many software architects and developers, and a lot of effort has been put worldwide in this area. However, only recently with the advent of Web services, SOA has found its route to real applications. Web services is the most prominent technology that forms a solid base to develop robust SOA applications. SOA has an inherent ability to apply itself efficiently across enterprises, being the most promising technology to form and operate virtual enterprises where different economic organisations are combining their strengths to provide a specific service traditionally provided by a single enterprise. In the following, we will examine in more detail SOA and Web services when applied to virtual enterprise integration.

Background

Gartner (1996) defined SOA as a software architecture that starts with an interface definition and builds the entire application topology as a topology of interfaces, interface implementations, and interface calls. Gartner states that SOA would be better named *interface-oriented architecture*. SOA is a relationship of services and service consumers, both software modules large enough to represent a complete business function. Services are software modules that are accessed by name via an interface typically in a request-reply mode. Service consumers are software that embeds a service interface proxy (the client representation of the interface).

Plummer, Blosch, and Woolfe (2002) defined Web services as modular business services with each module fully implemented in software and delivered over the Internet. The modules can be combined, can come from any source, and can eventually be acquired dynamically and without human intervention when needed.

SOA and Web services are complimentary technologies that represent the most recent step in the evolution scale, which started with distributed programming and object distribution technologies like CORBA, COM/DCOM, DCE and more recently J2EE. Web services represent a technology specification, meaning that an application must use its standards like Web Services Description Language (WSDL), simple object access protocol (SOAP), or universal description, discovery, and integration (UDDI) to be considered as Web services. SOA, on the other hand, is more considered as a design principle (Natis, 2005) meaning that Web services interfaces like WSDL and SOAP are suitable interface definition standards (Atkinson et al., 2002; IBM, 2001; SOAP, 2001; UDDI, 2001; WSDL, 2001).

SOA has an inherent ability to apply itself efficiently across enterprises, being the most promising technology to form and operate virtual enterprises where different economic organisations are combining their strengths (and thus minimising their weaknesses) to provide a specific service traditionally provided by a single enterprise. Such a development will offer, in the long term, immense influence on the economy and enterprise development strategies. The availability, through SOA on the Internet, of standardised SME information, relevant for participating in virtual enterprises, will dramatically multiply the number of business opportunities transformed into successful business ventures. The most important requirements for virtuality in virtual enterprises are (Protogeros, 2005):

- **Global visibility across the virtual enterprise:** There is a need to have an overall visibility on the entire life cycle of the products and/or services produced, starting from its development to its launch into the market. Such a visibility must be permitted to all the companies' personnel involved in the virtual enterprise operation and in particular to the Project Managers who often, in the traditional supply chain, cannot adequately follow the development of important subsystems, which are supplied by a subcontractor.

- **Uniform and consistent business model:** Gou, Huang, Liu, and Xiu (2003) define a business process of a virtual enterprise as a set of linked activities that are distributed at member enterprises of the virtual enterprise and collectively realise its common business goal. A uniform business model is very important for the viability of the virtual enterprise. It should support the evolution of the product, process, and organisation according to the increasing detail of the attributes representing the same concept (such as the status of an order, the categorisation of the order, the customer contact information, the customer account representation, etc.) in a consistent manner.

- **Uniform organisational model:** The organisational view of enterprises captures information about departments, roles, employees, partners, and entire organisations. The organisational model of the virtual enterprise should encompass ownership, privileges, and responsibility of messages, documents, and activities that are involved in the processes of the virtual enterprise. It also has to involve extensive security as well as personalisation requirements. Virtual enterprises can be thought of as an aggregation of processes. Thus processes use information, operations, roles, and sequencing of tasks to carry out specific objectives in the virtual enterprise.

- **Consistent process and data model**: The data model of the companies can capture various behavioural semantics of the business entities. Thus it is not sufficient to have just a consistent conceptual business model of the business entities for smooth operation (Setrag, 2002). Data semantics and operational behaviour must also be represented and applied consistently.

The large diversity in business practices reflected in the plethora of monolithic and legacy applications, along with the huge gaps in business scope and differences in working standards between the large enterprises and the SMEs make the integration process for virtual enterprises a real headache for analysts and developers. SMEs significantly contribute to the value chain by supplying to large enterprises the equipment and subsystems required. In Europe, for example, where a large number of SMEs exist, the need for harmonising the large and small/medium enterprises business approach and practices has been pointed out several times at European Community level. Technology should support the four main phases of a virtual enterprise life cycle, which are: creation/configuration, operation, evolution, and dissolution. By now a large number of projects are addressing various aspects of infrastructures for virtual enterprises including NIIIP (NIIIP), PRODNET II (Camarinha-Matos & Cardoso, 1999), VIRTEC (Bremer & Molina, 1999), Co-OPERATE (Azevedo,

Torscano, & Sousa, 2002), and BIDSAVER (Protogeros, 2005). Some of them are developing service-based reference architectures, for example the NIIIP.

SOA Technology and Standards

In recent years, a new trend has appeared related to the reuse of old applications in new type user-transactions. This style, being an alternative to the development of purely new applications, is known as composite development. In 2003, the majority of new business applications developed were composite applications (Natis, 2005). In taking that approach, wrappers are developed around legacy or other functionality that assemble those components into heterogeneous composite transactions. SOA is the natural place where these types of composite components fit together. SOA applications fit into two main types: user-client-oriented applications and system-oriented applications.

- **User-client-oriented applications** are used to expose back-office functionality to users mainly through a Web browser or any other client type. The main objective is to present an integrated view of the organisation across several office automation or business applications. Examples of this type of SOA are the enterprise portals, account aggregation systems (RSA, 2004), insurance claim submission and approval systems, and so forth.

- **System-oriented applications** are used to link enterprise systems among business partners or to link back-end transaction processing systems within the same organisation, both in a system-to-system interaction. Examples of such SOA applications are grocery-stocking systems, e-commerce transaction processing systems, and so forth.

In both types, SOA provides the natural basis for reuse of the back-end business logic by multiple styles of clients. Various user categories (customers, managers, operators), in the office or at home, can use SOA to request access to the same functional set of back-end business services. In cases where virtual enterprises operate, there is a need of multi-channel, multi-client application, and in that case SOA-based application design is pushed forward.

From an industry and standards perspective, SOA technologies are quite advanced. All major software vendors have at least some level of support for Web services in their products, providing Web service technologies with broad industry support.

On the other hand, the baseline standards underlying Web services—XML, SOAP, and WSDL—are stable and mature since they have been used for many years now (since 1998, 2000, and 2001, respectively). According to Gartner Group, these standards have reached the "plateau of productivity," a term Gartner applies to technologies whose value is demonstrated and accepted.

An important step towards interoperability in SOA is the formation of the WS-I, the Web Services Interoperability Organisation, an organisation driven by vendors. This organisation's

Figure 1. Various standards of service-oriented architecture

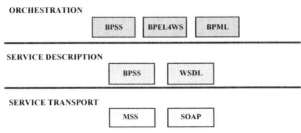

role is to assure that the "common language" of Web services (and the entire supporting infrastructure around it) is interoperable among implementations.

The WS-I has published a "basic profile" which describes how to build and use the base Web services standards to ensure interoperability. In addition, a version of the "security profile" has also been published.

BPEL has emerged recently as an effective and highly interoperable standard for Web services orchestration. Since the BPEL specification has been donated to OASIS by Microsoft and IBM, a large number of major industry vendors (including Microsoft, Oracle, IBM, SAP, Siebel, BEA, and Sun) have supported this standard, many of them having already commercialised products in the market (e.g., Oracle BPEL process manager). As the standards war in the business process modelling space appears to be over, many believe (Oracle, 2004) that this is a great thing for enterprise interoperability and integration at the business process level. BPEL can become for business processes the same thing as SQL is for databases.

Messaging Protocols and the Enterprise Service Bus

Since SOA was introduced in 1996, various protocols have been developed to allow services to exchange messages, both synchronously and asynchronously. Traditionally, messaging mechanisms have been built according to a queued architecture, that is, one in which incoming messages are held in a sort of electronic post office until the receiver is ready to retrieve and respond to them. This style of message exchange is suitable (and even optimal) for many non–real-time applications; Microsoft's MSMQ, Sun's JMS, and IBM's MQSeries technologies are examples of this style of messaging. Other type of applications such as device command and control for laboratory instruments generally requires a more immediate mode of messaging (McIntosh, 2004)

A new messaging paradigm that is rapidly gaining in popularity is variously called a messaging service bus or enterprise service bus (ESB). A key concept of this idea is that messages (usually XML-encoded) carry with them routing instructions that do not rely on a centralised server or rules engine to define how they are transported from one place to another. The bus infrastructure provides support for routing of these messages, along with service discovery, security, logging, and so on. In some implementations, such services are built into the core layer of the bus; in other implementations, some or all such services are provided as plug-in framework modules.

One very interesting open-source project that bills itself as an "enterprise service bus messaging framework" is called Mule and can serve to integrate many disparate messaging technologies, such as JMS (Java messaging service), HTTP, e-mail, and XML-RPC. Mule is Java-based and can interoperate with components running within the same Java virtual machine or with widely-dispersed components communicating over the Internet (and everything in between). Mule is designed around a very clean architecture based on the idea that incoming messages trigger events within the Mule server and can operate in any of the three primary messaging modes: asynchronous, synchronous, and request–response.

A lighter weight alternative to Mule is the "FreeSB" project (FreeServiceBus), developed by Spherion. It defines a standard ESB client implementation (by using the Apache Axis code base) that allows a variety of specialised services to easily "plug in" to the service bus. The bus itself is designed around SOAP messaging and comes pre-packaged with plug-ins to provide logging, authentication, and supervisory or management services (which implement registry and coordination functions for clients).

SOA as a Key Driver for Enterprise Integration: The Case of Virtual Enterprise

Ashkenas, Ulrich, Jick, and Kerr (2002) described the emergence of the "Boundaryless Organization" that increasingly requires organisations to consider four boundaries, vertical, horizontal, external, and geographic, in determining the shape of their enterprise. Web service environments can support horizontal integration by delivering the standardised technological infrastructure that will enable organisations to more effectively share knowledge and collaborate within and beyond organisational boundaries (Estrem, 2003).

Composite applications deliver a form of integration, and thus SOA and Web services can be the modern approach to the application integration problem for virtual enterprises. Moreover due to the many SOA benefits, a lot of expectation has been put to this technology. The reality, as always, is in the middle. SOA is very helpful in some cases of integration, such as real-time composite transactions, but is less helpful in other cases as in long-running transactions. In those cases, additional integration technology is typically required to reconcile the business information differences of the participating applications. Typical benefits that SOA brings to virtual enterprise IT are:

- **Interoperability:** Through the addition of a thin and transparent layer to existing software, Web service-enabled components can communicate with each other via a platform-independent messaging protocol. This ability, completed by a semantic interoperability, will enable two Web services to interact with each other despite their semantic differences. Only with semantic interoperability could different applications in members of a virtual enterprise build a composite application that exchanges data with each other's business systems.

Web services can provide the infrastructure that would support virtual enterprise relationships (Estrem, 2003). This would provide the flexibility and agility that could support manufacturing approaches by reducing the complexity and driving down the transaction costs associated with outsourcing and extended value chain operations between principals and their agents. The ability to dynamically integrate functions that are spread across the value chain would reduce the time, cost, and complexity associated with establishing the relationships needed to support virtual business processes. These capabilities could also enhance the operational efficiency of internal functions. Web services, which could be far less costly to support, could lower the barriers to entry and make it possible for small organisations to access and participate in sophisticated value chain activities.

- **Wide industry acceptance and compliance with standards:** The recently achieved standard in the orchestration layer, Business Process Execution Language for Web services (BPEL), provides enterprises with a powerful way for business process orchestration and execution. From a technical perspective, BPEL is a standard language for defining how to: interchange XML messages among remote services, manipulate XML data structures, receive XML messages asynchronously from remote services, manage events and exceptions, define parallel sequences of execution, and undo parts of processes when exceptions occur (Oracle, 2004). These are the constructs needed to compose a set of services into collaborative and transactional business processes. BPEL is based on XML schema, SOAP, and WSDL.

  Unlike process standards that have been proposed in the past, Business Process Execution Language for Web services, driven by the OASIS standards body, has achieved the critical support and endorsement from the industry's leading vendors. While earlier fragmented efforts fell short in developing a single, comprehensive standard that meets the needs of customers, BPEL is a comprehensive standard that satisfies real-world requirements and has the support of major infrastructure and application.

- **Flexible change and reconfiguration management:** Conventional monolithic IT systems apply many technologies and exchange data and requests via multiple connections. The resulting dependencies between systems are so numerous that system reconfigurations, for example, to support a new business requirement, are often extremely time-consuming. Tight coupling between applications may render conventional architectures so fragile that changes become prohibitively complex. SOA, in contrast, is much more flexible. Web services present many new potential opportunities to significantly reduce the complexity and costs of enterprise computing for developing and maintaining e-business applications (Huang & Chung, 2003)

  SOA permits fine-grained control over deployments across the virtual enterprise. Components within a process can be easily replaced by new or updated components, further reducing the time taken to modify or change an existing process in response to business requirements. Components are easier to develop because the semantics of each independent component are significantly less complex than the overall of a single, (usually large) monolithic application. Components can be developed by different teams of developers, each of whom focus only on their component without having to know the details of work done by others. Components can be dynamically deployed to remote nodes at run-time.

- **Reuse of business components in multiple services:** Since each component has well-defined interfaces, it can be developed, tested, and debugged independent of the other components. This not only speeds up virtual enterprise project implementations but, in the case of well-designed business components, also leads to significantly enhanced reuse.

- **Low-cost development of new business processes:** In the traditional software development process, translating requirements into working distributed systems is both time-consuming and difficult, requiring several stages of manual development and deployment. This complex, error-prone task can be effectively streamlined using a higher-level, component-based SOA architecture. SOA's components ease of development considerably lowers total development costs. Development of new business solutions for the virtual enterprise is reduced to an assembly of service components that does not require the in-depth technical skills needed when coding solutions from scratch.

- **Business-driven approach:** Traditional application design bound by conventional architectures has pursued a technology-driven approach to the automation of the enterprise's business processes. Under SOA, the emphasis is given to a business solution-driven approach, where created services are more meaningful and hence more accessible to business users. This approach shifts effort to a much closer alignment between the IT function and virtual enterprise member companies' business units.

The use of Web services is not a panacea. A lot of management and security challenges come up when dividing monolithic applications into collections of distributed services. As many early adopters have discovered (Actional Corporation, 2004), XML firewalls and Web services management products are necessary to preserve anticipated return of investment (ROI) and resolve the many infrastructure issues which appear, such as security, routing, versioning, provisioning, and transformation of Web services. The most important challenges fit into three contexts, which are economic, technological, and organisational (Estrem, 2003), as shown in Figure 2.

Figure 2. Virtual enterprise framework

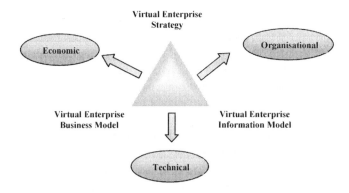

Technological Context

Generally speaking, standards do not guarantee interoperability. This is particularly true in software development and SOA where standards are designed to support many different uses across many different types of organisations. In the security standards, for example, many different types of credentials are allowed, related to the way a user is identified (e-mail, username, digital certificate, etc.). If both the sender and receiver do not understand the same types of credentials, then they cannot communicate. Thus there is an obvious need to agree on specific subsets of standards narrowing down the available options via policies and procedures.

Different teams of developers, each of which focus only on their specific functions, can develop SOA components. In such a development model, none has visibility into all of the moving parts that make up their overall application. This scenario is even worse in virtual enterprise integration development where different companies own services. This has a number of implications. For example, how does an application team ensure visibility across the services owned by various enterprises across a virtual enterprise, and how in that case can they ensure that their overall application is secure? If their application will be exposed to partners and customers via the Internet, how do they ensure that the services they use are not vulnerable to malicious attacks aimed at stealing or corrupting information? Further, who has a truly global view of all the interrelated services that are driving the member's applications overall? Who dictates security and business policy as it relates to shared services?

Economical Context

The valuation of Web services in the virtual environment is a multidimensional problem. While the analysis must include economic and financial factors, other factors must be considered as well. In recent years, strategic cost management methods such as total cost of ownership (TCO) have been employed as a means of evaluating information technology investment alternatives (Ellram & Siferd, 1998). However, Daghfous and White (1994) have shown that making decisions solely based on narrow differences in financial measures such as ROI, TCO, or payback period, could result in erroneous decisions. Instead, they suggested that an innovative technological concept, such as Web services, be evaluated in four dimensions: inventive concept, embodiment merit, operational practice, and market dynamics.

With traditional business applications or SOA development for internal use to the organisation, it is easy to estimate the initial implementation cost and ongoing operational and maintenance costs and thus the pricing policy. However, who pays for a service shared by many applications in various organisations participating in a virtual enterprise? A possible payment scheme would be that each line of business pay proportional to their use; those who use it most should pay the most. Essentially, this is a transfer-pricing model. However, the problem in such a case is how to track usage by each line of business; if you cannot measure usage, how can you charge for it!

Organisational Context

Web services are easier than previous generations of distributed computing innovations (Estrem, 2003). However, the dimensions of transformation and exploitation will be more challenging. According to Zahra and George (2002), transformation relates to the organisation's capability to harvest and incorporate knowledge into its operations, combining the newly acquired and assimilated innovation with existing organisational knowledge. Organisations that can successfully exploit Web services to transform their business processes could achieve significant competitive advantage. However, this process will require significant organisational learning and change.

In order to address limitations of Web services in real-time events and in handling long-running processes, many SOA technology vendors combine SOA with an event-driven architecture (EDA). In such architectures, SOA and EDA are delivered within a unified architectural framework. Organisations are using this approach to be able to send, receive, and respond to real-time business information and events asynchronously.

Researchers have also found that Web services can be combined with agent technology. Hao, Shen, and Wang (2005) propose a virtual enterprise framework which permits VE operation in a more flexible, scalable, and interoperable way. This framework is based on Web services and agent technologies, which are combined to provide an integrative solution for enterprise collaboration.

Future Trends

Virtual enterprise integration and operation will greatly depend on Web services and SOA standards adoption from a corporate perspective. How is corporate adoption progressing? An IDC's study from 2003 (just a few years after the SOA standards appeared) shows that among large organisations (those with more than 1,000 employees), 96 percent were actively pursuing Web services technologies. Of these organisations, 50 percent already had at least one Web service project in production, while the remaining 50 percent were either evaluating or running pilots with the technologies. Of the organisations with Web services in production, 81 percent had more than one Web service project in production.

Given that trend, it is safe to assume that the adoption of Web services and SOA has progressed even further than these figures indicate. Organisations are embracing these standards (Ziff Davis Media Custom Publishing, 2004) and deploying Web services for many internal projects and sometimes modern organisation schemes like virtual enterprises. However, most organisations and specifically SMEs have yet to fully capture the value available to them through a strategic use and reuse of services through a service-oriented architecture. SOA's true value escalates when organisations harness the economies of scale of consolidation and reuse. When an organisation moves from ad hoc use of collections of Web services to a more formalized SOA, the value of those services rises dramatically (Actional Corporation, 2004).

Furthermore the wide adoption by the industry of Oasis BPEL for the Web service orchestration layer will revolutionise business process integration the same way standards like SQL revolutionised access to structured data and HTTP and HTML standardised the way people access content and applications, Web services have the potential to transform the Internet into a true distributed computing platform and allow heterogeneous systems to cooperate simply and reliably.

Conclusion

Companies that work together need their applications and services to work together. This is driving the industry move to SOA and Web services, which promise significant benefits in terms of adaptability, ease-of-integration, portability, and interoperability.

Projects deployed with Web services and SOA can achieve an important level of business process abstraction. The interoperability and integration issues can successfully be addressed through SOA in a two-step process involving publishing services and orchestrating them. Publishing means making the Web services available through a supported interface/protocol, but does not require that all existing systems be "wrapped" with a new XML/SOAP Web service layer. Orchestration means assembling and coordinating these services into a manageable business application.

However, there is work to do, specifically to the wider standards adoptions between medium and small enterprises. The lack of custom and user-friendly tools drives developers to manually recode services or provide "glue code" so that they can interconnect with one another. Such painstaking labour deprives SOAs of much of their virtue—namely, rapid integration and composite application.

Wider virtual enterprise models acceptance tightly connects with the ease of integration at the business process level, and this in turn relates closely with SOA acceptance and adoption. BPEL promise for universal remote integration makes us more optimistic about the future of virtual enterprises.

References

Actional Corporation. (2004). *SOA command and control: The next generation of SOA enablement.* White paper.

Ashkenas, R., Ulrich, D., Jick, T., & Kerr, S. (2002). *The boundaryless organization: Breaking the chains of organizational structure.* San Francisco: Jossey-Bass.

Atkinson, B. et al. (Microsoft), S. Hada et al. (IBM), P. Hallam-Baker et al. (VeriSign). (2002, April). *Web Services Security (WS Security), Version 1.0, working draft.* Retrieved from http://msdn.microsoft.com/library/default.asp?url5/library/en-us/dnglobspec/html/ws-security.asp

Azevedo, A., Torscano, C., & Sousa, J. P. (2002). An order planning system to support networked supply chains. In L. M. Camarinha-Matos (Ed.), *Collaborative business ecosystems and virtual enterprises* (pp. 237-244). Kluwer Academic Publishers.

Bremer, C. F., & Molina, W. M. (1999). Global virtual business—a systematic approach for exploiting business opportunities in dynamic markets. *International Journal of Agile Manufacturing, 2*(1), 1–11.

Camarinha-Matos, L. M., & Cardoso, T. (1999). The PRODNET architecture. In L. M. Camarinha-Matos & H. Afsarmanesh (Eds.), *Infrastructures for virtual enterprises—networking industrial enterprises* (pp. 109-126). Kluwer Academic Publishers.

Daghfous, A., & White, G. R. (1994). Information and innovation: A comprehensive representation. *Res Policy, 23*(3), 267–80.

Ellram, L. M., & Siferd, S. P. (1998). Total cost of ownership: A key concept in strategic cost management decisions. *J Bus Logistics, 19*(1), 55–84.

Estrem, W. A. (2003). An evaluation framework for deploying Web services in the next generation manufacturing enterprise. *Robotics and Computer Integrated Manufacturing, 19*, 509–519

Gartner, Inc. (1996). *Service-oriented architectures, Part 1, Part 2* (SSA Research Note SPA-401-068).

Gou, H., Huang, B., Liu, W., & Xiu, L. (2003). A framework for virtual enterprise operation management. *Computers in Industry, 50*, 333-352.

Hao, Q., Shen, W., & Wang, L. (2005). Towards a cooperative distributed manufacturing management framework. *Computers in Industry, 56*, 71–84.

Huang, Y., & Chung, J. Y. (2003). Web services-based framework for business integration solutions. *Electronic Commerce Research and Applications, 2*, 15–26.

IBM. (2001). *WebSphere Business Integrator: Process Broker Services Concepts Guide, Version 2.1, IBM Product Manual.* Retrieved from ftp://ftp.software.ibm.com/software/btobintegrator/bizaam00.pdf

McIntosh, R. L. (2004, December). Open-source tools for distributed device control within a service-oriented architecture. *Technology Review*, PerkinElmer Life and Analytical Sciences, Downers Grove, IL, JALA, 404-410.

Natis, Y. V. (2005). Service-oriented architecture scenario. *Gartner, Inc.*

NIIIP project. (n.d.). Retrieved from http://niiip01.npo.org

Plummer, D. C., Blosch, M., & Woolfe, R. (2002). Untangling Web services. *Gartner, Inc.*

Oracle (2004, June). *Orchestrating Web services: The case for a BPEL server.* Oracle white paper.

Protogeros, N. (2005). *Virtual enterprise integration: Technological and organizational perspectives.* Hershey, PA: Idea Group Publishing.

Setrag, K. (2002). *Web services and virtual enterprises.* Chicago: Tect.

SOAP. (2001, December). *W3C: SOAP Version 1.2 Part 0-2, W3C, Working Draft.* Retrieved from http://www.w3.org/TR/soap12-part0

UDDI.org. (2001). *UDDI Version 2.0 API Specification, UDDI Open Draft Specification*. Retrieved from http://www.uddi.org/specification.html

WSDL. (2001). *W3C: Web Services Description Language (WSDL) Version1.1, W3C Standard*. Retrieved from http://www.w3.org/TR/wsdl

Zahra, S. A., & George, G. (2002). Absorptive capacity: A review, reconceptualization, and extension. *Acad Manage Rev, 27*(2), 185–203.

Ziff Davis Media Custom Publishing. (2004). *Service-oriented architecture and Web services: Creating flexible enterprises for a changing world.*

Chapter XIV

Knowledge Creation and Adaptive Collaboration Based on XML Web Services

Mayumi Hori, Hakuoh University Japan, Japan

Masakazu Ohashi, Chuo University, Japan

Abstract

This chapter introduces the adaptive collaboration (AC) and its potentials in the new para-digm of the 21ˢᵗ century networked society. It is an innovative information technology system for knowledge creation based on the XML Web services, which is essential to promptly meet the increasingly diverse needs and kaleidoscopic changes in economy. The AC is critical in the ubiquitous society, where constant improvement of business processes and cooperation and collaboration with both existing and new systems are required. Today's knowledge is considered ecological and organic in a way that it is flexible enough to swiftly sense numeral shifts in the environment. The new method that integrates a number of different systems and applications into one system to enable the AC has been generating much attention as it may meet the diverse and growing demands in the future of the ubiquitous society.

Introduction

In 21st century society, knowledge has attained independent value of its own. "Knowledge" in the networked society reflects the new value resulting from the dynamic interactions and sharing among knowledge of individuals and organizations.. Today, the rapid aging of the population amid extremely low birthrates is a pressing concern to the Japanese society as it may threaten Japan's most valuable assets for its established economy, its intellectual resources. This concern has spread among government, industries, and citizens alike. In this chapter, we introduce the adaptive collaboration and discuss its potentials in the new paradigm of the 21st century networked society. It is an innovative information technology system for knowledge creation based on the XML Web services.. It is strongly believed that the system will positively contribute to Japan's ability to cope with the aging/low-birth rates problem of the Japanese society. In other words, we aim to challenge a variety of problems posed to the networked society by promoting knowledge creation activities with the utilization of the adaptive collaboration. It is a new system that produces dynamic and valuable interactions among human resources through sharing, interlocking, and collaborating with different types of knowledge.

Building a New Social System by Knowledge Sharing

Depopulation, Aging, and Reconstruction of Human Resources

For six consecutive years, the Japanese labor force has been in decline. The post-war baby boom generation, born between 1947 and 1949, will become over 60 years old after 2007 and will start retiring. The overall workforce will dramatically decrease which will heavily influence the Japanese labor market. The population of the post-war baby boom generation is larger compared to that of other generations, accounting for 5.4% (6,900,000 people) of the national population. Furthermore, among the employed population, they account for 8.6% (5,400,000 people), which is 20% to 50% higher than any other generation. Therefore, as Japan faces serious depopulation and aging problems, maintaining and strengthening the development of and securing of human resources becomes the critical issue.

Today, the number of the people older than 65 years of age has reached its highest, 24,880,000, which accounts for 19.5% of the national population (127,690,000 people). At the same time, the birthrate, or the average number of births per woman (total fertility rate), has reached its lowest, 1.29. Depopulation and aging will also influence the Japanese economic growth and pension system. The Japanese welfare system entirely depends on the current workforce. Hence, the retired population is supported by the generations still working. As the aging and retiring population increases, the welfare system places a heavier tax burden on younger generations. The Japanese economy is anticipated to vanish if it is unable to develop a workforce or to find ways to improve worker's productivity (http://www8.cao. go.jp/kourei/index.html).

The following are the primary issues for the Japanese human resources:

1. Delay in the workforce development of women, the retired, and the physically-challenged to cope with the falling birthrate, the aging population, and the declining labor force

2. The increase of the unemployed youth such as Freeters (Japanese-English term for the youth in their late teens to early thirties whose main source of income is part-time jobs) and not in employment, education, or training (NEET)

3. Gender inequality in the workforce and the sexual division of labor based on traditional gender-roles in the Japanese society

4. The gap in working conditions and benefits between regular full-time, permanent workers, and irregular workers

5. The potentials and recruitment of foreign workers

As Japan faces a serious decline in population, human resources will be required to reach beyond the boundaries of conventional organizational management. That is, it has to depart from the belief in corporate loyalty among workers. Instead, it has to promote the liberation of workers from the organization so that they can exercise their full potential to facilitate diverse forms of self-actualization. Furthermore, their unique abilities and potentials need to be networked for the purpose of sharing and interaction (Hori & Ohashi, 2005a).

Dynamic Knowledge Creation Through Integration of Human Resources

A society based on information and communications technology (ICT) is frequently called a networked society, a ubiquitous-networked society, or a knowledge society. The term "networked" is not so new to many of us. The term is widely used to imply multiple connections among different entities such as people to people, organization to organization (e.g., schools, corporations, and government agencies), corporation to corporation, corporation to nation, and nation to nation. Originally, a networked society carries the connotation of one where valuable knowledge is created by the sharing of information or knowledge and collaboration through a computer network (Internet).

In other words, a networked society or a knowledge society is a place where people and organizations are able to freely exercise their creativity by sharing and examining different perspectives and values. The unique characteristic of a networked or knowledge society is that intellectual properties such as information, knowledge, and know-how that each individual and organization possesses can be digitalized, allowing it to be shared with anybody who needs it at any time, anywhere.

Knowledge has, of course, played a central role in industrialized society. Knowledge was essential to improve productivity and create a new market. However in many cases, knowledge of corporate management in the industrialized society is very specific, and not applicable to other areas. Specific knowledge often does not horizontally integrate with other knowledge. Instead, it remains within an individual or becomes useful only among specific groups maintaining a closed-system. In the closed-system society, the top priority of corporate management is the promotion of streamlining and efficiency. In order to pursue these, they have to excel in the vertical transfer of specific knowledge from experienced workers to inexperienced workers.

Since the 1980s, the nature of society has drastically changed. The advent and development of ICT, the increase in service economy, diversification of individual values, and globalization of society, economy, and politics all have contributed to a departure from traditional society. These shifts have also brought about the condition in which many problems cannot be solved by pursuing and promoting economic efficiency. In order to cope with issues that cannot be solved with existing solutions, it is indispensable not only to re-apply the existing knowledge for a temporal fix, but to create new knowledge. The development of ICT has doubled the potential of knowledge creation by networking (collaboration and sharing) and liberating conventionally-closed systems of knowledge (Ohashi & Hori, 2005b).

The 21st century is the era of great uncertainty. The society needs to utilize ICT not just for electronic infrastructure systems, but as the means to integrate diverse relationships over time, place, people, and organization. It is our mission to realize a society where knowledge is created and utilized through dynamic interactions.

Innovative System for Economics and Business Management: Raising Expectation for Adaptive Collaboration

Due to the drastic decrease in population along with a rapidly aging society, the role of human resources has been forced to be fundamentally reexamined. From the conventional problem-solving point of view, it needs to be reexamined from the legal, political, and strategic perspectives. On the other hand, recruitment of foreign workers, as previously mentioned, may negatively influence the working situation of the next generation. In order for Japan to overcome depopulation, it is critical to produce an innovative system for economics and business management based on the new paradigm for knowledge creation.. This paradigm for knowledge creation, in other words, is the development of ICT and a system that utilizes these technologies. Especially in the present century, the conception of human resources has been increasingly broadened along with the diversification of values among people. Furthermore, it is strongly required to reconstruct our networked society in a more humane, citizen-centric way to embrace these diversities for establishing an innovative role of human resources. It is essential that human resources utilize ICT to take advantage of the intellectual properties that individuals and organizations possess, including knowledge, experiences, and know-how (Hori & Ohashi, 2005c).

In this chapter, we explain that adaptive collaboration based on the XML Web services technology eliminates the knowledge attribution yet brings about the potentials of knowledge creation opportunities through collaboration and sharing knowledge that exists within individuals and organization in our ever-changing society.

XML Web Services and the Flexible Adaptive Collaborative Society

Building of a Seamless and Flexible Networked Society

The adaptive collaboration (AC) is not an extension of the development of ICT. Rather, it aims to further refine the social systems. Its mission is to reconstruct and digitize the Japanese society that is ideal for the 21st century, which values globalism as well as localism. For example, in terms of public administration, services should not be standardized, but be localized to sensitively meet the diverse needs of local residents (Hori & Ohashi, 2004a).

The adaptive collaboration based on the XML Web services that we advocate in this chapter essentially implies knowledge creation and growth through seamlessly connecting distributed knowledge of people, organizations, and communities via computer systems. The XML Web services we discuss is highly effective for sharing, exchanging, transforming, and mutually exploiting virtual resources including information, knowledge, and wisdom at a lower cost. This shift may enable us to increase the quality of information itself, as well as that of business. In other words, adaptive collaboration based on XML Web services distributes shareable data over the network, making it easier for network users to collaborate with each other. What is unique about XML Web services is not that its users are mutually connected via a network, but that the system intelligently manages the operation flow and data accumulation to optimize user productivity. XML Web services can be utilized for collaboration among organizations distributed in different communities, cooperative projects between municipalities, corporations, and external organizations such as education and research institutions, and as an application supporting telework.

 For a more concrete example, there is a model that used the technology for healthcare management. By using XML Web services, patients are able to manage their own health-related information in an integrated fashion. It is often very troublesome for patients to collect medical information because information is stored at different places depending on where they had medical treatment. XML Web services enables patients to collect their medical data without having to contact different medical institutions. Therefore, it becomes easier for patients to submit their medical history to doctors, which helps doctors to gain in-depth knowledge of patients so that they are able to provide prompt and appropriate treatment. As a result, by seamlessly integrating distributed medical institutions, patients autonomously manage their healthcare and take the initiative in handling preventive medicine and medical treatment (Hori & Ohashi, 2005a).

In the business sector, XML Web services seamlessly integrates organizations of different types such as business-to-business (B2B), business-to-consumer (B2C), business-to-business-to-consumer (B2B2C), business-to-employee (B2E), and business-to-government (B2G) to collaborate. Another advantage of utilizing this technology is that it enables organizations to connect to the new system without abandoning and wasting the old systems.

Adaptive collaboration based on XML Web services presents an innovative way to solve issues by flexibly integrating diverse organizations to facilitate collaboration. Therefore, it is highly beneficial for a number of fields including public administration, business, healthcare, and education. The society linked via adaptive collaboration based on XML Web services achieves the identical aims of a ubiquitous society.

The Potentialities of a Ubiquitous Society and XML Web Services

We can envision a future business world where an organization no longer functions on its own but collaborates with a variety of other organizations. In other words, organizations will no longer need to stick to specific data or applications. Rather, they will need to be flexible enough to adopt appropriate objects according to each business model and project. Likewise, in the ubiquitous society, continuous innovations are always required, and collaboration and sharing knowledge within and outside of the organization are essential for survival. We can realize this knowledge sharing and management system, adaptive collaboration (AC), by incorporation of XML Web services and iDC (Figure 1).

In terms of applying AC into e-government and e-local governments, it is imperative to build a system as a social system with the perspectives of users in mind instead of those of the system or service providers. The XML Web services based e-government and e-local government system will enable AC with utilizing SOAP/XML data sharing, dynamic data linking among governmental bodies, and automatic linking and execution between application modules on the Web (Ohashi, 2004).

The XML Web services enable us to automatically link the distributed applications online to realize AC. Automatically coordinating applications (objects) distributed on the Web may also present the optimum options for business and public services. Accordingly in the ubiquitous society, incorporating iDC and XML Web services will provide a bridge between the traditional top-down, hierarchical organization and the horizontal business models (Hori & Ohashi, 2005b)

Figure 1. Layer model (Source: Hori & Ohashi, 2005a)

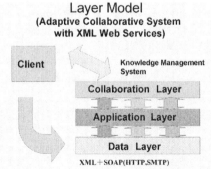

Potentialities of Adaptive Collaboration (AC)

The Concept of Adaptive Collaboration

Conventional business models had built information systems that operated only within the organization where interchangeability or interactivity was not necessarily considered. However, the rapid development of ICT has encouraged the creation of a seamless, networked environment regardless of an organization's type or size. It has also encouraged the development of a ubiquitous environment where public institutions such as government and local governments can freely utilize each other's information and collaborate together without the boundaries of time and space.

Today, in order for corporations and government agencies to achieve swift decision-making and innovation, they need to utilize a shareable system that simultaneously exists within and outside of the organization and office. Expansion of the versatility of ICT has allowed many corporations and administrative agencies to merge and collaborate with each other and has enabled them to enter into new business schemes. On the other hand, it has become extremely difficult to maintain the competitive advantage in the present market as the culture of sharing and collaboration has prevailed. Furthermore, government and local governments have been urged to meet the diverse needs of the people while improving economic efficiency. In accordance with these situations, we would like to propose adaptive collaboration (AC) as an essential concept for the new paradigm of knowledge integration and collaboration in a ubiquitous society.

Adaptive collaboration (AC) is defined as a system that efficiently relates, shares, and utilizes data, information, and knowledge in the ubiquitous society, where the amount of information created grows at an accelerated pace. This system would also allow entities of different ontological levels to be linked laterally, therefore making it easier for people in the organization to appreciate each other's expertise and know-how, which essentially encourages further development and innovation. Likewise, the system breaks the conventional relationships within and between organizations.

Adaptive Collaboration and Exercising Creativity

Traditionally, organizations tend to have regular full-time workers remain within the organizations. Moreover, operations have become further stylized, and organizations promote productivity by facilitating specialization and standardization. However, in today's uncertain working environment, it has become increasingly difficult to divide and distribute the work force, especially for those non-stylized projects requiring judgments based on in-depth knowledge and creativity.

As the working format has become progressively diversified, so-called "skill-workers" have emerged who engage in numerous projects to exercise their unique skills beyond the boundaries of conventional work format and organizations. In addition, highly efficient workers within or outside of organizations are required to be widely networked because the development and securing of human resources are essential to cope with today's depopulation. Adaptive collaboration is believed to realize a social system that supports a sustainable development for the future.

Below are the essential prerequisites for adaptive collaboration:

1. Clarify the operation distribution system by analyzing operations.

2. Create an evaluation system for skill-workers so that they can autonomously review their job operation.

3. Design a self-active education system for skill-workers to further develop their skills.

4. Archive information on skill-workers' experiences and achievement record.

5. Establish criteria on how to match project and skill-workers as well as a matching system.

The Benefits of Utilizing AC and Adaptive Collaborative Telework

Adaptive collaboration supports innovative methods for effectively using human resources of both in-house and outside staffing with ICT. Better managing human resources may enable in-house teleworkers to promote and maintain their mental and physical health. Furthermore, for in-house Teleworkers, a collaborative, group-work environment may help them maintain favorable working conditions as well as achieve better results in their work (Hori, 2003; Hori & Ohashi, 2004b).

Additionally, deconstructing the existing structure of an organization by adopting Telework would permit the viewing of the system and its internal relationships within the organization. This also encourages the discovery of new connections to be drawn between different branches of the organization of the same or different ontological levels. By doing so, they will be able to allocate financial and human resources appropriately and avoid bottlenecks. Furthermore, through efficient coordination and collaboration, organizations will be able to share the know-how and the expertise that each worker possesses.

The adaptive collaboration requires one to work toward common goals with other members of the group who have perspectives and values other than one's own. It can also assist group members in creating shared new value and understanding. Although collaboration requires harmony, it does not suppress or discard different perspectives and values. Sharing of common goals encourages each member to assume a responsibility and commitment for creating new knowledge that in turn benefits the group as a whole. Therefore, instilling this culture of "sharing" is critical for successful adaptive collaboration.

Today, municipalities and local organizations are required to seriously consider the implementation of telework in order to utilize the expertise within and outside of their organizations in a collaborative, networked manner. Additionally, like the private sector, municipalities are expected to increase their productivity and become more output-oriented. For those reasons, telework has drawn considerable interest in what could increase an individual's productivity, network the human resources, encourage the collaboration between different branches in the organization, and utilize the outsourced human resources for advanced knowledge and expertise.

Adaptive collaborative telework promotes rationalization and efficiency by enabling the distribution, sharing, and enhanced use of information through utilizing ICT. Hence, it would assist e-government and e-local governments in building a society that is sensitive enough to be aware of the social changes and flexible enough to respond to these changes appropriately while minimizing risks.

Adaptive collaboration makes a significant difference in the nature of the work of public officials, as it would change the way they carry out their job at home by aggrandizing the definition of telework. In other words, unlike the conventional unilateral services offered by the government, adaptive collaboration promotes new lateral services that link knowledge and expertise between public and private sectors of different ontological levels. It is also different from the telework center which only changes the location of work while the quality of work remains the same. On the other hand, adaptive collaboration divides and distributes work by its nature and quality that can be conducted outside of the conventional office. For instance, many software engineers utilize adaptive collaborative telework as a favorable working style because the nature of their work allows them to work independently, yet high-quality collaboration is enabled by the ICT so that they can remotely and continuously check their system's integrity with other engineers.

Although telework has been considered as a mere means of outsourcing, ICT has expanded its nature to enable adaptive collaborative telework. Consequently, as the global economy has moved further from a manufacturing base more towards a service base, we believe the demand for adaptive collaborative telework will grow. Telework will ultimately create an environment where organizations and individuals bring their expertise and generate innovative ideas, which will lead to new business opportunities, expansion of employment opportunities, and development of the ICT-related engineers; hence it will produce the driving force for local revitalization.

Experimental Pilot Study on Adaptive Collaboration

Implications of the Study

In the ubiquitous society, open networked information systems are vital as they enable people to collaborate with others regardless of location and type of business. In that environment, we will experience shifts in our communications both in terms of quantity and quality. Not only "human-to-PC," but a new pattern of "PC-to-PC" will expand the dimension of communications. The information we share with others will include not only textual information, but a disparate range of data and information, including knowledge that is essential for decision-making (Ohashi, 2003a).

Therefore, the primal benefit of collaboration is the sharing of knowledge, information, and data with others. In order to realize this, there needs to be a space or "*ba*" where a variety of applications help users to produce new knowledge, information, and data that are appropriately shared and reused among users. We conducted a demonstration experiment to examine technologies that are essential to build this knowledge sharing environment.

The information and knowledge sharing space has two distinctive attributes, static and dynamic. One is that it statically unifies the management of information and related behaviors, and the other is that it adds actions to make it adaptive to the dynamic operation processes. The stored data are structured for the purpose of reuse; hence it is also the "*ba*" that encourages knowledge recycling.

Since there are many possible operations imaginable that are suited for the adaptive collaboration, its goal is to provide users with a workspace to accomplish their own tasks instead of simply offering functions such as word processing or spreadsheet applications. The workspace may offer email and bulletin board services or document management services. The possibilities are infinite as it is also able to integrate specialized applications for each operation into the user interface.

Requirement and Purpose of the Study

For successful collaboration, it is essential that data, information, and knowledge are continuously stored and can be shared among many individuals. In order to do so, it is critical not only to build a reliable infrastructure and developed network, but also to consider how the data should flow on the network along with how the data should be applied and utilized. For certain fields, it is strongly preferred that contents will still be usable without depending on specific applications or software, or when values are changed 100-200 years from today. That is, data and content need to be constantly viewed, utilized, and processed by many users. Furthermore, the system needs to be flexible enough for the distribution and reuse of data and content, as they might be stored at dispersed locations at different times.

Therefore, the essential requirements for AC are the following: (1) Users are geographically-dispersed and belong to different organizations; (2) knowledge information is easy to store and retrieve, and long-term information storage needs to be safe and secure; (3) knowledge information needs to be available for high-level statistical processing and analysis; and (4) it operates uninterruptedly, and it is low in cost and highly reliable.

The purpose of the study is to realize the real-time AC environment through data sharing. For this purpose, we conducted the following experiments: (1) a demonstration experiment on the storage management which enables users to share information located in the iDC storage; and (2) a demonstration experiment on data management by applying XML Web services into the real-time collaborative work system through data sharing (Ohashi, 2003d, 2004).

Experimental Methods

For ensuring the durability and universality of data, it is important to standardize a character encoding scheme and data structure as well as a system that reconstructs and personalizes data according to the need of a user. In terms of data structure, it is necessary to standardize data format that is both open and global for the purpose of information transmission and distribution across the world. In terms of personalization, it is indispensable to consider how to systemize knowledge so that a system could tailor and reconfigure data for each user depending on a situation to utilize stored data. Collaboration can be divided into three categories from the perspectives of a long-term use, "ba" on the Internet, and application of the XML Web services technology into digital data: (1) intensive utilization of network infrastructure; (2) network utilization for information and knowledge; and (3) integrated utilization of distributed data in a large area.

In order to realize this open and flexible data structure and information distribution, it is necessary to conduct demonstration experiments in the following ways:

- Providing and integrating an *Active* utilization environment and a *Static,* long-term environment on the network, an *Adaptive* space
  - o Metropolitan area network (MAN) + Internet data center (iDC)
- Building an environment with the XML Web services technology that is independent of a system and application

In order to examine the feasibility of these systems mentioned above, we conducted a demonstration experiment. First, we examined the possibility of collaboration among corporations, universities, and research institutions by building an information-sharing environment prior to applying XML Web services into the data management system which utilizes the information stored within the iDC. Second, we examined the effectiveness of the data storage system and evaluated whether the external applications are capable of high-level utilization, such as its proficiency of producing knowledge out of information, presenting data effectively, and storing know-how (Figure 2) (Ohashi, 2004).

Figure 2. Collaborative system

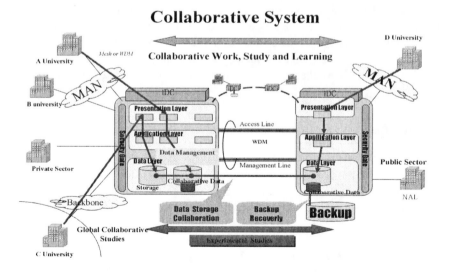

Results of the Experiment

The demonstration experiment proved that real-time discussion with sharing data and resources among the geographically-dispersed teams was possible. Furthermore, we confirmed that it is possible to collaboratively edit and process image data between remote locations using a high-speed network.

For the future agenda, if we plan the long-term use of the system, it is necessary to consider how to manage the Web services and how to develop and spread its computer architecture in corporations. In other words, in order to administer the relationship between different Web services on the multi-vendor delivery platform, it is necessary to consider how to manage many different components involved in this system such as network operation management, service management, and Web services management including ERP, CRM, SCM, EAI, and, EC.

Physically storing files and data and keeping them readable for a long time does not necessarily mean keeping them understandable for a long time. It is critical for a variety of systems to be able to cooperate in order to process diverse data while extensively accessing meaningful data. To facilitate this, it is essential to utilize a unified meta-standard technology such as XML, and to add auto-logical, self-explanatory descriptions onto data themselves (Ohashi, 2004; Ohashi & Hori, 2005b).

Conclusion

In this chapter, we discussed knowledge creation as a new paradigm to utilize human resources and to cope with the challenges which Japanese society faces today, the structural change of the society brought about by the rapid depopulation and aging that influences its economy, government, industries, corporate management, communities, lifestyle, and even values of people. We introduced adaptive collaboration based on XML Web services as a driving force to transform the threats of social and economic changes into opportunities for sustainable development.

In recent years, the growing network has presented more opportunities for collaboration. This working format allows people to work independently at a small office or home office (SOHO), and brings about greater synergy among them by integrating the expertise of different workers.. Hence, it fundamentally differs from the conventional working format where people gather and work in the office. The change in the nature of work with the network also provides more opportunities for those who prefer working at home including physically-disabled people, the elderly, and people who take care of children. Furthermore, it also allows a new venue for promoting welfare policies including nursing and healthcare according to the regional characteristics as well as employment and business activities.

It was also demonstrated that telework utilizing adaptive collaboration promotes comprehensive projects for business and promptly responds to the diverse needs of residents for municipalities by integrating the distributed expertise of individuals and organizations for the purpose of collaboration. Furthermore, distributing and integrating operations are also highly effective for avoiding risks of terrorism, natural disasters, and coping with environmental issues.

In the era of the 21st century networked society, a new working style without the restriction of time and place is in high demand. This requires changes in awareness, behavior, laws, and policies. It is critical to build a society where each individual's expertise is integrated with that of others in order to transform it into the wisdom of shareable form instead of crowding workers into an office and struggling to find harmony. It is also critical to build a society where people achieve a good balance between work and life. This chapter attempted to find a solution in the utilization of adaptive collaboration based on XML Web services to achieve this new society.

References

Hori, M. (2001). The development of IT and a new work format for women in Japan. In R. Suomi (Ed.), *Proceedings of t-world 2001, The 8th International Assembly on Telework, Labour Policy Studies,* (231), 43-58. Helsinki, Finland: Ministry of Labour.

Hori, M. (2003). *Society of telework and working for women.* Tokyo: Publishers of Chuo University.

Hori, M. (2005). The changes of social structure. In M. Ohashi (Ed.), XML *Web services for next generation and a view of citizen centric* (pp. 27, pp. 44, pp. 96-117). Tokyo: Kinokuniya Co., Ltd.

Hori, M., & Ohashi, M. (2004a). Implementing adaptive collaborative telework in public administration. In P. Cunningham & M. Cunningham (Eds.), *E-adoption and the knowledge economy: Issues, applications, case studies* (pp. 708-714). The Netherlands: IOS Press.

Hori, M., & Ohashi, M. (2004b). Telework changes working style for Japanese women. In *Proceedings of AWEEB, International Workshop on Advanced Web Engineering for E-Business,* Frankfurt, Germany.

Hori, M., & Ohashi, M. (2004c). Telework and mental health-Collaborative work to maintain and manage the mental health. In *Proceedings of the 37th Annual Hawaii International Conference on System Sciences,* HI.

Hori, M., & Ohashi, M. (2005a). Applying XML Web services into health care management. In *Proceedings of the 38th Annual Hawaii Conference on System Science,* HI.

Hori, M., & Ohashi, M. (2005b). Adaptive collaboration: The road map to leading telework to a more advanced and professional working format. *The Journal of the IPSI BgD. Transaction on Advanced Research Issues in Computer and Engineering* (pp. 36-42).

Hori, M., & Ohashi, M. (2005c). The potentials of adaptive collaborative work: A proposal for a new working style for Japanese women. In F. Grundy (Ed.), *The gender politics of ICT* (pp. 313-324). London: Middlesex University Press. Retrieved from http://www8.cao.go.jp/kourei/index.html

Ohashi, M. (2003a). *Public iDC and c-society.* Tokyo: Kogaku Tosho.

Ohashi, M. (2003b). *Time business.* Tokyo: NTT Publication.

Ohashi, M. (Ed.). (2003c). *Knowledge-based collaborative work.* Tokyo: The Report of Supplementary Budget Project of the Ministry of Post and Telecommunications, The Foundation for Multimedia Communications (FMMC).

Ohashi, M. (Ed.). (2003d). *The report of society for the advance study on e-society* (pp. 1-51). Tokyo: The Society of the Basis for E-Community.

Ohashi, M. (Ed.). (2004). *The report of the advanced studies for social capital of e-society.* Tokyo: The Society of the Basis for E-Community.

Ohashi, M., & Hori, M. (Ed.). (2005a). *The theory of economics for network society.* Tokyo: Kinokuniya Co., Ltd.

Ohashi, M., & Hori, M. (2005b). On the studies of adaptive collaborative work. *Journal of Policy & Culture, 12*, 83-112.

Chapter XV

Software Agent Technology for Supporting Ad Hoc Virtual Enterprises

Jarogniew Rykowski, The Poznan University of Economics, Poland

Abstract

This chapter introduces a new idea of using software agents for supporting ad hoc virtual enterprises and similar forms of temporal business-to-business collaboration. It seems that current information and telecommunication technologies, based on information interchange and local data processing, are not flexible enough to deal with modern business require-ments, especially dynamic and temporal business relations, heterogeneity of hardware, software and communication means, and data complexity. The proposed approach differs in the distribution of both data and programs for data treatment at-the-place and just-in-time. The distributed and remotely executed programs, software agents, are autonomous entities, targeted on obtaining preprogrammed goals, and working in the name and under the author-ity of their owners. The authors hope that the proposed techniques for agent preparation, distribution, and execution make the whole system safe and secure, providing an efficient environment for a wide spectrum of temporal and ad hoc business collaboration.

Introduction

The idea of a virtual enterprise (VE), a value-added business built upon different, distributed, autonomous units, resulted in the rapid evolution of traditional business models. As the technical possibilities grow, stable business units are becoming less and less geographically- and timely-restricted, and relations among these units are more and more dynamic and case-oriented. It looks like the VE evolution is going to change traditional enterprises into a set of autonomous business units, able to establish a virtual enterprise to achieve given business goals at a given place and time with minimum efforts and costs, and maximum profits.

Imagine such pool of autonomous enterprises, both real and virtual, ready to be in a business. The enterprises are heterogeneous, taking into account both their internal organization, and computer/telecommunication (IT) infrastructure. Suddenly, a business opportunity appears, for example, a possibility to organize a jubilee of a famous pianist. The cooperation is scheduled for two to three weeks only, and the coordinated activities, for example, a philharmonic concert and an official reception in a palace, are occasional, as they will probably never happen in the future. Moreover, the situation is changing all the time; there are new limitations and requirements coming that cannot be identified from the beginning, for example, a need for transportation for some disabled guests. In the future, another jubilee, for example, for a Nobel prizewinner, would require quite different activities, such as the organization of a scientific congress. Even if at the first view the jubilees are similar, the business activities and relations are completely different, and the business partners to be involved cannot be determined in advance.

Current, fixed, and costly IT technologies are not well-suited to deal with such temporal and evolving VEs. Existing proposals for building a virtual enterprise, mainly distributed applications based on such technologies as CORBA (2002) and Voyager (SOA platform, 2005), multi-databases (Hurson, Bright, & Pakzad, 1993), Web services (2002), and Semantic Web (DAML, 2006), are built upon two basic assumptions: (1) The relations between different VE units are quite stable and long-lasting; and (2) the client-server model is a dominant way of interaction among VE units. As a consequence, each unit implements a set of well-defined services (interfaces, programs, etc.) to be used at request by other business parties. This approach seriously limits an efficient implementation of evolving relations among cooperating units for at least two reasons. First, the information flow must be initialized by the client party in the online mode (information polling). Due to this poll-only mode, automatic detecting of server-side information changes and "pushing" them to clients is hard to maintain. Second, it is quite difficult to adopt services and interfaces of a single unit to the specificity of another unit; the client must be ready to adopt itself to the server-side standards. Server-side parameterization is usually limited, due to both technical and economical reasons.

To solve the problem of supporting ad hoc VEs (ahVE), we propose autonomous software agents (Caglayan & Harrison, 1997; Franklin & Graesser, 1996; Nwana, 1996; Wooldridge & Jennings, 1995). The role of an agent is twofold. First, an agent is used as an information broker and wrapper, to adjust data format (both syntax and semantics) to the specificity of communicating units. The brokerage/wrapping algorithm may be programmed either by one or by both parties. Second, an agent may act as a monitor and asynchronous notifier about important data changes. What is "important" is programmed in agent code and variables.

The agents may interact with local IT systems of the VE units, as well as with other agents, and with humans. The agents are executed in the scope of agent computing environment (ACE) framework, being a set of agent servers (Rykowski, 2003a). An agent server may be located at any host, including dedicated hosts belonging to unit's local area networks. The agents may be moved among agent servers (Rykowski, 2005a), and according to the situation each agent may be executed at client-side (i.e., in unit's local area network), at server-side (i.e., in a network of another unit), or at an external network host (i.e., on a separate host outside units' networks).

How do the proposed agents differ from (for example) Web services and other competitive technologies? There are three main advantages to using the agents in comparison with the classical approaches: substantially reduced amount of work needed to establish a connection between two cooperating VE units, unrestricted individualization of relations among units, and a possibility of off-line, server-side monitoring of critical information changes.

Current fixed servers and services operate with a global schema, common for all the cooperating units and possible business cases. Thus, by default, such services must be able to deal with any data flow related with the internal unit's information. A complexity of such a general service is quite high. In contrast, an agent is created just for a single business case. Thus, such an agent operates on a restricted amount of data, just a part (usually small) of the global schema. As a consequence, a complexity of the agent code is substantially reduced, and the agent may be prepared in a short period of time, usually hours rather than weeks, as for most of the present systems.

The agents are created by and for particular VE units. Thus, a behavior of these agents may be exactly adjusted to the requirements and expectations of both cooperating parties. Moreover, as the agents may operate at both server- and client-side, the adjustment covers not only the receiver, but also the source of information. Individualization of agents is not restricted to a parameterization of a generic access to servers and services; each agent is programmed (both code and variables) to deal with an individual business case. Indeed, once programmed, an agent may be used in future collaborations, with the same or other units. What is different in such reuse in comparison with current systems is that each agent instance is different. Thus, a new agent instance built upon a previous one may be in turn (slightly) adjusted to new requirements and specificity of a new business case.

In contrast to the current client-server approaches, the server-side, "remote" agents may be executed autonomously, with no online control of the agent owner. Such agents may detect "important" information changes at server-side (i.e., in a network belonging to the corresponding party) and asynchronously inform the agent owner (other agents and humans) about such changes. Mixing off-line monitoring, asynchronous notifying, and online requests greatly improves the possible ways of data interchange.

Similar to current proposals, the agents may use a set of predefined tools and utilities, implemented as server- and client-side agents, or executed in a given place of a network. Such usage covers as well existing systems and servers, including Web services, and Semantic Web utilities. However, as agents may be used as programmable brokers to external information sources, it is possible to individualize an access to each independent resource/service, as well as to monitor information changes at server-side.

Taking into account technical aspects of ad hoc collaboration by the use of software agents, one may notice that some important problems, being main barriers for wide usage of traditional approaches, are tempered. First, there is no need for maintaining a global schema and ontology, common for all the VE units. Instead, a set of distributed agent-wrappers is provided, each of them implementing a cooperation of two parties at a time only. Second, individualization is possible for each interaction, on both sides of the communication link. Third, the network is able to continuously monitor critical information changes, with no need for manual, cyclic inspection. The monitoring agents are executed near the information sources, thus reducing the growing needs for powerful communication links. Due to the above features, using software agents one obtains a powerful mechanism to establish ad hoc efficient cooperation between units of a temporal virtual enterprise.

The remainder of the chapter is organized as follows. In the section, "Current Approaches for Building VEs and AHVEs," the principal restrictions of the current approaches to build VEs and ad hoc VEs are presented and discussed. In "Agent Technology for Maintaining Ad Hoc VEs," a way of creating and maintaining ad hoc VEs is presented based on software agents and the agent computing environment (ACE) framework. Several architectural and implementation aspects are discussed, mainly agent distribution, agent programming, supporting connections with external information systems and (tele)communication channels, and the overall security policy. Basic architecture and functionality of the ACE agent-based framework is presented, and a typical scenario is discussed of using the framework for establishing and maintaining a sample ad hoc VE. The "Related Work" section contains a comparison with similar work based on the agent technology and related with virtual enterprises, while "Conclusion" points out some conclusions and directions for future work.

Current Approaches for Building VEs and AHVEs

In this chapter, we discuss principal restrictions of current approaches to build a VE: (1) a necessity of providing global schema (view, ontology), common for all the cooperating business partners; (2) technical limitations related with the commonly-used client-server and similar models, (3) costs and efforts while providing cooperation and data interchange mechanisms; and (4) basic limitations related with the software agent technology.

In most of current implementations of a VE, a basic assumption is made that that a *global view* (schema, ontology) exists that is a super-view of all the views of business partners. Thus, to cooperate in the scope of a VE, a wrapper is needed to adjust private IT systems (both ontology and information exchange) to a common schema. Wrapper-based architecture is commonly used due to its numerous advantages: a clear and uniform implementation, well-documented information flow, well-defined interfaces to information sources, and so forth.

The term *global* does not have to be related with the centralized (i.e., single) place of data management, storage, exchange, and so forth. Thus, two global-view architecture subtypes are introduced: centralized information management, and common ontology. In the first case, a single software instance is provided to control information flow in the whole system. This architecture type was preferred in the early or prototype implementations of VEs, for example, Concordia mobile agent (2002). Simplicity of this architecture type usually contrasts with a lack of scalability and strong specialization for a specific business case. In the second case, a distributed approach is preferred; however, all business parties involved in the information exchange must a priori agree to a way of cooperation (data format, ontology, message passing, server interface, etc.). This architecture type is now more popular, mainly due to technical progress in the area of distributed systems and new technologies as software agents, Web services, Semantic Web, and so forth.

Regardless the architecture type and the implementation, the global-view approach is characterized by several disadvantages. First, the common view (ontology) is usually imposed upon business partners by the strongest partner, to minimize costs related with information and communication adjustment. Smaller business units have no choice and must obey the obligatory view unless they want to take part in a VE. In the case of relatively equal partners, a process of establishing a common view may take a lot of time, as everybody wants to cash in on a situation. The wider that a VE is, the lower are the chances to establish a single, consistent common view. Second, to minimize efforts related with future collaboration (with the same or other business partners), an owner of information source usually provides information in a general (universal) and extended (parameterized) way, even if some information/functionality is not needed at the moment. Thus, an interface/functionality of a local system of a business partner is usually quite complicated and, sometimes in a large part, unused for a long time. Moreover, an excess of parameters, modes, message types, and so forth, may substantially complicate an implementation of the information flow at the partners' side. And last but not least, changes in the view (ontology) may force re-implementing large system parts. Note also, that reengineering is usually not addressed by a community of business partners; an implementation of an information wrapper (from the global to a local, private view) is a private property of a party. Even if some parties slightly differ, their private information systems are kept disjoined.

On the contrary, in a non-centralized approach, only the business units directly interested in the specific cooperation agree on a common sub-view (ontology). Thus, individualized, small, specialized wrappers are used, related only with the information requested by the partners. So far, such architecture has not been widely discussed in the literature. However, in the reality many ad hoc implementations are based on such assumption, to minimize implementation costs and time. Note that it is hard to speak about global (data) consistency of a non-centralized system, due to a lack of a single management point. Note also that an ad hoc non-centralized system usually evolves to a centralized one, as one of the (at the beginning equal) business partners becomes more and more strong and eclipses the others, imposing new "common" sub-views, services, interfaces, and so forth. We think that our proposal may fill this gap, providing a reasonable trade-off between a centralized and non-centralized architecture, especially for "light" application areas and fuzzy, dynamically changed cooperation among different business partners in the scope of an ad hoc VE.

From a technical point of view of a cooperating business partner, a typical way of providing information is to provide a service to access the necessary information from the outside. Service providers, that is, owners of data sources, decide who is authorized to access the information and how the access is done. The software implementing an access to information is optimized from the information provider point of view, to achieve maximum system efficiency and security. On the other hand, the data source is used by several business partners, who are characterized by different requirements and possibilities, who are using different hardware, and who are connecting via different communication means. For the partners, a possibility of personalization of a way of accessing a data source and further using the collected information would be very useful. However, there is a trade-off between an abundance of different expectations of all potential partners, and software complexity. Due to hardware and software limitations, as well as costs of software development and use, software personalization is typically restricted to some simple built-in mechanisms including user (i.e., partner) authentication, stored profiles, preferences, dynamic cookies, sessions, and so forth. All these personalization mechanisms are internal parts of the server software. As such, they cannot be changed by the partners. As a consequence, from the business partner point of view, the level of individualization of the way of accessing a data source is often unsatisfactory. Therefore, unsatisfied partners must extra-process data at the client-side. In this case, data flow increases significantly though unnecessarily, because usually most of the transmitted data is filtered out during data processing at the client-side.

One may suppose that recently proposed n-tier architecture (CORBA, 2002), where several software layers are distinguished, responsible for storing, accessing, supplying, formatting, and presenting the information, may contribute to the solution of the personalization problem. However, if taking into account fixed functionality of the tiers and the fact that this functionality is common for all the business partners involved in the information exchange, one may see that the above-mentioned problem is not relaxed.

The second main limitation of most current data sources is a fact of forcing information polling rather than pushing. A data source passively waits for external demands, while the business partners must periodically poll for new information to compare with the previous one and eventually to detect information changes. This approach generates huge network traffic and consumes client and server resources. Thus, polling for information should be replaced by pushing information by the data source to the partners' systems, that is, making the source active. Some techniques have been proposed towards this goal, mainly in the domain of databases, namely, database triggers, and active databases. Database triggers are usually implemented as a set of procedures auto-executed by the database management system once a given event occurs. Triggers are widely used as a mechanism for online verification of database integrity (Oracle Triggers, 2006). Triggers may be used for personalization; however, as they were not designed to this goal, such personalization is restricted. First, triggers are common for all the database users. As such, triggers are usually made by system designers, while users cannot easily personalize them. Second, triggers cannot modify query results (including both the format and the contents of the information requested). Third, current trigger implementations are limited to "insert-update-delete" commands only; application of triggers to read-only queries (i.e., a casual access in the scope of VE application area) is not possible.

Active databases (Ceri & Franternali, 1997; Paton, 1999) are, in some sense, an extension of the triggering mechanism (in a sense of a concept; not as a historical successor). In active databases, an automatic system reaction is programmed by a set of mutually-connected event-condition-action (ECA) rules. The idea of active databases (ACT-NET Consortium, 1996) seems to be abandoned, mainly due to the impossibility of development of efficient methods of database/rules management. The prototypes never reached the commercial status, and a lot of basic functionality has never been implemented, including an efficient debugger for rules and actions triggered, query optimizer specialized for ECA rules, and multi-user engine. These facts, together with the technical difficulties of individualizing the set of rules for different users, makes the concept of active databases practically useless in the scope of individual efficient information access.

Using the above-mentioned "severe" software technologies as Web servers and Web services, database management systems, and so forth, together with the approach of providing a single generic service for all possible business cases, leads to a situation where the cost of providing a useful set of services is quite high. Thus, service owners tend to use the services for a long time, in a stable manner. A lack of dynamic adaptation of services to changes in both overall situation and individual business cases seriously limits the use of traditional technologies in the scope of ad hoc, thus highly dynamic and unpredictable VEs. As a result, short-term business relations are usually supported by a manual work of the human staff, with the minimal use of modern telecommunication and information technologies.

As follows from the above contradictions, a generic, "severe," "one place" centralized implementation is inadequate for an efficient implementation of a set of distributed, temporal, and ad hoc services of a VE. A better solution is to implement and use several individual instances of specialized sub-services, possibly distributed across the network, executed both off-line and online (i.e., on demand). Choosing a place, form, and time of execution of a given instance should be case- and user-dependent. In a typical case, the software related with the information sources (both passive and active) is to be executed preferably at the server-side, while the software related with the partner-specific information processing should be executed either at the client-side, or at a selected host in the network, if the end-user system/communication line is not powerful enough. However, the above assignment (as well as service complexity) should be adjusted to the specificity of a particular business case.

Nevertheless, a technology is needed to combine execution of distributed programs, owned by different business parties, and orchestrated to achieve case-specific business goals under different restrictions. It seems that the software agent technology may be suitable here. A software agent is a program, executed at a given place, characterized by: (1) autonomy—agents process their work independently without the need for human management; (2) communication—agents are able to communicate with one another, as well as with humans; and (3) learning—agents are able to learn as they react with their environment and other agents or humans. An agent may be programmed by its owner, thus allowing personalization of its behavior. Agents may be executed in different places, according to owners' needs and possibilities of the end-user hardware.

In the next sections, we discuss some architectural and implementation issues related with using a software agent technology to implement an efficient environment for maintaining an ad hoc VE. We also provide a comparison of several already proposed systems, both commercial and scientific prototypes.

Agent Technology for Maintaining Ad Hoc VEs

In this chapter, we discuss some basic architectural issues of an agent-based system to maintain ahVEs. We propose a generic framework capable of creating and controlling a set of ahVEs, implemented as distributed networks of cooperating software agents. The basic assumptions of the proposed framework are the following:

- Each ahVE has an individual set of the agents, and these agents are distributed across the network according to a specificity of the ahVE.

- The agents may be used as wrappers to existing software systems, and the information is owned by all the ahVE parties.

- The agents are executed in a safe manner, taking into account an overall security policy of the environment the agent is currently executed in, agent owner's access rights, and a specificity of a business case.

- The agents are under exclusive control of their owners, except for the situation where it is in a conflict with a security policy mentioned above. In particular, the agent owners are able to program agent behavior (i.e., program code and variables), as well as to choose a place and time of agent execution.

- The techniques to program agent behavior are adjusted to the needs and possibilities of the agent owners. In particular, there are some "light" techniques to program temporal and prototype agents, and some "severe" techniques to program agents offering stable, public, multi-user services. A stress is put on efficient reengineering of agents, both for parallel (i.e., multi-user) and future applications.

In the next subsections, a discussion is provided which is addressed to each of the above architectural issues.

Distribution of Agents

The key question related with mobile agents is how to distribute agents in order to perform the tasks in the optimum way. (Chess, Harrison, & Kershenbaum, 1995; Milojicic, 1999) Recently we observe an evolution in answering this question (Figure 1). Let us analyze this evolution taking into account applying software agents to classical client-server architecture (Figure 1A). In the first implementations, agents were executed at server-side, in a dedicated agent environment (Figure 1B). These agents, in a natural way, were prepared and controlled by the server owner. As a consequence, agent behavior and access policy were optimized from the server point of view (cf. section "Current Approaches for Building VEs and AH-VEs"). From the client point of view, this architecture seriously limits individualization of the access to the server.

Together with a progress in communication and personal computers, some tasks were in a natural way shifted to the client-side, at the beginning, mainly the tasks related with data formatting and presentation. Thus, it is also quite natural to execute agents at client-side, in a safe (from a point of view of the client) environment (Figure 1C). However, some new problems arise related with the information access, both technical and psychological. The main technical problem is to provide an efficient communication link. As the transfer rate is substantially increased (in comparison with the server-side approach), the communication costs rise. Note that some data are filtered out just after the transmission by the agent (imagine an SQL query executed at the client-side with tuples collected from the server ...); from the client point of view, and taking into account the final results, high transmission

Figure 1. Distributing agents—possible extensions of the classical client-server model

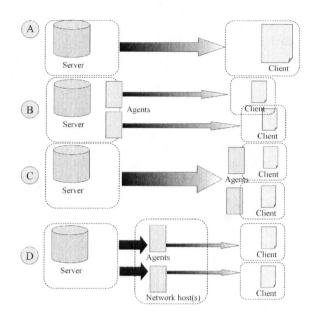

costs are usually unjustified. Note also that client environment may be not powerful enough to efficiently perform all the agent tasks (in turn, imagine a mobile phone running the above SQL query ...). Thus, a new architecture, already mentioned n-tier architecture, has been proposed, where agents are executed in a specialized host located somewhere in the network. In a natural manner, the n-tier architecture may be adjusted to the agent technology. An agent from a network host is able to contact the server in an efficient and non-expensive manner, and at the same time this agent may be contacted by the clients, also using different communication means. The basic restrictions mentioned above for both the case B and C are relaxed, as the agents are exclusively controlled neither by the server owner, nor by the clients. We think that moving agents to the network-side provides a reasonable trade-off between "pushing" (server-side) and polling (client-side) data access (cf. the discussion in section "Current Approaches for Building VEs and AHVEs"). However, choosing an optimum place of agent execution is user- and business-case dependent, and thus this decision must be left to the individual business partners.

We restricted the above discussion to the classical client-server architecture. Similar analysis may be performed for the P2P and other architectures as well; however, the conclusions would be similar.

Note that a new strategy is needed to store, maintain, and execute individual, migrating agents. A new set of agent interfaces, dynamically optimized according an execution place, access rights, accessible communication means, and owners' preferences is needed as well. In the next subsections, we discuss security policy and implementation issues of such an agent-based distributed system.

Basic Techniques of Agent Programming

In order to choose an optimum way of programming agents' behavior, we have to analyze four basic issues: (1) uniformity of an agent interface, (2) security aspects, closely related with (3) programming technique and language, and (4) agent code re-engineering.

Key issues of the network-side heterogeneous environment, portability and mobility of agents (Chess, Harrison, & Kershenbaum, 1995; Kotz & Gray, 1999; Milojicic, 1999; Schiemann, Kovacs, & Rohrle, 1999), force the agent interface to be unified for the whole system. A natural approach is to use a traditional single-method interface, used successfully for many years in the area of operating systems. Each agent is equipped with a single method parameterized by a set of invocation parameters. We do not analyze here all the "administrational" methods, that is, for verifying access rights, agent migration, storing and searching agents, and so forth. Number and types of parameters are not determined in advance. In such cases, only the syntax is unified, while the verification of the semantics of the invocation parameters is left to the agent owners, to be dealt individually for each business case. This approach is similar to an execution of an application by an operating system, except that some invocation parameters may be set dynamically at run-time, independently of both the agent and its owner. This is in turn similar to the set of operating-system-defined variables, except that current values of variables are set up for each individual execution separately, and some parameters depend not only on the operating system, but also on current communication mean, access rights, date and time, and so forth.

To choose an optimum way of defining agent behavior, that is, agent code, we may in turn take a look at a typical operating system. For such a system, there are usually two kinds of executable programs: compiled binary applications, and textual shell scripts. The applications are typically quite complicated and complex software, to be used by many users, sometimes in parallel, executed or accessed remotely, and so forth. These programs are "installed" in the system under several restrictions (user rights, security policy, disk size, etc.), usually by administrators or system designers. Ordinary users cannot interfere in the application code; such users are able to parameterize an invocation (execution) of this code only. In contrast, shell scripts are light textual files, sometimes prepared in an ad hoc manner by the ordinary users. An amount of work necessary to define a shell script is usually small; however, script functionality is thus restricted. Typically, shell scripts are used mainly for file manipulation and the invocation of other scripts and installed applications. Thus, scripting languages are not computational-complete, in contrast to application-programming languages, as for example C/C++ or Java.

We propose to use a similar approach for the agent-based environment for maintaining ad hoc VEs. Users are able to define two kinds of agents: public service agents, being counterparts of operating system applications, and Private Agents, equivalent to the shell scripts. Public *service agents* (SA) are agents created by trusted users (i.e., those users who have appropriate access rights), to be applied by many partners at a mass scale. SAs are treated as trustful system elements. Their efficiency is of primary concern. Thus, SAs are programmed in Java. Java was chosen for its universality, portability, efficiency, big support for using with different Internet services (built-in support and libraries for HTTP, XML, (2005), SOAP (2003), KQML (2003), SQL, and other standards), and openness for combining with other software (Bigus & Bigus, 1998). Standard Java security checking is applied. If needed, some additional security mechanisms may be added by programmers, including user account and password checking, token verification, ciphering, and so forth. A way of usage of a given SA cannot be changed by an ordinary user; however, it may be parameterized during the invocation. SAs are used once there is a need for mass access by many users to given information, providing this information in a standardized form and with optimum effort (from the system point of view). The most frequently used SAs are the following: wrappers, cache utilities, brokers, and so forth.

The *private agents* (PA) are created and controlled by their owners. There is not a single user, including system designers and administrators, apart from the agent's owner, who is entitled to execute private agent code and access private agent variables. Unless directly ordered by its owner, the agent cannot be accessed by any other agent and service. Several PAs belonging to the same owner (directly or indirectly, via other agents) and SAs may be used to compose a complex private agent (CPA). All the agents composing a CPA are arbitrarily connected, forming a directed graph. A single PA is distinguished to be an entry point to the CPA. The CPA composition and internal links among their components may vary in time (even at run-time). CPAs belonging to a given user may be activated either on the owner's demand, or after detecting an information change. In the first case, it is the CPA owner who initiates the agent activation, asking for some data. Once the execution of all component agent activities is over, the CPA response is generated and sent to the owner. Then the CPA becomes inactive until the next demand. In the second case, it is the CPA which initiates the activation, usually after detecting an information change in one of the periodically-observed SAs and external services. Once a change is detected of any interest to the CPA owner, an appropriate message is generated and sent. Thus, the CPA may be used for continuous monitoring of changes of information provided by the other agents (and indirectly, by external data sources).

As mentioned above, agents are created and executed on behalf of their owners. An agent is controlled by its owner, that is, the code is defined by the owner or by a programmer on behalf of the agent owner, and the internal agent variables (agent's state) are defined and accessible for the owner only. Agent's behavior, programmed in its code and variables, is determined by the owner and used for his/her/its individual purposes. Although theoretically owners have full control over the behavior of their agents, in reality they are not obliged to set up all their agents individually. There are three predefined classes of users (agent own-ers), taking into account users' ability to program agents' behavior. The non-advanced, naïve users use predefined, standard, fixed CPAs. The advanced users use standard CPAs as well; however, the level of parameterization is much higher. The experts are able to develop their own PAs (and SAs, on the condition that they have enough access rights).

As it was previously stated, for the system agents, Java is a natural candidate for a basic programming language. As for the "scripting" agents, the answer is not so obvious. Popular scripting languages are specialized in either providing an access to files and applications (operating system shells) or page formatting (JavaScript, PHP, and similar languages). It is quite difficult to adopt an existing scripting language to the specificity of an agent environ-ment. Moreover, as it is discussed below, according to the security aspects, standard scripting languages are not well-suited for unrestricted, user-defined, remotely-executed programs. For a trade-off between overall system efficiency, and agent privacy and efficiency, a spe-cialized language is proposed to program the behavior of private agents, based on XML and imperative programming. The language is equipped with several non-standard mechanisms to improve efficiency and security (cf. next subsections). Although there are many other possibilities to store agent code and variables, XML looks to be the optimum solution for the following reasons:

- XML permits to use a single language for all agent-related data: code, variables, and messages (communication). From the system point of view, the interfaces and mechanisms for storing, searching, migrating, and executing agents across the system are uniformed, as they all use XML data with no semantic checking.

- There are plenty of analyzers for XML syntax checking, that may be easily extended by the semantic analyzer (even individualized for each agent).

- XML-based analysis is independent of local resources and parameters (operating system, back-end database support, communication means, etc.).

- XML is easy to translate to any well-defined format, for example, WML or HTML, and also to the plain text, by the use of the XSL transformations.

- XML is supported by many software tools, for example, back-end database support, above-mentioned XSL transformations, and so forth.

Sample definition of an agent code and variables is given in Figure 2. Note that the agent code is similar to the popular scripting languages, except for the specificity of the XML format (i.e., a way of pointing tags and their parameters). The XML-defined agent code is interpreted and carefully checked during the interpretation; however, compiled parts of system code (i.e., other agents) may be called from it in a transparent way. Thus, assuming the system code (provided as a set of system agents with appropriate access tokens given to private agents) is safe and efficient, the execution of the agent code is also safe and ef-

Figure 2. Sample private agent (code and variables) defined in the XML dialect

```
<AGENT name="sending_sms">
<CALL name="send_sms">
  <PARAMETER name="recipient" value="48600123456"/>
  <PARAMETER name="message" value="Everything is OK..."/>
</CALL>
</AGENT>

<VARIABLE NAME="x1" VALUE="1"/>

<VARIABLE>
  <NAME>x2</NAME>
  <VALUE>1</VALUE>
</VARIABLE>

<VARIABLE>
  <NAME><CALL method="compute_name"/></NAME>
  <VALUE><CALL method="compute_value"/></VALUE>
</VARIABLE>
```

ficient, both from the system and the user points of view. Note that even if the agent code is interpreted, the overall system performance may be high due to the fact that most of the computations are performed inside the compiled Java-based system agents.

More details about the agent XML-based programming language are given in Rykowski & Cellary (2004), Rykowski (2003a), and Rykowski (2006).

Taking into account the above-mentioned programming techniques and languages, Java and XML, the question arises: Do we really need to program the agents in an imperative manner? Why not use any existing, declarative, agent-definition language? We choose the imperative approach for programming agents due to the following reasons. First, a single agent should have a possibility to combine several agents (and external systems and communication means, cf. the discussion below) of different input/output data, location, kind, and purpose. Moreover, such a combination has to follow frequent changes in the environment. Thus, it is not possible to use declarative or skeleton-based agents, as they are not flexible enough to deal with different agents and services, different user requirements, and dynamic changes of the environment. Instead, imperative programming should be used. Using imperative code, the agent's owner may program any behavior of the agent. In the declarative approach, code generation is limited by the declarations or skeletons defined by the system designers. Moreover, while collecting information coming from different sources, additional data processing is needed, wrapping, formatting, presenting, and so forth. Such processing must be defined in an imperative programming language, even if all the data sources are declarative-programmed.

Second, the data and knowledge interchange between agents and external data sources are not standardized (as in general they cannot be). There are some proposals for information-interchange standards (e.g., SOAP (2003) and FIPA (2006); (FIPA Personal Assistant, 2006); however, these proposals cover physical data transfer only, with limited support for semantic data processing. The knowledge representation and sharing standards (e.g., DARPA Agent Markup Language [2006], KQML and OWL [Web Ontology Language, 2004]) deal with data semantics and ontology. However, these standards do not concern data wrapping and formatting. As a consequence, while collecting data in different formats coming from different sources, additional data treatment is needed. This task must be performed in an imperative programming language, as one cannot foresee declarations for all possible standards, connections, communication means, and so forth.

Third, an environment for maintaining ad hoc VEs should be very flexible, due to the highly dynamic changes in the information flow. As one cannot foresee all the possible interactions among business partners, it is not possible to provide any base for creating and further using declarative agents. Moreover, for temporal and evolving cooperation, it is not justified to provide a set of agent declarations (skeletons, patterns, specialized ADLs, etc.) prepared in a traditional, "severe" manner. We think that the declarative approach would substantially reduce a possibility of individualization of agent functionality and behavior, forced by both the evolving user expectations and dynamic changes in the environment.

Fourth, as the cooperation is more and more stable, one may think about replacing "light" programming techniques with the "heavy" ones, for example, replacing a "scripting" prototype-agent with its Java-based compiled, much more effective counterpart. Thus, we propose to use XML-based private agents to start the cooperation, and Java-based system agents to provide a stable, efficient, long-lasting information exchange.

Combining two facts, imperative mode of agent programming, and individualization of agent behavior, we have found that reengineering of agent code is limited. As agents are independent entities, designed and used individually by their owners, it is very probable that a lot of programming work is repeated many times by different business parties. Many business tasks are similar, and thus there are many agents providing almost identical functionality. To avoid this problem, an *inheritance hierarchy* is proposed for the code and the variables of agents. This hierarchy links all the agents into a single directed graph. We propose to use late-binding for implementing agent hierarchy, based on identifiers of agent internal elements (e.g., a named part of a code, or a variable). A place of an agent in the hierarchy may be dynamically changed during its execution, even by the agent itself, as it is determined by one of its variables. Multiple inheritances are allowed, as defining an ordered set of "parent" agents from which the agent derives "missing" elements. Eventual cycles are detected at run-time, thus they do not block the execution.

Apart from effective reengineering, the inheritance mechanism may be used for three additional purposes: effectively storing the agent code, manipulating access rights, and auto-creating new agents. To the first goal, a set of agents is provided being "patterns" of other agents. These agents are equipped with standard code to serve typical business tasks; however, they are not directly executed by the users. Instead, the user's agents derive all the code from one or more "pattern" agents. As long as the code is not changed by the agent owner, private code of an agent is empty, and only the derived code is stored and further used (read, compiled, and executed). If, however, an agent owner modifies any named element, the modified value takes precedence over the inherited one and this modification is used, changing usual agent's behavior. Note that only parts of the code and some variables are usually changed, thus the space needed to store the changed parts is relatively small. Note also, that all the changes to the "shared" code and variables are immediately propagated to all the inheriting agents, allowing online and "hot-swap" actualizations.

To the second goal, the inherited access rights are used. Once an agent has a parent with a given access right, this right is inherited and acts as a private grant. Thus, it is enough to provide a few "empty", non-executable agents with certain access grants and add these agents to the inheritance hierarchy for the agent to grant or revoke access to given services for this agent. Note that it is similar to granting and revoking a single access right to a group of users at once, thus facilitating the administration of grants.

Finally, the inheritance mechanism may be also used to generate some "standard" agents automatically. A new "empty" agent is automatically created that derives code and variables (mainly access rights) from given "pattern" agents. As long as the newly-created agent is not modified by the agent owner, this agent shares all the system variables and the code with the parent(s), thus avoiding unnecessary use of disk space.

Gateways to External Software Systems and Telecommunication Channels

It is quite obvious that the agents must have a possibility of making contact with external software systems and with the humans (agent owners and users). To this goal, as well as for security and flexibility reasons, specialized system agents are provided, so-called gateways. There are two types of gateways: *gateways to external software systems*, and *telecommunication gateways*. These agents are able to provide bidirectional communication with external software systems, via a computer network, and with humans, via standard telecommunication facilities. As for the first case, gateways are able to connect with any network-accessible external software system, located at the same host, and remote ones, respectively (cf. section "Current Approaches for Building VEs and AHVEs"). To this goal, a gateway is programmed to fit to a specificity of a software system this agent is connected to, taking into account proprietary interfaces, communication standards, data formats, and so forth. Shifting this task to a system agent rather than leaving it for the system core improves overall system extensibility and flexibility.

Most of the gateways are used as brokers and wrappers between an external environment and the population of agents. A gateway is able to adjust the information collected as a result of cooperation with an external system to the specificity of the agents interested in using this information. There are three main advantages of such brokerage. First, the agents are not forced to deal with proprietary standards of external software systems. Gateways are able to provide a common, stable standard for accessing many different external software systems in the same, standardized way. As a consequence, the complexity of a private agent's code may be substantially reduced. Second, from a system point of view, an access to external systems may be supervised, if needed. Such supervision may cover specific external systems, communication means, agents and their users, and so forth. Third, the gateways are able to bill user agents (and, indirectly, agent owners) for each access to an external software system. The billing procedure, included in a gateway code, may be set up for a specific connection, communication channel, time, information content, user rights, and so forth.

Putting stress on pushing mode of executing agents and alerting their users, we introduced the second group of gateways, telecommunication utilities, connecting agents with selected public telecommunication systems, to enable contacts with humans via communication channels of different type and purpose. In general, two basic types of communication channels are available: textual and Web-based. A textual channel is able to exchange flat (unformatted) text messages, usually among humans and agents. Physically, textual channels may use such media as an e-mail SMPT/POP3 connection, short message system (SMS)/MMS connection with a telecommunication network, a voice gateway, and so forth. Once sent by a textual message, an agent acts as a chatterbot (Zillman, 2003), analyzing the message via keyword extraction and analysis (Jurafsky & Martin, 2000; Weizenbaum, 1976). The semi-natural access to an agent in a chatterbot manner (Rykowski, 2005b) is especially useful for non-advanced users, and for users who are temporarily handicapped due to limited hardware possibilities and communication costs. For example, an SMS message may be used to check the most important information during a journey, and a stationary PC is further used to get the complex information when the user is back at home.

Web-based channels are used to access an agent via a WWW/WAP page, and from specialized ACE applications. These channels use personal, semi-automatic formatting of both contexts and presentation of the data to be sent. To this goal, XSL-T technology (The Extensible Stylesheet Language Family, 2002) was adopted with XSL transformations defined in a personal manner and stored in private agent variables (Rykowski & Juszkiewicz, 2003). In a case of a conversation with a human, automatic detection of an end-user device may be used, thus restricting the communication. For example, a small textual message is sent to a mobile phone using WAP connection; a similar message with the same contents but with some additional formatting is sent to a PDA device; and a full text and graphic message is sent to a stationary PC.

The number and types of the telecommunication gateways used (including some specific parameters, as a phone number for an SMS center, an address for a SMTP/POP3 server, etc.) is local-administrator dependent. Note once again that these gateways are implemented as system agents; thus one may easily extend a given Agent Server by some specific communication means.

From a technical point of view, gateways may be used to collect information from any kind of an external software system, on the condition that there is a communication means available to the external system. In particular, information may be collected from a Web server, a Web service (Web Services Activity, 2002) and its extensions (e.g., UDDI directories [UDDI Version 2, 2005]), Semantic Web system (DAML Semantic Web Services, 2006), a database, and so forth. In such a way, agents may be used for combining several data sources of different type and purpose into a single, consistent service (Rykowski & Cellary, 2004).

Security Policy

The most important problem related with mobile, user-defined, imperative agents' code is to achieve a reasonable level of global system safety. Note that executing "remote" agents means, from a local system point of view, executing alien code, unknown and potentially dangerous. Maybe in several cases this is more psychological than real menace; however, imperative migrating agents are usually used in closed, mutually-trusted environments. As a consequence, additional mechanisms must be introduced to ensure that the system is resistant/immune to malicious agents. However, additional security checking lessens efficiency of code execution. Thus, a reasonable trade-off must be found between the level of security checking and the overall system efficiency. We think that the division to compiled, Java-based system agents, and interpreted, XML-encoded private agents solves this problem. A system agent is created by a trusted system designer, to be massively used by other agents. Here, the agents' code is trusted, so security checking may be relaxed; system agents may be executed more efficiently. On the contrary, private agents are carefully inspected at run-time, in order to avoid "dangerous" cases. The interpretation and security checking slows down agent execution; however, as most of the massive computations are performed by the compiled system agents, overall system efficiency is high enough.

The above-mentioned run-time inspection covers: checking access rights, mainly to access other agents and (indirectly) external software systems and communication channels; limiting a maximum time of a single execution of an agent; and quoting memory space required by an agent for its code and variables.

Checking access rights applies to both system and private agents. There are two types of access rights: system- and agent-based. System-based access rights are checked before agent execution. The most frequently used system-based access rights are the following: a right to execute an agent in a given place, a right to execute compiled code of an agent, a right to migrate to any other place, and so forth. Agent-based access rights are verified at run-time (i.e., during agent execution), by other agents, involved in a communication with a given agent. It is each agent's responsibility to verify appropriate access rights and to react in a case of access violation. An access right may be related with any part of agent code and any agent variable. For example, there may be a grant for modifying a variable value, for accessing an external information source, for human communication by given communication means, and so forth. Introducing agent-based access rights extends security level to the point required by the agent owner. Note that, as for the agent code, agent-based access rights, as well as a process of their verification, may be set up individually for each agent.

Verifying maximum execution time and memory quota is related with the private agents only; system agents rely on standard Java security mechanisms. In addition, system agents are executed as separate parallel threads, and there are some mechanisms to verify whether a running thread is still active and behaves correctly from the JVM point of view. The maximum execution time is set up for each agent individually, depending on overall security policy, current system load, and (to some extent) individual access rights. During an interpretation of each XML node, current execution time is compared with the maximum. Once the time is over, an execution is unconditionally stopped with an error indication. Thus, a malicious (or simply badly programmed, with no intention for unwanted behavior) agent trying to execute "forever" cannot block the whole system. Note that such feature is not a standard mechanism for any programming language, and must be programmed manually. Even if theoretically the above-mentioned execution threads may be stopped once it is executed too long, it is quite easy to break this protection by modifying standard Java security mechanisms. Similar, a check is performed after each modification of any private agent variable. A total amount of memory required by the agent variables is computed (in the delta mode, i.e., only the affected variable is recomputed) and compared with the quota. Once the quota is exceeded, agent execution is stopped and the new value of a variable is not set.

Agent Computing Environment

The architecture described in the previous sections has been implemented in the scope of the *Agent Computing Environment* (ACE) project. ACE system consists of a distributed set of *agent servers*, characterized by different functionality of system agents, and different communication means. Taking into account a specialization of an agent server for certain tasks and localizations, we may distinguish three basic classes of agent servers: source-side servers, connected directly to data sources and located at the same host (local area network) as a given data source is connected; middle-side servers located in the network, not directly linked with any particular data source; and client-side servers for personal usage of a given agent owner (Figure 3). The servers are connected to each other, and they are able to transfer private agents among each other as well as remotely execute the agents previously transferred to a given place.

A functionality of a *source-side agent server* is optimized towards reliable and efficient access to selected data sources, from the point of view of the information owner (i.e., given business party). For security reasons, using private agents in such a server is substantially limited. The system is reduced to a set of gateways, able to standardize an access to the data source(s) connected, with limited support for public telecommunication facilities. Gateways are equipped with several mechanisms supporting efficient, parallel, multi-user access to the

Figure 3. Distributed set of cooperating agent servers

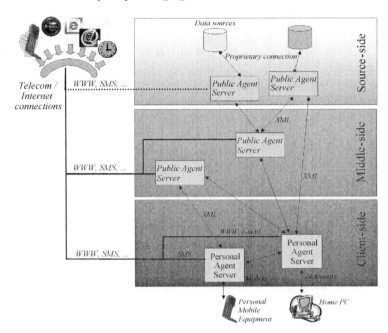

data sources as, for example, cache memories, proxies, synchronizers, semaphores, locks, query optimizers and serializers, and so forth.

Middle-side agent servers are located in the network, at a selected host. In contrast to the source-side agent servers, middle-side agent servers store and execute both system and private agents. A typical task list for system agents covers: brokering among source-side agent servers and user agents; wrapping and formatting messages exchanged by the population of agents; and providing access via different telecommunication means (WWW/WAP, SMS/MMS, e-mail, etc.). A stress is put on efficient access to the agents by many telecommunication channels and standards. User-defined agents from the private pool are usually devoted to the task related with comparing information and detecting changes that are "interesting" for users and other agents.

Architecture of a *client-side agent server* strongly depends on technical and communica-tional possibilities of an end-user hardware/software the server is running at. It is up to the user to locate his/her private agents either in a selected middle-side Agent Server, or in the private client-side server. In the first case, the network traffic may be substantially reduced; however, remotely-executed user agents are less secured (from the user point of view) and less efficient. In the second case, all the user agents are executed in a trusted (still, only from the user point of view) environment; however, a lot of information must be transferred among distributed agents.

For an agent server executed at a portable/mobile device, a stress is put on fast and user-friendly agent-to-human communication. The technical capabilities of the device strongly limit the possibilities of executing the agents (small memory, limited battery time, difficult management, etc.). Thus, usually only a few private agents are located in a mobile agent server capable of performing some simple tasks as, for example, final formatting of an alert message, filtering incoming messages, generating sound alerts, and so forth.

Typical Scenario of Creating and Maintaining an Ad Hoc VE

As already mentioned in the section, "Current Approaches for Building VEs and AHVEs," the system may be used by the beginners and advanced users at the same time, depending on individual preferences. Below, a strategy is proposed for personalization of the private agents according to the growing user level. The strategy assumes that at the beginning the user representing a business party is not able to program the agents. So, the VE representative (i.e., another business party) offers a set of predefined agents, with functionality common for all the users of the same kind. However, as time goes by, the user's expectations grow, and the system is ready to satisfy the user with new/extended functionality.

1. A client addresses a given ad hoc VE, determining some personal preferences: mobile and stationary devices used, identifiers (e.g., a phone subscriber number, IMEI device number, PKI signature, IP/DNS address, e-mail account, etc.), preferred communication means, and so forth.

2. The VE representative proposes a set of predefined SAs and PAs to be installed for the new VE member located in the local area network of the VE representative or in a selected network host. This set of agents is capable of serving the client's requests in a predefined way that is common for all the parties.

3. The VE representative proposes a set of PAs to be installed at client-side, to facilitate business contacts. It is up to the user to accept this set of agents or not. In the latter case, only the PAs executed remotely (from the point of view of the new member) are used. However, once a user accepts PAs agents in his/her private hardware/software environment, he/she may profit in using individual data treatment (cf. "Current Approaches for Building VEs and AHVEs"); better adjustment to end-user devices; more personalized formatting and presentation methods; and other functionality related with client-side information processing. Note that, as the new VE member may inform the VE representative about detailed characteristics of the devices used and preferable communication channels, the generated client-side PAs may be customized, even if the server-side PAs are quite standardized (at the beginning, however, cf. Point 5 below).

4. The set of accepted agents is installed and activated each time the change of information is detected related with VE. The detected changes are filtered and eventually sent to the client (usually, to an agent, and further via given communication channel directly to the end-user device, e.g., a mobile phone).

5. Once the client is not satisfied with a subscription or PA behavior, he/she has some rights to redefine both data and code of his/her agents. For advanced users, it is possible to fully personalize the behavior of the system, both at server-, and at the client-side. For non-advanced users, it is still a possibility to define preferable communication

channel, ways and timings of sending alerts, formats and contents of messages generated by the agents (e.g., small SMS alerting vs. formatted HTML e-mails). In this way, system functionality grows as user requirements grow.

Note that even if the users change the behavior (i.e., the code) of their private agents executed at the server-side, the overall system security is not reduced due to continuous run-time inspection of "untrusted" (user-defined) agents (cf. section "Agent Computing Environment"). Note also that private agents are executed only in two "trusted" (from a user point of view) environments: a VE representative local area network, and private "network" of the new VE member, mobile phones included. Sending messaging among user agents may be encrypted (e.g., using PKI cryptography), increasing the overall confidence level of business contacts.

As an example of using the above-presented scenario, we may consider a warehouse selling and transporting large amounts of items to ad hoc (i.e., single-transaction) customers. Each customer is interested in obtaining real-time information about payments, loading to the trucks, further position of these trucks, and exact date of delivery. In addition, some alerts would be quite useful, starting from eventual problems with money transfer, and finishing with just-in-time delivery reports and delays. In the traditional approach, mobile phones are used to get the latest info about the transaction and delivery state. In such a case, these are the members of the customer's staff who would initiate the telephone calls ("polling" mode). However, as this is an ad hoc business activity, it is not possible to make a direct call to the warehouse by an ordinary employee of the company. Only the employee directly responsible for this ad hoc business activity (usually one of the company's management staff) has detailed knowledge about the cooperation, knowing warehouse's telephone numbers, staff names, responsibility areas, and so forth. Thus, this person is overloaded by "setting up" telephone connections, propagating some important information changes (i.e., about delivery delays), and performing more similar low-level business activities, rather than concentrating on high-level management.

To improve the quality of the business process, we introduce ACE agents as being brokers between the warehouse and the customer. This process is well known by the warehouse, as it was already performed several times, however, with different business partners. Thus, the warehouse is in charge for proposing a set of standard agents, operating in one of the warehouse-owned hosts, and responsible for the support of the business activities between the warehouse and the customer. The customer accepts this set of agents, providing some parameters, such as telephone numbers of the employees directly responsible for particular sub-activities (i.e., a storeman, a driver, an accountant, etc.). Such information, in turn, is well-known by the customer, however, not necessary by the warehouse. Once the business process is started, these agents and telephone numbers are used for propagating useful information about the current state of this process, as well as some alerts if something goes wrong (i.e., not in a usual/arranged way). Note that the information messages and alerts are individualized, taking into account the area of responsibility of the employee to whom the message is addressed. For example, an alert about a delay of the money transfer is sent to the accountant, while the exact date and time of the delivery is sent to the storeman.

If both business partners are satisfied with the transaction, probably the process will be repeated in the future. In such case, the ACE agents prepared for the first cooperation may be reused. Moreover, both business partners may use just-gained experience to improve the agent functionality. For example, the storeman's agent may play a significant role in planning the transport, by setting up possible departure/arrival dates, layout of the items on a truck, additional protection, and so forth. To this goal, the agent is partially moved to the personal communication device of the storeman (e.g., a palmtop with GSM modem). In case of a significant delivery delay, the storeman's agent is able to send an alert to the management staff. In turn, agents of the management staff are able to generate alerts and inquiries to the agents of the warehouse staff. Note, however, that the above-mentioned additional agent functionality must be designed by the customer rather than the warehouse, even if the agents are to be executed in one of the warehouse's hosts. Thus, the costs of individualization and improvement of the customer-side agents are left to the customer. Note also, that the decision for the automatization and/or automated support for a particular business sub-activity is left to the business partner for which the sub-activity is realized.

Related Work

There were already some attempts to use agent technology in the scope of virtual enterprises. A good survey of using software agents, Web services with UDDI/WSDL, and other extension technologies to create VEs may be found in Petri and Bussler (2003). There are, as well, some scientific prototypes for an agent-based virtual enterprise; these are enumerated and discussed below.

Oprea proposed to use software agents for the coordination of different activities of business partners inside a VE (Oprea, 2003a). The concept resulted in a prototype of an agent-based environment for establishing and maintaining VEs (Oprea, 2003b). The basic assumption for the proposal is to use a stable set of predefined roles and software agents related with these roles, such as a coordinator, a member, a broker, and so forth. Agents are expected to coordinate the services and information exchange, to be able to follow complex negotiation protocols, and to perform other socially complex operations. Recently, the proposal resulted in a real-business application for establishing a set of VEs in the area of house-developers (Oprea, 2005).

The proposal concentrates on coordination of a set of autonomous agents; however, an evolution of agent roles is not taken into consideration. Due to the fixed set of roles and, in turn, agent types, the ad hoc and temporal activities are not modeled. Implementation of the prototype is based on JADE, a Java-based FIPA-compliant agent platform. The implementation allows for programming the agents in the imperative way; however, security aspects are not taken into consideration, and a priori assumption is taken that standard Java security mechanisms are enough for the distributed execution of the agents. In contrast, the ACE environment is concentrated on the security aspects for secure, remote execution of user-defined agents.

In the metaMorph II project (Shen & Norie, 2004), being an extension of MetaMorph I, ABCDE, and DIDE projects, agents are used as a mechanism for knowledge sharing in a distributed environment. The authors introduce a common vocabulary in order to provide efficient, global information sharing. The main project objective is to integrate the enterprise's activities such as design, planning, scheduling, simulation, and execution with those of its suppliers, customers, and partners into a distributed intelligent open environment. Two fixed classes of agents are introduced: resource agents, and mediator agents. As each mediator must contain detailed knowledge about the coordinated agents, the overall structure (network) of agents is fixed. The system behaves well in such stable applications as supply chain management. However, probably such a system would fail in a dynamically-composed and evolving structure of an ad hoc enterprise. Other drawbacks of the proposal in the scope of an ad hoc VE are related with fixed, generic way of representation of business knowledge (logic). As for an ad hoc VE, detailed, static representation of business knowledge of each VE business party would be quite difficult, because such knowledge cannot be collected in advance, and thus it is hard to represent in a formal way.

Petersen, Divitini, and Matskin (2001) extended a typical representation of business units to the uniform representation of different business partners, humans included. In the proposal, a VE is treated as a team of partners that have common goals and are committed to fulfilling these goals. A VE is a combination of entities: agents, human beings, and business enterprises. The classical VE life cycle is assumed with stable roles of business partners, fixed before any business cooperation. This assumption limits a possibility of establishing an ad hoc VE, because the final commitment of the whole ad hoc VE is hard to reach, and this evolving process takes some time to get to a stable state, involving several business-to-business activities among the partners.

The idea has been further extended to the AGORA proposal of an agent-based architecture for supporting VEs (Petersen, 2003; Petersen, Rao, & Matskin, 2003). In AGORA, several common predefined agent classes are introduced: initiator, partner, interested partner, and potential partner. Agents representing business partners are matched on the base of requirements (defined for a business goal) and skills and capabilities (defined for a business party). Fixed predefined algorithms allow for establishment of a VE as well as for contract negotiations inside the VE. The implementation is based on FIPA ACL and XProlog system, with a possibility of mapping Prolog clauses to FIPA messages. Similar to the MetaMorph system, AGORA proposal is not flexible enough to deal with ad hoc VEs.

Aerts, Szirbik, and Goosenaerts (2002) deal with the problem of modeling an ad hoc VE as a set of distributed agents. The authors put stress on the problem of high evolution of an ad hoc VE, in contrast to the stable and fixed supply chain management. The authors also discuss an interesting concept of an extended enterprise, stating that a company is made up not just of its employees, its board members, and executives, but also its business partners, its suppliers, and even its customers (Jagdev & Thoben, 2001). The project is concentrated on VEs that manufacture products, with an emphasis on fast and timely delivery, rather than on integration at the planning level. As a result, a group of enterprises is modeled that collaborate on the production of a set of related products, such as aircraft subsystems, whole complexity transcends the abilities of a single enterprise.

The main implementation issue of the proposal, docks and service bridges, seems to be less flexible than the agent servers of the ACE framework with specialized agent-gateways, as the docks form fixed system infrastructure. In such a way, a bridge serves as a single, multi-use wrapper to local software systems, with no possibilities of individualization. A common ontology is assumed, and a translation should be provided for each business partner. The bridges also serve as firewalls for incoming agents; however, nothing is said about security policies and inspection mechanisms to overcome security problems. For non-advanced and new-coming users, so-called agent providers are introduced, offering communication and application services to customers. We think that the derivation hierarchy of ACE agents is more flexible and easy-to-use. Moreover, ACE agents of a standard functionality may be generated automatically without direct human control, while the Agent Providers need a substantial amount of human management.

The DIP project (Data, Information and Process Integration with Semantic Web Services), started in 2004, has in mind to balance between ad hoc and global integration strategies (DIP, 2006). DIP's main objective is to develop and extend Semantic Web and Web service technologies by producing a new technology infrastructure in which different Web services can discover and cooperate with each other automatically. Although the implementation is based on Web services rather than agents, we think that the main goal of the DIP project is somehow similar to our evolving agent-supported cooperation in the scope of the ACE framework, being ad hoc and non-formal at the beginning and as time goes by, becoming more and more precise and stable. The idea of evolving ontology in the DIP methodology may be compared with the idea of evolving user-managed agents' code for the network of ACE agents. However, our proposal is concentrated on the ad hoc cooperation phase only. Thus, we put stress on the fact that the evolution of agents is managed by the agent owners as a result of evolving requirements and skills of the business parties, while the evolution of DIP ontology is more centralized and performed in a formal way.

Conclusion

Establishing and maintaining a VE requires a lot of efforts. The amount of work is substantially enlarged in a case of an ad hoc VE, with a highly dynamic environment and ongoing evolution of the requirements and expectations of the business partners involved. Due to the fact that the business activities related with an ad hoc VE will probably never happen in the future, using fixed, severe technologies as, for example, Web services is not economically justified. Moreover, as the individual goals of the business partners are frequently redefined on-the-fly, it is hard to provide a stable, commonly-shared knowledge about the business case. Such knowledge is a base necessary for most of the current attempts to provide an environment supporting creation and maintenance of VEs. Thus, the current proposals either assume a common, predefined ontology (and further common schema), to be set up by all the business partners before any cooperation takes place, or restrict the application area to such with well-defined generic business knowledge, for example, e-markets, supply chain management of a traditional enterprise, and so forth. In any case, all the business partners must agree with the common ontology and, as a consequence, the partners must either adjust their own way of doing business to the ontology specification, or to provide some mapping between "global" and "local" private ontologies.

In the case of an ad hoc VE, there is a limited possibility to establish a common ontology for the business partners prior to the start of the cooperation. First, the business case is usually not fixed, and the knowledge about this case is usually gathered on-the-fly, as the business evolves. Second, there are no generic rules and knowledge for similar business cases, as there were not present in the past, and they will probably never happen in the future. Third, the cooperation among business partners possibly involved in the cooperation in the scope of an ad hoc VE is usually restricted in time. Thus, it is not economically justifiable to invest in any severe technology dealing with generic knowledge (ontology) exchange and management. And fourth, if we take into consideration one-to-one relations between the business partners (a usual case for the ad hoc cooperation), only a part of the global knowledge is usually needed for a single relation. Then, instead of providing some complex tools for the ontology (schema) mapping and exchange, one need to precise only a part of the total knowledge with minimum efforts. Note, however, that this task must be individualized for both the business case and the business partners involved in this case. As a consequence, a need arises for a "light" technology to effectively and securely maintain such temporal and ad hoc business activities. We proposed to adopt a software agent technology, with a possibility of defining and controlling agents' behavior directly by the agent owners, that is, business partners involved in cooperation in the scope of an ad hoc VE.

Comparing with the other proposals related with using the agent technology to support VEs, the presented agent-based framework, based on agent computing environment (ACE) is much better suited for a specificity of ad hoc VEs. First, no assumption is made for creating common business knowledge prior to establish a VE. Instead, business partners develop individually their agents to use a part of this knowledge, necessary to establish one-to-one business contacts. As the control of agents' behavior is left to the agent owners, and there are no global restrictions related with a common schema and/or ontology, the agents may be quickly adopted to the changes in the environment and evolving expectations of the business partners. In such way, longer is the cooperation between business partners, better the contacts are supported by the partners' agents and their internal knowledge, and less work must be performed manually by the human staff.

Second, the ACE agents are imperatively programmed by their owners, being able to deal with any business case. Using the declarative technique of agent programming, which is a key for most of the current proposals, would strongly restrict overall system flexibility. The natural fear of remote execution of the imperative agents' code is tempered by introducing two classes of the agents: the public agents, designed by the trusted users and used as "black boxes" by the others, and the private agents, to be exclusively used by their owners.

Third, ACE agents make it possible to mix traditional, human-based cooperation and automated information exchange, by introducing several human-to-agent communication channels: from traditional (Web/WAP pages and e-mail) to modern mobile communication channels, as for example SMS/MMS, push-to-talk (PTT) and voice gateways for instant messaging. Even if the business activities are performed manually by the human staff, there is still a large application area for ACE agents being remote monitors and notifiers, sending alerts while "something interesting" happen. What is "interesting" is individually programmed by the agent owners, and may be dynamically changed as the overall situation evolves. For example, imagine an alert about a just-closed credit line, sent automatically by the use of a secret SMS message to the company's representative being in the train of business negotiations. Even if such information is not incorporated in the total knowledge about the VE, knowing this one fact may drastically change the style of cooperation between the business partners.

Fourth, the ACE framework does not control the internal functionality of the private agents provided by the business partners. The framework itself is a generic, safe environment for the establishment of an ad hoc VE of any kind and purpose. Thus, starting from a weak support for an ad hoc VE, the business partners may continuously enlarge agents' possibilities, either by providing gateways to existing and newly-proposed external software systems, or by incorporating the new ideas directly in the agents' code. Once enough knowledge is gathered about the business activities, some formal approaches may be adopted, replacing the manual work of a human staff by the automated data interchange according to well-defined business rules. The imperatively programmed ACE agents are well suited for both these cases. Note that the new functionality does not have to be provided for all of the business partners at once. Instead, at the beginning only a small group of business partners may be involved, and, as time goes by, more and more business partners incorporate new solutions in their business logic. For most of the current proposals, it is not possible to differentiate business partners in such a way.

It seems that the idea of a continuous evolution of the business relations, starting from manual cooperation of the humans, and finishing on automatized cooperation of standalone and individualized software agents, needs further research. The proposed ACE agents are, on one hand, a good starting point for beginning the cooperation by creating an ad hoc VE. On the other hand, several existing proposals may be incorporated dealing with stable and well-defined business relations, changing an ad hoc VE to "real," "severe" and long-lasting business relations. The ACE agents may be also used for providing a kind of a prototype of a VE. Once enough experience is gathered about business relations while using such a prototype, a targeted VE may be designed by the use of more sophisticated, but also more costly, software technologies.

References

ACT-NET Consortium. (1996). The active database management system manifesto: A rule-base of ADBMS features. *ACM Sigmod Record, 25*(3), 40-49.

Aerts, A. T. M., Szirbik, N. B., & Goosenaerts, J. B. (2002). The flexible ICT architecture for virtual enterprises. *Computers in Industry, 49*(3), 311-327.

Bigus, J. P., & Bigus, J. (1998). *Constructing intelligent agents with Java. A programmer's guide to smart applications.* New York: Wiley Computer Publishing.

Caglayan, A., & Harrison, C. (1997). *Agent sourcebook: A complete guide to desktop, Internet, and intranet agents.* Toronto: John Wiley & Sons.

Ceri, S., & Fraternali, P. (1997). *Designing database applications with objects and rules.* Addison-Wesley.

Chess, D., Harrison, C., & Kershenbaum, A. (1995). *Mobile agents: Are they a good idea?* Research report. Yorktown Heights, NY: IBM, T. J. Watson Research Center.

Concordia Mobile Agent. (2002). Concordia: An infrastructure for collaborating mobile agents. *Mitsubishi Electric ITA, Horizon Systems Laboratory.* Retrieved from http://www.cis.upenn.edu/~bcpierce/courses/629/papers/Concordia-MobileAgentConf.html

CORBA. (2002). *3- and n-Tier Architectures.* Retrieved from http://www.softeam.com/technologies_architectures_distribuees.php, http://www.corba.ch/e/3tier.html#Why%203-tier?

DAML Semantic Web Services. (2006). Retrieved from http://www.daml.org/services

DARPA Agent Markup Language. (2006). Retrieved from http://www.daml.org/

DIP on-going project—public deliverables (2006). Retrieved from http://dip.semanticweb.org/

FIPA. (2006). Retrieved from http://www.fipa.org/

FIPA Personal Assistant Specification. (2006). Retrieved from http://www.fipa.org/specs/fipa00083/XC00083B.html

Franklin, S., & Graesser, A. (1996). Is it an agent, or just a program? A taxonomy for autonomous agents. In *Proceedings of the 3rd International Workshop on Agent Theories, Architectures, and Languages*. Springer-Verlag.

Hurson, A., Bright, M., & Pakzad, S. (1993). *Multidatabase systems: An advanced solution for global information sharing*. IEEE Press.

Jagdev, H. S., & Thoben, K. D. (2001). Anatomy of enterprise collaborations. *International Journal of Production Planning and Control, 12*(5), 437-451.

Jurafsky, D., & Martin, J. H. (2000). *Speech and language processing: An introduction to natural language processing, computational linguistics, and speech recognition*. Prentice-Hall.

Kotz, D., & Gray R. S. (1999). Mobile agents and the future of the Internet. *ACM Operating Systems Review, 33*(3), 7-13.

Milojicic, D. (Ed.). (1999). Trend wars—mobile agent applications. *IEEE Concurrency, 7-8*, 80-90.

Nwana, H. (1996). Software agents: An overview. *Knowledge Engineering. Review, 11*(3), 205-244.

Oprea, M. (2003a). Coordination in an agent-based virtual enterprise. *Studies in Informatics and Control, 12*(3), 215-225.

Oprea, M. (2003b). The agent-based virtual enterprise. *Journal of Economy Informatics, 3*(1), pp. 15-20.

Oprea, M. (2005). A case study of agent-based virtual enterprise modelling. *Lecture Notes in Artificial Intelligence, 3690*, 632-635.

Oracle Triggers (2006). Retrieved from http://www-rohan.sdsu.edu/doc/oracle/server803/A54643_01/ch15.htm

Paton, N. (Ed.). (1999). *Active rules in database systems*. Springer-Verlag.

Petersen, S. (2003). An agent-based evaluation framework for supporting virtual enterprise formation. In *Proceedings of the IEEE 12th International Workshop on Enabling Technologies, Infrastructures for Collaborative Enterprises (WET-ICE2003)* (pp.159-164) Linz, Austria.

Petersen, S., Rao, J., & Matskin, M. (2003, October 13-16). Virtual enterprise formation with agents: An approach to implementation. In *Proceedings of the 2003 IEEE/WIC International Conference on Intelligent Agent Technology (IAT-2003)* (pp. 527-530) Halifax, Canada. IEEE Press.

Petersen, S., Divitini, M., & Matskin, M. (2001). An agent-based approach to modelling virtual enterprises. *International Journal of Production Planning & Control, 12*(3), 224-233.

Petrie, C., & Bussler, C. (2003). Service agents and virtual enterprises: A survey. *IEEE Internet Computing, 7*(4), 68-78.

Rykowski, J. (2003a, September). Agent technology for secure personalized Web services. In *Proceedings of the 24th International Scientific School ISAT 2003,* Szklarska Poręba, Poland (pp. 185-193).

Rykowski, J. (2003b). Databases as repositories for software agents. In B. Thalheim & G. Fiedler (Eds.), *Emerging database research in East Europe. Proceedings of the Pre-conference Workshop joined with the 29th VLDB Conference,* Berlin, Germany (pp. 117-123).

Rykowski, J. (2005a). ACE agents—mass personalized software assistance. *Lecture Notes in Artificial Intelligence, 3690,* 587-591.

Rykowski, J. (2005b, April). Using software agents to personalize natural-language access to Internet services in a chatterbot manner. In *Proceedings of the 2nd International Conference Language and Technology L&T'05,* (pp. 269-273), Poznan, Poland.

Rykowski, J. (2006). Management of information changes by the use of software agents. *Cybernetics and Systems, 37*(2-3), 229-260.

Rykowski, J., & Cellary, W. (2004). Virtual Web services - Application of software agents to personalization of Web services. In *Proceedings of the 6th International Conference on Electronic Commerce ICEC 2004,* Delft, The Netherlands (pp. 409-418). ACM Publishers.

Rykowski, J., & Juszkiewicz, A. (2003). Personalization of information delivery by the use of agents. In *Proceedings of the IADIS International Conference WWW/Internet 2003,* Algarve, Portugal (pp. 1056-1059).

Schiemann, B., Kovacs, E., & Röhrle, K. (1999, October). Adaptive mobile access to context-aware services. In *Proceedings of the 3rd International Workshop on Mobile Agents* (pp. 190-201), Palm Springs, FL.

Shen, W., & Norie, D. H. (2004). An agent-based approach for information and knowledge sharing in manufacturing enterprise networks. *International Journal of Networking and Virtual Organizations, 2*(2), 173-190.

SOAP. (2003). *Version 1.2, Part 1: Messaging Framework, W3C Recommendation.* Retrieved from http://www.w3.org/TR/soap12-part1/

Specification of the KQML Agent-Communication Language. (2003). *The DARPA Knowledge Sharing Initiative, External Interfaces Working Group.* Retrieved from http://www.cs.umbc.edu/kqml/kqmlspec/spec.html

The Extensible Stylesheet Language Family. (2002). *XSL.* Retrieved from http://www.w3.org/Style/XSL/

The Voyager SOA Platform. (2005). *Recursion Software.* Retrieved from http://www.recursionsw.com/Voyager/2005-09-13-Voyager_SOA_Platform.pdf

UDDI Business Registry Version 2. (2005). Retrieved from https://uddi.ibm.com/ubr/registry.html

Web Services Activity. (2002). Retrieved from http://www.w3.org/2002/ws/

Web Ontology Language OWL. (2004). Retrieved from http://www.w3.org/2004/OWL/

Weizenbaum, J. (1976). *Computer power and human reason. From judgment to calculation.* S.Franc.

Wooldridge, M., & Jennings, N. R. (1995). Intelligent agents: Theory and practice. *Knowledge Engineering Review, 10*(2), 115-152.

Wooldridge, M., & Jennings, N. (1995). Agent theories, architectures, and languages: A survey. In M. Wooldridge, & N. Jennings (Eds.) *Intelligent Agents* (pp. 1-22). Berlin: Springer-Verlag.

XML Extensible Markup Language. (2005). Retrieved from http://www.w3.org/XML

Zillman, M. P. (2003). *Chatterbot resources and sites.* Retrieved from http://chatterbots.blogspot.com/

Chapter XVI

Business Networking:
The Technological
Infrastructure Support

Claudia-Melania Chituc,
Faculty of Engineering of the University of Porto (FEUP), INESC Porto, Portugal

Américo Lopes Azevedo,
Faculty of Engineering of the University of Porto (FEUP), INESC Porto, Portugal

Abstract

The rapid evolution of information and communication technologies, the changing client's demands, and market conditions impelled enterprises to adapt their way of undertaking business, from traditional practices to e-business, and to participate in new forms of collaboration, such as networked organizations. In this context, standards, frameworks, technologies, and infrastructures supporting collaborative business, in a networked environment, become key factors in achieving environments with a desired high level of collaboration and inter- and intra-organization business processes alignment. The aim of this chapter is to underline the main issues, trends, and opportunities related to business integration from a technological perspective, analyzing and discussing the most relevant (existing and still under development) business integration reference models, frameworks, standards, technologies, and supporting infrastructures, and to briefly present relevant research projects in the area of business networking. A special emphasis is made on frameworks such as ebXML and RosettaNet, and the importance of papiNet, BPLE4WS, and freebXML is underlined. Challenges regarding self-forming networked organizations are also advanced.

Introduction

Current business trends and information and communication technology (ICT) developments determined enterprises to change their way of undertaking business, from vertically-integrated companies towards flexible collaborative networked organizations (CNOs). In this context, enterprise integration and interoperability emerge as key elements supporting real-time information flow and exchange, and intra- and interorganization business processes integration and alignment. CNOs represent a valuable and effective approach to achieve strategic objectives in a time-response and cost-effective manner, with a high level of quality of delivery and customer's satisfaction, while generating value to stakeholders.

CNOs represent a collection of heterogeneous organizations with different competences, but symbiotic interests that join, efficiently combining the most suitable set of skills and resources (e.g., knowledge, capital, assets) for a period of time in order to achieve a common objective, and make use of ICT to coordinate, develop, and support their activities. The term CNO is used in this chapter, in a broad sense, for other emerging business collaborative forms with similar proprieties, such as virtual enterprises (VE), virtual organizations (VO), or extended enterprises.

The aim of this chapter is to underline the main issues, trends and opportunities related to business integration, from a technological perspective, analyzing and discussing the most relevant (existing and still under development) business integration reference models, frameworks, standards, technologies, and supporting infrastructures, and to briefly present relevant research projects in the area of business networking in Europe and the USA. A special emphasis is made on frameworks such as ebXML and Rosetta Net, and the importance of papiNet, BPLE4WS, and freebXML is underlined.

The main research questions which motivated the present work are:

- **Question 1:** Which are the main benefits for technology integration, in a business collaborative environment formed by heterogeneous organizations with different goals, strategies, and technologies, but symbiotic interests?
- **Question 2:** Which are the main (existing or still under development) standards, technologies, and frameworks supporting business integration and interoperability?
- **Question 3:** Which are the most relevant developments/research projects in the area of business networking?

The remains of this chapter are organized as follows. The following section presents the main issues (e.g., benefits), opportunities and trends related to business integration and interoperability, from a technological perspective. The most relevant reference models, standards, frameworks, technologies, and supporting infrastructures for enterprise integration will be then analyzed, exemplifying with research projects developed in EU and the USA. A special emphasis will be made on ebXML, BPLE4WS, papiNet, freebXML, and Rosetta Net. The last section addresses the needs for further research and concludes this chapter.

Needs for Enterprise Integration and Interoperability in a Collaborative Business Networked Environment

CNOs represent a powerful mechanism to achieve competitiveness and agility in today's turbulent market conditions by comprising various entities with complementary competences, but symbiotic interests. They include geographically-distributed organizations, having different cultures, working methods, or supporting technologies. Although CNO partners aim at achieving a common business goal and following a common business strategy, each member organization has its own goal and strategy, which makes CNO coordination and management assume a critical role.

CNO have several advantages, the most relevant ones being summarized in Camarinha-Matos and Afsarmanesh (2003): agility, complementary roles, achieving dimension, competitiveness, resource optimization, and innovation.

However, the formation, development, and operation of any CNO, and its success, depends on some base commonality among its members, such as common goals, common or interoperable ICT infrastructures and supporting services, real-time information sharing and flow among CNO members, and common standards or common views in a number of areas (e.g., describing and orchestrating business process flows across multiple systems, trust, common system of values and common way to perform business processes) (Camarinha-Matos & Afsarmanesh, 2003). Adequate reference models, supporting infrastructures, and proper managerial and technological alignment of inter- and intra-organization business processes are required to achieve these common challenges.

Enterprise integration and interoperability aim at developing computer-based tools that facilitate coordination of work and information flow across organizational boundaries. While enterprise integration focuses on intra-enterprise distributed business processes (e.g., orchestration, communication) and flows, enterprise interoperability is focusing on inter-enterprise distributed business processes and flows. According to Vernadat (1996), enterprise integration (EI) refers to facilitating information, control, and material flows across organizational boundaries by connecting all the necessary functions and heterogeneous functional entities. It aims at improving communication, cooperation, and coordination in an enterprise. As a consequence, the enterprise behaves as an integrated whole, enhancing its overall productivity, flexibility, and capacity for the management of change. EI does not represent a new issue; evolving from physical integration to application and later business integration, EI has been a challenge for both information technology and manufacturing industries for several decades. IEEE (1990) provides a definition for interoperability, focusing on information exchanged and its use.

Major motivations for EI are mentioned in Vernadat (1996), and can be summarized as follows:

- The need for real information sharing
- The need for interoperability (e.g., the need to harmonize the operational networked environment)

- The need to improve task coordination or inter-working between organization units, individuals, and systems in interaction within an enterprise

In order to be competitive in a collaborative business networked environment, organizations should adopt a bipolar approach which allows them to fully benefit from the specific competences of each partner of a CNO (Chituc & Azevedo, 2005b):

- To develop a compatible organizational infrastructure allowing CNO members to join their competences while supporting the operations and functions to be performed
- To build up new management methodologies based on the most recent ICT developments, assuring high performance of the business activities with a minimum of human interaction

Enterprise Networking:
Relevant Initiatives in Europe and the USA

Several initiatives are currently being developed in the area of business networking in Europe and the USA, and also in Australia, Mexico, Canada, and more recently in Japan. As pointed out by Camarinha-Matos and Afsarmanesh (2003), the area of networked organizations/ enterprises is particularly active in Europe, and this can be somehow explained by the process of European integration. The European Union (EU), especially with the 6th Framework, supports a large range of research projects in the area of enterprise networking. Figure 1 illustrates the main "clusters" or targeted research initiatives in this field, as defined in VE-Forum (http://www.ve-forum.org):

- **Business networking cluster:** aiming at designing and developing reference models and technologies supporting organizations and professionals, enhancing their collaboration and agility, and at fostering the development of suitable VO breeding environments; relevant research projects in this area are: ECOLEAD (European COLlaborative networked organizations LEADership initiative, http://www.ecolead.org), CROSSWORK (Developing Cross-Organizational Workflow Formation and Enactment, http://www.crosswork.info), VE-Forum (the European forum for virtual organizations domains, http://www.ve-forum.org).
- **Enterprise interoperability:** aiming at developing open and secure technologies to connect system and enterprises. Enterprise interoperability is addressed at different levels: physical integration, syntactic application integration, semantic application integration, business process integration, inter-enterprise coordination. ATHENA (Advanced Technologies for interoperability of Heterogeneous Enterprise Networks and their Applications, http://www.athena-ip.org) and INTEROP (Interoperability Research for Networked Enterprises Applications and Software, http://www.interop-noe.org) are relevant research projects in this area.

Figure 1. EU targeted research clusters for enterprise networking (Adapted after VE-Forum http://www.fe-forum.org—The European Research Clusters for Enterprise Networking)

INTEROP	Enterprise Interoperability	Business Networking	Ambient Intelligence Technologies for the Product Life Cycle
	ATHENA No-Rest TrustCoM	CrossWork ECOLEAD 1st-Bonus Mosquito MyCarEvent MyTreasury XBRL in Europe	Co DesNet ILIPT MAPPER PARADISE' PROMISE Spider-Wiu V-CES VERITAS X-Change
	DigitalEcosystems		
	DBE Legal-IST SATINE		
	VE-FORUM		

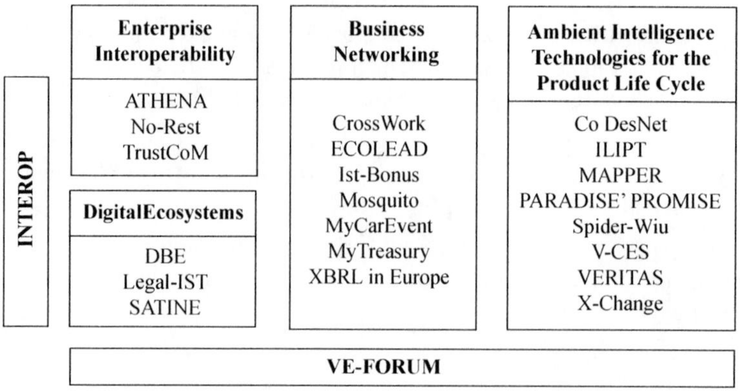

- **The ambient intelligence technologies for the product life-cycle cluster:** aiming at enabling organizations, in a networked business environment, to deliver better products to the market, in a more efficient way and faster, by enhancing the product and the product life-cycle processes using ambient intelligence technologies; CO-DESNET (Collaborative Demand and Supply NETworks, http://codesnet.polito.it) is a relevant research project in this area.

- **Digital ecosystems:** aiming at providing to small and micro-systems ICT applications and services which improve their efficiency and business integration within EU regions; SATINE (Semantic-based Interoperability Infrastructure for Integrating Web Service Platforms to Peer-to-Peer Networks, http://www.srdc.metu.edu.tr) is a relevant project in this area.

Reference Models, Standards, Frameworks, and Technologies Supporting Enterprise Integration and Interoperability

Several reference models, frameworks, and standards have been developed aiming at supporting enterprise integration and interoperability. This section concisely presents some integration reference models, frameworks, and standards referring to B2B domain, and relevant infrastructures and technologies supporting enterprise integration and interoperability. According to Vernadat (1996), a reference model represents a partial model, which can be used as a basis for certain model developments or evaluations. The term "framework" refers to a collection of elements (e.g., principles, methods, tools) put together for a certain purpose, and relevant for a given domain of application. Standards can be regarded as objects (e.g., hardware, software), which are accepted and shared within a community (i.e., business unit, value chain) (Crargill, 1989).

A. Reference Models, Architectures, and Frameworks

Purdue Enterprise Reference Architecture (PERA) provides the reference model of physical and informational interactions in enterprises (Li & Williams, 2000). An extension of the model is presented in Li and Williams (2003), which aims at enhancing the functionality of PERA as reference model for a distributed enterprises environment (e.g., VE), where the business processes in a group of enterprises are synchronously and simultaneously executed via information exchange.

Generalized Enterprise Reference Architecture and Methodology (GERAM) (IFAC/IFIP, 2000) defines a tool-kit of concepts for designing and maintaining enterprises for their entire life history. GERAM refers to the methods, models, and tools, which are needed to build and maintain the integrated enterprise, a single enterprise or a network of enterprises. GERAM encapsulates and orders previous architectures (e.g., CIMOSA, PERA, GRAI/GIM), providing an overall structure to use those methods and modeling techniques. GERAM is not a reference architecture; it is aimed at organizing enterprises' existing integration knowledge, and its framework has the potential for application to all types of enterprises by describing the components needed in all enterprises' engineering and integration processes. Generalized Enterprise Reference Architecture (GERA) is GERAM's most important component. It identifies basic concepts to be used in enterprise engineering and integration.

Supply chain operations reference model (SCOR) (http://www.supply-chain.org) is a process reference model developed by the Supply-Chain Council as a cross-industry standard for supply-chain management used to describe, measure, and evaluate supply-chain configurations. The SCOR model is organized around five primary management processes: plan, source, make, deliver, and return. It is composed by a hierarchic architecture of four level details: top level (process types), configuration level (process categories), process element level (decompose processes), and implementation level (decompose process elements).

Zachman's framework for enterprise architecture (Zachman, 1987) describes a holistic model of an enterprise information infrastructure from six perspectives: planner, owner, designer, builder, subcontractor, and working system. Its focus is to ensure that all aspects of an enterprise are well-organized and exhibit clear relationships that will ensure a complete system regardless of the order in which they are established.

Workflow reference model (Workflow Management Coalition, 1999) provides the general architectural framework that identifies interfaces and covers broadly five areas of functionality between a workflow management system (WfMS) and its environment: process definitions import and export; interaction with client applications and work-list handler software; software tools or applications invocation; interoperability between different WfMSs; and administration and monitoring functions.

B. Business-to-Business Integration Standards

In a broad sense, the term business-to-business (B2B) integration refers to electronic message exchange among trading partners. It includes issues such as product catalogs, classification systems, B2B protocol standards, synchronous/asynchronous communication, or back-end integration. According to Bussler (2003), B2B integration is the enabling technology and the necessary infrastructure to perform different operations: for example, automated supply chain integration, to send XML-formatted messages over the Internet, or to send messages in a peer-to-peer (P2P) pattern to trading partners.

According to SWWS (2003), B2B standards' scope can be roughly separated into catalogue and classification standards, document exchange, collaboration, and business processes, as follows:

- **Catalogue systems and classification standards** include: BMEcat (http://www.bmecat.org), eCX (Electronic Catalog XML, http://www.ecx-xml.org), OCP (Open Catalog Protocol, http://www.martsoft.com/ocp) as catalogue systems, and eCl@ss (http://www.eclass-online.com) or UNSPSC (United Nations Standard Products and Services Code, http://www.unspsc.org) as classification standards.

- **Document exchange** comprises electronic data interchange (EDI), electronic data interchange for administration, commerce and transport (EDIFACT), eXtensible Markup Language (XML, http://www.xml.org), XML common business library (xCBL, http://www.xcbl.org), Commerce eXtensible Markup Language (cXML, http://www.cxml.org), Open Applications Group Integration Specification (OAGIS, http://www.openapplications.org), RosettaNet implementation framework (RNIF, http://www.rosettanet.org), and Society For World-wide Interbank Financial Telecommunications (SWIFT) standard modeling (http://www.swift.com).

- **Collaboration** includes Electronic Business XML Initiative (ebXML, http://www.ebxml.org), Universal Business Language (UBL, http://docs.oasis-open.org/ubl), and RosettaNet (http://www.rosettanet.org)

- **Business processes** refer to executable business processes, ebXML business collaborations (http://www.ebxml.org), business process activities, or workflows. Business Process Modeling Language (BPML)/ Business Process Query Language (BPQL), Web Services Flow Language (WSFL), Business Process Execution Language for Web Services (BPEL4WS), XML Processing Description Language (XPDL), Unified Modeling Language, (UML, http://www.uml.org), and Process Specification Language (PSL, http://www.nist.gov.psl) are only some of the modeling languages dealing with business processes.

Other relevant developments for enterprise integration are: Open Buying on the Internet (OBI), Bolero.net, eCo framework, business transaction protocol (BTP), Transaction Authority Markup Language (XAML), and Microsoft BizTalk.

CNO require advanced infrastructures providing capabilities such as: multi-level support for interoperability, security, reconfiguration, and recovery mechanisms. The following section presents some relevant platforms and technologies for CNOs.

C. Infrastructures and Technologies

An overview of the current approaches and trends towards the establishment of flexible and configurable infrastructures for VE is presented in Camarinha-Matos and Afsarmanesh (2003). Emerging technologies for flexible VE infrastructures are grouped as follows:

- Open inter-operable underlying network protocols (e.g., TCP/IP, CORBA-IIOP, HTTP, RMI, SOAP)

- Open distributed object-oriented middleware services (e.g., J2EE Framework, CORBA Framework, Active X Framework)

- Information/object exchange mechanisms and tools (e.g., XML, ebXML, WSDL)

- Standardized modeling of business components, processes, and objects (e.g., EJBs)

- Business process modeling tools and languages (e.g., UML, UEML, WfMC XML-based Business Language, PSL)

- Open and standard business process automation and workflow management system (e.g., WfMC, OMG-JointFlow)

- Standard interfacing to federated multi-databases (e.g., JDBC)

- Intelligent mobile agents (e.g., FIPA, OMG-MASIF, Mobile Objects)

- Open and standard distributed messaging middleware systems (e.g., JMS, MS-message server, MQSeries, FIPA-ACC)

- XML-based e-commerce protocols (e.g., BizTalk, RosettaNet, OBI, WIDL)

- Web integration technologies (e.g., Servlets, JSP, MS-ASP, XSL)

Concerning infrastructures to support VE, Camarinha-Matos and Afsarmanesh (2003) illustrate two of the main approaches (from the software engineering perspective): transaction-oriented layer (TOL) based frameworks, and agent-based infrastructures (ABI).

TOL infrastructures add a cooperation layer to the existing IT platforms of the enterprises, and inter-enterprise communication is performed through layers interaction (e.g., transaction-oriented). Examples of projects developing such infrastructures are: National Industrial Information Infrastructure Protocols (NIIIP, http://www.niiip.org), Production Planning and Management in an Extended Enterprise (PRODNET II, http://www.uninova.pt/~prodnet), and Virtual Enterprises using Groupware tools and distributed Architectures (VEGA) (Zarli & Poyet, 2001), which aimed at designing open platforms to support the basic information exchange and cooperation needs in industrial VE.

For ABI, enterprises are represented as agents, and the interactions in a distributed multi-agent system determine inter-enterprise cooperation. Multi-agent Manufacturing Agile Scheduling Systems for Virtual Enterprises (MASSYVE, http://www.cordis.lu/esprit/src/962219.htm) and Dynamic Forecast for Master Production Planning with stock and capacity constraints (DAMASCUS, http://www.damascos.com) are examples of projects developing such infrastructures.

Table 1 presents infrastructure characteristics of PRODNET II, NIIIP, DAMASCUS, and VEGA projects.

A more in-depth analysis concerning trends in VE support infrastructures is available in Camarinha-Matos and Afsarmanesh (2003). The authors present also limitations for current VE/VO infrastructures and collaborative frameworks. The main problems identified concern the lack of effective approach to interoperability (e.g., software inter-operation, information exchange/integration), and the lack of standard definitions and mechanisms. As pointed out by Camarinha-Matos and Afsarmanesh (2003), most of the technologies supporting integration and interoperability in a networked environment are at their beginnings, and they

Table 1. Examples of infrastructure characteristics and typical services offered

Project	Project's aim	Infrastructure Characteristics	Supporting Technologies	Typical services offered by the platform/ architecture developed	Industry sector
PRODNET II	Design and develop an open platform and adequate information technology (IT) protocols and mechanisms to support virtual industrial enterprises	TOL	STEP, EDIFACT, Web and Internet technologies, Java	• exchange of commercial data via EDIFACT messages • exchange of technical product data using STEP • federated/ distributed information management • coordination module managing all cooperation-related events • monitoring of orders and production status • extended ERP/ PPC system adapted to interact with a VE environment • safe communications	SMEs in general
NIIIP	Solve incompatibility issues within VE, allowing organizations to collaborate with each other regardless of data structures or computing environments	TOL	STEP, OMG technologies (e.g., IDL, CORBA), workflow	• synthesizes collections of resources and technologies into a production system • control and flow of information • trap ORB (Object Request Broker) requests • inspect and validate the request NIIIP context • route requests to other components • dispatch rules and constraint-checking process associated with the request	Shipbuilding (with application in other sectors)
VEGA	Establish an information infrastructure which supports technical activities and business operations for VE	TOL	STEP, CORBA, SGML, EDI/ EDIFACT, Web technologies	• **Conceptual level:** STEP EXPRESS product data models supporting SGML documentary models and EDIFACT messages models • **Implementation level:** dedicated converters supporting the back and forth translation of SGML documents and EDIFACT messages towards STEP format, providing remote access to any kind of information for all actors involved in a construction project	Architecture construction and engineering
DAMASCOS	Design and develop an open platform providing adequate IT modules and mechanisms to manage customized supply networks in a multi-enterprise scenario	ABI	Workflow, Java	• enables customer relationship management at the sales level • supply chain management (inventory, production, logistics issues) and forecasting • interface between existing ERP systems	SMEs in general

require considerable effort to implement and configure reliable infrastructures supporting CNO creation and development.

Several research projects are currently being pursued in the area of grid technology. Grids facilitate the sharing, selection, and aggregation of geographically-distributed resources (e.g., supercomputers, storage systems), which can cross single or multiple organizations, aiming at solving large-scale computational and data-intensive problems in science, engineering, and commerce (http://www.gridcomputing.com). Unlike other approaches (e.g., clusters, where the resources' allocation is performed by a centralized resource manager and all nodes cooperatively work together as a single unified resource), in the case of grids, each node has its own resource manager.

In the USA, large projects developed in the area of networked enterprises focus on middleware and grid technology. Started in 2001, National Science Foundation Middleware Initiative (NMI, http://www.nsf-middleware.org) aims at designing, developing, deploying, and supporting a set of reusable, expandable set of middleware functions and services that benefit applications in a networked environment. Two system integration projects started in Fall of 2003: Grid Research Integration Deployment and Support (GRIDS Center, http://www.grids-center.org) and Enterprise and Desktop Integration Technologies (EDIT, http://www.nmi-edit.org). GRIDS Center develops, tests, deploys, and supports standard tools for authentication, authorization and policy, resource discovery and directory services, and remote access to computers, data, and instruments. EDIT consortium developed a set of core middleware tools in the areas of identity and access management architectures, standards for deployments, elated directories, schemas, and tools.

In Europe, the European Commission has been financing grid research since early 2000, when the first EU grid-related projects were launched under the 5th research Framework Program (FP5) (CORDIS, 2005, http://www.cordis.lu/ist/grids). Grid research projects under FP5 were focused on technology development and application pilots, and results of these research projects are now deployed in grid-enabled research infrastructures made available by FP6 projects (e.g., EGEE, DEISA).

The approach for grid research being pursued in FP6 (2002-2006) refers to CORDIS (2005):

- **Technology push:** aims at developing the underlying technologies and tackling issues such as integration, open standards and interoperability.

- **Application pull:** aims at developing the enabling technologies for real-world applications, such as modeling, simulation, data-mining, and collaboration.

According to CORDIS (2005), the most relevant current EU grid initiatives are:

- **GRIDCOORD:** (http://www.gridcoord.org)
- **InteliGrid:** (http://www.inteliGrid.com)—interoperability of virtual organizations on a complex semantic grid
- **OntoGrid:** (http://www.ontogrid.net)—paving the way for knowledgeable grid services and systems;

- **Data Mining Grid:** (http://www.datamininggrid.org)—data mining tools and services for Grid computing environments;

- **Provenance:** (http://www.gridprovenance.org)—enabling and supporting provenance in Grids for complex problems;

- **K-WF Grid:** (http://www.kwfgrid.net)—knowledge-based workflow system for Grid applications;

- **UniGrids:** (http://www.unigrids.org)—uniform interface to grid services;

- **HPC4U:** (http://www.hpc4u.org)—highly predictable clusters for Internet Grids;

- **SIMDAT:** (http://www.scai.fraunhofer.de/simdat.html)—data grids for process and product development using numerical simulation and knowledge discovery;

- **NextGrid:** (http://www.nextgrid.org)—architecture for next generation grids;

- **Akogrimo:** (http://www.mobilegrids.org)—access to knowledge through the grid in a mobile world; and

- **CoreGRID:** (http://www.coregrid.net)—European research network on foundations, software infrastructures, and applications for large-scale distributed grid and peer-to-peer technologies.

Despite the existence of a significant number of computer-based tools aiming at enterprise integration and interoperability, and the scientific developments in the business networking area, it is generally accepted that more work needs to be done since available solutions are usually cumbersome and lack in flexibility to respond to the most recent technological outcomes, very often focusing on very specific aspects. The scientific community agrees that questions related to formalization, conceptual development, and semantic integration (namely, concerning the formal description of the domain or ontology) need to be urgently developed (Camarinha-Matos, 2003).

Relevant Approaches

Relevant initiatives, such as papiNet, ebXML, freebXML, and RosettaNet are discussed more in detail in the fallowing paragraphs.

papiNET

papiNET (http://www.papinet.org) is an international paper and forest products industry e-business initiative. It is a set of standard electronic documents which facilitates the flow of information among parties engaged in buying, selling, and distribution of paper and forest products. The papiNet Standards Group has the vision of enterprises of any size and in any geographical location meeting and conducting the business of paper, printing, and publishing with each other through the exchange of XML-based messages.

papiNet aims at increasing efficiency in transaction and marketplace activities through documented business processes with supporting standard XML messages and consistent data definitions, common terminology and formats, real-time exchange of information through the Internet, in order to ensure standards' interoperability among trading partners (in the paper and forest products industry, or in other industries). papiNet standard is a set of common electronic formats and terminology for the paper and forest products industry, designed to facilitate application-to-application information exchange. Its interoperability guidelines are based on ebXML message service specification. Messages have a very uniform structure with common definitions contained in the file that is shared among all the message schema files. The most prevalently implemented message is delivery message, followed by the purchase order, order confirmation, and invoice (http://www.papinet.org).

papiNet has formally accepted from ebXML the message service and collaboration (CPPA) aspects. The internal integration information is used to determine how ebXML envelope (which acts as a common interface between systems) is used, when received, and how it is going to be created the ebXML envelope when sending. Figure 2 illustrates the papiNet interoperability approach. It is intended that any trading partner can open a message (payload) sent to them, regardless of the messaging service which was used.

ebXML and freebXML

eXtensible Markup Language (ebXML, http://www.ebxml.org) is a set of specifications that together enable a modular electronic business framework. ebXML vision is to enable a global electronic marketplace where enterprises of any size and in any geographical location can meet and conduct business with each other through the exchange of XML-based messages. Several industries endorse ebXML (e.g, computer/technology companies, banking, shipping).

One of the core values of ebXML is its vision of ubiquity from a technology perspective (Dournaee, 2004). ebXML is built around XML, SOAP, HTTP, and SMTP—all open standards.

Figure 2. papiNet: Interoperability standard approach (Adapted after papiNet, 2004)

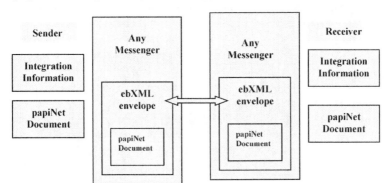

ebXML provides a complete framework for business interactions, all delivered as a set of vendor-neutral specifications, and the concrete set of ebXML specifications refers to the following concepts:

- **Centralized shared registry:** Registry information model (ebRIM), registry service specifications (ebRS)
- **Business processes and collaboration:** Business processes specification schema (ebBPSS), collaboration-protocol profile and agreement specification (ebCPPA)
- **Messaging:** Message service specification (ebMS).

ebXML registry is similar to a database, being able to represent a large range of objects (e.g., XML schemas, business process descriptions, ebXML core components, UML models, generic trading partner information). ebXML registry architecture is defined in terms of registry service and registry client. The first one provides two interfaces, defined using Web Service Description Language (WSDL):

- **Life-cycle management interface:** used to manage the life cycle of the objects
- **Query management interface:** used to make queries against a registry

ebRIM is defining and managing interoperable registries and repositories. The core information model used by ebXML registry is a tree-based classification scheme, and the information (e.g., information referring to business partners, industries) is arranged in a hierarchy.

ebBPSS is used to define the business processes (BPs) and business documents (BDs) involved. BPs and BDs are designed and documented prior to their use. They are usually composed from existing components and processes. Both of them are documented using ebBPSS, and stored in an ebXML registry so that they can be referred from other structures (e.g., PPs, CPAs).

ebBPSS is used to specify public business processes. It provides an XML schema to specify binary collaborations among parties. A binary collaboration may consist of multiple business transactions, each one of them being specified in terms of business envelopes, business documents, and business signals which are communicated among parties.

A collaboration protocol profile (CPP) provides the information needed to do business with a specific trading partner (e.g., business processes, document formats). When two parties trade for the first time, their CPPs are combined into a collaboration protocol agreement (CPA), which serves as the basis for the interaction. ebCPPA specifies the XML schema for CPP and CPA, and includes guidelines to form a CPA from two CPPs. CPP defines the technical capabilities of a partner engaged in electronic business collaborations with other partners by exchanging electronic messages. It includes elements such as: party's information (e.g., contact name), transport protocol, transport security protocol, messaging protocol. CPA is a special business agreement tied to a specific transaction, and makes explicit requirements derived from the intersection of the various CPP instances published by each of the trading partners.

In order to assure the communication among applications and business processes from different business partners, it is necessary to capture critical information upon which organizations must agree. An electronic trading partner agreement (TPA) registers such information. A TPA is an XML document that records specific technology parameters for conducting electronic business (e.g., partner identification, communication protocol, security for message exchanges).

ebMS specification defines the ebXML message service protocol, and it is designed to enable a secure and reliable exchange of business messages between trading partners. The specification for the message-based service invocation focuses on defining a communication protocol neutral method for exchanging electronic business messages, defining specific enveloping constructs for a secure and reliable exchange of messages, and a specific enveloping technique, allowing messages to contain payloads of any format type.

ebXML is designed to meet enterprises' needs to conduct electronic business, by providing: an *infrastructure* which ensures data communication interoperability (e.g., standard message transport mechanism, business service interface); a *semantic framework* supporting business interoperability (e.g., meta-model for defining business processes and information models, set of reusable core components); and a *discovery mechanism* enabling enterprises to discover each other, to reach an agreement and to conduct business (e.g., shared repository network) (Campbell, 2001).

A high-level presentation on how an ebXML interaction occurs can be framed in terms of ebXML's three functional phases defined by the ebXML technical architecture. Each functional phase defines its own security requirements and processes: implementation phase, discovery and retrieval phase, and run-time phase (Dournaee, 2004).

The implementation phase starts when a trading partner makes an active decision to do business using ebXML framework. During this phase, the trading partner will analyze its business processes and will publish them into a registry. An actual ebXML implementation is made then, aiming at attaining a working ebXML framework, and includes a set of published business processes, the CPP, and interfaces.

During discovery and retrieval phase, trading partners use the registry to discover business processes and interfaces published by other trading partners (e.g., the CPP for a specific partner is exchanged).

The run-time phase is concerned with the actual business transactions and choreography of messages exchanged between trading partners. Typically, there is no run-time access to the registry during this phase. Firstly, each trading partner is responsible for obtaining the necessary CPP document for a potential business partner. Usually, CPP is retrieved from an ebXML registry. Secondly, each partner derives the CPA, and finally the trading partners can start performing business transactions. Figure 3 illustrates run-time phase.

ebXML aims at creating a generic meta-model for business processes which allows it to model each business process in a machine-readable way. This can enable companies to deploy software that automatically adapts to specific business processes of different trading partners (SWWS, 2003).

ebXML specifications have matured rapidly over the past years, and its relevance for enterprise integration and interoperability in a collaborative business environment is emphasized by the augmenting number of research projects and technology infrastructures based on ebXML standard. Both OASIS and UN/CEFEACT pursued several standards developments,

Figure 3. ebXML run-time phase (Adapted after Dournaee, 2004)

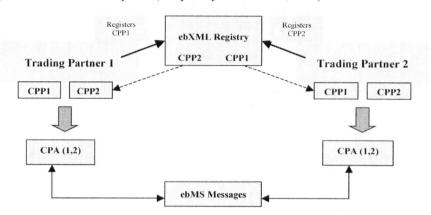

in real-world projects, combining ebXML with other technologies (e.g., Web services) in key industry sectors and government (ebXML, 2003). Examples of such projects are: JXTA Project, in the USA; COMOS Project (Cluster Of Systems of Metadata for Official Statistics), in Europe; and Kasumi B2B integration project in Japan. There is also underway a relevant project between RosettaNet (http://www.rosettanet.org) and ebXML, making use of ebXML BPSS, Registry, and ebMS. RosettaNet has adopted BPSS as they pursue the next evolution of the PIPs, and it is operating private registry with their technical dictionary content loaded. A more complete list of research projects focusing on ebXML is available in ebXML (2003).

Very few analytical comparisons are available concerning EI standards and technologies, based on different criteria. For instance, related to B2B standards, an interesting approach for the comparison of ebXML and RosettaNet was made by Pusnik, Juric, Rozman, and Sumak (2000), and Nurmilaakso and Kotinurmi (2004) compares XML-based B2B integration frameworks.

Comparing ebXML and Web Services, both of them use SOAP for message transport. XML Web services have a loosely coupled wire stack that consists of separate specifications for reliable transport and security, while ebXML rolls all this functionality into its messaging standard (ebMS), making use of different technologies. For the description of the discovery stacks, XML Web services use Web Services Description Language, (WSDL, http://www.w3.org/TR/wsdl) and universal description, discovery and integration protocol, (UDDI, http://www.uddi.org), while for ebXML these description and discovery mechanisms are part of ebXML registry. ebXML includes additional specifications for business process and collaboration. In fact, ebXML is a self-contained set of specifications, and does not rely on emerging standards and specifications (Dournaee, 2004).

freebXML (http://www.freebxml.org) is an initiative aiming at fostering the development and adoption of ebXML and related technologies through software and experience sharing. Its objectives are to create a centralized site for the sharing of "free" ebXML code and applications, and to promote ebXML as an e-commerce enabling technology. Relevant research projects have been developed, aiming at achieving these objectives (e.g., Hermes Message Service Handler, ebMail).

Messaging service is a key component of ebXML technical architecture. ebMS utilizes SOAP, Internet transport protocols, and other security standards, aiming at providing enterprises with a standardized, reliable, and secure infrastructure for the exchange of business documents.

Hermes B2B messaging server provides enterprises a standardized, reliable and secure infrastructure to exchange business data over the Internet. It supports secure messaging functions through security technologies such as XML signature, secure socket layer (SSL), and secure multipurpose internet mail extensions (S/MIME). Aiming at supporting different requirements from enterprises of all sizes, it implements reliable messaging, message packaging, message ordering, error handling, security, synchronous reply, message status service, and supports transport protocols, such as HTTP and SMTP. Hermes also supports the concept of "quality of service" by respecting in-force agreements, which are expressed as CPA.

ebMail is a GUI system. It makes use of open standards (ebXML), underlying GUI, in order to communicate with business partners. Business messages are composed and read in GUI form, so that enterprises do not need back-end integration. The project is platform-neutral; it is developed by using Java, and the GUI part is using Java Swing. For ebXML Messaging Service, ebMail makes use of Hermes project.

RosettaNet

RosettaNet (http://www.rosettanet.org) is a self-funded non-profit organization around a consortium of major IT, electronic components, and semiconductor manufacturing companies aiming at aligning business processes between partners in a given supply chain: Partners agree on partner interface processes (PIPs) to use, and are then ready to start a business scenario. RosettaNet implementation framework (RNIF) provides exchange protocols for quick and efficient implementation of PIPs. RNIF defines the overall RosettaNet business message format for business documents exchange, with elements to support authentication, authorization, encryption, and non-repudiation; details of the bindings for the transfer protocols (e.g., HTTP); and the specification for a reliable exchange of messages between business partners.

RosettaNet aims at aligning business processes of supply chain partners, a goal which is achieved by the creation of PIPs. Each PIP defines how two specific processes (running in two different partner organizations) will be standardized and interfaced across the entire supply chain. PIPs include all business logic, message flow, and message contents to enable alignment of the two processes. The purpose of each PIP is to provide common business/data models and documents enabling system developers to implement RosettaNet eBusiness interfaces. Each PIP includes: partner role descriptions (individuals/organizations); business data involved (and corresponding XML documents); and business process activities, a validation tool and implementation guide (http://www.rosettanet.org).

RosettaNet's standardization efforts refer to:

- **PIPs:** defining business processes between trading partners
- **PIP directory:** providing faster access to PIPs' information
- **Dictionaries:** which provide a common set of properties for PIPs. (e.g., **RosettaNet** Business Dictionary: designates the properties used in basic business activities, and Technical Dictionary provides proprieties for defining products)
- **RNIF:** providing specifications for packaging, routing, and transport of all PIP messages and business signals
- **Product and partner code:** which expedites the alignment of business processes between trading partners

RosettaNet does not provide a model for supply chain arrangements as a whole, but a model for linking supply chain members' information flows in a uniform manner, within specific business processes. The RosettaNet model describes several business activities that can be mapped to RosettaNet XML-framework. These activities are collected inside PIPs.

Web Services and BPEL4WS

Web services (http://www.w3.org/2002/ws) aim at achieving universal interoperability among applications by using Web standards. They use loosely-coupled integration model to allow flexible integration of heterogeneous systems in a variety of domains, including B2B, B2C, and enterprise integration and interoperability. Specifications derived from Web services include: SOAP, WSDL, and UDDI. SOAP (http://www.w3.org/TR/soap) defines an XML messaging protocol for basic service interoperability. WSDL (http://www.w3.org/TR/wsdl) introduces a common grammar for describing services, and UDDI (http://www.uddi.org) provides the infrastructure required to publish and discover services in a systematic way. All these specifications allow applications to find each other and interact following a loosely-coupled platform-independent model. However, system integration requires much more than the ability to conduct simple interactions by using standard protocols. According to Andrews, Curbea, Dholakia, Goland, Klein, Leymann, Liu, Roller, Smith, and Thatte (2003), the full potential of Web services as an integrated platform will be achieved only when applications and business processes will be able to integrate their complex interactions by making use of a standard process integration model.

Business Process Execution Language for Web Services (BPEL4WS, http://xml.coverpages.org/bpel4ws.html) provides an XML-based process definition language that enables the formal description of business processes and interaction protocols (Andrews, et al., 2003). BPEL4WS defines an interoperable integration model that facilitates the expansion of automated process integration in both intra-enterprise and B2B integration.

BPEL4WS is meant to model the behavior of executable business processes (which are modeling the actual behavior of a participant in a business interaction), and abstract business processes (which are process descriptions for business protocols). In this way, BPEL4W extends Web services' interaction model and enables it to support business transactions.

BPEL4WS depends on the following XML-based specifications: WSDL 1.1, XML Schema 1.0, XPath 1.0, and WS-Addressing. Among these, WSDL has the most influence on BPEL4WS:

P2P interaction between services, described in WSDL, is at the core of BPEL4WS process model, and both the process and its partners are modeled as WSDL services. The definition of business processes also follows the WSDL model of separation between the abstract message contents used by the business process and deployment information.

Conclusion and Further Research

Current market conditions and information and communication technology (ICT) developments determined enterprises to adopt new ways of undertaking business. As a consequence, new forms of collaboration emerged, such as collaborative networked organizations (CNO). In this context, the need to support enterprise integration and interoperability is increasing. Several conceptual frameworks, integration standards, technologies, and supporting infrastructures are being developed. Despite the relevant developments in the area of enterprise integration and interoperability, and the numerous scientific results in the business networking area, it is generally accepted that more work needs to be done, mainly concerning CNO creation or setting-up, support, and implementations (Camarinha-Matos & Afsarmanesh, 2003). Most of the technologies and infrastructures supporting CNO currently available are at their beginnings, and require considerable implementation and configuration efforts. In general, there is a lack of an effective approach to interoperability (mainly concerning software inter-operation and information exchange integration), and a lack of standard definitions and mechanisms.

Since it is very difficult (not to say impossible) to find a standard which is valid or easily configurable, supporting a wide range of services and operations concerning enterprise integration and interoperability, a convenient approach is to develop standards for specific industry sectors (e.g., papiNet for paper and forest industry), considering also the fact that a single process and document standard for communicating business transactions is critical to companies buying and selling products from the same industry. RosettaNet and papiNET are examples of successful standards developments supporting integration and interoperability for a specific industry sector: high-tech industry and paper industry, respectively.

Although several standards (e.g., ebXML) provide support for different requirements regarding enterprise integration and interoperability, in a networked environment, it would be naïve to consider that it is possible to convert everybody to a single platform (e.g., ebXML). Each technology or standard has its advantages and disadvantages. No true technology or standard can work as an isolated island; different technologies are combined or adapted to specific needs. It is therefore challenging to observe the rapid evolution of different technologies, standards, frameworks, and the development of emerging projects aiming at combining these standards and technologies (e.g., the development of research projects combining both ebXML and RosettaNet frameworks).

The questions that guided this work were answered. Major benefits for enterprise integration were identified. The most relevant standards, frameworks, technologies, and supporting infrastructures aiming at enterprise integration and interoperability were analyzed, and relevant research projects in the area of enterprise networking were briefly presented. Further research will be pursued to define criteria to be used to compare the available standards and frameworks. However, in the context of CNO, as mentioned by Bussler (2003), the grander challenge will be: how to achieve self-forming collaborative networked organizations (SF-CNO)—that is CNO where the detection of service provider, as well as their contracting, is automated.

Acknowledgment

The author, Claudia-Melania Chituc, would like to acknowledge Fundação para a Ciencia e a Tecnologia for PhD grant SFRH/BD/19751/2004.

References

Andrews, T., Cubera, F., Dholakia, H., Goland, Y., Klein, J., Leymann, F., Liu, K., Roller, D., Smith, D., & Thatte, S. (2003). *Business Process Execution Language for Web Services—Version 1.1.* White paper. Retrieved September 10, 2005, from http://ifr.sap.com/bpel4ws/BPEL%20V1-1%20May%205%202003%20Final.pdf

BPEL4WS. (2005). *Business Process Execution Language for Web Services Version 1.1.* Retrieved September 10, 2005, from http://www-128.ibm.com/developerworks/library/specification/ws-bpel/

Bussler, C. (2003). *B2B integration—concepts and architectures.* Springer.

Camarinha-Matos, L. M. (2003). *New collaborative organizations and their research needs in process and foundations for virtual organizations.* Kluwer Academy Publishers.

Camarinha-Matos, L. M., & Afsarmanesh, H. (2003). Elements of a base VE infrastructure. *Computers in Industry, 51*(2) 139-163.

Campbell, S. (2001). ebXML—the global standard for electronic business. Retrieved March 17, 2006, from http://www.gca.org/papers/xmleurope2001/papers/pdf/s03-2.pdf

Chituc, C. M., & Azevedo, A. L. (2005a) (in press). Enablers and technologies supporting self-forming networked organizations. *International Workshop on Enterprise Integration, Interoperability and Networking (EI2N),* Geneva, Switzerland. Hermes Publishing.

Chituc, C. M., & Azevedo, A. L. (2005b, September). Multi-perspective challenges on collaborative networks business environment. In L. Camarinha-Matos, H. Afsarmanesh, & A. Ortiz (Eds.), *Collaborative networks and breeding environments: Proceedings of the 6th IFIP Working Conference on Virtual Enterprises,* Spain (Vol. 186, pp. 25-32). Boston: Springer.

CORDIS. (2005). Building grids for Europe—a crucial technology for science and industry. Retrieved September 10, 2005, from http://www.cordis.lu/ist/grids

Crargil, C. F. (1989). *Information technology standardization: Theory, process, and organization.* Bedford: Digital Press.

Dournaee, B. (2004). *Introduction to ebXML.* White paper. Retrieved September 10, 2005, from http://dev2dev.bea.com/pub/a/2004/12/ebXML.html

ebXML. (2003). *ebXML adoptation update.* Retrieved from http://www.ebxml.org

European Commission. (2005). *Strengthening competitiveness through production networks—a perspective from European ICT research projects in the field of enterprise networking.*

IEEE. (1990). *IEEE standard computer dictionary: A compilation of IEEE standard computer glossaries.* New York: Institute of Electrical and Electronics Engineers.

IFAC/IFIP. (2000). GERAM: Generalized enterprise reference architecture and methodology. *IFAC/IFIP Task Force on Architectures for Enterprise Integration.*

Li, H., & Williams, T. J. (2000). The interconnected chain of enterprises as presented by the Purdue enterprise reference architecture. *Computers in Industry, 42*, 265-274.

Li, H., & Williams, T. J. (2003). Interface design for the Purdue enterprise reference architecture (PERA) and methodology in e-work. *Production Planning & Control, 14*(8), 704-719.

Nurmilaakso, J. M., & Kotinurmi, P. (2004). A review of XML-based supply-chain integration. *Production Planning & Control, 15*(6), 608-621

papiNet. (2004). *papiNet from top to bottom—an introduction to papiNet.* Retrieved September 10, 2005, from http://www.papinet.org/presentations.asp

Pusnik, M., Juric, M. B., Rozman, I., & Sumak, B. (2000). *A comparison of ebXML and RosettaNet.* White paper. Retrieved September 10, 2005, from http://www.ebpml.org/articles.htm

SCOR—Supply Chain Operations Reference Model. (n.d.). Retrieved from http://www.supply-chain.org

SWWS—Semantic Web-Enabled Web Services. (2003). *Analysis of B2B Standards and Systems: Deliverable D1.1 SWWS Project.* Retrieved from http://swws.semanticweb.org

Vernadat, F. (1996). *Enterprise modeling and integration—principles and applications.* Chapman & Hall.

Webber, D. (2004). The benefits of ebXML for e-business. In *XML 2004 Conference.* Retrieved September 10, 2005, from http://www.idealliance.org/proceedings/xml04/papers/44/webber.pdf

Workflow Management Coalition. (1999). *The workflow management coalition specifications: Terminology and glossary.* Retrieved from http://www.wfmc.org

Zachman, J. A. (1987). A framework for information systems architecture. *IBM Systems Journal, 26*(3), 276-292.

Zarli, A, & Poyet, P. (2001). A framework for distributed information management in the virtual enterprise: The VEGA project. In L. M. Camarinha-Matos & H. Afsarmanesh (Eds.), *Infrastructures for virtual enterprises—networking industrial enterprises* (1st ed.), (pp. 293-306). Boston: Kluwer Academic Publishers.

About the Authors

Goran D. Putnik received his DiplEng, MSci and DrSci from Belgrade University, both MSci and DrSci in the area of intelligent manufacturing systems. His current position is associate professor, Department of Production and Systems Engineering, University of Minho, Portugal. He teaches the subjects of CAD/CAPP, CAM, FMS, and virtual enterprises in undergraduate studies, and CAD/CAPP/CAM Systems, concurrent engineering, enterprise organization, IMS, and design theory in postgraduate studies. He served as director of the Centre for Production Systems Engineering (CESP) for four years and its deputy director for five years. He is director of the Master and Postgraduate Course on CIM, and is responsible of the Laboratory for Virtual Enterprises (LABVE), the Department of Production and Systems Engineering, University of Minho. His scientific and engineering interests are production systems and enterprises design and control theory and implementations: CIM, CAD/CAPP/CAM systems, intelligent production systems and enterprises, machine learning as a design theory model, design engineering, information systems management, formal theory of production systems and enterprises, and distributed, agile and virtual enterprises. He is supervising a number of PhD projects as well. He regularly publishes and participates in international scientific conferences. He serves as a member of editorial boards for several international journals, and has served in more than forty scientific committees of international conferences. He was also an invited lecturer at a number of universities.

Maria Manuela Cunha is currently associate professor in the Higher School of Technology, Polytechnic Institute of Cávado and Ave, Portugal. She holds a DiplEng in informatics and systems engineering, an MSci. in the field of information society and a DrSci in the field of virtual enterprises, all from the University of Minho. She coordinates the scientific domain of organizations and information systems in the Department of Information Systems and Technologies, and teaches subjects related with information systems and technologies, software engineering, and organizational models, to undergraduate and postgraduate studies. She supervises several PhD projects in the domain of virtual enterprises. Her scientific and engineering interests are electronic business, agile and virtual enterprises, and information systems. She regularly publishes and participates on international scientific conferences. She serves as a member of editorial boards for several international journals and has served in several scientific committees of international conferences.

* * * * *

G. M. Accacia is professor of mechanical engineering of the University of Genova, PMAR Lab, Italy. Her research activity covers different aspects in expert automation and robot technologies, especially with reference to computer simulation and virtual prototype investigation of the on-duty dynamical behaviour of the equipment, by extended exploitation of hybrid (causal and heuristic) models, through joint algorithmic routines and decision support procedures. She has contributed to the technical literature with some 150 publications.

Paulo Silva Ávila received his EngLic from the University of Coimbra in the domain of mechanical engineering, his MSc from the University of Minho in the domain of computer-integrated manufacturing and his PhD from the University of Minho in the area of resources selection for agile and virtual enterprises. His current position is assistant professor in the Department of Mechanical Engineering, at the High Engineering Institute of Porto, Portugal, covering the subjects of production system organization and management, computer-integrated manufacturing (CIM), and total quality management. He is a quality consultant, and his interests, besides that, are manufacturing systems and enterprise design, and management theory and implementation.

Américo Lopes Azevedo has a PhD in the area of advanced planning systems for networking enterprises. Since 1988, he has been teaching in the Electrical and Computers Engineering of the School of Engineering of the University of Porto, Portugal, and since 1995 he has been a researcher and project leader in INESC PORTO. He is the author of many articles in international journals and technical publications, and he has been active in preparing and participating in R&D projects involving industrial companies. His main research interests are in the collaborative business networking, business process management, and operations management.

Nicholas Beaumont works in the Department of Management at Monash University, Australia, teaching information systems management and electronic business. He worked in the computer industry for 12 years. His research interests include the effect of information and communication technologies on individuals, organisations, and society; a particular interest is electronic business and its ramifications. His major current project entails research on outsourcing in Australia. Other current projects are an investigation of service level management in Australia and the improvement of a particular kind of statistical analysis. He enjoys presenting at industry seminars, and meeting people who have to cope with the day to day problems of reconciling customers' changing requirements and limited resources with head office demands.

Jimmie Browne is the registrar and deputy president of the National University of Ireland, Galway, as well as the founder of the Computer Integrated Manufacturing (CIM) Research Unit there. He has many years experience of working in applied research and development, including extensive experience of EU and industrially-funded projects. His research interests are in the design, analysis, modeling, and operation of extended and virtual enterprises. He holds Bachelors and Masters degrees from NUI, Galway, and PhD and DSc degrees in engineering from the University of Manchester Institute of Science and Technology. His most recent book, co-authored with Dr. Hari Jagdev and Dr. Attracta Brennan, was entitled "Strategic Decision-Making in Modern Manufacturing" and was published by Klewer Academic Publishers in 2004.

Claudia-Melania Chituc is a PhD student at the Faculty of Engineering of the University of Porto, Portugal (Electrical and Computer Engineering Department), and researcher at INESC Porto. She received a MSc degree from the same university in June, 2004, in the area of information technology for enterprise management. Claudia-Melania has an inter-disciplinary background: She is both a computer engineer and an economist. She graduated from Politehnica University of Bucharest, Romania (computer science and engineering) in 2002, and the Academy of Economic Studies, Bucharest, in 2000 (being specialized in finances, banks, and stock exchange). Claudia-Melania's current areas of research include: collaborative networked organizations (CNOs), business process management, and networked organizations' performance assessment, and economic analysis.

Alexandre Félix-Alves is a mechanical engineer with additional qualifications in systemic and strategic modulation and reengineering processes for innovation. He started to work with a research scholarship in the University of Porto, and presently works as a senior consultant in Inovamais, S. A., as project manager. He has coordinated/managed several European research and development projects, in areas that range from innovative business models to industry-driven research activities. He has written some scientific papers and participated in one support manual for mechanical classes at university level (FEUP). He is currently finishing his MBA at EGP (Escola de Gestão do Porto).

Paul Folan received his BE, in 2002, and MEngSc degrees from National University of Ireland, Galway, in 2004, and is currently a PhD student at the same university. His main research interests include performance measurement, the extended enterprise, product life-cycle management, and reverse logistics.

Tor Guimaraes has been rated by several independent sources as one of the top researchers in the world based on publications in the top IS journals. He holds the Jesse E. Owen Chair of Excellence at Tennessee Technological University, USA. He earned a PhD in MIS from the

University of Minnesota and an MBA from California State University, Los Angeles. Tor was department chairman and professor at St. Cloud State University. Before that, he was assistant professor and director of the MIS Certificate Program at Case-Western Reserve University. He has been the keynote speaker at numerous national and international meetings sponsored by organizations such as the Information Processing Society of Japan, Institute of Industrial Engineers, Sales and Marketing Executives, IEEE, Association for Systems Management, and the American Society for Quality Control. Tor has consulted with many leading organizations including TRW, American Greetings, AT&T, IBM, and the Department of Defense. He is on the board of directors of several national and international business organizations and is a top strategic advisor to their CEOs. Working with partners in more than thirty countries, Tor has published over 200 articles dealing with the effective use and management of IS and related technologies.

Jennifer Anne Harding is a senior lecturer in the Department of Mechanical and Manu-facturing Engineering at Loughborough University, UK. She has substantial industrial experience having worked for over 15 years in the engineering and textile industries before joining Loughborough University in January, 1992. Her expertise includes knowledge management and reuse, tools to support knowledge sharing within collaborative teams, knowledge discovery and data mining applications in manufacturing, and "Best Practice" information and knowledge. Her research has been funded by Europe and in the UK by EPSRC and Industry. She has a wide range of academic publications and has supervised several successful PhDs in these subject areas.

Anja Hofer works as a research assistant and PhD student at the Institute for Information Systems (IWi) at the German Research Center for Artificial Intelligence (DFKI), Saar-bruecken, Germany. She holds a diploma in business science from the University of Saarland. Her research activities focus on e- and c-business, especially for small and medium-sized enterprises.

Mayumi Hori is a professor at Graduate School and Faculty of Business Management, Hakuoh University, Japan. She received the B.E. and M.E. degrees in economics from Rikkyo University, Japan, and Dr Policy Studies degree from Chuo University, Japan. Her research interest is telework (e-work). She is a director of the Web Services Initiatives and of The Infosocionomic Society in Japan. She may be contacted by e-mail at m.hori@ hakuoh.ac.jp.

Harinder Jagdev graduated from Indian Institute of Technology, Madras, in mechani-cal engineering in 1974. After working for two years as production engineer at Mercedes Benz, he joined UMIST in 1976. He gained MSc and PhD in manufacturing technology from Victoria University of Manchester, UK, in 1977 and 1980, respectively. Since 1980, he has been with UMIST, working in Manufacturing and Machine Tools Engineering Divi-sion, Control Systems Centre, and is presently teaching in the Computation Department. His research interests encompass all aspects of manufacturing/business activities, taken in the broadest sense. He is the editor of the journal, *Computers in Industry*, and also serves the editorial board of *Production Planning and Control*. Since 1980, he has researched for and been consultant to many organisations in Europe. Since 1980, he has been a regular reviewer of national, European and international research funding applications and the funded projects.

S. Kopácsi received his MSc degree in electrical engineering in 1990, Specialised Engineering Degree in measurement and control technique in 1992, PhD in technical sciences in 1995, and MBA in 2000 at the Technical University of Budapest, as well as Engineer-Economist Degree in 1996 at the Budapest University of Economical Sciences. He has been working for the Computer and Automation Research Institute of the Hungarian Academy of Sciences since 1986, where he has at present a senior researcher position. He was a visiting researcher in Seoul for three months in 1991 and in Germany for several months in 1996, 1997, and 1999. In 2002-2003 and in 2005, he worked for 13 months in Bremen, Germany. He has more than 50 scientific publications in national and international periodicals and conferences, mostly in English. His professional interest includes knowledge-based simulation, animation, artificial intelligence, graphics systems, and virtual reality.

Adamantios Koumpis heads the Research Programmes Division of ALTEC S.A., Greece, which he founded at 1996 (then as independent division of Unisoft S.A.). His research interests include quantitative decision-making techniques and info-society economics. He successfully lead many commercial and research projects in Greece in the areas of e-commerce, public sector and business enterprise reorganisation and information logistics, concerning linking of data/information repositories with knowledge management and business engineering models. He may be contacted by e-mail at akou@altec.gr.

G. L. Kovács graduated at the Technical University of Budapest, Faculty of Electrical Engineering, in 1966, received a DrTechn degree (PhD) in 1976, and was Habil. and Prof. at the same university in 1995. He received a Dr of the Academy of Sciences (HAS) degree (Design Problems of Manufacturing Systems) in 1997 at the Hungarian Academy of Sciences. Dr. Kovács was named research fellow in the Computer and Automation Institute of the HAS since 1966, and head of CIM Research Laboratory since 1990. Kovács was also professor at the Technical University of Budapest and at the University of Pecs. He was a visiting researcher in the USA (one year), Soviet Union (two years), West Germany (one year), and visiting professor in Mexico (six months) and in Italy (6+1 months). He has published more than 300 scientific publications in journals and conference proceedings. He is also a member of several Hungarian and international scientific organizations, as IEEE (senior member), IFAC and IFIP, as well as: a Hungarian IFIP TC5 representative and deputy chairman, member of the editorial board of five scientific journals, and often organizer and invited plenary speaker at international conferences. Dr. Kovács' scientific interests include: CIM, robotics, computer aided design and manufacturing, expert and hybrid systems, virtual manufacturing, industrial networks, and technology transfer. He is currently project manager of several Hungarian and international R&D projects, including European joint projects and bilateral research projects.

Florian Kupsch works as a research assistant and PhD student at the Institute for Information Systems (IWi) at the German Research Center for Artificial Intelligence (DFKI), Saarbruecken, Germany. He holds a diploma in business science for information systems from the University of Muenster, and focused his business studies on data management, databases, and management information systems. His main research interests are knowledge management and business integration.

Hsiao-Kang Lin received a BA degree in international trade and finance from Fu Jen University, Taiwan (1987) and an MSc degree in business system analysis and design from the City University, London, UK, in 1992. Between 1993 and 2001, she worked in global OEMs sales and marketing in the PC sector and also in global manufacturing investment consultancy, on behalf of Taiwan companies and official government agencies in England. In 2005, she received a PhD degree from Wolfson School of Mechanical and Manufacturing Engineering, Loughborough University, UK. Currently she is an assistant professor of the Department of Industrial Engineering and Management, I-Shou University, Taiwan. Her research interests include manufacturing system engineering moderator, ontology modelling, knowledge engineering, and Semantic Web applications for global enterprise integration.

Marcelo Machado is a special adviser on management of technology (MOT) and management of information systems (MIS) at Manaus City Administration, Secretary of Information Technology and Science, Brazil. He earned a PhD from the Japan Advanced Institute of Science and Technology, School of Knowledge Science, which was founded by Professor Ikujiro Nonaka, a pioneer of knowledge management. His research is placed at the intersection among the fields of strategic management of technology, strategic alliances, and knowledge management. He has a master's degree in production engineering and systems from Santa Catarina University in Brazil, and his master thesis examined the strategic processes of Brazilian manufacturers. He earned his Bachelor of Engineering major in electronic engineering while working as an industrial engineer for subsidiaries of technology-intensive multinational companies operating in Brazil such as Xerox and Sharp.

R. C. Michelini is professor of mechanical engineering of the University of Genova, PMAR Lab, Italy. His research activity develops in the areas of integrated design, robot technologies, industrial diagnostics, and expert automation, with attention recently moved on the growth sustainability and to the eco-conservativeness problems, suitably tackled through life-cycle service engineering and reverse logistics techniques. He has contributed to over 500 technical publications.

Masakazu Ohashi is the dean of faculty of policy studies and a professor at Graduate School and Faculty of Policy Studies, Chuo University, Japan. He received the BE, BS, ME, and DrEng degrees from Chuo University, Japan. His research interest is the system for the next generation networking social systems. He is the chair person of Time Business Forum, Web Services Initiatives, and a vice-president of The Infosocionomics Society in Japan. He is a member of UN/CEFACT TBG6. He may be contacted by e-mail at ohashi@ fps.chuo-u.ac.jp.

Keith Popplewell started his career in operational research, and specialised in computer-aided engineering and production planning systems design with Raleigh Industries and Boots Company plc. During this time, he took a doctorate in manufacturing engineering at the University of Nottingham. Subsequently, he became a technical director in a software house specialising in the design, development, and implementation of CAE systems, before joining the Department of Manufacturing Engineering at Loughborough University, UK, in 1985, and then becoming Jaguar Cars Professor of Engineering Manufacture and Management at Coventry University in 2000. His research interests include the application of intelligent computing methods to the modelling and design of both engineering products and manufacturing systems throughout the virtual organisation life cycle.

Jennifer Priestley is an assistant professor of applied statistics at Kennesaw State University, USA. She holds a PhD in decision sciences from Georgia State University and an MBA from Penn State University. She worked as a consultant in the financial services industry for 11 years with VISA, MasterCard and Andersen Consulting. She has published papers in the areas of knowledge management, interorganizational knowledge transfer, and statistical modeling and model evaluation methods.

Nicolaos Protogeros is a lecturer in electronic commerce, in the University of Macedonia, at Thessaloniki, Greece. He holds a PhD in information technology from National Polytechnique Institute in France, a DEA on image processing from the University of Paul Sabatier, Toulouse, France, and a BS in mathematics from the Aristotle University of Thessaloniki. He has worked in the information technology sector for many years specializing in electronic commerce applications. He has been the project leader for many research and development projects in the area of Web-based technologies, software agents, and virtual enterprises. He has published articles on electronic commerce, information technologies, and network management.

R. P. Razzoli is researcher at the Department of Mechanical Engineering of the University of Genova, PMAR Lab, Italy. His research activity is addressed to the mechanical design for intelligent automation and robotic systems, especially for the development of mechatronic devices with reference to virtual prototyping techniques and complying eco-compatibility constraints, through integrated design paradigms covering the life-cycle aspects, the expected on-duty reliability, and on-service intrinsic safety. He is author or co-author of about 80 scientific papers.

Peter Rittgen received an MSc in computer science and computational linguistics from University Koblenz-Landau, Germany, and a PhD in economics and business administration from Frankfurt University, Germany. He is currently a senior lecturer at the School of Business and Informatics of the University College of Borås, Sweden. He has been doing research on business processes and the development of information systems since 1997, and has published many articles in these areas. For further details, the reader is referred to http://www.adm.hb.se/~PRI/.

Bob Roberts, is Reader at Kingston University, UK, and a leader of the e-business group in the Centre for Applied Research in Information Systems (CARIS) and also course director for the MSc course in e-commerce in the Faculty of Computing, Information Systems, and Mathematics at Kingston University. His research and teaching activities are concerned with the implementation of e-commerce systems to support business to business (B2B) collaborative relationships as well as the socio-political and relational aspects of interorganisational systems and virtual organisations. His recently funded research interests cover a range of e-business projects in the telecoms, health, construction, and electronic sectors. He may be contacted by e-mail at R.Roberts@kingston.ac.uk.

Jarogniew Rykowski received the MSc degree in computer science from the Technical University of Poznan, Poland, in 1986, and the PhD degree in computer science from the Technical University of Gdansk, Poland, in 1995. From 1986 to 1992, he was with the Institute of Computing Science at the Technical University of Poznan. From 1992 to 1995, he worked as an associate professor in the Franco-Polish School of New Information and Communication Technologies in Poznan. Since 1996, he has been with the Poznan University of Economics, working as an assistant professor in the Department of Information Technology. He participated in several industrial projects concerning operating systems, networks, programming language compilers (assemblers, LISP), multimedia databases, and distributed systems for e-commerce. His research activities cover mainly software agents, concentrating on methods for efficient management and distribution of software components over the Web. His recent interests have gone towards user-defined, multiversion software agents, especially in the scope of mobile networks composed of non-intelligent and relatively small devices (mobile phones, palmtops, laptops with GSM/GPRS connection, etc.) He is the author and co-author of three books, over 30 papers in journals and conference proceedings, and two patents.

Subhashish Samaddar is an associate professor of managerial sciences in the J. Mack Robinson College of Business at Georgia State University, Atlanta, Georgia, USA. He is the director of PhD program in decision sciences. His recent articles have been published in several scholarly journals such as *Management Science, Omega, European Journal of Research, Communications of the ACM, Interfaces, International Journal of Flexible Manufacturing Systems, International Journal of Computer Applications and Technologies, International Journal of Operations and Production Management, Computers and Industrial Engineering: An International Journal*, and in many national conferences.

Dominik Vanderhaeghen works as a research assistant and PhD student at the Institute for Information Systems (IWi) at the German Research Center for Artificial Intelligence (DFKI), Saarbruecken, Germany. He holds a diploma in business science from the University of Saarland. His main research interests are business integration, especially interoperable, cross-organisational process modelling and process execution, as well as business process management.

Index

Single Journal Articles and Case Studies
Are Now Right at Your Fingertips!

Purchase any single journal article or teaching case for only $25.00!

Idea Group Publishing offers an extensive collection of research articles and teaching cases in both print and electronic formats. You will find over 1300 journal articles and more than 300 case studies on-line at **www.idea-group.com/articles**. Individual journal articles and cases are available for only $25 each. A new feature of our website now allows you to search journal articles and case studies by category. To take advantage of this new feature, simply use the above link to search within these available categories.

We have provided free access to the table of contents for each journal. Once you locate the specific article needed, you can purchase it through our easy and secure site.

For more information, contact cust@idea-group.com or 717-533-8845 ext.10

Databases, Data Mining & Data Warehousing

Distance Learning & Education

E-Commerce and E-Government

E-Government

Healthcare Information Systems

Human Side and Society Issues in IT

Information Technology Education

IT Business Value, Support and Solutions

IT Engineering, Modeling & Evaluation

Knowledge Management

Mobile Commerce and Telecommunications

Multimedia Networking

Virtual Organizations and Communities

Web Technologies and Applications

IDEA GROUP INC.   www.idea-group.com